A CULTURAL HISTORY OF GARDENS

VOLUME 3

A Cultural History of Gardens
General Editors: Michael Leslie and John Dixon Hunt

Volume 1
A Cultural History of Gardens in Antiquity
Edited by Kathryn Gleason

Volume 2
A Cultural History of Gardens in the Medieval Age
Edited by Michael Leslie

Volume 3
A Cultural History of Gardens in the Renaissance
Edited by Elizabeth Hyde

Volume 4
A Cultural History of Gardens in the Age of Enlightenment
Edited by Stephen Bending

Volume 5
A Cultural History of Gardens in the Age of Empire
Edited by Sonja Dümpelmann

Volume 6
A Cultural History of Gardens in the Modern Age
Edited by John Dixon Hunt

A CULTURAL HISTORY
OF GARDENS

IN THE
RENAISSANCE

Edited by Elizabeth Hyde

BLOOMSBURY

LONDON · NEW DELHI · NEW YORK · SYDNEY

Bloomsbury Academic

An imprint of Bloomsbury Publishing Plc

50 Bedford Square
London
WC1B 3DP
UK

175 Fifth Avenue
New York
NY 10010
USA

www.bloomsbury.com

First published 2013

British Library Cataloguing-in-Publication Data
A catalogue record for this book is available from the British Library.

ISBN: 978 0 85785 031 7 (volume 3)
978 1 84788 265 3 (set)

Library of Congress Cataloging-in-Publication Data
A catalog record for this book is available from the Library of Congress.

Typeset by ApexCovantage, LLC
Printed and bound in Great Britain

CONTENTS

LIST OF ILLUSTRATIONS

CHAPTER 2

CHAPTER 3

CHAPTER 8

GENERAL EDITORS' PREFACE

The volumes of this series explore the cultural world of the garden from antiquity to the present day in six particular periods. Each volume addresses the same eight topics, determined by the general editors for their relevance to garden history across different times and cultures. Thus a reader interested more, say, in planting or in types of gardens could read through the chapters devoted to those issues in successive volumes. Contrariwise, either of those interests might be contextualized by a volume's discussion of other aspects of the garden in a given period. There is therefore both a horizontal and a vertical way of using these volumes. Further, each volume includes both its editor's introduction, which rather than abstracting or summarizing the other contributions, surveys the period from a fresh vantage point, and a bibliography, which encompasses references from all the eight chapters augmented with that editor's additional readings.

HISTORY

These volumes are a historical enquiry and not an encyclopedia. They do not pretend to be comprehensive, either geographically or chronologically. The authors of the individual chapters have been encouraged to foreground what seem to be the most significant episodes and examples of their particular topic, leaving it to the reader to envisage how other sites that he or she knows better might further illustrate, challenge, or qualify the given analyses. But in every instance, we intend there to be some narrative of one particular theme as it exists, unfolds, or develops during a particular historical period. The definitions of these historical eras must be taken with some caution and elasticity, since a chronology of garden making does not always fit the divisions of time devised for and endorsed by other histories: André Le Notre did his work after 1650 but is arguably more usefully considered in a volume focused on the Renaissance than on the Enlightenment; similarly, Gertrude Jekyll and William Robinson were designing before 1920, but we understand their work better within the cultural content of the modern age.

CULTURAL HISTORY

There are of course many modes of history that have developed over the centuries. A relatively new one addresses the cultural context of human activity. "Culture" derives from the Latin *colere*, which has as some of its meanings "to inhabit," "to respect," "to pay attention to"; it emerges also in our words "colony" and "cultivation." Gardens, then, must be considered as driven by and evidence of a whole congeries of human concerns; they are not, above all, to be examined in terms of their merely visual appearance, materials, or stylistic histories. The diversity and density of human involvements with those sites we call gardens mean that the discipline of garden history draws upon adjacent disciplines such as anthropology, sociology, economic, and political history, along with histories of the arts with which the garden has been involved. So three large questions are posed: why were gardens created? How were they used or visited (there being no handy term for the "consumption" of gardens)? And how does their representation in different arts express the position and value of the garden within its culture in diverse periods? Regretfully, we were unable to extend the range of these volumes to include the garden making of China and Japan among other Eastern cultures, although inevitably the rich examples of such gardens have been invoked on occasion.

GARDENS

The range of places that can be envisaged within this category is enormous and various, and it changes from place to place, and from time to time. Yet this diversity does not wholly inhibit us from knowing what it is we what to discuss when we speak of the garden. Yet the garden is typically a place of paradox, being the work of men and women, yet created from the elements of nature; just as it is often acknowledged to be a "total environment," a place may be physically separated from other zones but answering and displaying connections with larger environments and concerns. Gardens, too, are often created, and subsequently experienced, as commentary and response: a focus of speculations, propositions, and negotiations concerning what it is to live in the world. Both the physical gardens and the ideas that drive them are cultural constructions, and their history is the topic of these six volumes.

John Dixon Hunt, University of Pennsylvania

Michael Leslie, Rhodes College

Introduction

Views and Perspectives of the Renaissance Garden, 1400–1700

ELIZABETH HYDE

In his *Oration on the Dignity of Man*, Pico della Mirandola described God's creation of humankind in vegetal terms:

> But upon man, at the moment of his creation, God bestowed the seeds pregnant with all possibilities, the germs of every form of life. Whichever of these a man shall cultivate, the same will mature and bear fruit in him. If vegetative, he will become a plant; if sensual, he will become brutish; if rational, he will reveal himself a heavenly being; if intellectual, he will be an angel and the son of God.[1]

The 1486 *Oration* is often celebrated as the most eloquent expression of the Renaissance liberation of humanity from its fixed link on the Great Chain of Being, the Christian hierarchical understanding of the world. Medieval theologians placed human beings near the bottom of that chain, just slightly above plants and animals, but far beneath the angels that resided with God in heaven. Pico della Mirandola, however, emphasized the free will that allowed humans to move up or down the great chain, as they so aspired. For Pico, then, humankind was distinguished by its potential. The essence of humanity, he maintained, lay in the seeds God had planted within human beings and in the human ability to cultivate those seeds.

One can think of the act of cultivating those seeds as the fundamental impetus of the Renaissance. For in celebrating human ability to grow through achievement and accomplishments, Pico della Mirandola was celebrating the process of becoming cultivated. A Neoplatonist, Pico della Mirandola imagined God's this-worldly creations as capable of becoming noble reflections of the ideals in heaven. The process of cultivating potential, for Pico, became a noble attempt to strive towards a heavenly ideal. In imagining such potential for humankind, the Renaissance thinker, like many of his humanist contemporaries, looked backwards, past the Middle Ages, to Antiquity for the language and metaphor of human growth. Since antiquity, the cultivation of the human mind and human virtue had been described as the nourishment of the seeds of potential into a tree of knowledge and wisdom. And the recognition of the importance of education to the proper nourishment of the intellect only became more important with the emergence of Renaissance humanism.[2] Education, or improvement, was key to the acquisition of skills and the development of the mind that both facilitated climbing the great chain of being and contributed to the building of an identity within Renaissance society. Indeed, the notion of cultivation at the heart of Pico's celebration of the dignity of man is central to the notion of Renaissance "self-fashioning," the term that modern scholars have appropriated to describe the self-conscious act of cultivating the self.[3]

In describing the lowliest state of human development as vegetative, Pico della Mirandola seems to have little praise for plants themselves. Like his medieval predecessors, he believed plants to be among the least sophisticated of God's creations. His metaphor is about potential—the potential for those plants (or the humans that they represented) to grow through the cultivation of the intellect into something greater. It seems too easy to apply Pico della Mirandola's metaphor of the seeds of human potential to the Renaissance garden. And yet the metaphor aptly represents the emergence of Renaissance garden art and, more precisely, the cultural uses of and meanings acquired by the Renaissance garden. In the Renaissance, the cultivation of plants and the landscape became entwined with the cultivation of the self. Renaissance men and women took full advantage of the opportunity to cultivate both literal and metaphorical seeds in gardens and landscapes designed in the period to reveal their own cultivated natures. They applied human intellect and curiosity to the collection and analysis of plant life, human ingenuity to the manipulation of natural forms and substances, and human creativity to the expression of aesthetic ideas through natural media. Indeed, the relationship between humanity and the natural world was explored from every angle, every perspective in the centuries leading up to the eighteenth century.

Historians have debated vigorously the extent to which the Renaissance can and should be understood as a unique moment in the human effort to know humanity's place in the world. Indeed, the term *Renaissance* for this period is a historiographically contested label. Scholars have argued over whether the period broke distinctly from the Middle Ages that preceded it or was the culmination of the feudal past. Scholars have questioned, too, how it is possible to apply such a label, based on cultural and intellectual developments, to Europe as a whole when disparate parts experienced this "renaissance" in different times over a period of two hundred years. Did Petrarch usher in the same movement from which came William Shakespeare—hundreds of miles to the north and two centuries later?

After over a century of debate (sparked initially by Jacob Burckhardt's *The Civilization of the Renaissance in Italy* in the nineteenth century), little agreement remains over how to establish the meaning and implications of the term itself, let alone the chronological boundaries.[4] Most scholars date the beginning of the Renaissance to the career of Petrarch, whose literary work marks the emergence of the cultural and intellectual movement that is humanism. Petrarch himself chose to focus on the discontinuities, seeing in his lifetime and in his own intellectual and literary example, a distinct break with the "darkness" of the Middle Ages. Although some historians may argue to the contrary, it is culturally and intellectually significant that Petrarch and his contemporaries believed themselves to be living in a distinctly new era, even if the "newness" came from a self-conscious looking backward. Equally contested is when to end the Renaissance—with Martin Luther's ignition of the Protestant Reformation? With the devastating sack of Rome in 1527? Or not until the end of the Thirty Years' War in 1648 marked an end to the devastating era of religious warfare?

In this series on the cultural history of gardens, and for this volume, in particular, the Renaissance has been defined as the period from the late fourteenth century through the achievements of André le Nôtre in the second half of the seventeenth century, from the emergence of humanism through the age of absolutism. Or more specifically, 1374, the death of Petrarch, by which time the garden was becoming understood as a humanist space, until 1683, the death of André Le Nôtre, whose work marked the culmination of the appropriation of the garden arts into the realm of the political.

Some will quibble with these dates. To the art historian, they encompass aesthetically distinct stylistic periods of the Renaissance through mannerism and the baroque to neoclassicism. To the scholar of literature, they encompass the humanist recovery of Latin and then Greek classical literature, to the triumph of neoclassicism and the rise of vernacular literature. To historians, they encompass the Italian Renaissance, the Reformation, the Scientific Revolution, the discovery of the Americas, and a subsequent shift of economic activity and power away from the Mediterranean where Renaissance culture, material and otherwise, had emerged to the Atlantic world. And yet there is an internal, historical coherence to considering the cultural history of the Renaissance garden from 1400 to 1700 (or 1374 to 1683). It is a chronological frame drawn around a stylistically similar (though not singular) period, with Le Nôtre's work representing the culmination of Renaissance, cum mannerist, baroque, and French classical, aesthetics in the garden, more so than a precursor to the eighteenth-century landscape garden. It was a period of artistic creativity and ingenuity in the garden arts just as in painting and sculpture and architecture. But just as important, it is a period marked by the embracing of new geographies (and the flora and fauna found within them) in the European landscape, and the emergence of new epistemologies for thinking about them. Further, it marks the growth of the meaning and reception of the formal garden to include expressions of intellectual sophistication, taste, and luxury to the political power of the monarch who saw in the garden the opportunity to represent symbolically and iconographically the totality of his (or her) rule over the land via the landscape.

The cultural history of the Renaissance garden comprises the history of the Renaissance itself. The Renaissance Europe that emerges from such an investigation is one peopled by men and women who were fascinated with the natural world, men and women who created new means to share and explore their fascination and who found ways to use the landscapes they created in the complicated social and political stages upon which they performed. More broadly, the garden that emerges out of this cultural landscape reveals a Europe self-consciously looking backward and forward, devotedly acknowledging a debt to the ancient past, while excitedly embracing the contemporary worlds being discovered and created. Using the Renaissance garden as a lens through which to examine the period from 1400 to 1700, a picture emerges of a Renaissance Europe consciously and systematically working out the place of man in the world. That world was changing rapidly in size, in scale, and in scope. And the garden provided an earthen palette on which to address these changes.

That Renaissance men and women drew creative and artistic inspiration from the natural was neither new nor surprising. Artists and craftsmen, studying sculptures, vases, and mosaics from antiquity, valued them for a naturalism that had been absent from Western art for a thousand years. The media used to create works of art in this period connected both artisan and patron to the natural world. As Michael Baxandall has made clear, the Renaissance patron understood and valued art in part through the media from which it was created.[5] Premodern paints were tempered in egg, pigmented with ground minerals reflecting their organic origins and relationship to nature. Fibers and fabrics were dyed with plant and animal substances. Buildings and sculptures were carved out of marble quarried from the ground. Colorful rocks taken from the earth were cut and polished to form the *pietre dure,* or stone mosaic masterpieces so highly valued at the courts of Europe.[6]

Baxandall's thesis, that the value of a piece of art in the early Renaissance was determined by the substances—gold leaf, rare pigments, silver threads—that went into making it, can also be extended to the Renaissance garden. By the end of the Renaissance, the parterres of elaborate broderie would be constructed of colored sands, stones, and soils that might be thought of as *pietre dure* designs writ large on the landscape. The challenge to Renaissance artists and artisans was to make art out of nature. The earth itself served as the artist's palette. But more importantly, one might think of the earth as the artist's canvas in the Renaissance, the value being determined by the land itself. Nothing was more financially, politically, and culturally more valuable than land. Over the course of the Middle Ages, land ownership had become key to the consolidation of noble power within the evolving political and social structure of feudal Europe. Even as the sale of political offices and noble titles in the late sixteenth and through the seventeenth century became a preferred means of generating royal revenues, the newly ennobled still sought to emulate their peers through the purchase of land.

If land embodied power, the landed could seek, as they did through the patronage of other forms of art, to convey that power through the fashioning of the land. But what might the application of the arts to the improvement of the land (as both palette and canvas) communicate? Renaissance thinkers and modern garden historians alike have worked hard to explain the relationship between art and nature as understood within the Renaissance garden. John Dixon Hunt has demonstrated that Renaissance humanists thought of the formal garden as a "third nature." Drawing on Cicero's *De natura deorum,* Bartolomeo Taegio and Jacopo Bonfadio each invoked the idea of a third nature to describe the formal garden and convey the degree of human action on the landscape, wilderness being the first nature, agricultural lands second nature.[7] Many have sought to define the cultural, intellectual, and aesthetic meanings of that third nature. Were Renaissance patrons and gardeners motivated by the desire to emulate a Ciceronian first nature within the garden? Were they trying, from a Christian perspective, to honor God's work in nature? Or were they seeking to demonstrate human ability to manipulate and improve on God's work through labor, thereby demonstrating status through the exhibition of power over nature? The Renaissance garden yields examples to support each of these hypotheses, making evident the remarkably malleable nature of its meaning and reception. That malleability made the garden an art form capable of communicating identity and power during the culturally dynamic period that is the Renaissance.

The Renaissance garden emerged out of the desire to make the landscape communicate the cultural values, wealth, and power of the patron. Historians of Renaissance garden design have demonstrated that the evolution of the formal garden park over the course of the Renaissance may be understood in context of both the impact of perspective in the axial design of the garden and the acquisition and consolidation of landed estates by noble families.[8] The reciprocal relationships between land acquisition, garden planning, and landed social stature found expression in cartographic demonstrations of power and design—new geographies of power, written on the landscape and recorded in surveys and maps and engravings. By the late seventeenth century, the measurement of land had become the measurement of power.

Those new geographies were being charted and diagrammed on European soil just as Renaissance Europeans created, wrestled with, and reacted to new geographies being mapped out across the globe as Europeans traded with, explored, conquered, and colonized new lands. The quest for new global geographies was driven largely, though not exclusively, by material concerns. As Lisa Jardine has demonstrated, the history of the Renaissance can be written from the perspective of the material.[9] The economic development resulting from trade in goods from the East by Italian merchants and the processing of woolen cloth from northern European sources by Italian mills led to the amassing of expendable wealth that could be and was spent on land and, on the land itself, to the creating and furnishing of gardens. The physical transformation of soil, plants, and stone into garden art, too, is revealing of the materiality of the Renaissance. The same materiality that drove curious Renaissance humanists to collect and study manuscripts led them to seek out, study, and display (increasingly, in the garden) the ancient Roman sculptures that had passed relatively unnoticed through the Middle Ages. And that same materiality led to the growing curiosity about and collecting of plants to fill those gardens and, eventually, to the creation of nurseries to fill the growing demand for increasingly widespread and sophisticated plantations. Most plants destined for Renaissance gardens came from European sources,[10] but as with spices, textiles, and porcelains from exotic places of origin, the desire for rare and visually stimulating plant species drawn from distant locales grew over the Renaissance. The increasing want for and cultivation and display of exotic trees and flowers (and even animals) in the garden demonstrates the relationship between Renaissance materiality and the evolution of new geographies in the period. The Renaissance, of course, coincided with the age of exploration. The desire for things—things that Europe could not produce on its own—drove Renaissance explorers to seek out new trade routes and establish new trade networks that altered the geographic range of European acquisition. Within decades of Columbus's initial voyages in the late fifteenth century, Europe found itself integrated into new geographies—a larger Mediterranean, the Indian Ocean basin, and the Atlantic world.

The Renaissance garden bore witness to the new geographies. As European ships plied ever-larger parts of the world oceans in search of faster and cheaper routes for the trade and transport of commodities bought in the East, they demonstrated a curiosity for the peoples, animals, and plants they encountered. Europeans brought back specimens from around the world to be studied and cultivated, both for agriculture and for the pleasure garden. Seventeenth-century collectors, a group that included scholars, nobles, and kings, increasingly sought plants from the Americas, in particular, to grace their gardens. The desire for American flowering shrubs and trees only grew into the eighteenth century, thereby bringing a unique character to the eighteenth-century English-style landscape garden. But Asia, too, piqued the curiosity of Europeans for whom the taste for chinoiserie invaded the garden: Louis XIV's 1670 construction of the Trianon de porcelaine was inspired by limited European awareness of pagodas and a taste for blue and white Chinese porcelains. Indeed the Renaissance garden, too, traces the evolution of new geographies within Europe: the oranges and lemons moving northward from the Mediterranean mirrored the spread of Renaissance humanism and aesthetics northward from Italy, while the late sixteenth-century acquisition of tulip bulbs by Carolus Clusius from Turkish sources led to the Netherlands becoming the center of tulip cultivation and trade (though to spectacularly disastrous economic consequences).[11] French gardeners, heavily influenced by Italian designers and style, exported formal garden style northward and eastward around Europe. Dutch gardeners, too, were influential in shaping the evolution of garden design in Scandinavia and in Russia, by which the history of the Renaissance garden reveals a dynamism within Europe, as well.[12]

The Renaissance garden also reveals a deep curiosity about and desire to play with and understand nature in all its forms. The acting on that curiosity presents the historian with a unique perspective from which to understand how knowledge was made. The cultural history of the Renaissance garden is also thus the history of new epistemologies through which the contents not only of the garden, but also of the larger world, were understood. Encompassing the centuries associated with the intellectual revolutions that fed the emergence of humanist philosophy and scholarship, the Renaissance is a period of dramatic transformation in how the physical world was understood and explained. Indeed, an examination of the making of gardens in the Renaissance is as much about making knowledge as it is about altering landscapes. The achievement of a formal garden required the accumulation of a breadth of knowledge and experience, ranging from the appreciation of Renaissance aesthetics of garden design and a knowledge of the iconographical language of classical mythology, to an understanding of hydrological engineering, an awareness of fashion in plants, an essential familiarity with the care of those plants, and an acquaintance of the even more mundane matters of pest control, weed management, soil preparation, and so forth. This array of information might be found within one Renaissance mind, but in most cases, it would have taken a team of men to assemble the information and the garden. And that information would have to be gleaned from a diverse set of sources. Following the trail of that information reveals the complex means by which knowledge was created and circulated.

One aspect of this can be seen in the treatment of plants in the garden. Through the Middle Ages, for example, understanding of plants—edible, medicinal, and ornamental—existed in the realm of the vernacular largely as wisdom and experience passed down through generations of peasant families and herbalist monks. Within the universities, medical knowledge of plants was largely received knowledge from the ancients—botany centuries old.[13] These traditions were challenged in the Renaissance not only because of the influx of new specimens from around the world, but also because of the newly placed trust in the powers of observation and experience in gathering knowledge. The curiosity about and collecting of rare and exotic plants, for example, led to a desire on the part of their growers and collectors to meaningfully name and categorize specimens so that distinct specimens could be distinctly labeled and identified.[14] Efforts to classify such plants culminated in the eventual adoption of the Linnaean system over the course of the eighteenth and early nineteenth centuries, but the wrangling of curious sixteenth- and seventeenth-century florists over how to name their many varieties of tulips and anemones must be seen in context of (and driving, even) the epistemological changes in classification.

Knowing and understanding a plant therefore became not only about what the ancients had written about it, but where it originated, how it could be cultivated, what its practical uses were, and what exactly it was, in context of the rest of the botanical world. At the same time, collectors and gardeners expanded the number and variety of plants to be studied through aggressive breeding of cultivars for increasingly visually impressive and hardier flowers.

Collectors and gardeners alike, though continuing to articulate an appreciation for both divine authorship and ancient knowledge of the botanical world, were increasingly willing to accept the challenge of and take credit for the ability to exert human power over the natural world through the selective breeding of plants and increasingly sophisticated taxonomy. Similar transformations, at work between the practical, artisanal world of doing and making, and the theoretical world of the scholar, took place in the realm of physics and engineering. Sixteenth-and early-seventeenth-century Renaissance gardens produced wonderment in those who visited them through their creative use of hydraulics in the production of water-driven automata. Frequently incorporated into grottoes, they were decorated to create the illusion that they were natural formations within earth. And yet, over the course of our long Renaissance, the mechanics hidden within the grotto walls became an increasingly featured part of the garden, as in the great water works at Marly.[15]

Modern scholars studying the culture of curiosity and collecting have shown the importance of the informal but serious, even rigorous, exchange of information and ideas through the republic of letters, the epistolary networks linking elite but highly educated and intellectually curious men.[16] The circulation of information among such men helped to build knowledge about the natural world, in particular, as plants—live, dried, and their seeds—were shared among the curious. Although the curious would eventually be denigrated as amateurs or pedants, their work contributed to the growth in stature of and generated momentum for more systematic study. But the Renaissance garden was the achievement of the collaboration of intellectual and "artisanal" expertise. Thus, knowledge was shaped by artisans carrying out the actual transformation of nature into art and by garden theorists who, in writing about the Renaissance garden, developed a language of garden aesthetics and theory that, too, would shape garden design. Artisanal traditions and techniques came first, theory later. Yet, artisans, gardeners among them, would seek to preserve their knowledge and posterity through their increasing entrance into authorship of treatises recording their knowledge.[17]

The Renaissance garden was, like so many other aspects of Renaissance culture, shaped by the appearance of the printed book. For in addition to the circulation of description and information among the curious via the republic of letters, garden technique, design, and theory found its way into printed volumes of all sorts of books from practical instructional literature to theoretical treatises. Such volumes offered aesthetic models, theory, and practical instruction on their implementation. And they ranged in style and content from the fictional *Hypnerotomachia Poliphili* to the more practically minded estate management books like Olivier de Serres's *Théâtre d'agriculture et mesnage des champs,* and eventually, to volumes dedicated to the construction of the pleasure garden like André Mollet's *Le Jardin de Plaisir.*[18] Some might be sumptuously illustrated, like the illustrated florilegia of Pierre Vallet.[19] Some books, like Ferrari's Latin *De florum cultura,* translated into Italian and published five years later as *Flora overo cultura di fiori,* on floriculture offered intellectual sustenance, aesthetic pleasure, and a healthy dose of "how to" all at the same time—evidence of the erudition and hands-on experience of curious collectors of the seventeenth century.[20] Increasingly, though, different volumes might speak to different needs of their readership, such as the cultivation of fruit trees, or the collection of flowers.

By the second half of the seventeenth century, the popularity, and apparent economic profitability, of garden literature was such that one Parisian printer, Charles de Sercy, assembled a large enough inventory of garden manuals that he requested and was granted permission to publish a series of garden manuals. He published a catalogue advertising his offerings and the series that included new editions of older works like Claude Mollet's *Theatre des Jardinages* and Pierre Morin's *Remarques necessaires pour la culture des fleurs,* as well as more recent volumes. The series included works covering a broad range of garden-related topics including Mollet's work on garden design, "Aristote's" *Instruction pour le jardin potager,* and Venette's *L'Art de tailler les arbres fruitiers,* and the anonymous *Secrets pour teindre la fleur d'immortelle en diverses couleurs.*[21] Charles de Sercy missed no opportunity to market his series: at the end of the fifth tome, he included his "Catalogue des Livres de Iardinages." Within that list, he demonstrated an awareness that his customers varied in wealth, indicating that Boyceau's *Traité de Jardinage* could be purchased in a "petit volume sans figures" for fifteen sols (the cost for most of the volumes he offered) or in grand format for seven livres.

Charles de Sercy's marketing of the books he printed reveals his awareness of and catering to a particular consumer base. He sought to appeal both to their desire for practical information, as well as to the taste for gardening. His books, and the many other manuals and engravings of parterre designs and famous gardens across Europe are revealing of an increasing desire for elites to be at least conversant in, if not knowledgeable in, the garden arts and the theory underpinning them. Indeed, the development of so many new kinds of intelligence (the practical and mechanical, the scientific and aesthetic, all necessary to and intersecting in the garden), made for new opportunities for Renaissance men to demonstrate expertise as a means of fashioning an identity.

If demonstrating an understanding of both the aesthetic and the practical could communicate one's cultivation, the garden arts were perfectly suited for doing so. As N. Valnay, author of a seventeenth-century flower-gardening manual (printed by Charles de Sercy) explained, "[W]hen one mixes reasons with taste . . . beautiful flowers hold the first rank amongst the pleasures of sight."[22] The crux of his argument here is that the appreciation and cultivation of flowers engaged one's senses and one's intellectual faculties. For the appreciation of flowers, he proclaimed, required both *raison et goût,* reason and taste, two qualities that were increasingly necessary to exhibit in elite circles in Renaissance Europe. Valnay's use of the word *raison* refers here to the fact that *raison* was necessary to bring those flowers to blossom—to literally cultivate them, to know how to make them grow. This required a specific *intelligence,* a practical knowledge that made flowers, trees, and other plants distinct from many other goods collected by the curious.[23] But when that practical knowledge was combined with a deeper understanding (*connoissance*) of flowers—their meaning in the natural world, the value of the labor needed to create them, or their aesthetic and even spiritual beauty—one could demonstrate a taste for flowers and all that it implied. By the end of the seventeenth century, the word *goût (goust)* had already come to imply both an interest in something and an ability to discern.[24] *Goût* could imply having an interest in or preference for something. It could be used to refer to a specific style, or it could be used to imply a superiority of quality or aesthetic pertaining to any object, including sculptures, flowers, trees in the garden—and even the garden itself. So taste as something that implied a degree of cultivation was in place by the end of our long Renaissance.

The demonstration of one's understanding of, and taste for, the Renaissance garden as a means to cultivating one's self or one's identity, also tells the historian how the cultural meaning of the garden was fashioned. If the Renaissance is about self-fashioning, then the Renaissance garden illuminates the many increasingly sophisticated ways by which modern man could lay claim to power and cultivation in Renaissance society. Nothing illustrates this better than the appropriation of the Renaissance garden for political purposes. Baldassare Castiglione, of course, argued in *The Courtier* that individual effectiveness as a courtier (and therefore at court) was contingent upon one's demonstration (with grace or *sprezzatura*) of wit, taste, and learning. By the end of the seventeenth century, certainly knowledge of and taste for gardens as well as their natural and artificial components had become essential. On a larger feudal level, the construction of formal pleasure gardens was inherently political to the extent that the garden was a means for great families to exhibit great wealth and taste. The gardens of the Medici and the Barberini demonstrate the role of gardens in the image making that accompanied the consolidation of power.[25] By the end of the Renaissance, gardens and garden iconography had become measures and symbols of power. Nowhere were gardens and their meanings more fully appropriated in expressions of political power than in the France of Louis XIV. Over the course of Louis XIV's reign, his panegyrists transformed expressions of the king's power from classically inspired Greek and Roman iconography to an iconography supplemented with, and eventually supplanted by, the material demonstrations of power over nature. In the first years of his reign, Louis XIV, cast as Apollo, the life-giving Sun King, was the mythological ruler over the gardens, his image and those of fellow Olympic deities providing the iconographical language of power that was expressed largely through the sculptures that formed the fountains in the gardens of Versailles. By the middle of his reign, those deities—and even Apollo himself—were being replaced with literal demonstrations of the king's power over the realm of nature. The collaboration of artisans, engineers, gardeners, and designers in the massive moving of earth, redirecting of waters, engineering of fountains, and forcing of plants to grow in and out of season were understood to be expressions of the reach of the king's power—the garden was a model of the state.[26]

In the 1680s, Adam Perelle designed a series of engravings titled *Veues des plus Beaux Lieux de France et d'Italie*. The collection was not unlike similar collections produced by his father and brother. The most beautiful places in France and Italy included important and aesthetically pleasing palaces as well as gardens in both countries. Featured prominently were the chateau and gardens of Versailles, both recognized and celebrated around Europe for their magnificence.[27] Perelle's set of engravings served as a visual catalogue of pretty places. But they are more than that: they are also a catalog of aesthetic, horticultural, and even political achievements of the Renaissance.

Perelle's images of Versailles included representations of individual *bosquets* and fountains within the garden as well as broader, more inclusive images offering an overview of the entire palace and gardens like that in Figure 0.1, the "veue et perspective" of Versailles. To represent the totality of the park, Perelle produced a "veue et perspective" of Versailles by raising the viewer's sightline into the sky, offering an aerial view of the palace and gardens that extended to a distant vanishing point. Thus, the perusal of the engravings of Versailles, including this one, would have taken the viewer from individual *bosquets* in the garden to the facade of the palace, and into the sky for an aerial view of the palace and the gardens extending to a distant horizon. By the definitions of Antoine Furetière in his *Dictionnaire universel,* Perelle's depiction of Versailles is a *paisage,* an "aspect d'un pays, le territoire qui s'estend jusqu'ua le veue peut porter," and a tableau "ou sont représentés quelques veues de maisons, ou de campagnes. Les veues des Maisons Royales font peint en *paisage* a Fontainebleau & ailleurs."[28] For Furetière, as Thierry Mariage has pointed out, the landscape and the view were nearly synonymous.[29] Perelle's view of Versailles is both a landscape (though engraved and not painted) and an image of a landscape. Perelle's *"veue et perspective"* offered the viewer a vantage point that could not be realized in actuality, but which allowed the viewer to see and comprehend the totality of the park and palace. This conundrum or paradox of Perelle's bird's-eye view is revealing of a deeper transformation in the meaning of the Renaissance garden. Antoine Furetière defines *veue* as

> the manner of looking at things. . . . In order to see well the perspective, one must be at the point of view, in the light of view, which is at the height of the eye which is looking. One also calls a perspective a view of a bird [hirondelle], when the point of view is so elevated, that the buildings, or other bodies which are ahead, [n'empechent point] cannot be blocked from that which one could not see if one were below.[30]

Obtaining this proper view, either by situating oneself at the right point to view something in perspective or by viewing something from above, was therefore intended to bring the viewer to some degree of understanding or comprehension.

Yet, a "perspective" might also deceive. In addition to describing the technique of using linear perspective to create the illusion of depth in a painting or drawing, *perspective* could also be used in seventeenth-century France to describe *trompe l'oeil* scenes painted on the garden wall. As Furetière writes, "[a *perspective* is a] tableau one ordinarily finds in gardens, or on the walls of galleries, which has been made in order to deceive/trick the view, in representing the continuation of an allée, ou du lieu ou elle est posée, ou quelque veue de bastiment ou paysage en lointain."[31] The *veue et perspective* offered by Perelle's images and the gardens depicted within them use the visual trickery of the bird's-eye view to make comprehensible the axial logic of the park in such a manner as to draw the eye outward, beyond the borders of the garden to the

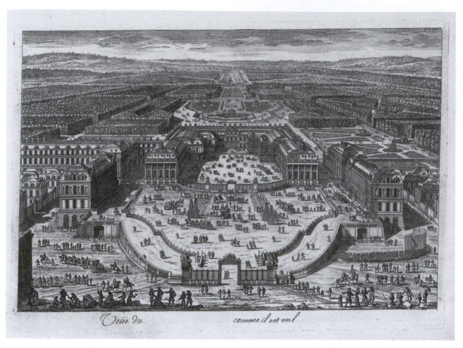

FIGURE 0.1: Perelle, "Veüe du Chateau de Versaille comme il est en la presente année 1687." Paris: Chez N. Langlois. Private Collection.

rest of the French state (as if the metaphorical bird kept flying to the vanishing point that stood for the king's domain). The image encapsulates the entirety of the garden, demonstrating the accomplishments of André Le Nôtre in the creation of the gardens at Versailles, and importantly, through him and the gardens, the glory of Louis XIV. The view, not actually visible to any viewer, has been constructed by Perelle. That construction, however, is the totality of what was Versailles, encompassing the whole of the garden—its physical layout and metaphorical meanings to which Versailles aspired and what the Renaissance garden had become.

The gardens of Versailles—the crowning achievements of André Le Nôtre and his patron, Louis XIV—mark in many ways the cultural zenith and chronological bookend of the Renaissance gardens that are the subject of this volume. Much has been made of Versailles and its gardens as creations designed by Louis XIV to demonstrate his power through the manipulation of nature: the massive movement of earth, the diversion of water, the construction of sophisticated engineering to pump that water into spectacular fountains, the cultivation of plants out of season and out of climate zone all articulated the finely honed message that Louis XIV and France (under Louis XIV's rule), had reached a cultural apogee in the West. That message, constructed as it was out of a seemingly unpromising piece of swampland, marble, lead, water, hedges, trees, and flora of all sorts, together with a very great deal of human labor, were collectively an organic palette from which that message was composed. Perelle's images were designed to circulate that message. But the grand park, indeed, the Renaissance garden that was achieved is, too, a palette from which to reconstruct European cultural history as it had evolved over the course of the Renaissance. For Perelle and for Louis XIV, the garden was not just about the garden, and so it is for us.

The illusion that is embedded in Perelle's *veue et perspective* is telling evidence of both the transformation of the meaning of things and words in the Renaissance, and what the garden came to represent over the same period. In *The Order of Things,* Michel Foucault dissects what he sees as a revolution in the understanding of the human sciences. He suggests that over the course of the Renaissance and into the "classical" age that followed, the relationship between words as signs had become more complex in that "[t]he relation of the sign to the signified now resides in a space which there is no longer any intermediary figure to connect them: what connects them is a bond established, inside knowledge, between the *idea of one thing* and the *idea of another.*"[32] Over the course of the Renaissance, the idea of the garden came to encapsulate a range of knowledges and concepts at which Perelle's *veue et perspective* hints. The act of transformation of landscape into a garden embodies a complex set of cultural ideas and historical developments of which Perelle's deceptive image represents. In that Perelle seeks to bring coherence through the unrealizable view, he is imposing order and making possible comprehension of what the garden represents. Foucault writes that

> The natural history room and the garden, as created in the Classical period, replace the circular procession of the 'show' with the arrangement of things in a 'table.' What came surreptitiously into being between the age of the theatre and that of the catalogue was not the desire for knowledge, but a new way of connecting things both to the eye and to discourse. A new way of making history.[33]

The transformation Foucault describes is the same transformation at work in the garden as it absorbs and makes sense of the new epistemologies and new geographies of the Renaissance. And one might see Perelle's impossible image as a visual attempt to connect eye and discourse—to make visual sense of what the garden encompassed.

The Renaissance garden, the garden as it evolved from 1400 to the late seventeenth century, presents us with an opportunity to turn the tables, to both follow Perelle's bird's-eye view beyond the boundaries of the garden and to simultaneously reverse our gaze back into the garden, using the garden as a means to better understand European culture and history in the period. The Renaissance garden, though constructed out of the building blocks of nature, is essentially the creation of people manipulating things. As such, it offers a unique means by which to explore how Renaissance men and women saw the landscape, the rapidly expanding world around and beyond them, and, at the same time, their place within it. Or, in Foucaultian terms, how the garden came to represent an idea. For like Perelle's image of Versailles that draws viewers' eyes both into the park and beyond it into the larger world, so can the study of the Renaissance garden reveal much of the larger European culture that produced it. Thus, accepting the challenges posed by Perelle's image by using the garden to look beyond allows us to ponder not only the cultural history of the Renaissance garden but also the history of Renaissance culture as revealed by the garden.

CHAPTER ONE

Design

LUKE MORGAN

It looks as though nature in her artfulness, to amuse herself, imitates the
imitation of nature.

—Torquato Tasso[1]

Leon Battista Alberti believed that "it is obvious from all that is fashioned,
produced, or created under her influence, that Nature delights primarily in the
circle."[2] For this reason, he argued in Book 9 of *De re aedificatoria,* that "circles, semicircles, and other geometric shapes that are favored in the plans of
buildings can be modeled out of laurel, citrus, and juniper when their branches
are bent back and intertwined."[3] A few years later in his *Trattato di architettura, ingegneria e arte militare* (after 1482), Francesco di Giorgio Martini
recommended that whole gardens be designed as geometrical figures (circles,
squares, and triangles).

Both texts were important sources for the design of the botanical garden
at Padua (established 1545), which was laid out as a square inscribed within
a circle. The Paduan garden was also a descendent of the monastic or cloister
garden of simples. It was partly conceived as a re-creation of the Garden of
Eden, a complete collection of the world's flora, which accounts for the revelation of the Greek cross in its layout. Most important, however, its perfect
geometry was a microcosmic expression of the intrinsic perfection and orderli-
ness of God's Creation.[4]

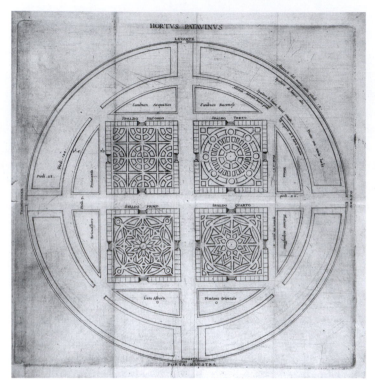

FIGURE 1.1: Plan from Girolamo Porro, *L'Horto de i semplici di Padova*, Venice, 1591. Courtesy of The British Library, London.

The geometry of the Italian Renaissance garden has always been regarded as one of its most characteristic features. Alberti's brief comments on garden design have often been interpreted as implying the received and still commonplace idea that the Renaissance sought to impose an artificial order on nature through geometrical plantings and compartment designs; that in other words, the geometry of the Italian garden is primary evidence of the period's belief in the pre-eminence of the individual human subject in an increasingly secular world. On this view, in the Renaissance garden nature submits to and is *improved* by art.

Obviously, the design of the garden at Padua does not follow this logic. Yet, perhaps this has more to do with its function as a comprehensive collection in which scientific imperatives and religious convictions mingle. What of the Renaissance pleasure garden?

Some time ago, Rudolf Wittkower dispensed definitively with the notion that Renaissance architects were more interested in aesthetic and formal issues than they were the sacred function of ecclesiastical buildings. Alberti's advocacy of centrally planned churches, for example, seemed to an earlier generation of scholars to imply a lack of interest in the practicalities of liturgy and worship (centralized planning makes the placement of the altar problematic, for example). Yet, as Wittkower argued, "in such centralized plans the geometrical pattern will appear absolute, immutable, static and entirely lucid. Without that organic geometrical equilibrium where all the parts are harmonically related like the members of a body, divinity cannot reveal itself."[5]

Wittkower's hypothesis has implications beyond architectural history. Although the imagery of Renaissance landscape design is almost exclusively profane (derived from Ovid's *Metamorphoses* in most cases), contemporary ideas about nature as God's Creation and of God himself as a "Deus Geometer" may well have informed the layout of sixteenth- and early-seventeenth-century gardens, as they did contemporary architecture. It seems worth proposing that an insufficiently acknowledged objective of Renaissance landscape design was to reveal the divine, that is to say, inherent geometrical order of the natural world, not to "improve" or supersede nature through the imposition of an artificial geometrical scheme. This is the sense in which Alberti's statement that "Nature delights primarily in the circle" should be understood. God's Creation is, indeed must be, inherently rational and constructed on geometrical principles. Landscape design of the period thus sought to *reveal*, not impose, nature's concealed order.[6]

This principle, along with the other characteristic tenets of Renaissance garden design, first emerged in Italy, before becoming established as the basis of a European style of landscape design during the late sixteenth century, which was disseminated by peripatetic Italian designers and engineers such as the Francini brothers as well as by foreign students of the Italian garden such as Salomon de Caus. Italian ideas also provide the essential foundation for the development of landscape design in France during the following century though a different cultural context led to transformations in the significance and meaning of geometry in the garden. Nevertheless, André Le Nôtre's designs are inconceivable without the precedent and ubiquity of the Italian garden style. What follows, therefore, is an account of the emergence and development of the Renaissance garden in Italy, focusing on two of the most influential examples, some comments about the diffusion of the style north of the Alps, and, finally, a discussion of the subsequent development of the garden in France, paying particular attention to Versailles.

FIFTEENTH-CENTURY GARDEN DESIGN

There is very little extant evidence for the reconstruction of fifteenth-century garden design in Italy. As a recent survey of Medici gardens of the period indicates, we must rely on a handful of literary texts and paintings.[7] Foremost among these is the *Hypnerotomachia Poliphili* (1499), one of the most influential books in early modern garden history (for its imaginative wood-cuts and descriptions of gardens), and probably the most useful, though by no means the most straightforward source of early Renaissance garden images and forms. In fact, Francesco Colonna's book might be appropriately described as Janus-faced: it looks backward as well as forward. It was published in the last year of the fifteenth century, although its ambience is closer in tone to the elaborate gardens of the mid- to late sixteenth century.

In her detailed study of garden design in the *Hypnerotomachia*, Ada Segre suggests that the garden of Adonis, a *hortus conclusus* or en-closed garden, is modeled on the fifteenth-century *verzieri de le mezane persone* (meadow garden for owners of average rank).[8] They share the

FIGURE 1.2: Woodcut illustration of the Garden of Adonis from Francesco Colonna, *Hypnerotomachia Poliphili*, Venice, 1499. Courtesy of Dumbarton Oaks Research Library and Collection, Washington, D.C.

same characteristics: "the lack of internal subdivision of the lawn, the presence of a water feature as a centrepiece, of a pergola and sparse trees."[9]

Other representations of designed landscapes from the period confirm that these were the distinctive elements of the fifteenth-century garden. In Jacopo del Sellajo's painting of the *Banchetto di Assuero (o della regina Vasti)* (Uffizi, Florence), for example, the banquet takes place under a pergola that closely resembles the one depicted in the *Hypnerotomachia* woodcut.[10] There is also a candelabrum-style fountain in the garden, which is enclosed by high brick walls and is sparsely planted with trees. A similar pergola appears in Domenico Veneziano's *Annunciation* (the predella panel of the *St. Lucy Altarpiece*) of ca. 1445 (Fitzwilliam Museum, Cambridge). The same simple layout of walls, a central fountain, and trees appears in other fifteenth-century representations of the Annunciation (by Fra Angelico and Alesso Baldovinetti, for example), and the Garden of Eden, such as *The Fall and Expulsion from Paradise* from the *Trés Riches Heures* of 1415–16 by the Limbourg Brothers (Musée Condé, Chantilly).

The kind of garden that these sources evoke has more in common with medieval cloister gardens than it does with the fully-fledged Renaissance gardens of Castello, Pratolino, Tivoli, Bagnaia, and elsewhere. Yet, Claudia Lazzaro and others have suggested that what we are accustomed to think of as the Italian Renaissance garden—a designed landscape and site of *villeggiatura* ("the withdrawal to the country of the urban Romans"[11])—emerged in the second half of the fifteenth century.[12]

This view has recently been challenged by Raffaella Fabiani Giannetto, who argues that there is simply not enough textual or visual evidence from the fifteenth century to enable a reconstruction of the early Medici villa gardens of, especially, Trebbio, Cafaggiolo, Careggi, and Fiesole.[13] The assumption of previous historians that the lunettes depicting these properties by Giusto Utens, which date from 1598–99, are records of gardens made nearly two centuries earlier is, she states, anachronistic and untenable. This is difficult to disagree with, especially given the very nature of garden design as a mutable medium, highly susceptible to change. More trenchantly, she also claims that the early Medici villas were

fortified buildings, rather than villas, and this explains why little attention was paid to their surroundings. Hence, the *orti* described by the primary sources were . . . simple orchards, rather than gardens. This consideration would explain the lack of archival sources concerning 'gardens,' in the search of which many scholars have neglected the plentiful information concerning orchards.[14]

The Renaissance garden, a cultivated landscape designed primarily for pleasure—the necessary condition for the emergence of the concept of *villeggiatura*—rather than utility, did not yet exist.

A key difference between the gardens of the earlier period and those of the sixteenth century, beginning with that of the Villa Medici at Castello is the fact that the latter were *designed* in the same way that buildings or other works of art were designed.[15] The unknown designers (their anonymity is in itself telling) of the landscapes associated with the early Tuscan villas most likely did not operate on the basis of drawings and models, but rather on the basis of received workshop practices and lore as well as empirical observation and decision making. At Castello, however, the garden of which was constructed from the 1530s, Nicolò Tribolo was commissioned first to provide drawings and models for fountains and then to design the whole garden, for which at least one sketch survives.[16] This is an important development that is corroborated by Giorgio Vasari's long account of the works at Castello in his biography of Tribolo. Vasari not only mentions Tribolo's designs but also approvingly compares the "labyrinth" of the Castello garden with painting. The introduction of a process of *disegno,* which presupposes a concept of the garden as a work of art, that is, a landscape of pleasure rather than use and composed according to aesthetic rather than utilitarian principles, is essential to the emergence of the Italian Renaissance style as a distinctively sixteenth-century phenomenon.

THE ESTABLISHMENT OF THE RENAISSANCE REPERTOIRE: THE VILLA MEDICI, CASTELLO

Utens's series of fourteen lunettes depicting the Medici villas and their gardens in Tuscany (Museo storico topografico "Firenze com'era") may be of limited use for the reconstruction of fifteenth-century landscape design but they remain an invaluable record of sixteenth-century gardens. They are bird's-eye views painted in an inventory style and are dedicated to recording the properties of the family in as much detail as possible, although Utens occasionally made cosmetic adjustments and corrections. The lunette depicting the Villa Medici at Castello together with Vasari's description give a good impression of the original appearance of the villa and its grounds. In fact, Vasari himself took over the direction of the works at Castello after Tribolo's death, adhering to the latter's original design. More than any other, Tribolo was responsible for establishing the repertoire of principles and elements that underpin the Italian Renaissance garden. His two major landscape designs are masterpieces of the

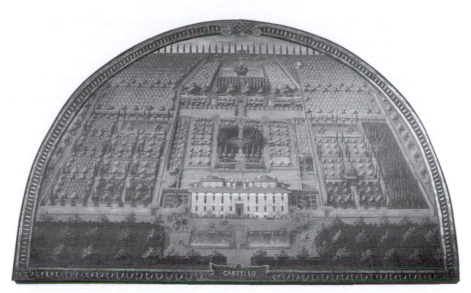

FIGURE 1.3: Giusto Utens, *Castello* (1599). Courtesy of Museo di Firenze com'era, Florence.

style: the garden at Castello (for which Tribolo received the commission in February or March of 1538) and the Boboli garden in Florence (the commission is dated 1549).[17] The former is the focus of this section.

The garden at Castello was Cosimo I de' Medici's first significant act of patronage as duke of Florence.[18] As Vasari states, it was necessary to build an aqueduct (1537–41) before anything else could be done, which indicates the fundamental importance of an adequate water supply to Renaissance garden design.[19] Without water, plants, flowers, and trees cannot flourish, and fountains, *giochi d'acqua, scale d'acqua,* cascades, and grottoes lack their raison d'être. Cosimo's new aqueduct was designed to collect all the waters of the hill of Castellina and was probably deliberately intended to associate the Medici duke with his Roman predecessors: the town of Castello was the site of an ancient Roman *castellum* (cistern or reservoir).[20] Lazzaro has noted that sixteenth- and seventeenth-century visitors to Castello were most impressed by the large number of fountains, grottoes, and other water features distributed throughout the garden. As early as 1549, for instance, William Thomas, visiting from England, thought it probable that "every flowre is served with renning water."[21]

Not unlike Poliphilo's progress from the dark wood to the paradisiacal concentric gardens of Cythera in the *Hypnerotomachia,* the visitor to the Medici garden at Castello first ascended the hill at the back of the villa before beginning his or her descent from Bartolommeo Ammannati's Apennine

Fountain (installed in 1565) and the *boschetto* ("a wood of cypresses, mulberry trees, yews, laurels and other evergreen trees, finely spaced out," according to Vasari), through gardens of increasing sophistication and ornamentation.[22] The route properly begins at the highest point of the garden, therefore, which must first be reached, suggesting that the visitor's experience was initial uncomprehending ascent followed by comprehending descent.[23]

The general layout of the garden could also be apprehended from the upper floors of the villa, although this was not aligned on the central axis, despite Utens's silent correction of what must by the end of the sixteenth century have seemed a "flaw." Tribolo's chief organizing device was the central axis, which divided the garden in two. The main ornamental and iconographical elements were all located on this axis and included the personification of the Apennine mountains beyond the *boschetto* at the top, the Grotto of the Animals, the Garden of the Labyrinth with its fountain and the Fountain of Hercules immediately below. The main east–west cross axis from the lawn below the Fountain of Hercules led to two large gardens, both of which are divided into square planting beds.

The axes imply symmetry. On close analysis of the Utens lunette, however, the west and east sides of the garden are discovered to be nonidentical, despite the modular repetition of the beds throughout. To the east, for example, a rectangular strip of evergreen trees runs along the length of the boundary wall, which is not mirrored on the western side of the garden. Utens also depicted an octagonal pavilion on the eastern side of the garden that is absent in the west. These subtle differences and variations within the modular order introduce what Alberti described, in another context, as "copiousness and variety."

In *On Painting*, Alberti advises artists to inject variety into their compositions through the inclusion of male and female figures of all ages, as well as animals, yet at the same time, he warns against excess and confusion (in the Latin edition of the treatise, he states that nine figures are an ideal number). According to him, "[t]hat which first gives pleasure in the *istoria* comes from copiousness and variety of things. In food and in music novelty and abundance please, as they are different from the old and usual. So the soul is delighted by all copiousness and variety. For this reason copiousness and variety please in painting."[24] Until the emergence of the Le Nôtrean style in France, gardens were generally organized as a series of loosely related, episodic spaces in which copiousness, variety, and contrast rather than unity and homogeneity were the controlling aesthetic concepts.[25]

This compositional principle recalls another, more ancient source that was also known to Renaissance designers: Pliny the Younger's well known letter to his friend Domitius Apollinaris. For Pliny, a garden was ideally characterized by what he calls "harmonious and regular variety."[26] Tribolo's layout of the Medici garden at Castello might almost have been meant as a demonstration of the idea: it is broadly harmonious and regular, but simultaneously copious and various in its detail and experience.[27]

The point should be made here that the Renaissance had access to very little information about ancient villa gardens. Pliny, despite the influence of his concept of "harmonious and regular variety," is extremely vague about what his gardens actually looked like, and Vitruvius has almost nothing of use to say on the subject. The other main sources were the agricultural treatises of Cato, Varro, and Columella.[28] Needless to say, no garden had survived from Antiquity. This lack should, however, be regarded as a fertile one. With only the slightest hints to go on, sixteenth-century designers developed a garden type that is an authentic product of the Renaissance but involved little revival or "rebirth." There was no elaborate system of rules governing garden design, as there was for architecture for instance, which followed Vitruvius. If there had been, it is unlikely that there would have ever been a *Sacro bosco,* or *Parco dei Mostri,* as it is now referred to, at Bomarzo.

Taking one of the two flint staircases down from the uppermost garden, the visitor to Castello would have encountered a lawn, dotted with orange trees (and depicted in the Utens lunette). Set into the wall was the grotto of the animals, which Vasari barely mentions (it was not finished until 1572), and a fountain to each side representing Mt. Asinaio and Mt. Falterona. The water then flowed underground from these two fountains to personifications of the Mugnone and Arno below, alluding to the relationship between the mountain source and river in both cases. Next comes what Vasari refers to as the "principal garden" or the "garden of the labyrinth." According to him,

> In the middle of the garden are high and thick cypresses, laurels and myrtles growing wild, and forming a labyrinth surrounded by a hedge two and a half braccia high, so regular that it looks as if it had been produced by the brush. In the middle of the labyrinth Tribolo made a beautiful marble fountain, as the duke desired.[29]

The fluvial theme is continued here. In his later, more detailed description of the fountain, Vasari notes that Tribolo "proposed to erect a bronze statue three braccia high on the top, to represent Florence, to which the waters of Arno and Mugnone flow."[30] (Florence is personified as Venus Anadyomene wringing out her hair.[31])

The basin of the fountain is circular. At the center of Tribolo's design, therefore, is a circle squared: two perfect geometrical forms, which are roughly

contemporaneous with the botanical garden at Padua and often signify, respectively, heaven and earth or the macrocosm and the microcosm. Tribolo's
Garden of the Labyrinth may invert the ground plan of the Paduan garden,
but it remains no less an image of natural perfection, albeit on a smaller scale.

Vasari's observation that the box hedges of the Labyrinth are so artfully
grown (and clearly pruned), they look as if they have been "produced by the
brush" amounts to high praise: the gardener's art is the equal of the painter's,
the implication being that painting is normally capable of greater perfection.
It is also suggestive of the complexities attending the relationship between art
and nature in the Renaissance garden, a point underlined by the presence of
two monkeys in the grotto of the animals (a monkey also appears in Bernardo
Buontalenti's Grotta Grande in the Boboli Gardens). It is probable that the
frequent inclusion of monkeys in the artificial grottoes of the Renaissance is
meant to recall the well-worn idea that art is or should be the "ape" of nature,
a particularly appropriate garden concept, and one that can also be understood
in terms of Renaissance ideas about the intrinsic perfection of Creation.

More often than not, the relationship between art and nature in the Renaissance garden is a collaborative one. John Dixon Hunt has noted that the idea
of the garden as a *terza natura* (third nature), which is the result of the collaboration of art and nature, is first mentioned by Jacopo Bonfadio in a letter of
1541, followed by Bartolomeo Taegio in his 1559 treatise *La Villa*.[32] Cicero's
discussion of "second nature," by which he means agricultural landscapes, inspired the development of the concept. "First nature" is the untouched natural
world. The relationship between art and nature may be weighted differently in
individual gardens and periods, but there is always, to a greater or lesser extent,
some form of cooperation between art and the organic, even if it occasionally
takes on the character of *paragone*. This is an important theme of early modern
landscape design, sometimes implicit rather than explicit, but always present.

Vasari remarks that the pavement around the fountain of the labyrinth was
filled with "slender jets, so that by turning a tap all those who come to see
the fountain are sprinkled, and escape is not easy."[33] Even Alberti thought
that a garden should be a "festive" place, where humour and comedy are ac-
ceptable.[34] From the *giochi d'acqua* or trick fountains of the *Hypnerotomachia,* to the more sophisticated wit of the epigram over the Mouth of Hell at
Bomarzo—"Lasciate ogni pensiero voi ch'entrate"—a reformulation of Dante's
"Lasciate ogne speranza, voi ch'intrate," Renaissance garden designers sought
to inject humor into their designs. The combination of serious conviction and
light comedy that characterises Tribolo's design—geometry and joviality—is a
recurring feature of the Renaissance garden.

On leaving the Garden of the Labyrinth, which is the physical and conceptual heart of the design, the visitor would have immediately encountered another fountain, with a sculptural group at its apex depicting Hercules squeezing the life out of Antaeus. As Vasari puts it, "[f]rom the mouth of Antaeus water issues in a great quantity, instead of his spirit." This is a paradoxical image: water, which is after all an element necessary to life, is here made to represent Antaeus's last exhalation before expiration.

The subjects of the two main fountains very obviously belong to what Elizabeth Blair Macdougall has described as the topoi of Italian Renaissance garden design.[35] Venus and Hercules are among the most common and repeated figures in the fountains and statuary of the Italian garden. At Castello, they also provide a good example of the way that this standardized lexicon of Ovidian subjects could be inflected with local significance, which is to say that although the iconographical themes of the garden may seem quite limited, they actually constituted a flexible and adaptable language that could be made to express patriotic, political, and propagandistic ideas.

The garden at Castello is the first garden of the Renaissance to express a coherent political message, which Vasari claims was formulated by Tribolo with the assistance of the humanist Benedetto Varchi. The garden's imagery was dedicated to extolling the virtues of the duke and his family, as well as their close association (indeed near interchangeability), with the city of Florence. Venus, at the centre of the composition, is also Florence, a Florence dominated by, or under the protection of, the Medici (goat heads, alluding to Cosimo's sign of Capricorn, and the arms of the main cities of Tuscany adorn the fountain's shaft). Hercules is a commonplace princely symbol, but the Fountain of Hercules and Antaeus at Castello may specifically celebrate Cosimo "having routed his enemies at Monte Murlo in his first year," as Vasari put it.[36] The whole garden is therefore a kind of emblem of the continuity of the Medicean peace under Cosimo.

Bernardo Buontalenti's garden design for Cosimo's son Francesco I de' Medici at the Villa Medici, Pratolino (now the Villa Demidoff), suggests the extent to which Tribolo's approach at Castello became normative. Many of the principles that Tribolo first essayed at Castello are also present at Pratolino (axial layout, variety and copiousness, and the generation of meaning through dispersed topoi), but they had by 1569 (the date that work on the garden began) become so familiar that Buontalenti could treat them ironically, in the knowledge that contemporary visitors would understand his point of departure.[37]

For example, as at Castello, visitors to the garden marveled at the abundance of water that Francesco and Buontalenti managed to bring to what had previously been a barren and unpromising site. Fynes Moryson, another English traveler, surmised that at Pratolino water probably cost more than wine.[38] However, where Castello's fluvial iconography cohered in a grand theme of ducal munificence (Cosimo redirecting water from the mountains to the people of Florence), at Pratolino, the culmination of the progress of the waters down the hillside was deliberately prosaic, even scatalogical. As Utens's lunette reveals, at the lowest end of the central axis, which is aligned with the main entrance of the villa and bisects the garden, was a figure of a laundress and a pissing boy by Valerio Cioli. According to contemporary accounts, the boy continuously soiled the washerwoman's laundry: a distinctly mundane image compared with Giovanni da Bologna's Venus Anadyomene/Florence on her pedestal at Castello.[39]

The provision and manipulation of large quantities of water, a marked tendency toward axial layout, the controlled variety of plantings, which becomes extreme to the point of disunity at Pratolino, geometrical design (especially near the villa or palace, as Alberti recommended), a fascination with the interactions of art and nature and the use of conventionalized topoi to express local and personal meaning(s) all become central characteristics of Italian Renaissance garden design. The importance of Tribolo's design for Castello lies in the fact that he brought these ideas and principles together in a lucid and integrated whole for the first time.

THE TERRACED GARDEN *ALL'ANTICA:* THE VILLA D'ESTE, TIVOLI

Michel de Montaigne remarked on the "gushing of an infinity of jets of water" at the Villa d'Este, Tivoli in his *Travel Journal* of 1580–81.[40] He also noted, however, that he had seen similar waterworks elsewhere on his trip, especially in Florence. In fact, Montaigne writes that the Villa d'Este was built in deliberate rivalry of Pratolino. According to him,

> As to the richness and beauty of the grottoes, Florence is infinitely superior; as to abundance of water, Ferrara [by which he means the garden at Tivoli of Ippolito d'Este, Cardinal of Ferrara]; in variety of sports and amusing mechanisms derived from water, they are equal, unless the Florentine has a little more elegance in the arrangement and order of the whole body of the place; Ferrara excels in ancient statues, and in the palace, Florence.[41]

Indeed, most of the ornaments and effects of the d'Este garden have their antecedents in the Medici villa gardens. The basic principles of Tribolo's approach
to garden design are of equal importance to the late-sixteenth-century gardens in and around Rome. Yet, even so, the designs of Pirro Ligorio for Tivoli
amount to more than a simple redaction or transplantation of the Florentine
style to the Lazio region. Unlike Tribolo's garden at Castello or Buontalenti's
at Pratolino, Ligorio's garden was conceived as an antiquarian paradise. Ligorio was the leading antiquarian of his generation and his original plan for
the garden at Tivoli (which is the focus of the following discussion), was full
of erudite scholarly allusions and references. Before considering the growing
importance of the theme of the cult of Antiquity in the Renaissance garden,
however, some comments on Ligorio's design are in order.

Cardinal Ippolito d'Este commissioned Ligorio to design the garden, which
was constructed between 1550 and 1572 at vast expense. The cardinal demol-
ished parts of the old town of Tivoli, including more than one church, to make
way for the terraces. These were indebted to Donato Bramante's design for the
Belvedere Court (1504–13) in which monumental staircases and other architectural features link three terraces along a central axis.[42] This elegant solution
to the problem of integrating different levels, which Bramante himself derived
from ancient architectural complexes such as the Sanctuary of Fortuna at Palestrina, was adopted in numerous subsequent terraced gardens of the sixteenth
and seventeenth centuries.

As at Castello and Pratolino, the provision of water to the new d'Este garden
was of fundamental importance and, likewise, became a key theme of Ligorio's
iconographic scheme. The main source of the Villa d'Este's water was the River
Aniene, which Montaigne described as "muddy" and an "extreme misfortune."
The cardinal also had an aqueduct built to convey water from the purer Rivel-
lese spring to public fountains in the town of Tivoli and his own garden.[43]

The principal fountains, which were also the main vehicles of the garden's
themes, were related axially to one another. In Étienne Dupérac's idealized engraving of the Villa d'Este of 1573, which includes features that were planned
but never realized, the garden is bisected by a central longitudinal axis that
begins at the top of the hill at the entrance to the villa and ends at the lower
entrance to the garden in the foreground (not visible). On the other side of the
villa, aligned to this axis, is a fountain of Venus, asleep, which can be interpreted as the source of the garden's waters. The axis recalls the one at Castello,
although there is at Tivoli a much closer relationship between the villa and the
garden.

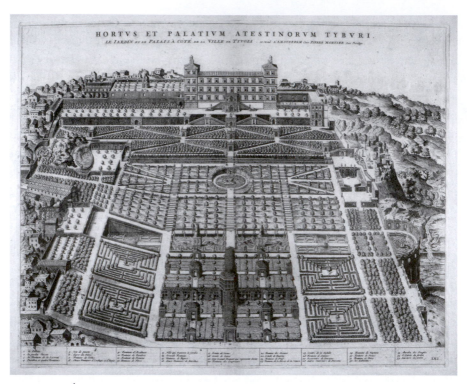

FIGURE 1.4: Étienne Dupérac, Villa d'Este, Tivoli, 1573. Courtesy of The British Library, London.

At Tivoli, in approximately the place of the Labyrinth at Castello, there is a circular basin containing the Fountain of the Dragons. The fountain may have been constructed in honor of Pope Gregory XIII, who visited the villa in September 1572, but its primary significance derives from a recurring topos of Renaissance garden design in general: the idea that the Villa d'Este garden is a new Garden of the Hesperides. On this basis, the Fountain of the Dragons represented the hundred-headed dragon Ladon who guarded the entrance to the mythical garden.

Visitors to the garden frequently commented on the Fountain of the Dragons. Fulvio Testi, for example, thought that it demonstrated how "human ingenuity has thrown the elements into confusion, and known how to attribute to water the effect of fire."[44] He was referring to the way in which the four dragons, instead of breathing fire, project great plumes of water into the air. This is, as Testi recognized, a contradictory concept: the element of fire is represented at Tivoli by its antithesis—water. In this sense, it shares a family resemblance with the Fountain of Hercules and Antaeus at Castello, in which water is paradoxically made to represent Antaeus's last breath. It also suggests that in the *paragone* between art and nature, here the former has succeeded in manipulating the latter against itself. The figure of the Goddess of Nature, however, depicted as Diana of Ephesus, embodies the opposite idea. The goddess with her rows of breasts (which in the original cultic statues may have actually been meant as bulls' testicles, making them extremely potent images of fertility) originally decorated the water organ, which played "real music" according to Montaigne. The implication was that nature is the source of the organ's music and, by extension, the other artifices of the garden.

The d'Este garden was laid out as a right-angled grid, which divides the terrain into regular units.[45] The garden was thus compartmentalized in a similar but more rigorous way to that at Castello. The Dupérac engraving makes this compartmentalization and the overall geometry of Ligorio's plan extremely clear, perhaps clearer than it ever was in reality. It may not be coincidental, given what has been said about the revelatory character of the geometry of the Renaissance garden that the patron of the garden of the Villa d'Este was a high-ranking cardinal and that the villa itself began life as a monastery.

The geometry of the gardens at Castello, Tivoli, and elsewhere should not be regarded as an intransigent strait jacket or as a stifling, self-imposed imperative. The principle is one of "harmonious and regular variety" to recall Pliny or, as Annibale Caro put it in his 1538 description of Cardinal Giovanni Gaddi's garden in Rome, a "disorderly order."[46] The central axis of the d'Este garden, though it is perfectly aligned with the villa, does not divide the garden into equal halves. The left side differs significantly from the right in size, topography, and ornamentation, as the Dupérac engraving shows. This contrast is established immediately at the lower entrance to the garden where there are two rustic wall fountains facing one another: the niche of the one on the right is made of travertine and that of the one on the left *tartari* (much used in rustic decoration in Rome).[47] Both fountains are constructed from materials that are well known natural products of Tivoli and therefore appropriate to the decoration of the garden, but in their difference within a similar structural type they also establish at the outset the principle of contrast—orderly, but nonetheless, identifiable—that the garden as a whole, like most Italian Renaissance gardens, is founded on.

Cardoli, who published a description of the Villa d'Este in 1588, was "at a loss in such variety what first to admire. Each object in itself captures the eye of the visitor and holds and delights it, unsatiated."[48] The most important of these objects—fountains and architectural features—were located at the ends of the cross axes, with the exception of the Fountain of the Dragons.

For this reason, instead of a steady, linear passage toward the villa on the crest of the hill or toward the large pergola at the lower entrance, the visitor would have crisscrossed the garden so as not to miss any of its key features. The layout was noncoercive in the sense that visitors made their own choices about their progress despite the organization of the garden around a central axis.

Most visitors would probably have lingered at the Rometta, which was located at one end of the d'Este garden's major latitudinal axis—the Alley of the Hundred Fountains. The Rometta is unusual in sixteenth-century garden design for the exactitude with which it was designed and executed (much of it has since been destroyed). The engraving by Venturini shows that the chief monuments of the seven hills of ancient Rome were all represented by models in a kind of compressed capriccio, with an emphasis on *castelli* and other monuments to water. It clearly reflects Ligorio's interests, but it is worth adding that Ippolito d'Este was himself an aficionado and avid collector of ancient statuary and that the garden of his villa was an open-air sculpture gallery. This also had a famous Florentine precedent: Lorenzo de Medici's sculpture garden and "school" at San Marco in Florence, which was instrumental in Michelangelo's early development. As David Dernie has shown, Ligorio's design for the

FIGURE 1.5: G. F. Venturini, Rometta, Villa d'Este, Tivoli, 1691, from G. B. Falda, *Le Fontana di Roma*. Courtesy of Dumbarton Oaks Research Library and Collection, Washington, D.C.

Cardinal's garden also deliberately associated it with the numerous archaeo-logical sites in and around Tivoli.[49]

Nicolas Audebert and Fulvio Testi both thought that the Villa d'Este sur-passed everything in its immediate vicinity and, indeed, anything that the an-cients had ever done.[50] Yet, as has been suggested, almost nothing concrete was known about ancient garden design during the Renaissance. What then was the status of Antiquity in the sixteenth-century garden?

Once again, the *Hypnerotomachia* provides some clues. Colonna's narra-tive, which takes place in a series of gardens, is, among other things, a dream of Antiquity, almost a lament for its irretrievable loss, which can only be accessed via the medium of the dream or, more accurately, a dream within a dream. It has been described as an architectural treatise rather than a romance (though it might be better thought of as an architectural romance), the third to be printed in the Renaissance after Alberti and Vitruvius himself and the first to be printed with illustrations.[51] Yet, although Poliphilo's descriptions of "antiquity" are ex-traordinarily detailed, they are generally not archaeologically accurate, even by the standards of the time, as were those of Alberti. For Colonna, the extant re-mains of antiquity evoked a kind of wonderland, removed in time and place but retrievable through reverie, whereas for Alberti, the same fragments comprised an essential ingredient in practical architectural education. In other words, Col-onna's approach is fantastic and imaginative whereas Alberti's is practical and scholarly (in his writings on architecture, though not in his comments on gar-den design, which are as vague as Pliny's before him). In many ways, however, Colonna's antiquarian landscapes are closer in spirit to the Renaissance garden, which was rarely a place of exact architectural knowledge anyway.

Roman Renaissance gardens were laid out according to the same basic principles as their Florentine equivalents, but with more emphasis on Antique statuary and allusion, which is not surprising given the greater availability of Classical architecture and material culture, however fragmentary, in Rome and its vicinity. At Tivoli, as at Castello, water, with the added significance of *renovatio* or revival (another allusion to the antiquity and ancient significance of the town), was of great importance. In both cases, fountains established the main themes. As in Tribolo's designs for both Castello and the Boboli Gardens, Pirro organized his garden around a central axis, although at Tivoli the trans-verse avenues assume more importance in the iconography. The relationship between art and nature, which is sometimes more collaborative and at others more antagonistic, is equally important in the d'Este and the Medici gardens. Finally, there is a similar attempt to give specificity to generic topoi through regional imagery and personal allusion.

DIFFUSION: THE ITALIAN RENAISSANCE
STYLE AS EUROPEAN STYLE

The Italian Renaissance garden style was well on the way to becoming a de facto European style by the end of the sixteenth century. Visitors to Italy sought to lay out similar gardens on their return home. Italian architects, engineers, and gardeners also became peripatetic to an unprecedented degree, often dominating court positions, much to the chagrin of local practitioners. This is an understudied phenomenon that deserves its own treatment. As Lyn White Jnr. has argued, "[t]heir [Italian engineers] impact upon the general culture of Europe was as great as that of the contemporary Italian humanists, artists, and musicians, yet their history remains almost completely unwritten. This is the single greatest lacuna in our understanding of the Italian Renaissance."[52] An apposite example is provided by the figure of Costantino de' Servi.[53]

When in 1610, Prince Henry Stuart requested that someone trained by Tommaso Francini, the designer of the Italianate royal gardens at Saint-Germain-en-Laye near Paris, be sent from the Florentine court to London to design the garden at Richmond, de' Servi was dispatched. Once there, he was involved in the design of the prince's garden, which was to include a colossus three times larger than Giovanni da Bologna's Appennino at Pratolino as well as elaborate and automated but not always successful theatrical spectacles and fêtes.[54] Clearly, and the accounts reflect this, de' Servi's expertise was valued more highly than anyone else's at Henry's court, including that of Inigo Jones, due to his Florentine training. Similar patterns emerge at other European courts during the period.

If bona fide Italians were unavailable then the next best option was to employ someone who had studied in Italy, or who had at least visited. Salomon de Caus, the Dieppois hydraulic engineer, theorist, and garden designer is perhaps the leading example of the period. Although we know little about his early career, it is almost certain that de Caus spent some time in Italy towards the end of the sixteenth century, where he familiarized himself with the design principles and topoi of the Italian Renaissance garden. He subsequently became, through his published and built works in Brussels, London, and Heidelberg, one of the early seventeenth century's main exponents of the Italian Renaissance garden style.

De Caus's *Hortus Palatinus* in Heidelberg was referred to as a "Northern Pratolino," despite the fact that its cultural context could not be more dissimilar to the Italian gardens discussed previously. The *Hortus Palatinus* was commissioned by the Protestant elector Palatine Frederick V on the brink of the Thirty Years War as a gift to his new wife Elizabeth Stuart, yet it was a

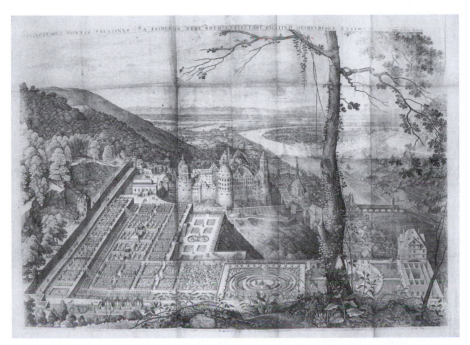

FIGURE 1.6: Matthias Merian, Scenography, from *Hortus Palatinus*, Frankfurt, 1620. Courtesy of Dumbarton Oaks Research Library and Collections, Washington, D.C.

thoroughgoing Italianate garden, implying, on one hand, that the style was not associated with a particular religion or politics and, on the other, that its reach had by the beginning of the seventeenth century become pan-European. It thus exemplifies the diffusion of the design principles articulated earlier and is the epitome of the transplanted Italian Renaissance garden.

Like the Villa d'Este at Tivoli, the *Hortus Palatinus* was to be a terraced garden *all'antica,* although the close relationship between villa (or, in this case, *Schloss*), and landscape is here nonexistent. The main principle behind its composition is one of "rareté," to use de Caus's term, which is the equivalent of the Italian emphasis on variety and copiousness. Every part of the garden was to be carefully individuated. *Parterres en entrelac* are juxtaposed with *parterres en broderie;* Narcissus, the embodiment of sterile *amour-propre,* is contrasted with Ceres and Pomona, goddesses of the fertility of the earth. Even within a single parterre of knots, each of the four beds was to be uniquely designed. Similarly, each terrace of the *Hortus Palatinus* consists of parterres and other features (which include fountains, grottoes, a water parterre, and a mount), all derived from the Italian repertoire of garden forms and elements. The imagery of de Caus's design also exploited the conventional topoi of the Italian

Renaissance garden: there was a fountain of Neptune; figures of Venus, Ceres, Pomona and the Muses; an attic frieze depicting the labors of Hercules; and a mount, which alludes to Parnassus and is based on the one at Pratolino.

Although the *Hortus Palatinus* is probably the most complete example of an Italian Renaissance garden north of the Alps, the country where the style exerted the most widespread and consistent influence was France. From Philibert de L'Orme onward, Italian ideas were quickly absorbed into the design language of the French garden, resulting in what is sometimes referred to as the Franco-Italian style.[55] This started to occur very early on in the sixteenth century and is the essential foundation for the development of the garden in France during the following century.

JARDINS DE VOYAGE: LE NÔTRE AND THE FRENCH GARDEN

In one of Abraham Bosse's illustrations for *Manière universelle de M. Desargues* (1648), nature has been completely transformed into a geometrical environment. Bosse depicts a garden in which the organic elements have been reformed, corrected even, to such an extent that it is almost impossible to tell the difference between the stone circle and square in the foreground and the natural volumes of the *palissades* bordering the central allée. In his important study of seventeenth-century French landscape design, Thierry Mariage has drawn attention to an anonymous manuscript of approximately the same period, which expresses a similar concept of nature to that of the Bosse image in the literary form of a dialogue: "'Nature' retorted Pamphile 'is not always good to imitate; a painter must select it according to the rules of his art, and if he does not find that which he seeks, he must correct that which is presented to him . . . an able painter must by no means be a slave to nature.'"[56]

If these sources are compared with the ground plan of the botanical garden at Padua and Alberti's comments on nature as the artist's guide and model with which this chapter began, then a cultural shift begins to emerge: from the imitation (or revelation) of nature as the goal of garden art to the correction of an imperfect nature by art (just as Alberti's remarks are transferable to garden design so too are those of "Pamphile"). This shift or mutation in the perceived significance of geometric design differentiates the seventeenth-century French garden from its Italian predecessor. Unlike Tribolo and Cosimo at Castello, Le Nôtre and Louis XIV at Versailles were less interested in the revelatory than they were the regulatory: "Le *jardin,* c'est moi" perhaps.

FIGURE 1.7: Abraham Bosse, illustration for *Manière universelle de M. Desargues*, 1648. Courtesy of Houghton Library, Harvard University.

André Mollet's short definition of a "perfect" pleasure garden in *Le Jardin de Plaisir* (1651) remains the most succinct itemization of the principles and elements of seventeenth-century French landscape design. It is difficult to surpass and is thus worth quoting at length as a theoretical context for Le Nôtre's work at Versailles. According to Mollet,

> First we should say that the royal house must be sited to best advantage, in order to ornament it with all things necessary to its embellishment; of which the first is to be able to plant a big avenue with a double or triple row of female elms, or lime trees (which are the two species of tree which we esteem most suited to this effect) which must be placed in line at right angles to the front of the château . . . Then, facing the rear of the house must be constructed the *parterres en broderie,* near to it so as to be easily seen from the windows, and gazed upon without obstacles such as trees, *palissades,* or any other elevated thing which can prevent the eye from embracing its full extent.
>
> Following the said *parterres en broderie* will be placed the parterres or compartments of turf, as well as the *bosquets, allées* and high and low *palissades* in their proper place; made in such a way that most of the said *allées* lead to something and always terminate in a statue or the centre of a fountain; and at the extremities of these *allées* put fine perspectives of painted canvas, so as to be able to remove them from damage by weather when one wishes to. And to perfect the work, statues should be placed on pedestals, and grottoes built in the most suitable places. Then raise terrace walks according to the convenience of the place, without forgetting aviaries, fountains, water jets, canals, and such ornaments which, duly being carried out, each in their place, form the perfect pleasure garden.[57]

Mollet's first point, that the "royal house" must be well situated, recalls Alberti. Yet, when work at Versailles began in earnest in 1661 (the date of the first enlargement), the available territory was distinctly unpromising. The marshy site was hemmed in by forest and the royal house was not much more than a hunting lodge. As Kenneth Woodbridge notes, Le Vau's plan for the redesign of the château involved enclosing the existing building in an "envelope consisting of two new north and south wings, linked by a terrace which left the old west front exposed."[58]

The great achievement of Versailles, however, lies precisely in Le Nôtre and his team's creation of a vast and complex garden ex nihilo. Unlike the Medici

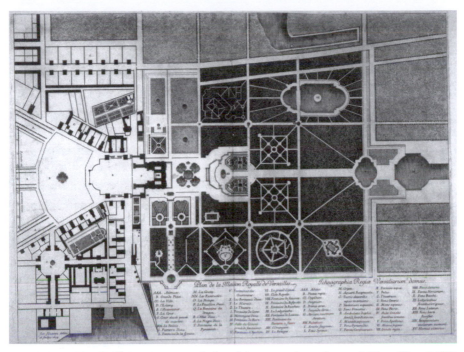

FIGURE 1.8: Israël Silvestre, map of the château and gardens of Versailles, 1680. Courtesy of Musée du Louvre, Graphic Arts Department.

garden at Castello or the d'Este garden at Tivoli, the site at Versailles was characterized by more natural disadvantages than advantages. Certainly, at Castello and Tivoli, "problem solving," especially regarding water and its provision on a large scale, was important to the general effect of the garden on visitors. Even so, the point always was that art and nature pooled their resources, collaboratively evolving a design that maximized the potential of both in unique circumstances. The regional imagery of the Italian Renaissance garden might be interpreted as embodying this basic tenet. In contrast, at Versailles, there was no reference to the undistinguished local terrain. The creation of the garden was not a collaborative act; it was imposed.

In his *Science de la géographie* (1652), Père Jean François defines "place" as "an immobile expanse which precedes the things placed on it, and is capable of supporting them . . . an expanse for which the essential feature, difference, and primary notion of place is to contain created beings and their extensions."[59] This is a very different concept to the earlier idea that nature must be inherently orderly and geometrically constructed; for François, nature was essentially blank—a support or "material envelope," as in Mariage's phrase, which has "lost all symbolic value."[60] The creation of the garden at Versailles out of such poor natural materials suggests something very similar. Le Nôtre's design, of course, has symbolic value—the garden is willed into existence through autocratic fiat—but the site has little or none at all.

Next, Mollet recommends that a "big avenue" be constructed and lined with trees. The main axis at Versailles, known as the Allée Royale, is the descendent of Tribolo's axes at Castello and Boboli, but is much larger. Indeed, the sheer scale of Versailles, like Vaux-le-Vicomte and other designs by Le Nôtre, distinguishes it from its Italian predecessors. These are gardens in which the Albertian principle of proportion and environments scaled to the human subject is no longer relevant. Erwin Panofsky put this best perhaps when he commented that a garden by Le Nôtre was designed to be driven around (by horse and carriage), rather than walked through.[61] They are *jardins de voyage*.[62]

Variety remained an important desideratum. The Allée Royale at Versailles is augmented by numerous additional perpendicular and diagonal allées. Likewise, the parterres adjacent to the château leading down to the Bassin d'Apollon have symmetrical elements but others that differ considerably. This is the principle articulated by Antoine-Joseph Dézallier d'Argenville, who probably derived it directly from Le Nôtre himself: "variety is necessary not only for the general design of a garden, but also in each separate component, since it would be disagreeable to find the same design on both sides . . . [O]ne should not repeat the same components on both sides except in exposed areas where the eye can compare them with each other and judge their conformity."[63]

Mollet states that *parterres en broderie* (flowing foliate patterns of box or colored gravel or earth that from above resemble embroidery, hence the name), should be laid out to the rear of the house. Le Nôtre departed from this principle at Versailles, however, installing a water parterre instead, which offset the monumentality of the château through its reflection of the sky.[64] In Mollet's directions and Le Nôtre's design, this is followed by more parterres (or compartments), as well as *bosquets, allées* and *palissades*.

There were numerous *bosquets* at Versailles, the history of which is highly complex due to the fact that they were regularly altered.[65] *Bosquets* were stylized versions of the Italian *bosco,* incorporated into the geometric design rather than, as at the Villa Lante, Bagnaia for example, functioning as a kind of foil or contrast to the "third nature" of the garden as a whole. Many of the *bosquets* at Versailles were enclosed by carefully trimmed hornbeam hedges that rose to a height of ten feet, not unlike those depicted in the Bosse illustration. The hedges thus appeared as virtual walls made out of natural materials: architecture rather than horticulture. They are essentially geometrical volumes whose material just happens to be organic.

The remaining garden ornaments in Mollet's definition include fountains, statues, grottoes, aviaries, water jets and canals, all of which were installed at Versailles in large quantities. As in the designs of Tribolo, the main axis was the most important from the point of view of the garden's iconography. At Versailles, the principal theme was dictated by Louis XIV's self-identification with Apollo. Indeed, there are numerous allusions to the Apollo myth throughout the garden, from the Bassin d'Apollon, containing Baptiste Tuby's group of Apollo and his horses (installed in 1670), which terminates the Tapis Vert, to the reliefs of west façade of the château facing the garden.[66]

A fundamental difference between the Italian Renaissance garden and the seventeenth-century French garden as conceived by Le Nôtre is the much greater scale and extension of the latter. Mollet, for example, makes the interesting point that at the extremities of the allées of a garden "fine perspectives of painted canvas" should be installed beyond (presumably) the statues or fountains that every allée culminates in. These were intended as *trompe l'oeil* extensions of the garden proper.[67] Their purpose was to augment the already expansive extension of the allées, to suggest that the garden had no boundary or wall (not unlike the *saut-de-loup* or English ha-ha in effect). The scale of the classic French garden was in this way increased still further through illusionistic painting.

In more general terms, if the "exterior rooms" of the Italian garden were comparatively intimate and the garden a private paradise that, through its enclosure and demarcation from the surrounding territory (a third nature), preserved, however vestigially, the earlier notion of the *hortus conclusus,* the allées and canals of the French garden brooked no obstacle. Perceptually at least, Versailles extended to the horizon line. The idea of *villegiatura* is, in a sense, here inverted: Versailles was not intended so much as a restorative retreat from city life (as was the Italian villa garden) as it was a generative model for the regulation of the territory of France at large. As Pierre-André Lablaude has argued, the garden at Versailles became "the very heart and the driving principle behind a new kind of land management. Like a spider weaving its web, the garden was at the centre of a radiating mesh of channels furrowing through the forest. Soon converted into thoroughfares, these roads extended beyond the confines of the garden to the very frontiers of the provinces, dividing, classifying, organizing and exploiting the entire land."[68] The garden thus "unites with the countryside," as Dézallier put it, or, perhaps better, *determines* the countryside.[69] In other words, Versailles corrects or even supersedes nature on a regional scale. The humanistic and syncretic principles behind the Italian garden in which geometric design had a revelatory purpose and art and nature are held in dynamic equilibrium, give way to the autocratic imperatives of *le roi soleil*'s self-fashioning.

CHAPTER TWO

Types of Gardens

RAFFAELLA FABIANI GIANNETTO

In his 1962 seminal study on architectural typology, art historian and critic Giulio Carlo Argan wrote that "the birth of a type is . . . dependent on the existence of a series of buildings having between them an obvious formal and functional analogy."[1] When the definition of type was first formulated in the second half of the eighteenth century, it implied not only the notion of form, which, in the case of building types, needed to be expressive of a building's character or purpose,[2] but also the idea of origin, exemplified by the aesthetic ideal of the archetype, from which all other building structures were thought to descend. With regard to garden studies, the most immediate application of typology often involves the comparison of numerous gardens in search for common formal characteristics, with the objective to identify the one garden that served as a model for all the others.

In order to go beyond formal analyses of gardens, however, it is useful to recall the more complex definition of type as was formulated by Quatremère de Quincy in the third volume of his *Encyclopédie méthodique* of 1825. "The word type" wrote Quatremère, "presents less the image of a thing to copy or imitated completely than the idea of an element, which ought in itself to serve as a rule for the model . . . The model . . . is an object that should be repeated as it is; the type, on the contrary, is an object with respect to which each artist can conceive works of art that may have no resemblance to each other. All is precise and given in the model; all is more or less vague in the type."[3]

From Quatremère's definition, it follows that the word *type* does not describe a precise and definite form, but rather an idea of form, or the most elemental scheme, that is deduced from a series of examples.[4] This means that a type is not formulated a priori, but rather preexists its definition. Thus, in the process of comparing and juxtaposing all the forms of individual gardens for the definition of the type, all the specific characters of each garden are eliminated, and only the common elements remain. This way the type is a schema deduced through a process of reduction of formal variants to a common form. And this form must be understood as "the principle that contains the possibility of infinite formal variation and even the potential for the modification of the type itself."[5] In addition, Quatremère's definition allows us to take into account not only the way form relates to function but also the genesis of the form itself, which is a response to specific ideological, religious, or practical questions posed at a certain cultural and historical time. In fact, historic garden types are not only created to respond to practical and contingent exigencies, but they also answer deeper questions that are deemed fundamental within a certain civilization.

The vagueness that characterizes the definition of type implies also that the morphological configuration of gardens, their function, and their symbolic and cultural meaning may have variable degrees of importance according to the type under consideration. In some cases, such as the countryside garden across Europe, form may be the determining factor for the identification of the type, considering that each villa garden, or estate garden, may have had more than one function in time and that its meaning and the cultural premises that generated it may be different from country to country. The genesis of botanical gardens, on the other hand, shows a more balanced relationship between function, form and the symbolic meaning embodied by it, whereas in the case of hunting parks, function, or better yet the rules and rituals of the sport, define the type more so than the morphology of the individual examples and their ideological content. The examples of suburban gardens, botanical gardens, and hunting parks that I describe in this chapter problematize the word *type* and reveal that Renaissance gardens are often characterized by a combination of one or more types.

COUNTRYSIDE GARDENS

Our first type under consideration is the countryside garden, which includes villa gardens, château gardens and the gardens of countryseats. As we shall see, countryside gardens are often characterized by formality of design, and their layouts obey to a certain degree the rules of symmetry and number. These qualities first emerged in the villa gardens of Renaissance Italy, and eventually informed the design of French château gardens and the gardens of countryseats typical of England, although each country adapted Italian forms and experiences to autochthonous traditions thus producing multiple subtypes of the countryside garden.[6]

In Italy, *vigne* and *orti* are the predecessors of Renaissance villas. The term *vigna* was mostly used around Rome to describe farms and vineyards. *Orto* was more common in Tuscany and elsewhere in Italy, where it was used to indicate both a small, cultivated field and a *giardino* or garden. Among the most famous *orti* are those the Medici owned on the outskirts of Florence. The purpose of the Roman *vigne,* as well as that of the Medici *orti,* besides the obvious agricultural profit, was to serve as a retreat away from the city where the owners could go to enjoy the harvest, the mild climate during the summer months, or to escape from the plague. In the fifteenth century, as well as earlier, it was common for a learned individual to engage directly in the practice of agriculture. Vespasiano da Bisticci tells us how both Cosimo de' Medici and Pope Boniface IX were known for their eagerness to prune vines with their own hands in their respective residences, the Medici *orto* at Careggi and the papal palace in Rome. The reason for this was the observance of a morally impeccable lifestyle, one in which the cultivation of the land corresponded to the nourishment of the soul and the obedience to the command of God. Thus, Leon Battista Alberti advised, "Buy the villa in order to provide for your family, not for the delight of others . . . furnish the house with that which is and might be necessary. Do not buy any of those goods that your fields produce."[7]

The symbolic content of the villa was known to Renaissance humanists from Roman classical literature produced from the time of the Republic to the early Empire. In particular, the writings of Republican writers such as Cato's *De agricultura* and Cicero's *Epistolae ad Atticum* or *De senectute,* exposed the first humanists to the classics' celebration of villa life and offered them a model for the pursuit of an ethical conduct that conformed to the moral principles of their times. But the ancients' lifestyle was not the only lesson considered worthy of imitation. In fact, the embellishment of gardens by means of statuary was also a practice inherited from the Romans. As Lorenzo de' Medici's persona reveals in Poggio Bracciolini's dialogue *De vera nobilitate,* the Romans were known to adorn their villas and gardens with statues, some of which representing their ancestors, in order to illustrate their glory and the nobility of their lineage.[8] From the fifteenth century onward, therefore, the practice of collecting sculptures, especially classical ones, and arranging them in gardens, became not only a means to ennoble a place and with it its owner but also a way to display someone's classical learning, which was often associated with virtue, for the acknowledgment of the contemporaries as well as for the remembrance of posterity. One of the earliest sculpture gardens of the Renaissance was included in the *vigna* that Pomponio Leto purchased in the second half of the fifteenth century on the Quirinal Hill. The garden's inscribed stones were meant to create a setting suitable to contemplation and study. Like Cosimo de' Medici at Careggi, Leto emulated at his *vigna* the moral life of Republican Rome. He was a reader of Cato and Varro, and in his commentary on Columella's treatise on agriculture, he advocated that scholars and rulers should devote themselves to the cultivation of their gardens.

The display of sculpture in villa gardens continued through the following century, although collecting antique statuary was a consequence of a new archaeological and scientific interest. The new attitude is represented in a painting of the *vigna* Cesi by Hendrick van Cleef III. The painter populated the canvas with numerous characters, all engaged with Cardinal Cesi's collection in different ways: some dig, some study, some draw, and some carry away seemingly heavy fragments. The urge to collect was not only motivated by an interest in antiquity, for marbles were not the only things that aroused curiosity. This is the time when also exotic plant species were gathered, catalogued, and cared for within the walls of gardens probably in an attempt to create

FIGURE 2.1: Hendrick van Cleef III, *View of Cardinal Cesi's Antique Sculpture Garden*, 1584. Courtesy of The National Gallery, Prague.

a sublunar version of paradise, which was the place thought to house the most complete of the collections. According to Ulisse Aldrovandi, the Bolognese naturalist who visited Rome in 1550, on entering Cesi's garden, a visitor would have experienced astonishment, marvel, and delight, as if entering "*un paradiso.*"[9]

Toward the middle of the sixteenth century, collecting ancient statuary became a highly commercialized pursuit and men of power and wealth felt the need to distinguish themselves and their gardens by commissioning new artwork that would be assigned a precise location within their gardens, and together, they would form a narrative ensemble. The new trend is particularly evident in Florence and Rome and is tied to cultural, political, and economic changes. In Florence, for example, the type of the villa as a *luogo di delizie* appears in connection with the fact that primary economic activities, such as agriculture, hunting, and fishing, soon became "useless" aristocratic pastimes when the Republic became a duchy in 1537. Thus, when the Medicis were granted ducal title over the entire city, their villas were no longer just a combination of farmland and *orti*. Rather, their gardens embodied a clear allegorical program carried out through the integration of sculpture, grottoes, fountains, and plant specimens within the overall design.[10] The most important example of this is the villa at Castello (see Figure 1.3). There, each section of the garden represented an event connected with the life of the duke. For example, the group of Hercules defeating Anteus was meant to represent Cosimo's victory against the anti-Medicean party. Venus located at the center of a labyrinth stood for Florence and springtime and was meant to suggest a parallel between Cosimo's renovation of the city and the Roman emperor Augustus's *renovatio imperii*. At this time the ideal villa of imperial Rome, as described by the Younger Pliny, along with the lifestyle associated with it, were taken as models more than the writings of the Republic's *scriptores,* which offered answers to questions that were no longer asked, nor did their descriptions conform to the prevailing taste.

The new villa, therefore, becomes a propaganda vehicle for sovereignty as city palaces had been in the past. Of course, the purpose of the new garden was not only representational, and some of its parts were the result of practical choices dictated by horticultural exigencies and specific functions connected with the life style of the duke. Although members of the earlier generation were directly involved in the practice of agriculture, their successors engaged in less "righteous" activities, and indulged in less-productive pastimes. At this time, *orti* and *vigne* of notable members of the laic and papal aristocracy were no longer the locus of labor and toil carried out by few for the benefit of the household or of the collectivity, but they were rather the work of art of an elite of intellectuals, usually hired by one client, such as the duke or the pope, for his own benefit and for that of his entourage.

In Rome, before the Counter-Reformation, the members of the church had started to spend lavishly in the construction of their summer residences urged, according to David Coffin, by the several foreign (i.e., Florentine) cardinals elected pope in the first half of the sixteenth century. An exemplary case is that of Villa Giulia, built for Pope Julius III just outside the walls of Rome. Elected pontiff in 1550, Cardinal del Monte "enjoyed a rather simple hedonistic life, delighting in rustic food and pleasures, such as peasants' dances and the festivities of the vintage."[11] In 1551, the pope started to acquire land around the *vigna del Monte,* his family property, until he owned the area from his old *vigna* to the edge of Monti Parioli and down to the Tiber. Unlike earlier, more modest *vigne,* the size of Villa Giulia was exceptional. In fact, the villa was planted with 36,000 trees during the years of construction and until the pope's death in 1555. Most of the elms and white poplars were planted across the hillside in order to form a wooded background around the villa. Ammannati reports that the property included "delightful woods for hunting thrush where one walks every where under the foliage so that the sun does not disturb the hunting."[12]

As Mirka Beneš has pointed out, because of its scale and its mixture of formal gardens, parkland, and farmland, the Villa Giulia can be interpreted as the prototype of the new estate villas, or villa parks, constructed in the last decades of the sixteenth century.[13] The most famous of these are the Villa d'Este at Tivoli and the Villa Lante at Bagnaia. While these villas present aspects of former *vigne,* such as agrarian lands planted with olives, grains and vines, like the Villa Giulia, they also represent an evolution of the prototype that has to do with their formal configuration. Previous villa gardens included at least three zones: a secret garden of compartments, which was usually adjacent to the house; a central garden or meadow that may or may not have included a labyrinth; and a *selvatico* with its *vivaio* usually in the highest portion of the property.[14] Each of the three garden sections or rooms was clearly separated from the others by means of walls, hedges, or changes in the topography. These villas were also characterized by a peculiar longitudinal section that visually linked the first floor of the buildings to the highest part of the gardens along the major axis of symmetry.

The Medici gardens at Castello exemplify the layout of the villas from the first half of the century (see Figure 1.3). The oldest part of the garden, or *giardino segreto,* coincided, at the time of the Medici's purchase of the property, with an existing *orto* planted with trees and grapevines.[15] The latter were replaced with simples during Tribolo's redesign of the garden in 1537. In spite of the transformation it underwent, the secret garden, so called because the most private, retained some of the features of the preexisting *orto*, such as the surrounding wall and the ordered layout. By means of axial design and symmetry, equally sized compartments replaced the old, regularly spaced vines and fruit trees. In Tribolo's original project, the central portion of the garden was occupied by a circular labyrinth of cypresses, myrtles, laurels, and boxwood. The evergreens emphasized the theme of the ever-lasting spring, that is, the wish of eternal peace and prosperity for the city of Florence under the duke's rule. The gardens were also meant to be seen from afar, in particular from the windows of the upper floors of the building, from which Cosimo I, and his guests, would have been able to appreciate the unfolding of the allegorical program narrated by the garden rooms following each other on the central axis of the composition. On the other hand, the details of the sculptural elements within the garden would have called for a closer look, perhaps during a stroll in the gardens.[16]

The same subdivision of the grounds into three main garden areas is found at Boboli, the difference being that here the design of the gardens is more integrated with the design of the building in that they are both aligned on the same longitudinal axis. Also, a *teatro di verzura* ringed by rows of evergreens, instead of a labyrinth, occupied the central portion of the gardens. The amphitheater was aligned on the central axis of the palace and culminated in a wide alley ascending through the trees to a marble fountain and fish pond. All around it was a cluster of orchards, muscatel vineyards and vegetable plots interspersed with groves for bird hunting, the so-called *selvatico* that characterized Castello.[17] The same longitudinal axis is found at the Villa Giulia, where it visually links the building with the rear courtyard, the nymphaeum, and the private garden.

Unlike the earlier gardens, the Villa d'Este and the Villa Lante were located in the feudal seats of the old titled aristocracy, so they included and recreated the landscape typical of the hills around Rome, which was characterized by natural forest of native oaks, firs, chestnut and hazelnut trees, holm oaks, elms, and beeches.[18] Moreover, because the palaces-castles of most fief towns were located on hills, or at least at such elevations as to afford a commanding prospect of the countryside, the new villas presented an inverted longitudinal section if compared to earlier examples (i.e., Boboli, Castello, and Giulia), and their terraced layout was a clear response to the topography of the existing site. The Villa d'Este, for example, reverses the traditional sequence of

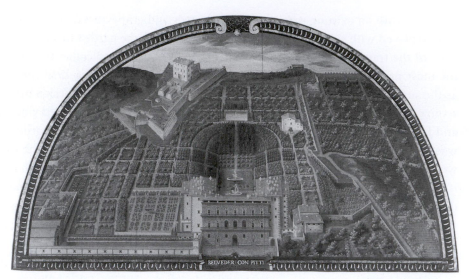

FIGURE 2.2: Giusto Utens, Veduta di Palazzo Pitti e del Forte di Belvedere, Museo Storico Topografico "Firenze com'era," Inv. 1890 n. 6314. Courtesy of the Ministero per i Beni e le Attività Culturali.

compartments, *prato*, and *selvatico* that is found in earlier villas, presenting an opposite longitudinal section. From the balcony on top of the loggia on the rear façade of the building, in fact, the cardinal would not face the woods of his property, in this case located right below the balcony; rather, he would enjoy "a magnificent prospect . . . to the mountainside beyond on whose slopes lie the terraced remains of the ancient villa of Quintilius Varro almost on axis with the gardens of the Villa d'Este."[19] A similar configuration exists at Villa Lante, where two *casini* instead of one building are located halfway the sloping hill, and the formal gardens are laid out on the lowest portion of the property.

In the decades around 1600, the villa type evolved as a consequence of the social transformations that were taking place in the upper tiers of the Roman landowning aristocracy.[20] Estate villas no longer included the formal elements that used to appear in the traditional *vigne*, such as the garden of compartments planted with fruit trees and flowers. Planting beds were increasingly replaced by tall trees, such as umbrella pines, firs, and holm oaks, and the parklike character of the traditional *selvatico* was also emphasized. The Villa Borghese, designed by Flaminio Ponzio for the Cardinal Scipione Borghese from 1606 onward is an example of such transformation. The villa, and especially its *barco*, or hunting park, summarized aspects of both the Roman *campagna*, which included farms and meadowlands for grazing cattle, and the forestlike landscape of fief towns. On one hand, by accentuating the parklike character of his estate, the Cardinal was appropriating a formal characteristic of the villas that the landed

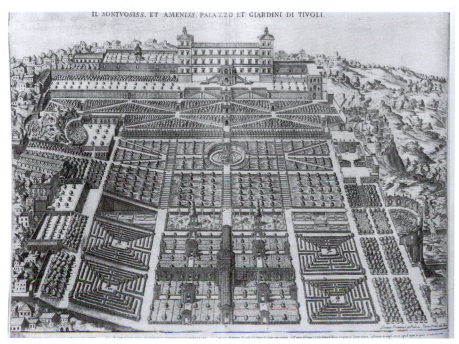

IL SONTVOSISS. ET AMENISS. PALAZZO ET GIARDINI DI TIVOLI.

FIGURE 2.3: Étienne Dupérac, Villa d'Este, Tivoli, 1573. Courtesy of the American Academy in Rome, Photographic Archive.

aristocracy had built in their fief towns, which were characterized by native forests of tall trees. The difference, however, between earlier villas and the Borghese's was that the latter was located just outside the city walls, in a landscape of vineyards. Therefore, as Beneš has demonstrated, the evolution of the villa type was dictated by the urge to represent the social status of the new wealthy families, especially the *famiglie da papi*, who acquired the aristocratic and hereditary rank of the old baronial families by investing in their lands.

It is also possible, however, that a change in the typology of the villa occurs because of foreign influences, although tree gardens had been planted earlier in Tuscany in villas located close, if not within, the city walls, such as Boboli. By the beginning of the seventeenth century, many villa patrons had the opportunity to travel and visit the most important royal gardens that members of the European aristocracy were founding in their respective countries. Among the most famous examples was the country residence of the Spanish king Philip II at Aranjuez. In the early seventeenth century, Cardinal Camillo Borghese, Scipione's maternal uncle, visited Aranjuez and "found it simply splendid and unique."[21] Indeed, the landscape at Aranjuez was unique, in that it did not conform to a local, Castilian type. Rather, it summarized the most notable features of European country estates without

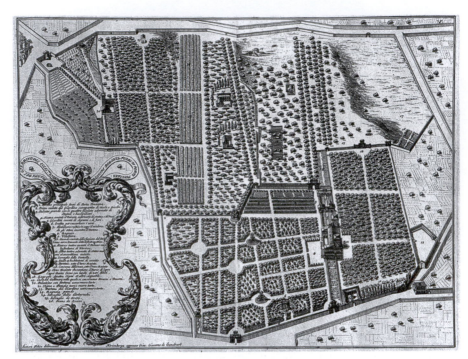

FIGURE 2.4: Simone Felice, bird's-eye view of Villa Borghese, ca. 1675. From G. B. Falda, *Li giardini di Roma*. Courtesy of the Bibliothèque Nationale, Paris.

directly imitating any one of them. Philip hired foreign designers and arti-sans who were supposed to handle those tasks for which they were famous in their countries of origin. So, French, Flemish, and Italian designers were employed to execute those landscape elements deriving from France, Flan-ders, and Italy respectively. In particular, three elements were characteristic of the new royal estate: the use of squares planted with trees—which were imitated at Villa Borghese—and long tree-lined avenues that connected the house to the surrounding landscape were features borrowed from France; shaded avenues and hedgerows were also used in Flanders; and the use of sculptures, fountains, and geometrical plantings symmetrically arranged around an axis were obviously Italian elements, though by this time they were to be found elsewhere in Europe at considerably larger scale. Notwith-standing the borrowings, Aranjuez was still original because of its departure from its numerous models. For example, unlike most Italian villas, including Villa Borghese, the estate was not bounded by a wall, but rather merged with its surrounding landscape. Moreover, at Aranjuez, plazas opened along the tree-lined avenues, and together they formed a system that was superimposed

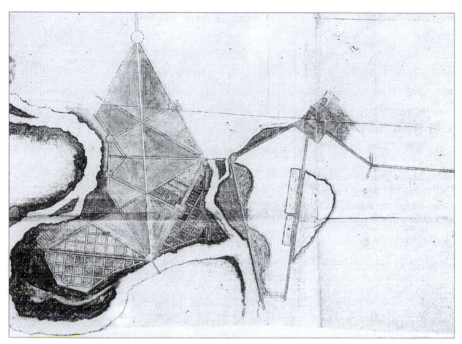

FIGURE 2.5: Juan de Herrera (attributed), map of the estate of Philip II at Aranjuez, c. 1570. Real Biblioteca (Madrid) IX/M/242/2 (4). Courtesy of the Patrimonio Nacional, Madrid.

on a landscape of cultivated fields, which was not to be found in northern European parks.

It has been pointed out that the coexistence of foreign design influences on the Spanish country estate is a sign that different European landscape designs were considered of equal value by the middle of the sixteenth century. If this is true from a stylistic point of view, however, the functions and meanings of countryside gardens across Europe differed considerably. In fact, the most important feature that distinguished Italian villas from foreign country seats was their being created for the purpose of *villeggiatura*, that is, for brief stays during the summer, to take a break from city affairs and usually to indulge in literary *otia* or more frivolous pastimes. French châteaux, on the contrary, were intended to be inhabited for longer periods. In the fifteenth and sixteenth centuries, they housed the itinerant royal court who could choose among the castles of the Loire valley first and, later, during the kingdom of Francis I, among the châteaux around Paris, such as Fontainbleau, Madrid, and Saint Germain-en-Laye. France was one of the European countries in which the old feudal system was most firmly established, and "the format of country life for the privileged classes derived from the feudal château."[22] Since the Middle Ages, the château was intended as an economically independent structure, which bore no relationship to the urban capitalism and money economy of the city. "The social character of the château did not change substantially as the monarchy gained in power, drawing the aristocracy into a dependent position at the court, where competition for royal favor made rustic retirement [e.g., villa life] a risky option."[23] A slightly different situation existed in Spain. Here, members of the aristocracy preferred living in their city palaces rather than on their lands, which were incorporated into municipalities, and "this practice may have discouraged the building of permanent residences in the country," whether castles or villas.[24] The existing country buildings were unpretentious dwellings set amid modest gardens. Aranjuez, of course, was an exception. But because it never served as a seat for the court, not even temporarily, as in the case of French châteaux, its existence and function depended on the center of government in Madrid. In this sense, its existence was more similar to the villas of central Italy, which were conceived primarily as retreats. However, unlike the villas of central Italy, Aranjuez was, from an economic point of view, a self-sufficient establishment. The estate "produced its own wheat and barley, and it raised goats, cows and fowl. Most of the produce was consumed by the king and the court or was shipped to Madrid or wherever the king was staying."[25] Moreover, the major difference of this countryside garden was that its elements were conceived for multiple functions: "a meadow might be grazing land, the site of a hunt or the destination of an outing for the queen."[26]

In sum, the gardens of the countryside created during the Renaissance across Europe fit the vague definition of type given by Quatremère de Quincy in his *Encyclopédie méthodique*. The gardens of Italian villas and those of French châteaux, as well as the gardens of Philip II at Aranjuez, were different in scale and purpose, for they all responded to functional exigencies and local cultural and economic traditions. Yet, they presented a similar formal vocabulary of parts arranged according to the rules of symmetry and proportion that Italian humanists had derived from their interpretation of the Roman classical villa. However, as Ackerman has pointed out, "Renaissance designers would have been disappointed and disoriented had they discovered that most Roman villas were not classical. The normal ancient example . . . lacked the axial symmetry, rational integration and proportion that supported their conception of the heritage of antiquity."[27] Rather than characterizing Roman gardens, axial symmetry and proportion were the formal characteristics embodied by most

Renaissance villa and château gardens, which is an indication of the fact that the definition of type is never objective, rather it always implies a translation that "tells us as much about the translator as about the original disposition of the . . . [types] themselves."[28]

BOTANICAL GARDENS

Unlike the villa garden, the botanical garden type that emerged in the Renaissance did not develop out of Renaissance archaeological and literary knowledge of antiquity. The type that precedes the botanical garden is the herb garden, which was mainly associated with monasteries in Medieval Europe and was included within villa gardens—often called *giardino segreto*—during the Renaissance.

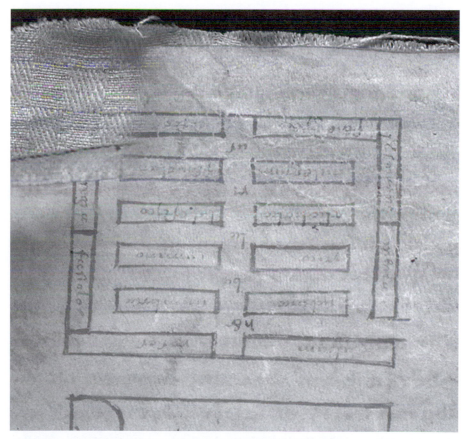

FIGURE 2.6: St. Gall plan of an ideal monastery, detail. Abbey Library of St. Gall, Switzerland, Codex Sangallensis 1092 recto. Courtesy of the Stiftsbibliothek St. Gallen.

Monastic orders were responsible for the introduction and exchange of "simples," which were cultivated for their medicinal and healing properties. Herbs, or simples, were the simplest ingredients used by apothecaries for the preparation of *remedia composita*. The earliest document showing what a *hortus medicus* may have looked like is the famous plan for an ideal monastery found at St. Gall, Switzerland. The plan, which was likely drawn up in several stages between 816 and 836, includes a vegetable garden, a smaller herb garden, and an orchard. The garden of simples, located to the northeasternmost portion of the site, includes eight rectangular plant beds surrounded by a longer and continuous bed that opens along the southwest corner to allow for access. Whether or not the ideal complex was ever built, its plan is the earliest known example of a garden drawing that includes a list of the plants cultivated in each bed. This information allows us to say that most of the plants recommended for the medical herb garden were natives.

The transformation of the *hortus medicus* into a botanical garden occurred in the moment at which exotic and nonmedicinal species were added to the collection of natives typical of the herb garden, and when foreign plants were sought after and domesticated for their own sake, rather than for their potential ability to cure diseases. Of course, this transformation took place over a long time and was due to several factors, including the scientific approach to the study of plants based on direct observation rather than on ancient written descriptions and the consequent foundation of botany as a discipline distinct from medicine.

The curiosity toward novel plant species imported from foreign countries was not an exclusive prerogative of monks and nuns. In fact, many wealthy individuals and rulers of both western and eastern countries across the centuries engaged in the exchange of seeds and cuttings and contributed to the naturalization of plants outside of their native environment. One of the earliest records of an attempt to naturalize exotic species in Western Europe dates to the eighth century. Abd al-Rahman, the first Umayyad emir of Moorish Spain, is said to have initiated expeditions for the import of foreign plants, such as the pomegranate from Syria, into al-Andalus, especially for cultivation within the precincts of his country palace estate.[29] In addition to plants being imported from distant geographical locations, the exchange of authoritative texts on medicine, which often included sections on plants, also contributed to the dissemination of botanical knowledge. We know, for example, that a copy of Dioscorides's *De materia medica* was sent to Abd al-Rahman III in 337/948 as a gift by the Byzantine emperor Constantine

VII Porphyrogenitus. The text, which was the most authoritative treatise on the practice of medicine and the use of medicinal plants from 78 C.E., contained plant descriptions and illustrations that had been based on direct observation. However, Dioscorides's text was in Greek and the identification of the plants described by him presented numerous difficulties in countries outside of the Byzantine Empire.

In addition to the problem of translation, plant identification in the pre-Linnean period was complicated by the fact that very often herbalists would have conflicting opinions with regard to what plant species matched Dioscorides's descriptions. The study of botany became even more complicated when herbalists found more than one match for each of Dioscorides's plants. An early attempt to organize the study and teaching of simples dates to the sixteenth century when Francesco Bonafede instituted the *lectura simplicium,* or chair of simples, at the University of Padua, Italy. In 1543, Bonafede petitioned the Venetian republic for the establishment of a garden of simples for didactic purposes. Being close to Venice, Padua had access to the trade links established by the Venetian government with regions of the Eastern Mediterranean, such as Constantinople, Egypt, and Syria, in addition to Crete and Cyprus that were part of the Republic. From these regions, Padua received plant specimens that were sought after for their pharmacological potential. Therefore, Bonafede's garden of simples, which was approved for construction in 1545, allowed him to expose his students to the direct observation of living specimens or *ostensio simplicium,* thus complementing his *lectura simplicium,* or botanical lesson that was based on the commentary of ancient texts, such as Dioscorides's and Galen's. Soon the garden at Padua became a well-known center for scientific research, especially after rare and exotic plants, in addition to medicinal herbs, were imported and acclimatized, and the *hortus medicus* transformed into a botanical garden.

Following the example of the garden at Padua in the following years, similar botanical gardens were created at other European cities, most notably at Bologna, Leiden, and Pisa. The Pisan garden, located in Via Santa Maria, between the university and the cathedral, was patronized by a Medici grand duke.[30] In 1592, Ferdinand I entrusted the construction of the garden to a Flemish botanist named Joseph Goedenhuize, known in Italy as Giuseppe Benincasa or Casabona, who was also in charge of Ferdinand's botanical garden in Florence.[31]

Unlike the gardens at Padua and Pisa, the Florentine garden did not have a didactic scope, for it was established for the private enjoyment of the grand duke. The existence of this garden is particularly important because it shows that the botanical garden of the Renaissance was not a rigid type. Although as early as the fourteenth century Pier de' Crescenzi wrote that the cultivation of medicinal herbs should be pursued in private gardens, thus implying that the cure of simples is not only a prerogative of monasteries, sources show that private individuals also grew exotic species within the walls of their residences or within those of the gardens entrusted to their care. A well-known example is that of Niccolò Gaddi, a learned naturalist and collector of scientific curiosities, who was credited by Agostino del Riccio as having been among the first private individuals to establish a garden

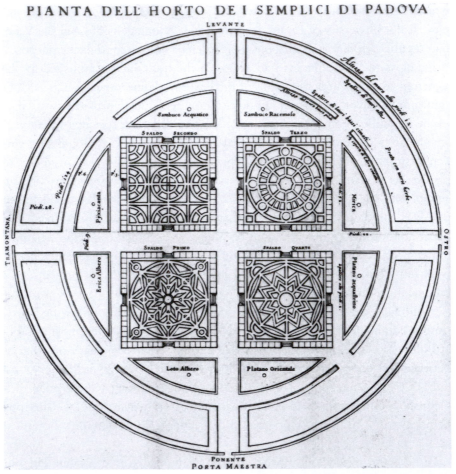

FIGURE 2.7: G. Porro, *L'horto de i semplici di Padova*, Venice, 1591. Courtesy of the Herzog August Bibliothek, Wolfenbüttel.

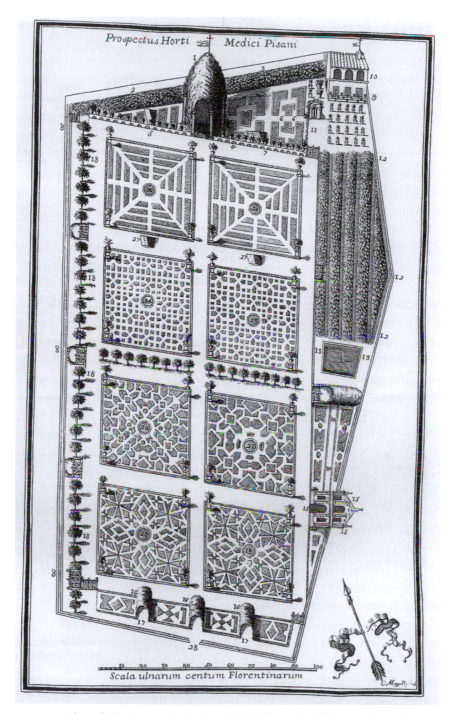

FIGURE 2.8: Plan of the Botanical Garden at Pisa from M. Tilli, *Catalogus Plantarum Horti Pisani*, 1723. Courtesy of the Biblioteca Nazionale Centrale di Firenze.

of simples in Florence in Via del Melarancio, next to the convent of Santa Maria Novella.[32] It was apparently Gaddi who recommended Casabona to the Medicis. In addition to Gaddi, there were other Florentine citizens who were involved in the cultivation and exchange of foreign plants. According to Targioni Tozzetti, the Tornabuonis introduced the first tobacco plant to Florence in the second half of the sixteenth century, and they cultivated it in their private garden, together with the first agaves imported from the new continent.[33] Antonio Salviati, like Gaddi, grew simples and rare plants, among which the highly sought-after red double-flowered poppy anemone, at his garden in Borgo Pinti, whereas Giovan Vettorio Soderini grew rare and exotic plants at his villa outside Florence.[34]

Whether for private enjoyment or public instructional purpose, these botanical gardens did have something in common, besides the nature of the plants cultivated in them. In fact, they usually presented ordered layouts in most cases consisting of an overall quadripartite arrangement determined by two paths crossing each other at a right angle. A curious exception is that of the *Giardino delle stalle* in Florence, which presented four, rather than two paths, crossing each other at the center and thereby creating eight, instead of four compartments. But this may be due to the fact that Casabona had to work on an already existing layout created for different purposes.[35] Gaddi's garden, on the contrary, displayed the more conventional plan of four quadrangles as we learn from an inventory of his possessions drawn up in 1591, the year of his death.[36] The botanical garden at Padua also consisted of four quadrants, although their outer perimeter formed a circle with a square inscribed in it as described by Gerolamo Porro in 1591.[37] Some seventeenth-century botanical gardens adopted the four quarters arrangement as in the formal section of the *Jardin de Roi* in Paris, described by Guy de la Brosse in his *Description du Jardin Royal des plantes medicinales,* and in the botanical garden at Oxford. In some cases, the number of quadrants was multiplied as at Pisa, where eight quadrants instead of four appear on the map drawn by Michelangelo Tilli in his *Catalogus Plantarum Horti Pisani* of 1723. According to Tongiorgi Tomasi, the layout of the garden had not changed since the time of Casabona.[38]

Drawings of layouts for botanical gardens and templates for the shape of their flowerbeds circulated between the sixteenth and seventeenth centuries across European cities and were used as guides by those entrusted with the creation of new botanical gardens. The correspondence between the numerous *Praefecti Horti* across Europe and their frequent travels, which allowed them to become familiar with the most well-known gardens, probably explains the

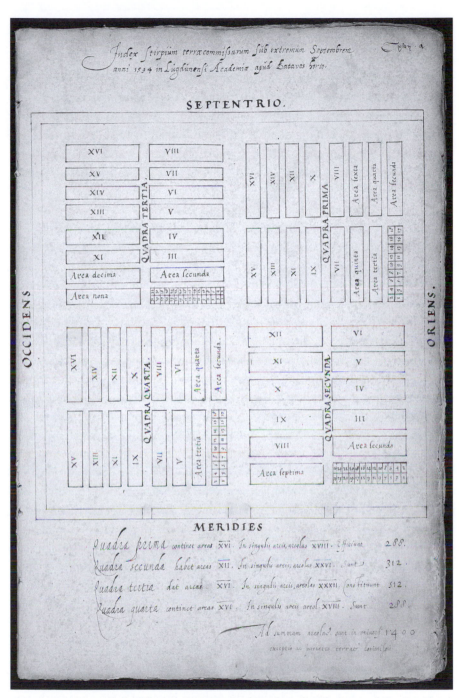

FIGURE 2.9: Plan of the Hortus Botanicus of Leiden. C. Clusius and D. O. Cluyt, manuscript, 1954. Courtesy of Leiden University Library.

similarity of the gardens' layouts. In 1591, for example, when Bernardus Palu-
danus, a famous doctor and plant collector, was offered the position of director of the botanical garden at Leiden, he sent drawings to the university that
were based on the design of the garden at Padua. Although most of the gardens
were laid out according to the quadripartite arrangement, however, there was
room for innovation and creative expression in determining the shape of the
smaller beds included in the quadrants. These ranged from simple squares and
rectangles, as was the case at Leiden, to more elaborate geometric figures. Some
of these are illustrated in the *Hortorum Viridariorumque Elegantes Formae*,
published in 1583 at Antwerp by Jan Vredeman de Vries, architect of Rudolph II
of Hapsburg, and in Daniel Loris's *Le Thrésor des Parterres de l'Univers*,
published in Geneva in 1629. Similar drawings of flowerbeds, labyrinths, and
ground plans for botanical gardens are found in the codex 646 of the University
library at Pisa. The manuscript, called *Libro di compartimenti di giardini*, dates
from the end of the sixteenth century. It was likely brought to Pisa by Casabona,
who was probably responsible for some of its drawings or for their commission.

In addition to the circulation and exchange of templates for the design of
gardens, the similarity in the formal arrangement of western botanical gardens
is also due to the fact that their ordered layout was the most practical. The
subdivision of beds composing the quadrants into smaller compartments was
dictated, for example, by the need to facilitate the cultivation and separation
or grouping of the simples. Furthermore, the smallest compartments were usually associated with letters, each of which corresponding to a specific plant.
The best example of this system is illustrated by the *Index Stirpium*, the first
inventory of the garden at Leiden drawn up in 1594. The document includes
a detailed plan and a numbered list of plants. Each number was meant to cor-
respond to one of the *pulvilli*, or small cushions, the smallest units composing
the plant beds or *areae*. The arrangement and shape of the beds resembles the
earliest layout of an herb garden known through the plan of St. Gall. In fact,
three of the four quadrants at Leiden double the layout visible on the monastery's plan by presenting sixteen rectangular beds instead of eight. The fourth
quadrant is subdivided into twelve beds as in one of the plates included in the
first book of Loris's *Le Thrésor*, which illustrates the parterres of Dutch and
German gardens. As at Leiden, Loris's template is characterized by a ninety-
degree rotation of the beds included in adjacent quadrants. Although the authorship of the *Index* is uncertain, there is evidence showing that the layout of
the garden is due to Carolus Clusius, the famous botanist, who apparently sent
his plan for the garden to Leiden before taking up the position of *Praefectus
horti* there in the autumn of 1593.[39]

The practice of numbering the beds and drawing up a corresponding inventory of plants seems to have been fairly common in the botanical gardens of Renaissance Europe. According to Agostino del Riccio, at the time of the refashioning of the *Giardino delle stalle* in Florence, each of the eight *quadri* or compartments was assigned a letter of the alphabet for the allotment of plants.[40] Also, the codex 464 of Pisa includes drawings of flowerbeds that are associated to numbers and names of plants. The purpose of this practice was to record the plants' exact location within the garden in order to facilitate their identification. But the writing of plant lists was also part of a larger aspect of Renaissance culture that has to do with the urge to collect, and classify every object, plant, mineral, or animal that could be considered representative of a corner of the world. Thus, for example, in his description of the garden at Padua, Porro said that "they were collecting the whole world in a chamber," and as late as the eighteenth century, Herman Boerhaave described the plants at Leiden as "being derived from the whole world."[41] It is also significant that knowing whether or not an individual possessed a considerable plant collection was one of the criteria for choosing the scientific director of a botanical garden in that the private collection automatically became part of the *hortus* once the *praefectus* took up the position.

As de Jong has pointed out, the botanical garden, with its gallery of *naturalia* and *artificialia* often attached to it, visualized an image of the world.[42] And it was a world full of wonders, some of which, unknown even to Dioscorides and Galen, had been recently discovered on the new continent or imported from Africa and from the East. The gathering and shipment of nonmedicinal species, such as the tulip, a purely ornamental garden flower introduced by Clusius at Leiden, gave new impetus to the development of botany as a science in its own right, as distinct from medicine. The purpose of the botanical garden, therefore, derived from the need to synthesize the increased variety of plants known and the botanist's task was to create a system of nature, the world at a smaller scale, near the classroom, and ready to be dissected. But, in some cases, the idea behind the Renaissance passion for collecting, ordering, and naming all manners of *naturalia* was also to regain a knowledge that man thought to have lost after the Fall. In the seventeenth century, someone like John Evelyn believed that "men began, with the indulgence of heaven, to recover that, by Arte and Industrie, which was before produced to them spontaneously."[43] God was thought to have revealed himself in his creation. Therefore, gathering all the plants into one place accounted for a greater knowledge of the Lord. Incidentally, the very layout of the botanical microcosm, especially in its most popular quadripartite form, may have represented not only the whole world symbolized by the four continents, but also an image of Paradise.

Paradise was, of course, a model of perfection, and the most perfect of the Renaissance gardens that a private individual would have wanted to create was going to combine features typical of existing botanical gardens, as in the Elysium envisioned by Evelyn that combined the narrow rectangular plant beds of Leiden, set out in a regular pattern, with a mound constructed at the *Jardin du Roi*. Of course, Evelyn's intentions were entirely different from those of Clusius or of Guy de la Brosse, founder the medicinal herb garden at Paris. Collecting plants representative of all the geographical locations was not only motivated by scientific and pedagogical interest, as in the case of public botanical gardens founded by European universities. It was also a desire of many wealthy individuals, those addressed by Evelyn in the *Elysium Britannicum,* whose urge to possess a "Compendium of what the whole Globe of the Earth has flourishing upon her boosome"[44] may have been dictated by a desire to express their power over nature, and through it, their social status. But this, as we shall see in the next section, found expression also in the exclusive use of places set aside for one of the most aristocratic pastimes, that is, hunting.

HUNTING PARKS

In the *Cortegiano* Baldesar Castiglione says that hunting is a pleasurable pastime for the courtier, and his remark that the sport "*ha una certa similitudine di guerra*" is a reminder that since the middle ages hunting is pursued by the nobleman in lieu of and in preparation for war.[45] Machiavelli also stresses the importance of hunting for the prince, in that through hunting the latter can experience directly the topographic diversity of the landscape, which was necessary knowledge for a good strategist.[46] That Renaissance hunting was restricted to the upper classes, if not exclusively to royal and princely families, is evident from the legislation of the period that forbade the practice of the sport within preserves where the right to hunt was reserved to those in power. In 1396, Charles VI of France announced that hunting was a privilege reserved for the king and for those aristocrats who received concessions from the king. In 1516, Francis I instituted a law that punished whomever carried harquebus, crossbows, nets, or traps. In sixteenth- and seventeenth-century Tuscany, similar laws forbade hunting and carrying weapons within the confines of game preserves and within a ten-mile radius from the city of Florence. The purpose of these laws was to protect certain species, such as boars, deer, fallow deer, roe deer, hares, pheasants, gray partridges, quails, and the latter's eggs and nests.[47] These animals were always at risk of being killed by peasants and sharecroppers who wanted to secure their fields against wild beasts' damage. But if, on one hand, the new legislation protected these species, on the other, it granted the seigniorial elite the exclusive right to practice the chase.[48]

Hunting was a typical aspect of a gentleman's education. At age twelve, Ludovico Sforza, Il Moro, wrote a detailed report of his hunting at the *parchetto,* which was a portion of the park created by the Visconti at Pavia after their conquest of the city in the second half of the fourteenth century.[49] Hunting training was also part of the education of the king of France's eldest son. In 1609, Henry IV accompanied the French dauphin, then aged seven, in his first hunting expedition in the woods of Vincennes. As his doctor's diary reports, the future Louis XIII practiced hunting regularly at Vincennes, Boulogne, and the Tuileries.[50]

In addition to having strong associations with the training for war, hunting had "cultural connotations important to the continuing prestige of the magnates as well as a functional utility in the political style which the aristocracy wished to promote."[51] The prestige and display of power associated to a well-organized event such as a hunt in a game-rich preserve explains the many diplomatic hunts organized by members of the upper classes for their most illustrious visitors. In the first half of the sixteenth century, Federico II Gonzaga asked the duke of Chartres to lend his hunting dogs and mastiffs so that he could organize the most magnificent hunt to impress the emperor Charles V during his visit at Mantua.[52] In the same way, hunts were part of the welcome receptions organized by the nobles for Charles V's son, the future Philip II, while traveling through the Empire. Of course, the size, duration, and ritual of the event depended on the kind of hunt.

Among the several types of hunt practiced in Renaissance Europe were falconry or the use of birds of prey to catch game animals; fowling or the capture of wild birds; fishing; and venery, which involved the hunting of wild boars, wolves, bears, and especially deer. This type of hunt was usually carried out on horseback and with the aid of dogs. The rules informing the practice of each type of hunt required different degrees of involvement of the seigneur and affected the configuration of space in various ways. The hunting of stag and game, for instance, often required paths that would be wide enough for horses and dogs. It also necessitated wooded areas to provide shelter and shade for the animals, and sources of water. These elements are listed by Pier de' Crescenzi in his description of a hunting preserve attached to a royal garden: "vi si pianti della parte del Settentrione una selva di diversi arbori, nella quale fugghino e si nascondino gli animali selvatici che saranno nel giardino . . . vi si faccia ancho una Peschiera, nella qual si nutriscono diverse fatte di pesci, e vi si ponghino Lepri, Cervi, Capriuoli, Conigli, e somiglianti animali non rapaci."[53] In order to prevent the animals from running away a wall was often constructed to enclose the space set aside for the hunt. This type of walled hunting park, called *barco,* developed in the north of Italy in the fourteenth century. An example is visible on a map engraved by Iacopo Cotta, which reproduces the *barco* of the Visconti at Pavia. The residence included a castle and a park of more than six thousand acres, which extended to the back of the castle. The property was entirely surrounded by a crenellated brick wall, with a series of doors with towers and drawbridges. The vegetation included meadows, woods, unplowed land, cultivated fields, and orchards. The park was traversed at its center by the Vernavola River, which, together with the *naviglio,* an artificial water channel created by the Visconti after their conquest of the city, fed a hydraulic network that included marshes and fishponds. Moreover, two axial roads that meandered along a north–south axis on each side of the Vernavola traversed the park and connected to a secondary system of roads that, meeting beyond the gates of the *barco,* extended into the surrounding territory. According to an inventory drawn up in 1451, the park included fallow deer and fawns, does and roe deer, hares, partridge, pheasants, and hundreds of rabbits. And it is possible that these animals were assigned separate spaces within the *barco,* as a description written in 1515 by Pasquier le Moine seems to suggest.[54]

The hunting parks of the duchy of Milan inspired the construction of similar types in the Veneto region, most notably, the *barco* of Caterina Cornaro, the queen of Cyprus exiled at Asolo.[55] The *barco,* whose construction started in 1491, consisted of three walled areas, the largest of which was parallel to the existing Roman *centuriatio* of the first century B.C.E.[56] The first wall included a rectangular area of more than one hundred acres that was set aside for hunting and pasture; within the hunting preserve was a smaller area of five acres, again enclosed by a wall and including a garden, a well, and a fountain; the third and smallest enclave included the building and the kitchen garden, which extended for one acre. Because of the existence of three concentric enclosures, it is not possible to separate the hunting preserve from the other two types to which it is attached, namely, the house and the garden. It is likely that, in addition to knowledge of the hunting parks in the Milanese territory, and possibly in Urbino, the Cornaro were familiar with the description of the *barco* included in Filarete's contemporary treatise on architecture, which the Florentine architect dedicated to Francesco Sforza. In fact, Filarete's ideal *barco* was enclosed by a

FIGURE 2.10: Giusto Utens, Veduta della Villa medicea La Magia, Museo Storico Topografi co "Firenze com'era," Inv. 1890 n. 6319. Courtesy of the Ministero per i Beni e le Attività Culturali.

wall and included two areas surrounded by shorter walls that allowed for the separation of predatory animals, such as wolves and bears, from preys, such as deer and boars. As at Asolo, Filarete's *barco* also included a building with a courtyard and a walled garden.[57]

The existence of multiple enclosures is not only a characteristic of the Italian *barco*. Several examples of hunting parks including multiple subdivisions also existed in England and France. Deer parks, and venison farms in general, were created in England since the early medieval times. They could be attached to manorial residences or extend at a distance from them. In either case, deer parks were surrounded by deer-proof fences and often contained sections of woods and fields separated by fences or hedging. The subdivisions gradually disappeared when some of the parks were redesigned later in the centuries following the rules of the landscape park, as Horace Walpole noted in his essay on the *History of the Modern Taste in Gardening*.[58]

In France, one of the earliest walled preserves, located near Paris, was the *bois de Vincennes* created by Philip II Augustus in 1164. The park contained several sections, each of which assigned to a certain animal or group of animals. Boars and the fallow deer, for example, were separated from stag, which were confined to the large woods, and from hares and wild goats, according to a mid-fifteenth-century description by Nicolas de l'Astesan.[59] These subdivisions continued to exist until the seventeenth century. Unlike Vincennes, the

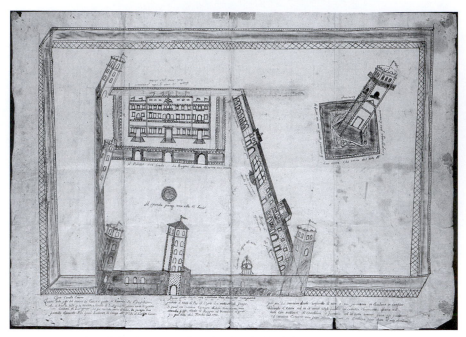

FIGURE 2.11: Plan of the *barco* at Altivole (first half of the eighteenth century). Courtesy of the Museo Civico di Asolo.

bois de Boulogne to the west of Paris, originally called *bois de Rouvray,* was not enclosed by a wall. A reason for this may be that, although it belonged to the king of France, the latter did not have exclusive hunting rights here as at Vincennes. In fact, concessions were made to the nuns of Longchamp and Montmartre, and the inhabitants of Boulogne also had the right to use the park for pasture. In the first half of the sixteenth century, when Francois I returned from his Spanish captivity, the chateau de Madrid was constructed at the *bois de Boulogne* in order for the king to "prendre notre plaisir et desduit a la chasse aux grosses bestes,"[60] and ten years later the property was enclosed by a wall.[61]

Although walls surrounded the woods at Vincennes and Boulogne, French royal hunts also took place outside of the parks' confines, as the presence of warrens in the surrounding territory shows. In addition, the predilection of French kings for the *chasse à courre,* which consists in the chase of an animal for several hours with the assistance of numerous hounds, required spaces that were larger than those enclosed by the walls. In fact, during the course of the sixteenth and seventeenth centuries, Vincennes and Boulogne became part of a hunting system called *capitainerie royal de chasse,* which also included the territory between and around them. Within this territory, hunting rights were reserved for the king and carrying hunting weapons was forbidden. But if the creation of these protected territories was a way to secure game animals for the king, it may also have been an excuse to disarm the peasants around Paris.

Similar concerns may have determined the creation of open hunting preserves in sixteenth-century Tuscany. The Medici villas, for example, were surrounded by *bandite,* or legal enclaves, which were sections of territory particularly rich in game but whose spatial extension went beyond the Medici's agricultural possessions and their gardens in that they included woods, marshes, and other agricultural fields. Although some of the territory of the *bandite* belonged to the collectivity, in addition to the portions that belonged to the duchy and to other private owners, no one was allowed to hunt in them except for the duke. Among the Medici *bandite*, those of Cafaggiolo and Trebbio, instituted in 1550 around the old family properties in the Mugello, and Pratolino, instituted in 1568, occupied a large area north of Florence. Other large preserves extended to the west of Florence and south of Pistoia, and included the *bandita* of Poggio a Caiano and La Magia on the left bank of the Arno, and that of Cerreto Guidi and Montevettolini on the right bank. A *barco reale* was eventually institutionalized on May 7, 1626, astride the latter *bandite* and around the Medici villa at Artimino.[62] Unlike the other preserves this new park was enclosed by a wall long more than eighteen miles that was created in 1624 in order to prevent the animals from destroying the surrounding fields; it included several woods and other lands acquired by the Medici since the time of Lorenzo il Magnifico.[63] Large openings in the woods, where carriages could stop and allow for the duke and his guests to follow the hunt from a distance, were the main formal characteristics of these hunting parks together with long, straight avenues. In France, these avenues were often arranged in a starlike shape or in *pattes d'oie,* which would become a characteristic of some Italian hunting preserves, such as the Savoia parks in Piemonte, later in the seventeenth and eighteenth centuries.[64]

Among the types of hunt, fowling, and the structures associated with it, such as the *ragnaie* used to capture thrushes, blackbirds, and warblers, also had a tremendous impact on the configuration of the landscape, particularly in Tuscany. According to Crescenzi and others after him, a *ragna* is composed of several rows of shrubs that form long rectilinear masses, separated by paths, and perfectly pruned in order to form green walls or *spalliere.* Meshes are stretched along the inner surfaces of the walls so that they can be closed down on the birds once these are lured between the hedges, attracted by berry-bearing plants and channeled water. These structures could stretch for several miles and their visual impact on the landscape was accentuated by the lack of woods, and the horizontality of the vineyards and cultivated fields by which they were often bordered. The two *ragnaie* built at Poggio a Caiano occupied, at the time of Francesco I, a surface of more than twenty acres. One of them was located on the right bank of the Ombrone and it included three segments forming a zigzag. The second one, L-shaped, was in the *Cascine* created by Lorenzo il Magnifico. The narrower segment bordered the Pavoniere, a square *barco* containing the black fallow deer that Lorenzo had imported from the Indies. The wider *ragnaia,* called Il ragnaione, was used to breed pheasants and woodcocks.[65]

Although *ragnaie* and other structures for fowling were most common in Tuscany, they were also found in Rome, and it is possible that their construction was encouraged by the Medici cardinals, such as Ferdinand, who had *ragnaie* built at La Magliana, the famous papal hunting lodge in the Roman countryside, and at the Villa Medici on the Pincio. Other *ragnaie* were built at the Villa Borghese respectively in 1606 and 1620. The later one was constructed by a Tuscan gardener, Domenico Savini from Montepulciano, and it was composed of multiple rows, long more than sixteen hundred feet, equipped

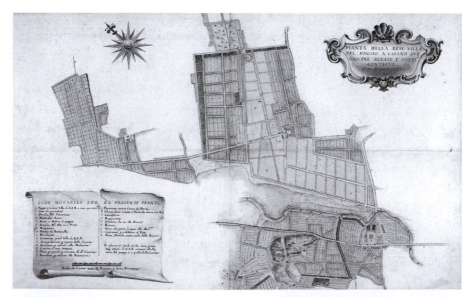

FIGURE 2.12: Plan of the villa and the *cascine* of Poggio a Caiano (1738). Florence, Archivio di Stato, Mannelli, Galilei, Riccardi. Courtesy of the Ministero per i Beni e le Attività Culturali.

with channeled water and surrounded by fig trees.[66] This fowling structure was located in the *barco* attached to the villa, which also included a *paretaio*.[67] As I mentioned earlier, the type of the estate villa or villa park, which is exemplified by the Borghese property, was anticipated by the earlier Villa Lante at Bagnaia, which also included a park. However, an unusual characteristic of the *barco* at Bagnaia was the absence of animals.[68] Although the park was enclosed by a wall and crisscrossed by long avenues with occasional clearings, its function was more symbolic and decorative, rather than cynegetic. The strong association of the sport, and the places where it was practiced, with the aristocracy, justified the presence of *barchi* attached to the villas of popes and cardinals, who were eager to adopt the forms, when not the activities, of the old baronial families in order to strengthen their new social image. However, toward the end of the sixteenth century, the interest in hunting was slowly decreasing, and in some occasions hunting parks were turned into tree gardens, or farms. Cardinal Luigi d'Este, for example, transformed into a farm the hunting park that his uncle, the Cardinal of Ferrara Ippolito d'Este had created at the Bagni di Tivoli in the first half of the century. The few exceptions were the new *barchi* created by French or Francophile cardinals. A reason for this transformation may be that in the seventeenth century, the chase was no longer the Italian clergy's favorite entertainment (hunting habits of popes and cardinals had been restricted since the Middle Ages by canon law) nor was it the nobility's preferred pastime. "The hunt had made its appeal to a society in which war was central to its existence,"[69] and even when the aristocracy was no longer directly involved in martial affairs, pushed aside by new military technology, hunting was at least a great psychological prop because it allowed the nobles to keep contact with part of the prestige system of the old way of life.[70] However, in central Italy, the increase in population converted the countryside to gardens and pasture and, in addition, game itself had been decimated by the increasing use of firearms. The situation was different in those regions that presented a more wooded landscape, such as the Piedmont, and in the countries of central and northern Europe. For these, hunting was not only a matter of recreation, but also a necessary source of supply for the households. In England, for example, the food-producing function of parks continued to be exploited until the seventeenth century along with their symbolic role of "signifiers of wealth and privilege."[71] Moreover, hunting rituals continued to play an important part in the layout of royal estates, as was the case at Aranjuez, although hunting was not the only function that these parks carried out. In fact, the long tree-lined avenues of Aranjuez, and in particular the large clearings that opened along them, were not only used to trap game, but also to stage other outdoor entertainments. Also in Italy hunting parks were versatile spaces where the court could hold tournaments, processions, and alfresco banquets that may, or may not, have followed a successful hunt.

Finally, the flexibility of the hunting park type is not only related to the different functions it allowed for, but also to its form. We have seen examples of hunting parks that were enclosed by walls and others that were open and encompassed larger sections of the landscape. Some consisted of long shaded avenues that radiated from a hunting lodge, but the number, length, and design of the avenues varied. Unlike venery, fowling required other structures that changed in scale from the extremely long *ragnaie* to the relatively small *paretai* and *boschetti da tordi*. These structures, moreover, could very well be integrated within the design of villa gardens, as is the case in Tuscany, where the labyrinth that occupies the central portion of the Medici villa at Castello was, in fact, a device for catching birds. It is precisely the overlapping of types that characterizes the gardens of the early modern period. Even the predecessor of the botanical garden type, the *hortus medicus,* was often found within other types, especially when medicinal herbs were grown within the walls of *giardini segreti.*

Ultimately, the multiplicity of functions of the hunting park type and their amorphous layouts, the more rigid and stable geometry of countryside gardens vis-à-vis their changing cultural meaning, and the ubiquitous existence of botanical gardens within universities, private villas, and monasteries, exemplify why—as Quatremère de Quincy maintained—"all is precise and given in the model" whereas in the type "all is more or less vague."[72] This vagueness has allowed us to take into account the social, political, and economic conditions that determined the birth of selected garden types, or favored their transformation. When the Medici became Dukes of Florence and the papal families in Rome sought the social status of the old landed aristocracy their *orti* and *vigne* developed first into Renaissance *ville di delizie,* which were used for less-productive pastimes, and then into villa parks endowed with representative power and meaning; the passion for collecting and classifying old and new plant species typical of Renaissance culture, and the consequent emancipation of botany from medicine, prompted the foundation of the first botanical gardens; and the association of hunting with the practice of war explains why, when the aristocracy ceased to be directly involved in matters of war, some of their hunting parks were turned into tree gardens and farms. These considerations warrant an understanding of types not as rigid formal and functional models, but rather as flexible spaces capable also of turning into one another given certain cultural and ideological conditions.

CHAPTER THREE

Plantings

MARGHERITA ZALUM

At the end of the sixteenth century, the friar Agostino del Riccio lamented on more than one occasion the fact that husbandry, once pursued by honest and virtuous persons, was now left in the hands of the ignorant, men who had no love for the land and growing things. The earth, the friar maintained, gave back in equal measure what was given to her; to those who treated her with loving consideration, she would bestow an abundant harvest of flowers and fruit, but to those who exploited her heartlessly she would grant only thorns and weeds.[1]

His words allow us to appreciate the importance that was assigned to plants in the late medieval, humanist, and Renaissance periods. In this chapter, I examine the evolution of the European garden between the early fifteenth and the middle seventeenth centuries to show how the plants exerted a crucial influence not only on the design of the garden but also on social customs and the development of the arts and sciences, serving as a vehicle for the most up-to-date expression of culture in every field.

PLANTS IN THE EARLY RENAISSANCE GARDEN

The principal characteristic of the early-fifteenth-century garden seems to be its continuity with those of the late medieval period in terms of typology and layout, choice of plants, and gardening techniques. For example, the

traditional division of the land according to the different types of cultivations (crops, orchard, vegetables, etc.)—which was a heritage from the Middle
Ages—persists; although it may not always take the form of an actual separation of the plot, it is always present on a conceptual level and is carried over in
many sixteenth-century gardening treatises.[2] In the same way, the classification
of the garden's typology based on the owner's census or the types of crops
grown there is not abandoned until the late sixteenth century.

In the fifteenth century, the garden generally consists of a piece of land
of variable size on which flowers, vegetables, herbaceous plants, shrubs,
fruit plants, and perhaps a few trees are planted. Often two perpendicular
paths that may broaden at their point of intersection to create an open space
where garden seats, a fountain, or other decorative elements can be placed
traverse it.

Other common features are the espalier and the *cerchiata* (or pergola),
wooden latticework frames against which climbing plants are trained to cast a
welcome shade in the summer months. These are regarded as the most appropriate way for cultivating plants such as vines and citruses, and therefore are
utilized extensively for this purpose up to the end of the seventeenth century.[3]
Furthermore, the pergola and espalier reflect the harmonious relationship that
man is seeking to establish with the world around him, in which the unruly
forces of nature can be shaped and brought under control through his skill and
ingenuity. They are consequently viewed by many authors as essential components in any garden worthy of such a name.

Frames and trellises are used with great imagination to cultivate a variety of
plants from fruit trees to roses, jasmine, and other ornamental species. Shrubs
such as rosemary, lavender, myrtle, and sage too are trained on lower espaliers
to create hedges and borders. The use of boxwood in particular, with its evocation of the pageantry of ancient Rome, comes to be the object of great debate
and in recent times has come to be associated in the collective imagination with
the humanist and Renaissance garden.[4]

In the gardens of the wealthy one may also find low stone parapets demar-
cating grassy expanses or large flowerbeds where the most valuable plants such
as roses or citruses are cultivated (*cassoni*). When a separate area cannot be
set aside for an orchard, fruit trees are planted in the open space of the garden, usually together with some other trees. In larger gardens and on country
estates, these sections of the garden will take on the semblance of wild thickets
or groves.[5]

Due to the lack of documentation, however, any attempt at the reconstruction of the fifteenth-century garden must remain somewhat vague. Most of

FIGURE 3.1: "Emilia in her garden." Courtesy of ÖNB / Wien–image BA11-0369.

the actual sites have disappeared or undergone radical modification (one rare exception being the Medici villa of Trebbio),[6] while the written and visual testimony is decidedly meager, particularly when compared to the wealth of material that has come down to us from the following centuries.

Especially difficult to evaluate is the degree to which the literary and visual descriptions of gardens are influenced by the symbolic meanings (religious, philosophical, literary, courtly, etc.) that are ascribed to them in the medieval and protohumanist periods; indeed, the garden can be found as a motif in countless poems, romans, and epic texts. Single plants are very frequent in altarpieces, portraits, and statues of the period too, and they bear symbolic connotations that are often crucial to understand the works themselves.[7] In some cases, the weight of this symbolic value is so great that it can shape reality itself. It is the case, for instance, of the cloisters and other monastic gardens, that adhere to a uniform typology in which the choice and layout of the plants lends form to a rich symbology associated with the monastic life and the vision of the world on which it was based.

This represents an extreme example, however. "Lay" gardens are infi-
nitely more complex and nuanced, and the many variables that influence their
design—from the size, location, and setting (urban or rural) of the garden to
the economic, social, and cultural background of the owner—make it necessary to exercise great caution when transposing literary and pictorial models
to reality.[8] In particular, the importance of the symbolic meanings can lead to
overlooking the utilitarian function of the plants in favor of their purely ornamental role, and therefore to underestimate the essential unity of the garden (as
an enclosed space) with the surrounding landscape.[9]

In fact, during the fifteenth and early sixteenth centuries, the garden is often
referred to as the *hortus conclusus:* in the past decades, scholars have tended to
focus more on the implications of the seclusion from outside world implied by
the word *conclusus* rather than paying attention to the original meaning of the
term *hortus*—a place where common herbs and flowers are grown for practical
purposes, to which ornamental qualities are lent through a skillful disposition
of the plants and the use of specific cultivation techniques, such as espaliering,
pruning, and grafting.

This continuity in terms of the flora, in which economically useful species
are cultivated side by side with flowers, can still be seen in the late sixteenth
century—for example, in the garden of the Villa Lante at Bagnaia, of which we
have enthusiastic accounts by more than one visitor. In the principal parterre
opposite the Palazzina del Cardinale there were "twelve plots all with espaliers
of *lontaggine,* within each there were eight different fruit trees . . . ", while
strolling through the grounds one came across "a wall covered with different
fruits, such as plums, medlars, pomegranates, and quinces, [. . .] a large avenue
with a wooden espalier covered with vines, and a row of fig trees"; "an olive
grove with an espalier of roses"; and "a fountain called La Tazza with a jet in
the middle surrounded by olive trees with its seat [and] next to the *conservone*
there is a grove of fig trees. On the left side of this fountain is an avenue with
various sorts of fruit trees, . . ."[10]

The literature of the period confirms this picture of a harmonious landscape in which the vegetation of the garden, fields, and orchards intermingle;
agricultural treatises (such as Michelangelo Tanaglia's treatise in verse, *De agricultura*[11]) often begin with a description of the ideal site on which to erect
a villa and discuss topics relating to the maintenance of the garden and fields
together rather than separately. The country villa serves as a residence for the
landowner who wishes to live on his property in order to better supervise its
activities. The villa therefore is central to the functioning of the estate and
will continue to be so until the end of the eighteenth century, particularly in

regions such as Veneto, where the cultivation of crops for market has replaced subsistence farming. And certain plants such as the olive, the vine, and the fruit tree are so important to the economy of the estate that they can be found growing in close proximity to the villa. On the other hand, since in this period agronomy and horticulture still share the same methods for partitioning, laying out, cultivating, and maintaining the land, the fields surrounding the estate bear many of the characteristics of the well-tended garden.

However, man's ability to control and exploit nature is growing rapidly, and the progress that leads to improved farming methods and increases yields also breathes fresh life into the concept of the garden. As techniques such as grafting and espaliering are perfected, gardeners find themselves able to cultivate a greater variety of plants and emphasis begins to shift to the ornamental uses of many different species. One of the earliest expressions of this decorative dimension is the revival of topiary[12]—the technique of molding plants into completely unnatural zoomorphic, geometric, and symbolic shapes. Topiary art is greatly admired because it is considered the highest expression of gardening in ancient Roman times, and images of sculpted shrubs appear in late-fifteenth-century paintings, while documents attest to their presence in the Medici garden in Florence and at the Rucellai family's villa Lo Specchio.[13]

The geometric motifs that are used to shape shrubs are repeated on a larger scale in the garden as a whole. Detailed plans are drawn up for the arrangement of plants, in which the latest principles of perspective and mathematical proportions are applied with meticulous rigor. The harmonization of the criteria for the design of the villa with those of its green spaces is the principal element that differentiates the fifteenth-century garden from its medieval predecessor. This precept is sanctioned by Leon Battista Alberti in *De re aedificatoria* and applied in the construction of gardens all over Europe during the fifteenth and well into the sixteenth centuries.[14] Thus, the garden becomes an integral part of the villa, and the form and disposition of the plants are subordinated to the creation of magnificent vistas that can be admired from its rooms. In this way, the architect initiates a dialogue with the landscape, one in which perspective and the rules of proportional relationships serve as the connecting elements between outside and inside, between the natural and the artificial.

By imposing order on nature through the application of mathematical principles, man transforms the garden into a microcosm of the universe, a vehicle for ascending step by step through the hierarchical cosmos of the humanists toward a knowledge of divine law and, eventually, of God himself. Also, the garden becomes the place where an idealized version of nature can be created, one that offers a setting for refined, classical *otium,* or the pursuit of aristocratic pleasures.[15]

The elaborated concepts that lay behind the design of Humanistic garden give the measure of how innovative it is; at the same time, the analysis of its vegetation has also shown its unbroken ties with the tradition and its substantial continuity with the rural context.

PLANTS IN THE AGE OF DISCOVERY

The carefully balanced equilibrium between nature and art that is embodied in fifteenth century gardens is destined to change radically during the course of the following century, due to the discovery of the immensely rich and varied flora of the Americas and the Near and Far East.

The vast amounts of botanical, zoological, and ethnographic data that reach Europe from distant shores induce men of science to start a process of identification and classification that eventually leads to a gradual revision of the entire system of knowledge inherited from antiquity. This process is given additional impetus by the humanist movement and in particular by artists' exploration of the perceptible, material world.[16]

The study of plants becomes one of the domains in which the new sciences and a new epistemological system are forged. The practice among herbalists, chemists, and physicians of gathering plants to make healing remedies gradually evolves into a more systematic approach to botanizing and within the space of a few decades Europe's most illustrious universities—in Padova, Pisa, Firenze, Bologna, Leiden, Leipzig, Heidelberg, Oxford, Montpellier, and Paris—found the first chairs in botany and the earliest *giardini dei semplici*.[17] In the absence of any preexisting models, botanists feel free to experiment with new designs for the construction of these gardens, adapting them to the requirements of new methodologies for the study and teaching of the *materia medica*.

Around the central decades of the sixteenth century, the design of the gardens is undergoing radical changes. Although maintaining the traditional quadripartite layout, areas that had once been left as grassy expanses are now divided into small plant beds laid out in patterns based on the principal geometric forms. This development is the result of many factors, one of the most important being the process of geometrization that affects architectural design as well as many other arts and sciences. To this must be added the influence of antiquity, which is transmitted through authors such as Sebastiano Serlio, whose *Quarto libro* applies ornamental designs from antique monuments to the decoration of coffered ceilings, marble floors, and garden parterres.[18]

The division of the terrain into many small plant beds that is becoming current turns out to be particularly suited to the *giardini dei semplici,* because it allows botanists to arrange their plants in a rational and systematic manner; this is demonstrated by the ground plans of the botanical gardens constructed in Padova (1545, Pisa (in its third and final version around 1592), and Leiden (also during the last decade of the sixteenth century). The layout of the plant beds is gradually simplified, as functionality takes precedence over aesthetic considerations, and the botanical garden of Leiden may be considered wholly modern in its conception.[19]

It is in these *giardini dei semplici* that men of science begin to study the exotic plants brought back by explorers from distant lands. The introduction of these new species in Europe is slow, because initially only a handful of sovereigns or those sponsored by them can afford the privilege of owning such rare plants. The grand duke Cosimo I de' Medici is one of the first heads of state to take an interest in botany; he becomes a knowledgeable collector and

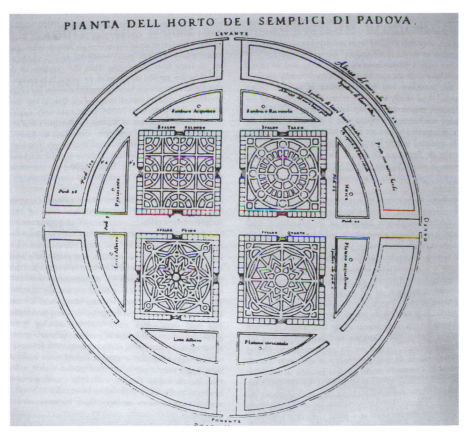

FIGURE 3.2: "Pianta dell'Horto de' Semplici di Padova," in G. Porro, *L'horto de i semplici di Padova* (Venezia, 1591).

seeks to acclimatize new species from the New World and Africa in the garden of his Villa di Castello, which becomes the object of great admiration and attracts illustrious visitors from all over Italy and Europe.[20] Cosimo's example is followed by his son Francesco I, who retains the services of the botanical artist Jacopo Ligozzi to portray the rare plants and exotic birds in the Medici collections.[21]

Cardinal Ferdinando de' Medici shares his family's love of botany and has a splendid garden constructed at the Medici villa on Pincian Hill in Rome, which he plants with the exotic specimens that the grand duke's *semplicista,* Giuseppe Casabona, sends to him regularly from his herborizing expeditions.[22] A fresco in the *Stanzino dell'Aurora* painted by Jacopo Zucchi in the late 1570s shows that, according to the original plan for the restoration of the villa, a large section of the garden is to be devoted to the cultivation of these plants; in the final project, though, they are moved to a safer place, in consideration of their great economic value. When he succeeds his brother Francesco as grand duke and returns to Tuscany, Ferdinando continues to pursue his botanical interests and expands the gardens of many of the family's villas. One of these is L'Ambrogiana, whose grounds at the front (as can be seen in a lunette painted by Giusto Utens in 1598–1599) are divided into four sections demarcated by vine-covered pergolas. Each of these sections is divided into four quadrants containing flowerbeds (*pulvilli*) laid out in geometric patterns, whose bright colors lend a touch of vivacity to the verdant scene.

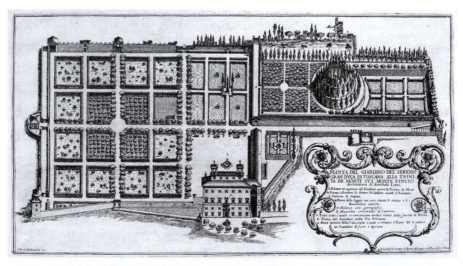

FIGURE 3.3: G. B. Falda, "Plan of the Gardens of Villa Medici in Rome." Courtesy of Biblioteca Nazionale Centrale, Firenze.

The Dominican friar Agostino del Riccio, who for many decades frequents the court of the grand duke and its circle of artists, documents the introduction of exotic flowers at an early date in Tuscany. He is the author of a ponderous treatise, *Agricoltura sperimentale e teorica,*[23] which was never published but whose aim is to describe procedures and techniques for the cultivation of all the types of plants then to be found in the gardens of Florence, from trees and fruit plants to vegetables and, of course, exotic flowers. Sifting through the manuscript's contents one comes across lists of plants, which the friar takes evident pleasure in drawing up, and that include non-European varieties of hyacinths, tulips, nasturtiums, jasmines, and citruses and information on the patrician gardens in which these plants are cultivated, which belong to some of the most eminent families in Florence.[24]

As they are successfully acclimatized and their cultivation spreads, many exotic species become more affordable and, beginning in the 1580s, members of the bourgeoisie, ecclesiastics, merchants, apothecaries, and artists join the ranks of scientists and sovereigns with an interest in botany.[25] Within a few decades, a veritable collectors' fever breaks out throughout Europe as gardeners from every social class seek to gain possession of what is the most fleeting thing in the world, the beauty of a rare flower.

One of the countries where this phenomenon develops first is the Netherlands. Thanks to the peculiar economic and social structure and to the early expansion of maritime commerce, the Low Countries are the place where the riches coming from the eastern world are amassed and then distributed across Europe. Many people from all social ranks involve themselves in the exchange and collecting of exotic plants: so, side to side with nobles and courtiers, scholars and humanists, apothecaries like Christian Porret from Leiden, rich bourgeois and merchants like Johannes van Hoghelande from Leiden and Guillelmo van de Heuvel Bartoletti or Emanuel Sweerts from Amsterdam can be found among the first owners of specific varieties of ornamental flowers, particularly tulips.

One of the consequences of this form of collecting is that the harmonious integration of garden and landscape that had been ensured for centuries by the continuity of vegetation is now interrupted. The indigenous flora is invaded by a multitude of exotic plants whose sole function is ornamental (attempts to make tulip bulbs palatable by caramelizing them fail signally[26]) and the distinction between *giardino* (garden) and *orto* (vegetable plot) as they are conceived today begins to take form. It must be said, nonetheless, that this process is anything but fast or straightforward: vegetables and kitchen plants are still to be found alongside precious ornamental plants for many decades to come, as it is clearly shown by the catalogue of John Tradescant's collection published in 1656.[27]

The introduction of new plants, in addition to changing the function and significance of the private garden, profoundly alters its appearance. In the beginning, following the model of the academic garden, the layout tends to be based on simple geometric patterns. Gradually, however, these rigid, purely functional schemata are abandoned and the garden becomes increasingly elaborate to befit its ornamental purposes. Geometric shapes are created, interwoven, and broken up, generating a sophisticated play of line and color in which each flowerbed is a distinct entity and at the same time forms a part of a larger design. The modular configuration means that a garden can be designed to fit any piece of land, no matter how large, small, or irregular in shape. This gives architects free rein to experiment and their creativity in this period knows no bounds, as is demonstrated by the projects drawn up at the end of the century by Hans Vredeman de Vries.[28]

The new type of garden is generally denominated *giardino di fiori,* and often planted on the site of a previously existing *giardino segreto,* sometimes as an autonomous entity (e.g., the garden of a palazzo in an urban setting) and sometimes as part of a larger whole (the garden of a country estate). Treatises written during the second half of the sixteenth century document a gradual separation of the areas dedicated to ornamental flowers from those where vegetables and herbs are grown, although this process is anything but linear. The *Dieci giornate d'Agricoltura* by Agostino Gallo and the *Trattato della coltura degli orti e giardini* by Gianvettorio Soderini (ca. 1588)[29] describe gardens still laid out in the traditional manner, with flowers growing alongside lettuces and other *herbe gentili,* while the garden in Charles d'Estienne and Jean Liebault's *Maison rustique* (1566)[30] already has a *parterre* for the more precious plants that is separated from the orchard and the kitchen garden by a tall hedge. A short time later in his *Villæ* (1592),[31] Giambattista Della Porta confirms that a distinction should be made between the area of the garden devoted to vegetables and that reserved for the more refined products of nature, such as flowers.[32]

The typology of the flower garden is not codified until the end of the sixteenth century, when the cultivation of exotic bulbous species and shrubs assumes vast proportions in Europe and is taken up by a large number of flower lovers. Its layout is characterized by a new formal complexity that can be linked to the development of the Renaissance principles of architecture, as well as to the dense symbolism connected with certain visual formulas. However, practical considerations also play a role; the reduced dimensions of the flowerbeds can be attributed to the fact that the most sought-after species are extremely costly but small in size; it is therefore important that they be arranged so that every bulb can be easily reached by the gardeners, and seen to its best advantage when in bloom.

The construction of the flower garden requires a whole range of skills, beginning with the ability to draw up a pleasing design, generally containing a graceful allusion to the owner, his family, or his intellectual and social milieu. However, the garden is not merely an abstract design on paper; it is a repository for growing things and in order to decide how they should be arranged it is necessary to imagine the effect that the plants will create when in bloom, considering the sequence of their flowering periods and the juxtaposition of different colors. It is even more vital to take into account the requirements of each plant in terms of soil, water, sunlight, and fertilizer, as well as possible incompatibilities between species.[33]

The most costly bulbs are only planted after a detailed layout of the flowerbeds has been drawn up and the exact position of each flower marked. The bulbs are then set in the ground using a grid of reeds or twine to ensure that the spacing is uniform, and a reed is placed to mark each spot. The more delicate species are cultivated in pots. Great skill and expertise are required of the gardener, particularly if one considers the experimental nature of much of his work, which consists of coaxing into bloom species accustomed to very different climates and habitats.

A manuscript compiled by Francesco Pona in 1618–1619 testifies to the complexity inherent in the planning of a flower garden.[34] Among its miscellaneous contents are some designs for flowerbeds prepared for Count Giusti, the owner of the most beautiful garden in Verona. The drawings explore a series of variations in pattern and size for flowerbeds in a garden divided into quadrants. In addition, there are sketches of the single quadrants that show how the plants might be arranged in each flowerbed. These reveal the care with which every detail is planned; for example, there are sketches of the same flowerbed with the bulbs planted more closely together or further apart to analyze the different effects that would be created.

Tuscany seems to have been one of the cradles of botanical collecting, and from thence, the practice spreads quickly throughout Europe. It is perhaps due to the presence at court of Maria de' Medici that the kings of France are among the first sovereigns to build their own, truly regal flower gardens, whose plants will be immortalized in one of Europe's earliest illustrated flower books, the florilegium published in 1608 by Pierre Vallet.[35] Another botanical collection owes its fame to an exceptional florilegium: *Hortus Eistettensis* depicts more than a thousand species growing on the bishop Johann Conrad von Gemmingen's estate in Eichstätt, presented following the order of the seasons.[36]

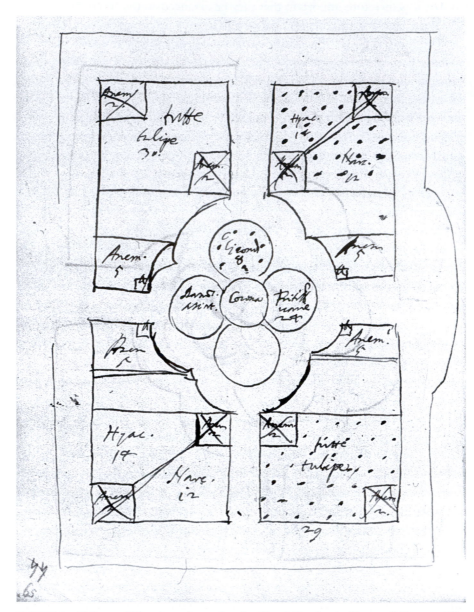

FIGURE 3.4: F. Pona, "Planting scheme for the Giusti Garden in Verona," Firenze, Biblioteca Medicea Laurenziana, Ms. Ashb. 380, c. 36v. Su concessione del Ministero per i Beni e le Attività Culturali. E' vietata ogni ulteriore riproduzione con qualsiasi mezzo. By permission of Ministero per i Beni e le Attivita' Culturali. Any reproduction with any means is forbidden

The most famous gardens of this period in France are probably those of Gaston d'Orléans, in Blois. Despite his disputable role in the politics of the century, Gaston surely deserves a citation as a collector of antiquities, coins and mostly of natural rarities. He is indeed the possessor of a garden whose fame spreads across Europe and also the patron who ordered the execution of the earliest *vélins,* the famous collection of botanical watercolors now kept in the Musée d'Histoire Naturelle.

The *hortus* planned to be built in Vienna under the direction of Clusius, on the contrary, is never actually realized due to the premature death of the emperor.[37] Beside these princely examples, many private gardens are founded, belonging sometimes to very wealthy members of the European courts, sometimes to less famed and powerful people. To the first of these categories belongs the Prince-Count of Arembergh, Charles de Ligne (1550–1616), one of the earliest collectors of ornamental and exotic species. After a brilliant diplomatic and military career, in 1606, the prince acquires the fief of Enghien, where he retires and plants a magnificent flower garden. One of the first in Europe, it exemplifies the transition between the encyclopedic garden of the botanist and the new typology of the garden exclusively dedicated to ornamental plants.

Arembergh's activities as a plant collector are described in some letters that he wrote to the celebrated floriculturist Matteo Caccini of Florence. A dealer in rare plants and a tireless intermediary in the exchanges between wealthy garden owners, Caccini creates a network of ties with botanists all over Europe that can be retraced in his correspondence over the course of four decades.[38] As was the custom, together with their letters the prince-count and Caccini exchange plants and *chipully,* as Arembergh refers to "flower bulbs" in his Spanish-tinged Italian. Caccini sends to the prince many species that are still quite rare in Flanders and in return receives bulbs and shrubs, most of them from the Americas, which the retired diplomat is able to obtain thanks to his social position and extensive network of contacts.[39] Before he begins corresponding with Caccini, Arembergh also exchanges specimens with the eminent Flemish botanist Carolus Clusius.[40] This spirit of collegial reciprocity is the rule among the earliest collectors of rare plants, although it will fray somewhat as collecting spreads beyond the confines of the scientific community.

Arembergh's garden boasts a vast collection of anemones, then a rare and coveted plant in the Flanders; indeed, the first documented specimen of *Anemone coronaria* is sent to Jean de Brancion by Alfonso Panza (the director of the botanical garden of Ferrara) in 1597, just nine years before Arembergh establishes his garden in Enghien.[41] The prince's enthusiasm, as well as his interest in the practical details connected with gardening and horticulture, is palpable in a letter dated 1 January 1609, in which he thanks Caccini for having sent him several specimens that "quite adorn a Garden when the bulbs have finished their Course, which for the Majority is usually at the end of June except for the anemones, for here a way has been invented to have them in every month of the year, and I assure you that I have at this moment some that are in flower and for this reason I beg Your Lordship to send me more sorts."[42]

In another of his letters, Caccini inquires whether there is anyone in Flanders who knows how to obtain double blooms from plants that usually produce only single blooms. The prince replies that "up to now I have never witnessed this miracle," but promises to look into the matter and send him any information he may find.[43] Collectors are fascinated by the possibilities of new horticultural techniques, whose aim is to acclimate species from exotic regions but also to develop new varieties with characteristics that occur only by chance in nature.

Very interesting in this context is a series of letters written to Caccini by Giovanni da Salò, a Capuchin friar. Fra' Giovanni eagerly discusses cultivation techniques, shedding an unexpected light on the practices of the botanists and horticulturists of the period[44]: he provides an account, complete with sketches, of "the secret of how to make variegated roses." The friar claims that he has succeeded in obtaining flowers of different colors from a single rose plant, and similar results in fruit trees, vines, and oleanders. A vine subjected to his treatment has produced clusters containing up to eight different types of grapes, while in his "giardinetto di fiori"—the friar maintains—there is a rose tree that can generate six different kinds of blossoms![45]

The growing interest of floriculturists in topics relating to the manipulation of plants is an implicit reminder of the complex relationship established between natural world and man in the early seventeenth century. The discovery of the inexhaustible creative powers of nature offers man both an invitation and a challenge—an invitation to admire her wonders, a challenge to study and classify them, and to compete by producing artificial *meraviglie*. Horticultural experimentation, which had always formed an integral part of agricultural and gardening practices, is now encouraged by the rise of the natural sciences and, at the same time, finds reinforcement in the theme of metamorphosis, which looms so large in the cultural imagination of the period. Transposed from the literary sphere to that of natural history, the myth of transmutation with its hermetic and cabalistic roots coexists with the modern scientific methods being developed in this period.[46]

PLANTS IN THE AGE OF THE *VIRTUOSI*

If so distinguished a *condottiero* and diplomat as the prince-count Arembergh does not consider it beneath him to take an interest in the day-to-day problems of gardening, it is not surprising that in the following decades, European princes, cardinals, merchants, friars, physicians, chemist-herbalists, artists, and voyagers to far-flung continents are all prepared to dirty their hands planting their own gardens. Indeed, toward the end of the sixteenth century and in the early decades of the seventeenth, alongside the well-recognized figure of the virtuoso in the arts, music, and poetry emerges that of the *giardiniere,* not in the modern sense of the professional gardener, but the enthusiastic student of nature, amateur horticulturist, and collector of unusual plants. Fully conscious of the dignity and worth of his role, the *giardiniere* moves in circles where "it is deserving of Princes to lay down the law in the realm of flowers as in that of men"[47] and transforms his interest in nature into a vehicle for the expression of his intellectual refinement and social standing.

By the 1620s, no villa or palace in Europe is complete without its *giardino di fiori* and the mania for acquiring the latest varieties has infected gardeners everywhere, giving rise to the excesses typical of collectors. This peak of the phenomenon is well illustrated in the letters of a well-born ecclesiastic from Naples, Monsignor Giuseppe Acquaviva, who declares himself to be extremely fond of flowers, but who shows no hint of any genuine appreciation of plants or nature for their own sake; the prelate's sole purpose in filling his garden with expensive plants is so that he can boast of them to others.

Many collectors fall prey to similar feelings of unappeasable cupidity, envy, and discontent. Andrea Matteo d'Acquaviva, prince of Caserta and a relative of Monsignor Acquaviva, owns a garden that, as we know from indirect sources, contains some unique specimens, including a tuberose called the gia-cinto tuberosa radice and an *Amaryllis belladonna* that flowers for the first time in Italy in his garden. Nonetheless, in the letters of Monsignor Acquaviva, the prince is reported to complain incessantly about how few plants he has in comparison to his rivals.[48]

Nonetheless, botanical collecting is not merely a pastime limited to the privileged few. Religious orders have a long tradition of cultivating gardens of simples and some of their members become highly respected botanists. The friars of Trinità dei Monti in Rome are well known in the seventeenth century for their expertise on botanical matters and divide their activities between research and the preparation and sale of herbal remedies. Caccini notes in a letter to Duke Francesco Caetani (1621) that the community possesses some very valuable plants, and their botanical collection is also cited, just after 1650, by the art historiographer Giovan Pietro Bellori.[49]

Physicians and pharmacists are another group whose professional interest in medicinal plants quite naturally with time extended to exotic species and their potential pharmacological properties. One of the most prominent of these is Johann Faber, a German physician and surgeon who becomes director of the Vatican's botanical garden and is happy to undertake projects such as advising Cardinal Pio of Savoy on the layout of his private garden. He occasionally serves as an intermediary in the exchange of specimens between plant lovers from his homeland and powerful Roman collectors as Cardinal Borghese, or even more modest ones like Alessandro Rondanini.[50] Another member of the circle of naturalists to which Faber belongs is Enrico Corvino, owner of one of the most important pharmacies in Rome. Behind Corvino's busy establishment is a garden that has no doubt been set up as an adjunct to his profession, but soon the number and types of species growing there greatly exceed what is required for his dispensary. As late as 1664, this garden is considered worthy of mention by Bellori in his *Nota delli Musei*.[51] Apothecaries from all the other European countries can also be mentioned, like the Flemish Jean Mouton, Christian Porret, Peeter van Coudenberghe, Joachim Levenier, Jeroen van Wingen, or the British Hugh Morgan, James Garet, Thomas Penny, and many others.

Botanical collecting leads to the emergence of a new profession, that of the dealer in ornamental plants and flowers, as exemplified by the figure of Matteo Caccini. Equally prominent in Italy is Tranquillo Romauli, whom Giovanni Battista Ferrari praises more than once in his treatise *De Florum Cultura*. Romauli runs a nursery together with Fabrizio Sbardoni, and when the latter withdraws from the partnership to join the retinue of Cardinal Pio, Romauli buys out his share of the business, which consists of "multas et diversas cepollas et plantas diversorum florum magni et notabilis valoris" (many different bulbs and plants of different flowers of great and noteworthy value) that Sbardoni had gathered during the course of his voyages to different parts of the world. The termination agreement lists more than two thousand bulbs, including tulips, on which Romauli is recognized as the greatest authority in Rome. In the document some plants that Romauli himself has introduced to the gardens of Rome are also recorded, among them "a tuberous [plant] shaped like a turnip" from India; an exotic narcissus called the marzolino; two jasmine plants, possibly with double blooms; and twelve different specimens of the yucca, a truly impressive number if one considers how rare this shrub still is at the time in Italy.[52]

Another celebrated floriculturist is the Belgian Emmanuel Sweerts, who is the first to exploit on a full scale the practice of selling plants by correspondence. For the benefit of his clients, he has a beautiful florilegium prepared, that shows the hundreds of species available from his nursery, accompanied by an explanatory table in four languages.[53]

With the demand for exotic plants and flowers growing rapidly, the business of flowers soon expands beyond these exclusive vendors; within a few years, the Morin family in Paris and the Tradescant family in England establish the first large-scale nurseries. Alongside these gardeners many entrepreneurs appear, who enter the market purely as a business venture. In one of his letters to Caccini, the friar Giovanni da Salò notes that he had seen with his own eyes a blue hyacinth bearing eighty flowers on a single stem; the owner of this marvel is a banker, Ludovico Arrighino from Brescia, who after going bankrupt turned to the cultivation and sale of flowers as a profitable business. There is also a Flemish painter whom Arembergh describes as "one of the greatest, and best supplied herbalists" in the country, who has been recently identified with Raphael van Coxcie.[54] The prince-count sends Caccini a copy of the artist's catalogue, which enumerates 167 different bulbous flowers, including eight varieties of anemones, ten crocuses, five fritillaries, seventeen hyacinths, six irises, eleven Turk's-cap lilies, fifteen varieties of narcissus, and five types of peonies. An entire section is devoted to tulips, of which the artist-horticulturist possesses seventeen different varieties.

Thus, the passion for unusual plants and the desire to amass enviable collections seems to have drawn a wide range of people into gardening, from enlightened aristocrats to cultivated amateurs and professional men. Their growing numbers leads to another development, particularly in northern Europe—the formation of national guilds and professional associations. In regarding this phenomenon, though, it is important to distinguish between northern countries, like Great Britain and Flanders, where official organizations with statutory codes are established, and other countries: in France, for example, a community of passionate, but strictly amateur flower lovers, springs up, bound by shared interests with no regard to rank or occupation.[55] It is the case, for example, of François Filhol, a person of humble origin, who nonetheless devotes himself to the collecting of rarities and who, thanks to his interest in rare flowers, comes in direct touch with Gaston d'Orléans.[56] He also exchanges flowers with many other aristocrats of other countries, among which the famous Spanish nobleman Vincencio Juan de Lastañosa.[57]

Italy as well does not see the formation of commercial associations; the community of flower lovers is instead the product and expression of an elite culture that represents the evolution of the typical *Wunderkammer* collecting, where the rare and exotic are amassed more as a sign of wealth and power of the owner and less on the grounds of scientific interest in nature. This trend begins to take form in the last decades of the sixteenth century and reaches its apex during the reign of Pope Urban VIII. The vogue for flowers is reflected in every sphere, denoting intellectual curiosity, refined taste, and an enlightened interest in the latest scientific developments. In a process that begins during the sixteenth century and accelerates during the first three decades of the seventeenth, flowers are invested with multiple layers of meaning, becoming a symbol of the complex cultural universe of the Baroque period.

On a purely worldly plane, the cultivation of rare flowers is seen as a means of enhancing one's personal prestige. This is, for instance, the motive underlying the publication of *Exactissima descriptio,* a catalogue of some of the rare plants to be found in the Farnese gardens on Palatine Hill overlooking Rome.[58] Renowned since the sixteenth century for their botanical collection, the Orti Farnesiani reach their moment of greatest splendor under Cardinal Odoardo (1575–1626). Many bulbous species are cultivated there, as well as plants and shrubs from the Americas and Asia, for example, the Jerusalem artichoke (*Helianthus tuberosus*), which is called the *flos farnesianum* by the eminent botanist Fabio Colonna,[59] and the acacia (*Acacia farnesiana*), so named because it flowers for the first time in these gardens.

Rome has become an important center for the publication of fine books and *Exactissima descriptio* constitutes a magnificent example of the printer's art. The work, which is generally credited to the Roman botanist Pietro Castelli despite the "official" authorship of the gardener Tobia Aldini, presents in separate chapters sixteen of the most rare and beautiful plants in the Farnese gardens. Each chapter contains a detailed botanical description, practical information (including applications in medicine and cooking, recipes for ointments and perfumes, etc.), and a realistic engraving of the plant with its roots, branches, leaves, and flowers in various stages of opening. Smaller illustrations provide details helpful to the identification of the species, such as its fruit and seeds.

Although *Exactissima descriptio* still retains many features of the traditional herbals, in the earliest decades of seventeenth century, treatises are being written that mark the definitive transition to a new approach to the study of plants. Eminent *giardinieri* begin to share the fruits of their knowledge by writing manuals for the cultivation of specific categories of plants. Examples include *Propagazione e Governo della Rosa della China* by the Jesuit botanist Giovanni Battista Ferrari,[60] *Modo et ordine per propagar et conservar li Giacinti* by Fabrizio Carra of Brescia, and Alessandro Caetani's *Modo di custodire fiori tanto bulbi quanto tuberi, et Argemoni et Anemoni e altri fiori.* Matteo Pandolfini, the director of the botanical garden of Pisa, is the author of a *Lettera* on the cultivation of flowers together with an interesting manual titled *Modo di far ne Pavimenti e massime di Chiese historie composte di fiori come à Musaico che fu messa in opera in S. Pietro da messer Benedetto Drei fiorentino.*[61]

Also worth mentioning are the *Breve Instruttione per Vasi, e Spalliere di Cedrati e Lumìe* by Filippo Magalotti[62] and the *Discorso del modo di governar diversa sorte di fiori* by Tranquillo Romauli. The latter discusses anemones, hyacinths, narcissi, tulips, garofoli (carnations), primroses, and other rare plants including the "liene di Costantinopoli" and the cardinal's plant or *Lobelia cardinalis,* which is named after Francesco Barberini. The cardinal possesses another work by Romauli, *Delli Gelsomini e delle Rose,* which he has bound in gold-tooled leather, stamped with his coat of arms, a measure of the great value that he places on this work.[63]

Most of these *Discorsi* and *Istruzioni* are arranged in similar fashion, the author providing the name or names by which each plant is known, a botanical description, and instructions on its cultivation in simple and direct language, including advice on soil conditions and the best planting period, pruning techniques, methods of propagation and so on. Emphasis is placed on the practical aspects of horticulture, and the reader can profit from the direct experience of the author, who has personally tested all of the techniques he is recommending.

In fact, the vital importance of experimentation and the sharing of ideas and information is understood by the entire community of savants in Europe, who seek to create a common store of knowledge to assist them in the difficult task of acclimating new plants whose characteristics and requirements are still unknown. Through this process, a pragmatic approach focusing on the direct observation of nature is introduced into the botanical sciences, in keeping with the empirical methodology that is being developed in the study of all branches of natural history. These new botanical treatises produced in Italy and France generally exclude any reference to magical, alchemistic, or astrological elements, in marked contrast to the situation in northern Europe where such esoteric currents would remain influential for many decades to come.[64] The importance of these texts in facilitating the transition from a form of knowledge based purely on associative and metaphorical links to one based on direct experience must not be underestimated, especially if one considers that this was neither an immediate nor a linear process.

All the same, the primary audience for these works is not professional floriculturists, but the wealthy owners of private gardens. By both addressing such a public, and evoking the authority of classical writers as their model (that is introducing an erudite cultural dimension in their works), the *giardinieri* seek to elevate a branch of knowledge that, because of its associations with manual labor, had been considered an illiterate art up to the end of the sixteenth century.[65] They reconcile the transmission of useful information with an elegant writing style to produce works that are the expression of a refined culture of botanical dilettantism, which is itself the manifestation of a new relationship between man and nature. The theme of man locked in struggle against a hostile environment is modulated as the gentler aspects of nature come to be appreciated and channeled into the creation of propitious settings for moments of relaxation, social intercourse, and cultivated gatherings.

In the pursuit of these aims, gardeners are encouraged to develop techniques that allow them to obtain the so much appreciated *meraviglie*. The garden thus becomes a theater in which nature is brought under control not only to create special effects from labyrinths, waterworks, and grottoes but also to produce rare blooms, and it is from this perspective that we must interpret the shift in emphasis from botany to horticulture in these treatises.

By now, botany is regarded as the ideal pastime for cultivated persons with an inclination for the sciences, which in this period include some of the most powerful princes of the church. One of the most famous gardens in Europe in the second quarter of the seventeenth century belongs to two high ecclesiastics—Francesco and Antonio Barberini, the cardinal-nephews of Pope Urban VIII. The villa on the slopes of Quirinal Hill that the family acquires and renovates in magnificent style not only houses an extensive collection of antiquities and Francesco's private library, but is surrounded by a vast garden in which rare plants are cultivated, exotic animals such as camels and ostriches roam, and theatrical and musical performances are staged in which floral themes often serve as a source of inspiration.

Many flowering bulbs obtained through exchanges with botanists in every part of Europe are grown in the Barberini gardens, including the prized Narciso Iacobeo (*Sprekelia formosissima*), the Narciso detto Donna bella (*Amaryllis belladonna*), the Narciso Suertio (*Haemantus coccineus*), and the Iacinto tuberoso (tuberose). There are ornamental shrubs such as the yucca, the "trachelio americano o pianta cardinale" (*Lobelia cardinalis*), the passiflora or passionflower (which by the 1630s is actually quite common in Italy), the Virginia creeper, the acacia, the rosa della China or hibiscus, and many other species. In addition, the garden becomes renowned for the successful acclimatization of plants never before seen in the papal city and that can be found in no other garden: the Albero Americano del Corallo, the fagiolo del Brasile or sweetpea, the meringa malabarica, the Caio or Caioo, the tamarind, and the gelsomino giallo indiano odoratissimo, a prized plant that is as beautiful as it is difficult to grow.[66]

The importance of the Barberini gardens in seventeenth-century Rome cannot be overestimated; they become a point of reference for the intellectuals and scholars who gravitate to the Barberini court (among them Cassiano dal Pozzo and the second generation of Lincei academicians) and by extension for many intellectuals and men of science across Europe, such as Nicolas-Claude Fabri de Peiresc of Provence, who often sends naturalistic gifts to the young cardinal Francesco.[67] These gardens represent the highest expression of the floral culture of the seventeenth century or—as Giovanni Battista Ferrari would have said—of the new kingdom of Flora, returned to earth to inaugurate the "century of flowers."

The most refined testament to this new era in European culture are Ferrari's horticultural works, *De florum cultura* and *Hesperides*, which are printed in Rome in 1633 and in 1646; the first of the two has also had an Italian translation, published in 1638.[68] Running more than five hundred pages divided into four books, *De florum cultura* describes many ornamental and exotic plants, cultivation techniques, modalities for designing a garden, and the "uses and wonders" of flowers. The beauty of its layout and illustrations and the richness and complexity of its contents make this work the quintessential expression of a refined culture in which the study of nature is regarded as an instrument of worldly delight. The engravings are commissioned from some of the most well-known artists in Italy and range from simple illustrations of gardening tools to botanical drawings of rare species (including the first botanical image drawn with the aid of a microscope), elaborate floral compositions, and charming vignettes that illustrate mythological tales conceived by the author in the style of Ovid's *Metamorphoses*.

The presence of these tales is especially relevant to understand the role of plants in seventeenth century's culture. Just as Ulisse Aldrovandi, to name but one of his predecessors and colleagues, had been completely unaware of a rigorously "scientific" approach,[69] Ferrari chooses to insert all of the information he provides on gardening and plants, however new and unfamiliar, within a traditional cultural framework. By investing the species he describes with an antique pedigree (inventing one when there were none from classical mythology to draw upon) and providing his readers with an 'encyclopedic' background that spans from botanical and horticultural information to literary references, he sets these exotic plants within a context that his readers can understand. Ferrari does not perceive a separation between traditional and modern knowledge; to him, the latest scientific methods and instruments of research (such as the telescope and microscope) represent further modalities of

FIGURE 3.5: "The creation of the hibiscus plant," in G. B. Ferrari, *Flora overo cultura dei fiori* (Roma, 1638).

understanding the world that can help to amplify those already established by centuries of tradition.

The relationship that is created between antique culture and the new culture of the natural sciences in the early seventeenth century is unique, because the two spheres are not yet perceived as separate. They are instead integrated at every level, leading to exceptional results in the printed books and figurative arts of the period. Masterpieces that demonstrate the popularity of mythological themes connected with botany include Caravaggio's painting *Narciso;* Cassiano dal Pozzo's *Museo Cartaceo,* an encyclopedic synthesis of *natura* and *cultura;*[70] and two canvases painted by the young Nicolas Poussin just before the publication of Ferrari's *De florum cultura.* The complex significations of *The Triumph of Flora* (Paris, Louvre) and *The Kingdom of Flora* (Dresden, Gemaldegalerie)[71] can be fully appreciated in this context, especially if one recalls that the second canvas, whose interpretation has arisen many discussions between art historians, was according to contemporary sources originally entitled *The Metamorphosis of Flowers.*[72] Like Ferrari, Poussin chooses to narrate the stories of various flowers through mythology with an accent on the Ovidian theme of metamorphosis. The difference lies in the fact that, while the painter draws directly upon classical sources and re-elaborates them, the Jesuit invents the episodes that he recounts in his treatise.

The centrality of the theme of classical mythology to both Poussin and Ferrari is a coincidence that bespeaks the lively curiosity and multitude of interests that animates the intellectual life of the period, where a completely modern component of scientific research could exist side by side with and shed fresh light on the more traditional component of classical and antiquarian culture. Although Ferrari shows how far an interest in botany could carry a scholar who was an erudite polymath rather than a scientist, the obverse is true as well. The passion for botany and collecting in its various forms is not merely an expression of taste and social status. It forms an integral part of the culture of the period, a branch of knowledge that no savant could ignore.

In its every dimension, therefore, Ferrari's *De florum cultura* represents the summa of a civilization. With its meticulous editing and layout, its fine illustrations and refined prose, and its subject matter, which could not have been more à la page, it serves as a vehicle for some of the most important manifestations of early-seventeenth-century culture. Yet, at the heart of this tour de force lies an inherent contradiction, one that will contribute to the eventual fragmentation of knowledge into increasingly specialized sectors. Ferrari himself makes clear *a priori* distinctions between different areas of knowledge; unlike Aldrovandi or Clusius, who engaged themselves in encyclopedic projects of cataloguing nature, his interest is limited to a handful of brilliant chapters in "the great book of nature": ornamental plants and flowers. This choice, like every other aspect of Ferrari's treatise, allows us to appreciate the full extent of the transformations brought about by flowers and plants in European culture, from science to the arts, between the sixteenth and the seventeenth centuries.

CHAPTER FOUR

Use and Reception

ELIZABETH HYDE

In 1580, Michel de Montaigne, on tour in Italy, visited the palace and gardens of the Grand Duke Francesco I de Medici at Pratolino.[1] Montaigne (via his secretary) had faint praise for the palace: "[t]he house is called Pratolino. The building is contemptible to see it from far off, but from near it is very beautiful, though not up to the most beautiful in France. They say that there are six score furnished rooms; we saw ten or twelve of the finest. The furniture is pretty, but not magnificent."[2] But he found much to admire in the gardens and devoted lengthy passages of his travel journal to describing his impressions of the garden's features, including the grotto about which he wrote,

> There is one miraculous thing, a grotto with several cells and rooms; this part surpasses all that we have ever seen elsewhere. It is encrusted and formed all over of a certain material which they say is brought from certain mountains, and they have joined it invisibly with nails. There is not only music and harmony made by the movement of the water, but also a movement of several statues and doors with various actions, caused by the water; several animals that plunge in to drink; and things like that. At one single movement the whole grotto is full of water, and all the seats squirt water on your buttocks; and if you flee from the grotto and climb the castle stairs and anyone takes pleasure in this sport, there come out of every other step of the stairs, right up to the top of the house, a thousand jets that give you a bath.[3]

Montaigne followed the report of his exhilarating descent into—and water-soaked escape from—the grotto with a literary surrender to Pratolino: "The beauty and richness of this place cannot be described in detail." Of course, Montaigne's literary capitulation was only temporary, and he went on to describe other features of the Pratolino garden. Montaigne portrayed a garden with features designed to engage and to be used and experienced by its visitors. When John Evelyn visited the garden decades later, he also noted that "the whole place seemes Consecrated to pleasure, & retirement in Summer." Like Montaigne, he was fascinated by the grottoes and fountains, writing, "Here having been well wash'd for our Curiosity, we went down a large Walk, at the sides whereof gushes out of imperceptible pipes, couched under neath, slender pissings of water, that interchangeably fall into each other Chanells, making a lofty arch, so as a man on horseback may ride under it and not be wet with one drop, nay so high, as one may walk with a speare in ones hand under each spout, this Canopi or arch of Water, was mi thought one of the surprizings magnificences I had ever seene . . . ."[4]

Della Bella executed a series of six engravings depicting views of Pratolino that in many ways illustrate the experiences of Montaigne and Evelyn. He produced renderings of the grottoes, fountains, a tree house, and the colossal figure of the Apennines, the sculpted giant by Giovanni da Bologna that seemed to emerge from the rocks, soil, and vegetation of the mountain.[5] Like the images of gardens produced by most of his contemporaries, Della Bella's engravings show them peopled with fashionably dressed seventeenth-century men, women, and children who stroll down the avenues. By the time Della Bella depicted these visitors in the Pratolino garden, the garden and its spectacular features were already decades old. They were no longer a novelty, and yet they were filled with visitors not only occupying the space but also clearly taking in, "consuming" the garden. One must be skeptical about reading Della Bella's etching as a literal representation of the activities taking place in the Pratolino garden: artists typically included figures in landscapes. And yet Della Bella's figures echo Montaigne and Evelyn: they are not passive descriptors of the landscape. Rather, they are experiencing or consuming the garden and its features. Within the etchings, Della Bella's figures seek rest on walls and benches, take in garden vistas from the palace, ascend the staircase into the tree house, hesitate before walking under arcs of water extending along an allée lined with fountains, and get wet when surprised by playful jets of water. In Della Bella's engraving of the Apennino alone, figures converse in small groups as a small child chases a dog, figures look into both distant perspectives and the water of the pool immediately below the colossal giant. Other figures lean

FIGURE 4.1: Stefano Della Bella, *Appennino, Medici Villa at Pratolino*, 1652. Private Collection.

into the water, perhaps feeding ducks swimming in it, while two women stand in front of Bologna's giant, their gaze directly on him.

We cannot, of course, eavesdrop on what conversations, observations, or thoughts Della Bella might have imagined for them, but Montaigne, Evelyn, and Della Bella all remind us that although the Renaissance produced self-conscious attempts at a theory of landscape, the Renaissance garden was no sterile, theoretical exercise in design, perspective, and hydraulics or botany. Rather, these gardens were functional sites, meant to be walked, meant to be observed, meant to be used for physical labor, for retreat and relaxation, for entertainment and stimulation. Their fruits were meant to be consumed, their refreshments taken, and their surprises gloried in; in other words, Montaigne's buttocks were supposed to get soaked! But we also know that Montaigne's reactions were not entirely unanticipated, that he likely reacted to the garden in the manner of a sixteenth-century European man actively seeking out what the garden had to offer. As series editors Michael Leslie and John Dixon Hunt have articulated, we do not have a vocabulary to express how gardens were "consumed." We can attempt, however, an archaeology of the experience of the Renaissance landscape by exploring how gardens were used and the corollary reception of them. At its simplest, the Renaissance garden was a piece of land used for the cultivation of the soil, a place to display the fruits of that cultivation, and a place of pleasure where those fruits might be consumed. These uses inform the reception of the garden in the Renaissance. As a space for the labor of cultivation, the garden was received as a space where agricultural, intellectual, and aesthetic cultivation work could be carried out. Used as a space for display of the fruits of that labor, it was received simultaneously as a means to display one's cultivation. And used as a place of pleasure, the garden was received as a stage on which the cultural and political dynamics of Renaissance society could be—and were—played out. In hopes that one can begin to understand Montaigne and Evelyn's reception of Pratolino—and almost imagine the conversations of Della Bella's figures in the landscape— this chapter is an explication of use and reception in the Renaissance garden through an analysis of the garden as a place of cultivation, display, and performance.

CULTIVATION

At its core, the garden is a landscape manipulated through the labor of cultivation—but cultivation understood in all senses of the word: agricultural, cultural, and intellectual. During the Renaissance, cultivation very much implied improvement or development of one's self. But the much older agricultural meaning still had relevance and resonance in Renaissance Europe. For the cultivation of the soil, or the working of or laboring in the soil in order to transform wilderness into civilization, barren into fruitful soil, and seeds into plants and fruit-bearing trees, remained essential to a primarily agrarian society, a large portion of which continued to subsist precariously from harvest to harvest. It was well understood that labor was required to transform the earth from its wild first nature into what John Dixon Hunt has referenced as "second" and "third" natures.[6] The transformation of a landscape through the stages of natures, from the untouched to the agricultural to the formal garden suggests both a progression of development of the landscape based on the degree of human intervention (i.e., toil), and a progression from the utilitarian but essential agricultural landscape towards increasingly sophisticated cultural uses—the politically and culturally charged royal gardens, for example.

Within such transformation, the Renaissance garden did not lose sight of its agricultural origins or the requisite human toil and labor necessary in developing it. Indeed, the Renaissance formal garden played with both the idea of utility and the notion of labor, with the knowledge of the labor necessary to make a garden informing its reception and meaning. While Renaissance humanist culture emerged out of a notably urban Italian world of the fifteenth and sixteenth centuries, most people even within those urban areas lived close enough to the soil to appreciate the garden primarily as the source of food. The peasant gardens of the European countryside and growers' gardens that ringed Europe's cities and fed their inhabitants bore little resemblance to the pleasure gardens of the Renaissance. And the life experiences of those who labored in and depended on peasant gardens bore little resemblance to those able to build formal gardens. But it is significant that the formal pleasure garden explored its utilitarian roots with increasing creativity as new fruits and vegetables, some imported from the Near East, others from the Americas, still more newly bred cultivars of older species, captured the attention of gardeners, their patrons, and collectors alike. Within the formal garden, the lines between the ornamental and the edible were deliberately blurred. Fruit trees, for example, were a vitally important part of the Renaissance garden. Orange trees, in particular, were highly sought after, the difficulty of cultivating them in northern climates serving to heighten their desirability and leading to the development of increasingly sophisticated orangeries. Apple trees and pear trees were manipulated into fashionable and difficult to achieve forms such as the espalier. The fruits themselves were also valued: by the seventeenth century, for example, pears had become highly fashionable, and a number of cookbooks dedicated to the preparation of fruit preserves were published.[7] Extensive literature on grafting, a procedure intended to graft desired varieties onto heartier trunks, was published in order to lead gardeners and collectors alike through the process.[8] In France, the kitchen garden was elevated to an art form by Jean-Baptiste de La Quintinie whose *potager du roi*, begun at Versailles in 1678, became a showplace. The fruits and vegetables produced at Versailles graced the table of the king and his courtiers, who marveled at the royal gardener's ability to coax fruits and vegetables from the *potager* at all seasons of the year.[9]

While over the course of the sixteenth and seventeenth centuries the Renaissance garden was becoming a site in which agricultural labor could produce marvel, it was also growing in the consciousness of European states as a site of economic potential, the management of which was deemed worthy of bureaucratic attention. In the early seventeenth century, Olivier de Serres and Henri IV famously advocated the planting of mulberry trees in French pleasure gardens in hope of stimulating the silk trade in France.[10] More important, states began to realize the importance of managing their wooded parks and forests. John Evelyn composed and published his 1664 *Sylva, Or a Discourse of Forest-Trees, and the Propagation of Timber in His Majesties Dominions* after gathering information and advice on the management of forests and timber for the British Commissioners of the Navy. In the work, he advocated the careful management of forests in order to maximize timber production for the benefit of British naval power.[11] By the reign of Louis XIV, Jean Baptiste Colbert, finance minister to the Sun King, realized the importance of managing French forests to simultaneously protect against over harvesting and deforestation and encourage the growth of French timber for shipbuilding and other military priorities, and enacted royal policy accordingly with the passage of the *Grand Ordonnance des eaux et forêts* in 1669. And at the same time, he put his mercantilistic economic principles into practice in the construction of a nursery in Toulon, on the French Mediterranean coast, where immature bulbs could be purchased cheaply from Mediterranean sources, raised to maturity in the favorable climate there, and then shipped north for plantation at Versailles and other royal gardens.[12] From Colbert's perspective, then, proper management of French arboreal and horticultural resources could advance both French gardens and the French state. Plants and trees were becoming recognized as economic resources necessarily managed in the race for European supremacy.

The utilitarian, therefore, had an important place in the formal Renaissance garden, as did an acknowledgment of the labor carried out on the earth to bring forth from it flowers, trees, and waters. Laboring in the gardens was ancient work, of course, rooted in the production of food. As the Renaissance pleasure garden grew in size and complexity, so did the workforce necessary to build, furnish, and maintain the garden. The majority of those who entered the garden did so out of necessity. They were the gardeners by trade whose fathers had trained them in the requisite skills. Or they were women who worked as weeders. The work was neither glamorous nor well paid, with a very few master gardeners and designers, like André Le Nôtre in seventeenth-century France, the exception to the rule. And yet professional gardening grew sufficiently over the course of the Renaissance to warrant increasing corporatization. By the end of the seventeenth century, separate guilds existed for seeds men, gardeners, and women flower sellers.[13]

The labor of these gardeners was in many ways ordinary: weeding, raking, digging, and transplanting were simple but necessary. But the reception of that labor could be anything but pedestrian. Toil in the garden meant a livelihood for many, but it served as a diversion many at the other end of the social and economic spectrum, to the extent that some were criticized for overindulging their passions for gardening. But they defended themselves by celebrating the labor entailed in the act of cultivating. Collectors of flowers, or "curious florists" as they were becoming known, defended their passion for flowers on the grounds that the labor necessary to care for and bring to blossom the flowers in their gardens served a more important goal. To the author of a 1692 flower gardening manual titled *La Culture des fleurs,* those who labored at gardening would find tilling the soil comparable to cultivating the soul: "You know well (my dear reader) that your parterre is a figure of your soul, and that one day it will serve in your condemnation in the judgment of God, if you neglected to cultivate the Plant of your Garden . . . . The world is a garden, or the nursery of the great God, it is there that he opens every day that flowers to be placed on the altars of his glory, and in making the ornaments of his Paradise."[14]

This association with the Christian faith is important here, as the medieval legacy of the garden is that of a space associated with reflection, contemplation, and retreat. The monk's garden of simples was an expected part of a monastic compound. As the source of herbs thought useful in the healing arts, the garden, too, was a repository of useful and valuable botanical specimens—and knowledge about them. The monastic repository also had Biblical resonances, for it, too, served as a reminder of the Garden of Eden where every sort of plant blossomed and bore fruit without any human toil being necessary. The idea of the Garden of Eden remained powerful in the Renaissance, as Columbus and his successors sought lands to the east that, in addition to being rich in silks, spices, and jewels, were also, according to medieval maps of the world, the geographical location of paradise from which Adam and Eve and all botanical specimens had sprung. The expulsion of Adam and Eve and the scattering of its botanical wealth could be reversed only in the body of the Virgin Mary, who's Immaculate Conception and virginity came to be represented visually by the closed garden. Indeed, much of our visual knowledge of fifteenth- and sixteenth-century gardens derives from gardens depicted in medieval and Renaissance renderings of the Annunciation, as in Hans Memling's *Annunciation.* Executed in the second half of the fifteenth century, the painting depicts Mary, whose reading has been interrupted by the angel Gabriel, in the foreground, while in the background a window opens onto a garden with geometric beds and geometrically clipped and shaped trees, one of which appears to be tended by a woman.[15]

Labor in the garden was not just healthful to the soul: it could also feed the intellect. The humanist revival of Virgil's *Georgics* led Renaissance writers to attempt to emulate the classic celebration of labor both in Latin and in the vernacular. Early Renaissance examples of georgic literature included Rucellai's work *Le Api* and Luigi Alamanni's 1546 *La Coltivatione,* a work written in Italian and published but Paris while Alamanni worked in the court of Francis I.[16] Interest in the genre survived into the seventeenth century, even as the use of the Latin language was beginning to decline. The Jesuit René Rapin published his *Hortorum libri IV,* a georgic verse celebration of flowers, forests, water, and orchards, in 1665. Composed and published in Latin, the work described the very ordinary but honorable labor needed to cultivate the realm of nature, but in eloquent verse. Rapin was aware that attempting such a feat in Latin in the seventeenth century would not be easy as the style, methods, and subsequently, language of gardening had evolved since Virgil: "Nor was I a little discouraged by the defects of the Latine Tongue, since it is an insufferable arrogance to write of a thing in Latine, of which the Latines were wholly ignorant: For the method of Gardening which is now in vogue, either of disposing Flowers in Beds, or the planting, and ordering of Wall-Fruits, was not used among them."[17] But Rapin was determined to try, promising that "if I transgress either through the penury of the Language, or my own ignorance; I am so vain as to hope, that our Age which so admires Gardens above all others, will forgive me, if I fall short in an Essay which none have made trial of before me."[18] He maintained that because gardens were enjoying greater esteem than ever before, it was important to pay literary tribute to both the practice and pleasure of gardening."[19] Rapin's verses proved popular; they were translated into English and French and continued to be reissued in Latin through the eighteenth century, demonstrating simultaneously the desire to emulate the ancients, the desire to engage in the arts of gardening as it had evolved through the Renaissance, and the desire to celebrate the nobility of labor in the garden.

Labor in the garden was honorable and sustaining if performed in the proper spirit. And its results were to be marveled at: visitors to the Trianon gardens at Versailles marveled that flower plantations could be changed overnight to produce a remarkably different effect that seemed magical, the work having been performed after courtiers had retreated inside. In 1694, André Félibien wrote that the Trianon de porcelaine "was regarded first, by all the world, as an enchantment; because even though it had not been started at the end of winter it was found done at springtime, as if it came out of the earth with the flowers in the gardens that accompany it."[20] Saint Simon remarked that in the Trianon gardens, "[a]ll of the compartments in each of the parterres were changed every day."[21] To achieve such an effect required increasingly sophisticated hothouses and nurseries capable of bringing such large numbers of plants to flower out of season, the results eliciting comparisons to the perpetual springtime promised by Virgil's prophetic *Fourth Eclogue*. Jean-Baptiste Colbert took care to note in his *Ordres et règlements pour les bâtiments de Versailles* on October 24, 1674 to "[v]isit Trianon often, see that Le Bouteaux has flowers for the king during all the winter, that he has a number of boys who are obliged to him whom he can press to achieve all the worlds for the winter. He must render to me an account each week of the flowers he has."[22]

To achieve such a magical effect, it sometimes was deemed necessary that magician gardeners be hidden from sight, as when Louis XIV toured the garden and his fontaniers employed a system of whistles to signal his imminent arrival so that fountains could be turned on just before they entered his view.[23] But despite the delight taken in astonishing courtiers with the labor of "invisible" workers, labor did not have to be hidden entirely. The aesthetic of the Baroque delighted in the difficult and the acknowledgement of difficulty. Depictions of gardens might include workers laboring along side well-to-do ladies and gentlemen strolling through the gardens. Pieter Brueghel, in his depiction of Spring, depicted men and women hard at work in a formal garden planting and weeding and preparing the soil.[24] At Pratolino, Buontalenti even played with the idea of labor in the gardens though his incorporation of a sculpture of a washerwoman whose work allowed for water to drain from a fountain to large basin. Montaigne described the feature, writing, "At the bottom there is a woman washing. She is wringing a tablecloth, also of white marble, the droppings from which keep the basin full. Near this is another vessel, where the water seems boiling, to make lye with."[25] One should not romanticize the labor of the garden—distinct social, economic, and political rank sharply divided the Pratolino washerwoman and the boys who sank Louis XIV's flowers into the ground from the courtiers who whose astonishment they sought to generate. But tilling the soil was regarded as honorable work—even French nobles who risked derogation, or loss of rank and privilege, by engaging in trade, could safely work the land.

But the garden was also seen as an appropriate place for other kinds of work to take place. The religious and the secular intersect in the notion of the garden as a suitable, even desirable setting for reading: the mystic marriage of St. Catherine was frequently depicted with the Virgin Mary, holding an infant Jesus, accompanied by St. Catherine and other elite young women, at least one of which is shown reading.[26] By implication, then, the garden, as an appropriate place for reading, was, therefore, a space conducive to the transportation of the soul to heaven or the imagination to distant lands and times. The Renaissance garden was understood to be a suitable setting for debate and discussion of the Latin texts being collected, edited, and studied by humanist scholars. Cosimo de Medici's villa and garden at Careggi has long been regarded as the setting for the convening of the Neo-platonic Academy in 1439, and, subsequently assumed to have imbued the Renaissance garden with Neoplatonic ideals. Raffaella Fabiani Giannetto has questioned the historical veracity of Careggi as the site of the academy.[27] Even if correct, the persistence of the perception of the garden as the site of the emergence of Neoplatonic debate in the

Renaissance is nevertheless evidence of a strong association of the villa garden as a site of humanist thought. The association of the garden with conversation and debate proved lasting. Fictional works such as Madeleine de Scudéry's *Clélie,* among others, demonstrate that the idea of the garden as a space suitable for intellectual stimulation endured into the seventeenth century, with gardens serving as sites of debate, exchange, and friendship in the literary works associated with the Parisian salons and the *salonnières.*[28]

The Renaissance garden, by its design, encouraged debate. Its design could be manipulated to provoke intellectual, moral, and spiritual stimulation as one moved through the space. The entire garden design could be complicit in the exercise, as in the example of the Villa d'Este in Tivoli, built by Pirro Ligorio for Ippolito d'Este in the middle of the sixteenth century. The garden's iconography, organized around Hercules, required the visitor to choose iconographically (and spatially) between virtue and vice as he or she moved through the garden.[29] More commonly, gardens might contain a labyrinth as one of its features, through which a visitor could either wander or seek moral or ethical truths. The labyrinth, created by carefully planned hedges, could take one of two forms: either as a long and meandering path through which one passed on the way to the destination at the center or as an *irrgarten,* a maze the navigation of which required making choices along the path in order to find the path to truth.[30] Labyrinth designs had been incorporated into Gothic cathedrals to encourage spiritual contemplation. Within the Renaissance garden, the purpose of the labyrinth was more varied. Although a labyrinth could encourage spiritual growth, it might, as in the labyrinth constructed at the Palazzo del Te in Mantua (dating to the first half of the sixteenth century), serve its visitors as a quest and celebration of secular love—the love of Federico II Gonzaga and Isabella Boschetti, in the case of the Palazzo del Te.[31]

The labyrinth survived as a feature of the garden into the seventeenth century and the taste for them spread beyond Italy. Claude Mollet included designs for them in his *Théâtre des plans et jardinages* (written around 1595 and first published in 1652).[32] Salomon de Caus included a labyrinth in the form of concentric circles with an obelisk at the center in the upper terrace of the *Hortus Palatinus* (commissioned in 1614). And a labyrinth was constructed at Versailles for Louis XIV. The labyrinth at Versailles, begun in 1665 by André Le Nôtre, was designed by Charles Perrault to provide moral instruction to the dauphin. It consisted of a maze of allées each leading to a sculpture illustrating one of Aesop's Fables, with descriptive quatrains, by Isaac de Benserade, painted on plaques beneath each sculpture. The visitor to the labyrinth of Versailles had no predetermined path to follow or final destination to reach.

Rather, he or she was free to explore, moving from statue to statue, fable to fable, each interpreted in Benserade's verses. And yet Benserade's interpretation of the fables within the setting of the labyrinth was not the only one in circulation. Charles Perrault composed for publication in 1677 a competing interpretation of the labyrinth that emphasized not morals, but gallantry and love. Popular editions of Jean de La Fontaine's *Fables,* first appearing in 1668, were read at court and in literary circles in Paris.[33] The circulation of multiple readings of the labyrinth of Versailles demonstrates that, even at the court of Louis XIV, in a programmatically determined part of the garden, neither designer nor king could determine the reception of, or commentary on, the garden by its visitors. The fruits of the intellectual laboring in the garden, then, could not always be anticipated, manipulated, or controlled by their creators.

DISPLAY

The Renaissance garden was also fundamentally a place for display. It displayed the fruits of the labor carried out on the landscape, but during the course of the long Renaissance, it also became a space used to exhibit things brought into or made for the landscape. Displays of both sorts stimulated the Renaissance intellect and shaped the reception of the garden. The Renaissance emphasis on the recovery of antiquity led to the excavation of ancient Roman sculptures, and Italian collectors began to gather and display these antiquities in their gardens. Over time, however, the sculptures became less the raison d'être of outdoor spaces, and more a crucial element of the planned landscape. Garden historian Elizabeth Blair MacDougall describes the transition of the *giardino all'antico* in which, "[a]t first, the possession of antiquities was sufficient, and neither their condition nor the manner of their display was important. In the sixteenth century, however, the attitude towards these objects gradually changed as did their role in the garden."[34] Gardens were designed specifically to incorporate such sculptures into the larger whole. If ancient sculptures were not available, then copies of Greek and Roman works could be used. Francis I, for example, commissioned Vignolo to cast bronze copies of ancient works for the garden he was creating at Fontainebleau.

If the *giardino all'antico* was a space dedicated to the veneration of classical antiquity (and to the Renaissance itself as an era cognizant of its role in the rediscovery of its ancient roots), display in the garden also serves as an important reminder that the Renaissance did not only look backwards. Through the sixteenth and seventeenth centuries, Europeans continued to celebrate the ancients, but at the same time, increasingly sought to demonstrate the progress of the moderns—their own advances in the arts and the sciences. Indeed, the Renaissance garden was very much a space in which the metaphorical battle between the ancients and the moderns could be played out in concrete terms. In tangible material ways, the Renaissance garden became a showcase for both the fascination with the past and the accomplishments of the present.

Just as the Renaissance garden adapted to the incorporation of sculptures into the landscape, so the Renaissance garden created spaces for the display of botanical collections. The humanist passion for antiquity fed a new culture of collecting and curiosity. Collectors of ancient sculptures, medals, and manuscripts also, however, began to turn their attention to objects of natural history—fossils, corals, shells, and skeletons, as well as botanical specimens in dried, seed, and living plant form. Flowers, for example, were the obsession of many collectors. The garden offered an aesthetically and intellectually appealing space for the display not only of flowers, but also of other curious objects, as well. In 1644, John Evelyn described the Parisian garden of flower collector and seller Pierre Morin as a repository for all the objects of his collecting impulse: the garden was "an exact oval figure, planted with cypresse cutt flat & set as even as a wall: the tulips, anemonies, ranunculus's, crocus's, & c. are held to be of the rarest, and draw all the admirers of such things to his house during the seasons. He lived in a kind of Hermitage at one side of his garden, where his collection of purselane and coral . . . is much esteemed."[35] John Dixon Hunt has shown that Morin was not unique in integrating his collecting impulses into the garden.[36]

Over the course of the late sixteenth and seventeenth centuries, the collection and cultivation of flowers became increasingly fashionable among European elites, to the extent that garden designs dedicated spaces specifically to their display. The small, enclosed *giardino segreto* of Cardinal Antonio Barberini, built at the Roman Palazzo Barberini in the early seventeenth century, made for a suitable setting for increasingly valuable collections[37] of narcissi, hyacinths, dianthus, anemones, ranunculi, and tulips—the "florists' flowers," most favored by elite collectors. The French garden, too, made spaces for floral display. At seventeenth-century Versailles, the gardens of the Trianon de porcelain and then the Trianon de marbre were characterized by their floral plantations, while the *jardin du roi,* a parterre accessible only through Louis XIV's quarters in the Trianon de marbre was filled with an extensive display of expensive and "very rare" hyacinths.[38]

The impulse to collect and display flowers was not only driven by fashion and aesthetics. The Renaissance garden, as a repository of plant specimens amassed by collectors, was also a living laboratory dedicated to the advancement of botany and horticulture. "Curious florists" (as flower collectors were called) like Pierre Morin were "moderns" in that their collections were built not only from flowers bought, traded, and shared with fellow collectors but also from new varieties bred and perfected as curious florists engaged in the study and selective breeding of the plants they treasured. The botanical work conducted by such gardeners was formalized in botanical gardens in Italy, and then around the continent in the sixteenth and seventeenth centuries. The first formal botanical gardens were established in proximity to or in conjunction with European universities where their contents could be studied by faculty and students alike.[39] Among the earliest were the botanical gardens established in Padua and Pisa, established in 1543. These gardens were followed by similar establishments across Italy and beyond the Alps in Leiden, Montpellier, Oxford, and Paris, among others, built in the late sixteenth and early seventeenth centuries. Not only did many of these early botanical gardens have museums dedicated to the curiosities of natural history attached to them, but they also served as spaces for and the subjects of instruction.[40] The botanical gardens served simultaneously as repositories of plant specimens, laboratories of botanical study and breeding, and inquiry into the medical applications of the plants grown there. That the Jardin Royale de Plantes in Paris was open to the public suggests that botanical gardens, too, were places of leisure.[41]

Thus the scientific revolution played out in the garden itself. This was not lost on Renaissance monarchs who seized on the power of scientific knowledge and sought increasingly to harness that power through their support of scientific academies and, in the realm of the botanical, their patronage of botanical gardens. Guy de la Brosse, physician to Louis XIII of France, understood the importance of such a garden and convinced his king of the same: in 1626, the Jardin Royal des Plantes Médicinales was founded in Paris with the support of Louis XIII. The garden proved capable of weathering political revolution to become a lasting institution and home to the leading botanists of the eighteenth and nineteenth centuries.[42] Absolutist monarchs understood that power would be contested on a global stage as they vied with each other in the exploration of new lands and raced to establish new trade partnerships in territories with which they had become newly acquainted. Botanists and gardeners alike sought specimens from the distant corners of the globe. Indeed, the air of exoticism heightened the desirability of such specimens, as the acquisition of the tulip from Turkish sources, and the subsequent "tulip mania" demonstrates.[43] Increased contact with eastern and Mediterranean sources brought highly desired botanical specimens from those regions. European explorers, merchants, and diplomats brought specimens from Asian and American sources, as well. Indeed, the gathering of specimens from around the world became increasingly systematized—in the eighteenth century, the botanists at the *jardin du roi* both instructed French diplomats around the world to gather specimens from their host countries and dispatched botanists to do the same. Special spaces were created for the fashionable exotics they obtained: a plantation of American plants, for example, was attempted at Marly, one of Louis XIV's auxiliary palaces at Versailles.[44] In displaying collections of botanical and other curiosities, the Renaissance garden both piqued the curiosity of visitors, and established a reputation of curiosity for the owner. Possession was not a guarantee of curiosity: as N. Valnay explained in a seventeenth-century flower gardening manual, "I know that Monsieur the Prince and Monsieur the Marquis de Seignelay [the son of Jean-Baptiste Colbert] . . . have many anemones, but I do not know if they are curious about them."[45]

Montaigne's and Evelyn's reactions to the fountains at Pratolino described at the beginning of the essay demonstrate that curiosity extended beyond the natural to include artifice, as well. Fountains were appealing for the forms they took, frequently indulging the taste for the antique in the representation of classical nymphs, deities, or mythological characters. Or natural forms and forces might be allegorized, as in the case of the Apennino, an allegory of the Apennines Mountains, at Pratolino. If such iconography was remarkable, however, real marvel was reserved for the engineering that made possible the brilliant displays of water, the music the water made, and the automata. The desire to reach new and increasingly creative hydrological feats of engineering was, in itself, partly homage to, partly inspired by, the ancient world. For example, in 1575, Bernardo Buontalenti, designer of Pratolino, commissioned the scholar Oreste Vannoccio Biringuccio to translate the recently recovered *Pneumatica,* an ancient Greek treatise on automata, from Latin into Italian so that he could make use of its contents.[46] Advances in the art and science of hydraulics were explored and circulated in new books such as Agostino Ramelli's 1588 *Le diverse et artificiose machine* and Salomon de Caus's 1615 *Raisons de forces mouvantes avec diverses machines tant utilles que plaisantes ausquelles sont adjoints plusieurs desseings de grotes et fontaines,* a work that not only promoted his own innovations but also explored the science and engineering behind them. These texts reveal the growing sophistication of both the practice and theory of hydraulics in the art and science of gardening.[47]

Artifices and the engineering underlying them drew the respect and admiration of humanists whose attentions were usually focused on antiquity.

Renaissance thinkers such as Alberti, Lorenzo Valla, Marsilio Ficino, and Jean Bodin cited the printing press, the compass, and the gun as evidence that Renaissance creativity and ingenuity were as worthy of celebration as that of ancient Rome.[48] While humanist scholars did not single out technology in the garden, engineering in the garden made for an aesthetically pleasing way to celebrate it. Modern scholars, working such sites as Pratolino, the Hortus Palatinus, and Versailles, have come to recognize the Renaissance garden as a site through which the scientific and technological history of Europe can be traced and understood.[49] But this was understood, too, in the Renaissance. For just as water, carried in miles of aqueducts to the center of Rome, illustrated the triumph of Roman engineering that enabled empire building and a sophisticated urban lifestyle, so water in the early modern garden was used to demonstrate the ability of monarchs to harness engineering, hydrological and otherwise, in service of the state. Sophisticated water features were an important part of the Renaissance garden. And their importance was demonstrated in the careers of men such as Tommaso and Alessandro Francini and Salomon de Caus, whose expertise in the creation of original fountains, grottoes, and automata, led to their employment by the most illustrious and powerful leaders in Europe. Tommaso Francini was responsible for the water works and automata at Pratolino. He and his brother Alessandro both left Italy for France where they created the impressive fountains and grottoes for the gardens at Saint-Germain-en Laye, the Luxembourg Palace, and Fontainebleau in the first decades of the seventeenth century.[50] Salomon de Caus, also active in the late sixteenth and early seventeenth centuries, created works for members of the Stuart dynasty of England at Greenwich Place, Richmond Palace, and Somerset House, as well as for the Elector of Palatine, Frederick V, at the Hortus Palatinus in Heidelberg.[51]

Salomon de Caus also demonstrated the utility of his hydrological work in a proposal for the creation of twenty new Parisian fountains that were to contribute to a cleaner and healthier city.[52] Although the project was never realized, they demonstrated the larger applicability of engineering—a point not lost on those monarchs who patronized their work. The sons of Tommasso Francini, François and Pierre de Francini, went on to work at Versailles for Louis XIV. At Versailles, the Francini brothers helped to create the unequalled water works that contributed so much to the garden's character. The king's engineers struggled, as has been well documented, to transport enough water to the gardens of Versailles. Canals, aqueducts, and even the famous pumping machine completed at Marly in 1684 were not sufficient to allow all the fountains at Versailles to play simultaneously, let alone continually. And yet they remained among the most important attractions of the gardens. The fountains were to be played not only when the king passed them in the garden, but also for important visitors. Charles Perrault wrote to Jean-Baptiste Colbert, "The King wishes that all this that is said for His Person [regarding the playing of the fountains] be observed for people of consequence who are in the park or to whom His Majesty has ordered the waters be shown."[53] A proper garden tour with fountains playing was reserved for the king or those he deemed important enough to warrant the necessary logistical arrangements. Those arrangements included the deployment of a system of young gardeners armed with whistles to signal each other to turn on the fountains when the king approached (and turn them off when he was out of view) to maintain the illusion that the fountains played continually. That the Machine de Marly became itself the subject of engravings and a destination to be included on any tour of the Versailles gardens is revealing of how important engineering had become to the reception of Versailles. Despite the failure to secure sufficient water to the fountains of Versailles, the technical achievements of the king's engineers were brilliant for their time.[54] As a recent exhibition titled "Sciences et curiosités à la cour de Versailles" demonstrates, the gardens and palace became a site for the display of scientific experimentation and achievement.[55] Those achievements were intended to be received as evidence of the king's political and economic management of the state.[56] Displays in the Renaissance garden, then, whether of antique sculptures, or modern botanical collections and hydrological feats, were material demonstrations of both cultural sophistication and scientific knowledge.

PERFORMANCE

For all of the intellectual and physical labor carried out and put on display in the garden, however, neither the figures in Della Bella's engravings of Pratolino nor those depicted in Israel's Silvestre's "Veue de la cour des fontaines de Fontaine Beleau" appear to be doing much work. Silvestre depicts courtiers walking under the trees, reclining on the lawn, returning from the hunt, and embarking on short voyages in canopied boats across the water and back.[57] Collectively, the members of the royal court are tasting the many pleasures that garden had to offer, engaging in courtly play in the open air. Just as Michel de Montaigne and John Evelyn demonstrated at the beginning of this chapter, pleasure could be derived simply from taking in the delights, surprises, and curiosities the garden offered. For many, the Renaissance garden was defined by its role and function as a place of play and pleasure.

FIGURE 4.2: Israël Silvestre, "Veue de la Cour des Fontaines de Fontaine Beleau," 1665. Private Collection.

The theoretical characterization of garden spaces as distinguished by pleasure emerged in the sixteenth century, as books on estate management began to draw distinctions between "kitchen" gardens and gardens defined by the delights they afforded. For example, in his *Théâtre d'agriculture et mesnage des champs,* Olivier de Serres advised his readers on the construction of four types of gardens: the vegetable, medicinal, fruit, and flower gardens. The flower garden, in particular, which he labeled the *bouquetier,* was to contain "all sorts of plants, herbs, flowers, shrubs in compartments or parterres, and . . . cabinets, according to the inventions and fantasies of the lords, [and was intended] more for pleasure than for profit."[58]

But the use of gardens for the pursuit of pleasure, with roots in classical and medieval courtly behaviors, was much older than such texts. In feudal Europe, the knighted nobility distinguished itself through the demonstration of military skills—riding, hunting, and killing that took place outdoors. Hunting parks, the preserve of nobles on whose estates they were located, were used by hunting parties that grew in size and fashion through the seventeenth century.[59] European nobles and kings hunted all manner of animals in brutal and spectacular fashion. Accompanied by large packs of dogs and courtiers, such parties required large wooded spaces to shelter the game that would be their prey. The distinctions between the hunting park and the formal garden could be blurred, as in the garden of the Villa Lante in Viterbo, created out of the *barco,* or hunting park, of Cardinal Rafaele Riario. Wooded areas were retained and incorporated iconographically into the garden created in the sixteenth century for Cardinal Francesco Gambara, in which the movement into and out of the wilderness spurred visitors to contemplate the transformation of nature into art.[60]

Of course, gardens were also used for less bloody sporting, serving as spaces for tournaments or outdoor games. Illuminated manuscripts dating to the fifteenth and sixteenth centuries depict gardens as the settings for games such as "blind man's bluff" or archery contests.[61] Gardens could include spaces dedicated to particular games such *jeu de paume,* an early form of handball, or *paille-maille* (pall mall), an early form of croquet. In the early seventeenth century, Abraham Bosse depicted fashionable nobles engaged in a game of *paille-maille* in a plate in his *Iardin de la Noblesse Françoise dans lequel ce peut ceuillir leur maniere de Vettements.* St. James Park in London also included a court for the game in the seventeenth century. Indeed, by the second half of the seventeenth century, public landscapes with gaming spaces specifically labeled "pleasure gardens" were created in London. New Spring Gardens (renamed Vauxhall Gardens in 1785), provided spaces for public promenades, entertainments, and refreshments.

But pleasure seeking in the garden was largely confined to those with access to formal gardens of the elite. The gardens provided the setting for all sorts of play. Yet the play could be serious play, for the Renaissance pleasure garden was used for highly choreographed amusements that were at once social, cultural, and political. A stroll in the garden was rarely a simple stroll in the garden. A promenade offered the possibility that one might interact with or be seen by other courtiers. Thus it required that one be observant of courtly etiquette: for example, Antoine de Courtin, author of the 1671 *Nouveau traité de la civilité qui se pratique en France parmi les honnêtes-gens,* offered instruction on how to promenade in the garden in small groups of men of varying rank, including how to turn elegantly when one's group reached the end of an allée. The author reminded his readers that it was bad form to pick any fruits or flowers in the garden, although if one was presented with a flower or piece of fruit, one should accept it.[62] As such, the garden was used as a courtly stage: a place to see and be seen, to walk, to play, to dance, and to eat—according to social convention.

FIGURE 4.3: Abraham Bosse, Gentleman playing *paille maille*, from *Le Iardin de la Noblesse Françoise dans lequel ce peut Cueillir leur manierre de Vettements*, Paris: Melchior Tavernier, 1629. Private Collection.

Such social performances might also entail attending theatrical performances in gardens, as the garden was increasingly used as a theatrical space for the performance of rituals and entertainments that served to reinforce Renaissance notions of political and cultural power. The ancient Roman practice of building performance spaces in the garden was revived with the 1503–1504 construction by Bramante of a garden space linking the Vatican palace to the Belvedere villa that had been constructed as the summer residence of Pope Innocent VIII. Bramante designed a covered corridor linking the two buildings that was also used to house Julius II's impressive papal collection of antique sculptures. Meanwhile, the corridor bordered a large courtyard suitable for performances for which amphitheatre seating was constructed at one end.[63]

The space created by Bramante demonstrates the layers of utility and functionality of the Renaissance garden. For Bramante not only solved the practical challenge of linking the papal palaces, but he also created a space for the display of antiquities that established the cultural authority of the papacy, and a stage upon which that authority could be acted out. It was not only the papacy, of course, that used formal gardens in such ways. Leading Italian political families made use of them, too. The garden became an important site for Medici rituals and festivities designed to accentuate the power of the family. Importantly, as Raffaella Fabiani Giannetto demonstrates, rituals and festivities that traditionally had been carried out in the streets and public squares of Quattrocento Florence were, by the sixteenth century, increasingly staged within the private gardens of the Medici dukes. The transition both increased the importance of the garden as a politically legitimating site, and enhanced the power of the ducal family. Giannetto argues that "from a political point of view, the garden became a propaganda vehicle for sovereignty, as city palaces had been in the past."[64]

By the mid-sixteenth century, the garden had become a useful agent in performing politics. Such practices were received as successful enough to spread across the European continent, but at the same time, were malleable enough to meet the needs of European monarchs operating in different political and cultural contexts. Such performances of power traveled to France with Catherine de Medici on her 1533 marriage to the French king Henri II. As queen and then as regent after the 1560 death of Henri II, Catherine became a significant patron of architecture and the garden arts. Under her supervision, gardens became important sites for royal festivities. At Chenonceaux celebrations staged in 1560, 1563, and 1577 marked important political and military events, including the 1560 entry of François II and his queen Mary Stuart and a 1563 celebration of the (temporary) peace in the French wars of religion.[65] In 1573, the Tuileries gardens were used for festivities in honor of the arrival of the Polish delegation who had come to offer the throne of Poland to the duc d'Anjou; the entertainments staged in the gardens included fireworks, feasts, and entries, as well as performances of masques and ballets, all of which required the construction of sets, stages, and specially designed arches, grottoes, fountains, and artificial mountains. Such theatrical "props" shaped the evolution of French garden design, as they increasingly became permanent components of the land-scape.[66] Just as importantly, Catherine de Medici established French precedents for using the garden space in politically legitimating rituals. Those precedents would be exploited by Catherine's Bourbon successors, and most effectively by Louis XIV, whose early use of the gardens at Versailles was shaped by the staging of the fêtes of 1664, 1668, and 1674 celebrating, respectively, his new queen, Maria Teresa; the peace treaty of Aix-la-Chapelle; and the king's victory in the Franche-Comté. As the garden evolved in the next decades, the garden rooms or *bosquets* created at Versailles were stage like and theatrical both in design and function.[67]

By the seventeenth century, then, the garden, with its sculptural, architec-tural, and botanical elements, provided an earthen canvas upon which political iconography of (growing) princely power could be articulated. That iconogra-phy could be as simple as the plantation of boxwood or other plant material in the form of royal symbols or crests, or more sophisticated ideas like those explored at the Hortus Palatinus for Frederick V, the elector of Palatine, and his queen Elizabeth Stuart. Scholars have tried to read into such gardens com-plex hermetic and alchemical ideas, but Luke Morgan has convincingly argued against such an interpretation, seeing instead different elements of the garden speaking to larger themes of the power of art to improve nature and of love and its associated fertility that promised dynastic succession to the elector.[68] As Morgan argues in this volume, in very few gardens could one find a com-plex iconographic narrative informing an entire garden; yet large, malleable iconographic ideas and allegories like those explored at the Hortus Palatinus were politically potent and valuable in giving verdant expression to the politi-cal agendas of the princely elites. One example of a broadly interpreted but politically valuable theme was the Virgilian notion of the second Golden Age. The prophesied return of peace and prosperity under effective leadership was a case that could be made effectively in the garden. Reinforced with creative use of iconography, it could remind the visitor, not so subtly, whose leadership and patronage had made possible the vegetal prosperity on display. Scholars have identified the mythology of the Golden Age in Medici gardens at Poggio a Caiano, begun for Lorenzo de Medici in the late fifteenth century, and those at Castello (commissioned in 1537) built for Duke Cosimo, through to the end of our period, in the gardens of Louis XIV.[69]

The performance of political power in the garden did not, however, look only backward to Antiquity for inspiration. The growing horticultural so-phistication of the Renaissance garden, together with the increasing use of

technology in its service, allowed the garden to communicate a more sophisticated message: kings and princes could perform and display their power not
only through ancient deities but also with modern botanists and engineers.
Gardens, in that they embraced the languages of both the ancients and the
moderns, were symbolically thick, offering an economical means to communicate princely power. Louis XIV and his panegyrists argued that the reign
of Louis XIV had ushered France into a golden age like that foretold by Virgil via Louis XIV as Apollo, the Sun King, whose light brought warmth and
life. As his reign wore on, however, his panegyrists turned increasingly to the
notion of the perpetual springtime that characterized the second golden age.
In emphasizing the advances in the art and science of gardening, the French
king could argue his superiority over the ancients. Through the creation of an
extensive system of nurseries, greenhouses, and orangeries, Louis XIV's gardens at Versailles were celebrated for their ability to bring flowers to blossom, and trees and vegetables in the *potager* to bear fruit, out of season. Such
horticultural marvels became themselves objects of celebration that were, in
turn, drafted into the glorification of the king: In 1689, the Trianon gardens
at Versailles, known for their extensive floral displays, served as the setting for
the performance of the ballet *Du Palais de Flore*. In the libretto of the ballet
distributed at the performance, the ballet was set in "The Palace of Flora &
eternal Springtime which until now have [existed] only in the imagination of
Poets, [but which] are [now] veritably found here." The text continued, "these
Parterres are always filled with all sorts of flowers. One cannot remember that
it is the middle of Winter, or one believes that he has been transported all of a
sudden to another Climate, when one sees the delicious objects which denote
so agreeably the abode of Flora."[70] In the libretto of the ballet the audience
was reminded that while in the ancient world, perpetual springtime existed
only within the realm of Olympian mythology, it had been materially realized
in seventeenth-century France.

The garden facilitated the political power of the king (or queen or duke or
pope) precisely because it offered an aesthetically pleasing stage on which to
display the more serious issues of state: mastery of the science, engineering, and
botany. Such displays could be articulated in different modes, including the appropriation of garden iconography, the use of garden spaces for royal rituals,
or through the granting of access to garden spaces. For example, the garden
could be used to reinforce domestic social and political rank through access to
exclusive spaces or special displays within the garden, as with the playing of
the fountains at Versailles. A royal tour of the gardens was not simply a matter of the king deciding to take his guests for a walk. Being treated to a tour

of the gardens, and especially to a show of the waterworks within them, could be taken as a sign of favor. And the tour thus became a diplomatic tool. As such, the king could decline to offer a tour (as in the case of Muscovite envoys denied the pleasure of seeing the gardens in 1687), send guests on a truncated tour, provide diplomats with a knowledgeable guide to lead them on a tour, or, for those deemed most worthy, personally guide visitors through the park.[71]

Louis XIV's use of the gardens to show favor demonstrates the desire to control reception of the gardens and the power they communicated. Louis XIV himself drafted several itineraries according to which tours of Versailles were to be taken. Scholarly analysis of the itineraries reveals the preference given to the fountains, suggesting the importance of demonstrating achievements in engineering.[72] Attempts were also made to shape reception in more fixed formats. Scenes from the fêtes of Versailles of 1664, 1668, and 1674 were recorded in engravings by Israel Silvestre and circulated among the print-buying and collecting public. The horticultural triumphs of royal gardeners were also recorded in print, as in La Quintinie's *Instruction pour les Jardins Fruitiers et Potagers*. Jean Donneau de Visé's *Mercure Galant* published descriptions of the gardens of Versailles as part of a special issue of the court journal recounting the tour of the gardens by the ambassadors of Siam,[73] and works such as Madeleine de Scudéry's *Promenade de Versailles* offered descriptions of the gardens folded into fictional stories. Indeed, the example of Versailles illustrates the extent to which the king and his iconographers both utilized symbolic meanings in the garden, and sought to influence its reception. Louis XIV commissioned two series of tapestries on the four seasons and the four elements. Designed by Charles Le Brun and Jacques Bailly, they simultaneously drew inspiration from the king's specific horticultural accomplishments and appropriated the iconographic potential offered by demonstrations of the power of art to improve nature by incorporating garden-themed symbols and emblems into the celebration of the elements, seasons, and, most important, Louis XIV. The designs were engraved and explicated in an accompanying text by André Félibien and printed by the Imprimerie royale in lavish folio format in 1670 under the title *Tapisseries du Roi, où sont représentés les quatre éléments et les quatre saisons* by the Imprimerie royale in 1670 in Paris.[74] The royal tapestries communicated the greatness of the king while the printed text, issued again in 1679, disseminated for a much wider audience how the garden emblems in the tapestries were to be understood. That audience became wider, still, when the text was published again in 1687. This time the book included a German translation of the text and was printed by Johann Kraus in Augsburg.[75] The publication of the *Tapisseries du roi* both in Paris and Augsburg

XVII.

POVR LE PRINTEMPS.

DANS LA PIECE DE LA SAISON DU PRINTEMPS.

Des Fleurs printanieres dans vn Parterre, qui ont pour Ame ce Mot, TERRÆ AMOR ET DECUS; pour signifier que si la Terre aime les Fleurs, comme ses premieres productions, & celles qui font son plus bel ornement, Sa Majesté n'est pas moins l' amour & l' ornement de toute la Terre.

Auf den Frühling.

In dem Stuck der Jahr-Zeit deß Frühlings.

Einige Früh-Blumen in einem Garten-Betth/ mit dem Denck-Spruch: Der Erden Lust und Zier/ befindet sich in mir. Anzuzeigen/ daß gleich wie die Erde ihre Blumen/ als ihre erste Gewächse/ und schönste Zierde liebet : Also ist auch seine Majestät nicht weniger der gantzen Welt Liebe und Zierde.

Si lors que la Terre se pare	Waß nun der Erden-Schoß sich überlieblich schmücket
De ce present des Cieux si charmant & si rare,	Daß ihre Blumen-Lust den Menschen gantz entzücket/
Elle l' aime si tendrement ;	So ist man höchst verliebt in solchs Geschenck und Gab/
N'est il pas juste qu'on la voye	Welchs von dem Himmel selbst gesändet wird herab ;
En faire ses plaisirs, son amour, & sa joye,	Ists dañ nicht wol gethan/ daß mans mit Danck entr fange/
Comme elle en fait son ornement ?	Und wol betracht/ wie sie hierinnen stutz und prange.

not only demonstrates the perceived audience for such texts, but also serves as yet another reminder of the international proliferation of garden culture, knowledge, and design. The performance of the garden in print material of all sorts is a reminder that printed texts and images, as well as people, influenced the reception of gardens across cultures and national boundaries.

Use and reception of the Renaissance garden can neither be disentangled from each other, nor from Renaissance European culture. Just days after visiting Pratolino, Michel de Montaigne visited Castello, another estate belonging to Grand Duke Francesco I de Medici. As with Pratolino, Montaigne (again via his secretary) wrote that "[t]he house has nothing worth while about it; but there are various things about the garden." Although visiting in "the most unpropitious season for gardens, and [therefore] . . . all the more amazed" at what they saw, Montaigne and his party noted "the duke's escutcheon here high over a gateway, very well formed of some branches of trees fostered and maintained in their natural strength by fibers that one can barely discern." They saw many different kinds of trees growing in the garden, and a reservoir containing a "natural-looking artificial rock, and it seems all frozen over, by means of that material with which the duke has covered his grottoes at Pratolino." Montaigne's secretary also recorded the following:

> Elsewhere they had the very amusing experience of seeing what I have noted above; for as they were walking about the garden and looking at its curiosities, the gardener left their company for this purpose; and as they were in a certain spot contemplating certain marble statues, there spurted up under their feet and between their legs, through an infinite number of tiny holes, jets of water so minute that they were almost invisible, imitating supremely well the trickle of fine rain, with which they were completely sprinkled by the operation of some underground spring which the gardener was working more than two hundred paces from there, with such artifice that from there on the outside he made these spurts of water rise and fall as he pleased, turning and moving them just as he wanted. This game is found here in several places.[76]

FIGURE 4.4: Jacques Bailly, "Printemps," from Johann Ulrich Kraus, *Tapisseries du roy, où sont representez les quatre élémens et les quatre saisons, avec les devises qui les accompagnent et leur explication. Königliche französische Tapezereyen, oder überaus schöne Sinn-Bilder, in welchen die vier Element samt den vier Jahr-Zeiten . . . an den Tag gegeben und verlegt durch Johann Ulrich Krauss*, Augsburg: gedruckt daselbst durch J. Koppmayer, 1687. Private Collection.

The game was playful, to be sure. One can imagine the gleeful gardener surprising the guests with a good soaking. But the visit to the garden was also, as Montaigne's journal demonstrates, an opportunity to examine sculptures and other "curiosities" displayed in a rich and apparently lush plantation of fruit and other trees, and a chance to investigate the use of hydraulics to make fountains and other automata play. It was a demonstration of the artful and mechanical manipulation of the natural world into the performance of ducal power. And, as the gardener and his fountains played to the delight of Montaigne and his party, Montaigne was provided with an opportunity, in documenting it, to record his knowing comprehension of all the artifices at work.

By the seventeenth century, as we have seen, such artifices had been drafted into more overt political service of dukes and kings. Yet, the ability of the garden to communicate the greatness of dukes or kings via the aesthetic, the symbolic, the botanical, and hydrological in a synergistic effort at glorification did not mean that the language of the Renaissance garden was not malleable enough to allow for alternative, or even subversive, uses and meanings to emerge. Nor can it be assumed to function with equal success across the early modern period. Marie Antoinette's infamous *Hameau* must be understood as part of a tradition in which queens of France, beginning with Catherine de Medici in the sixteenth century, patronized the construction of elaborate working dairies that produced milk in architecturally beautiful agricultural settings. The dairies, richly decorated with iconographies intended to remind visitors of the queen's fertility,[77] showcased the labor carried out in the garden estate while allowing the queen to perform her dynastic role in the production of an heir. Catherine de Medici's dairy set a precedent that would be followed by queens of France to the French Revolution. And yet, by the late eighteenth century when Marie Antoinette constructed her dairy at the *Hameau*, its real connection to labor and cultivation had been lost: the entire project smacked of illusion and artifice. Efforts to control reception failed in making the royal case to an audience no longer willing to make the symbolic connections between cultivation in the garden and the cultivation of power.

In the seventeenth century, however, the political utility and power of the garden arts to perform the wealth, taste, and scientific knowledge of the patron/monarch no doubt contributed to the desire of European monarchs to the north and east of France to seek to emulate what the Sun King had achieved at Versailles. And while the printed and woven demonstrations of Le Nôtre's accomplishments made it possible to do so, one must not overlook the complexity of reception across political, economic, and national divides. One must not oversimplify the spread of Renaissance garden culture from

Italy, northward to France, and outward to the north and east from there. Although such a trajectory did take place, much work remains to be done in exploring and analyzing the complex networks, media, and people that facilitated the reception and dissemination of the garden arts across boundaries and time. The relatively familiar careers of gardeners and engineers like Salomon de Caus, who worked in England, France, and the Palatinate, and André Mollet, who worked in France and Sweden, demonstrate the geographical proliferation of gardening as an art of kings. Less-familiar gardeners and networks that functioned on different trajectories need to be brought into context within this trend. Recent research, like that of Erik de Jong on Swedish and Russian gardens, demonstrates that Dutch networks of knowledge, design, and materials were as important as French models of the political uses of the garden, in eastern and northern Europe. Such networks should not be overlooked in accounting for reception of gardens across the continent.[78] And, as the example of Marie Antoinette's *Hameau* reminds us, to understand and comprehend the use and reception of the Renaissance garden, both must be considered in context of space (geography) and time (chronology).

CHAPTER FIVE

Meaning

LUKE MORGAN

> Like a large labyrinthine garden, a work of art permits one to take many
> different routes, whose number is increased by the criss-cross of its paths.
> —Umberto Eco[1]

THE RENAISSANCE GARDEN AS A CULTURAL OBJECT

Gardens are inherently ambiguous. They are often construed as heterotopias or as sets of polarities.[2] James Elkins, for example, has suggested that "gardens, more than paintings or sculptures, are often intentionally vague or ambiguous in reference . . . It may be that the next generation of scholarship will find the adjudication of various theories, and the investigation of conscious and unconscious ambiguities, to be a profitable focus."[3] This ambiguity precludes the possibility of interpretative closure or definitiveness. It means that any given garden will be continually reassembled by each new visitor, whose experience will always be unique.

The descriptions of the garden designed by Nicolò Tribolo for the Villa Medici, Castello, by Giorgio Vasari (1568) and Michel de Montaigne (1581) provide examples. Vasari, more accustomed perhaps to writing about painting, gives a lengthy account of the iconography of the garden, which he claims was dedicated to extolling "the greatness of the Medici house."[4] Montaigne, however, mentions nothing of the kind, dwelling instead on the fountains and *giochi d'acqua,* and noting the garden's "curiosities" and "amusements," but not the apparent political or propagandistic purpose of its imagery.[5]

The point is not that Montaigne missed something important, but rather that a Renaissance garden was never only or solely an expression of the personal power of its patron or, for that matter, an alternative form of theater and site of social interaction, a place of contemplation, a memorial, a productive patch of ground, a laboratory or an encyclopedic collection of botanical specimens. Potentially, it was all of these things and more at once.

In its multivalency, the Renaissance garden resembles Roland Barthes's concept of a text: "etymologically, the text is a tissue, a woven fabric."[6] Just as the experience of a garden involves several senses, which cannot be separated from one another, so too is meaning in the garden rarely simple or singular. One of the paradoxes of the Renaissance garden is that it makes use of a standardized repertoire of forms and images, which is repeated at sites all over Europe, but nonetheless elicits idiosyncratic responses.

For the Renaissance garden designer, the *Metamorphoses* was the indispensable sourcebook of imagery and themes, to the extent that it is difficult to think of any example from the period that does not make some reference to Ovid's text, and despite the fact that Pope Paul IV consigned the *Metamorphoses* to the *Index Librorum Prohibitorum* in 1559.[7] The acceptability, even normality, of Ovid in the garden can be partially explained through an appeal to the Renaissance aesthetic doctrine of *decoro* (decorum), which specifies that certain kinds of subject are appropriate to certain kinds of site.[8] Yet, the apparent immunity of the garden to Counter-Reformatory asceticism, its status as a privileged site in which ordinary strictures and structures did not apply, does not mean that it was a secular or even profane product of the Renaissance.[9] During the sixteenth century and into the seventeenth, one of the tasks of garden design was to reveal the concealed logic of nature, which was conceived in geometrical terms. Alberti, for example, believed that "Nature delights primarily in the circle" in his brief comments on garden design. Two centuries later, Salomon de Caus thought that architects should imitate "la vraye nature" (true nature).[10]

Despite, therefore, the pagan imagery of the Renaissance garden, its design was informed by religious conviction. It is also worth mentioning that in early modern Europe, any garden would inevitably have recalled the first garden and its loss. The original and most perfect garden was Eden and the first gardener was Adam who was charged with maintaining this idyllic, timeless realm. Time and therefore change and death begin with the Expulsion; prior to that catastrophic event, the Garden of Eden was presumably immutable and unchanging. Mutability, atrophy, and loss are thus implicit features of the postlapsarian garden—the legacy of original sin. Consequently, the Renaissance garden, as the product of a Christian culture, was always attempting to fix its elements, or halt its degeneration (through the construction of orangeries, constant replanting, and the gradual superseding of organic elements in parterre design by gravel and other inorganic materials)—a Sisyphean task.

Once again, however, this sense of loss is an ambiguous one. Eden and the prototypical *locus amoenus* in the Classical tradition—Arcadia—have always been problematic ideals.[11] Basil, for instance, described Adam's state in the Garden of Eden as "apathetic" and Polybius considered Arcadia to be a poor, barren place. For Philostratus, the Arcadians were "acorn-eating swine."[12]

Loss and change were of course very real features of the Renaissance garden. Even when the explicit aim was to "conquer" the seasons or to institute a *Ver Perpetuum* (eternal spring) as in Francis Bacon's ideal garden, change was unavoidable.[13] The same garden can never be reentered or reexperienced. Gardens are always in a state of flux, due to their partial construction out of and inscription within nature.

Raymond Williams once described "nature" as possibly the most complex word in the language.[14] Certainly, the relationship between art and nature in the Renaissance garden is a complex one. John Dixon Hunt has noted that the idea of the garden as a *terza natura* (third nature), which is the result of the collaboration of art and nature, was first mentioned by Jacopo Bonfadio in a letter of 1541, followed by Bartolomeo Taegio in his 1559 treatise *La Villa*.[15] Cicero's discussion of "second nature," by which he meant agricultural landscapes, inspired the development of the concept. "First nature" is the untouched natural world.

In the garden, the relationship between art and nature may be weighted differently in individual examples and periods, but there is always, to a greater or lesser extent, some form of cooperation between art and the organic, even if it occasionally takes on the character of *paragone*. This is a fundamental theme of early modern landscape design, sometimes implicit rather than explicit, but always present. In 1543, for example, Claudio Tolomei, lavished praise on those fountains in which it was difficult, if not impossible, to distinguish between art and nature due to the closeness with which the former had followed the latter.[16] Baccio Bandinelli, in contrast, opined that "the things one builds must be the guide and superior to those one plants," when he was asked to design a fountain for the Boboli garden in 1551.[17]

Bonfadio makes another important point. He regards the three natures as "representing" the history of human development from "the wild, hard people . . . made as much of stone and oak as of man, and who live on chestnuts the greater part of the year" to the "civilized people, gentlemen and *signori* who live on the shore."[18] Representation in the Renaissance garden was of two main types. First, individual elements within a garden of the period clearly referred to or represented subjects and concepts that were not restricted to the designed landscape itself. In the garden of the Villa Medici, Castello, for example, there were personifications of local mountains (the Apennines, Mount Asinaio, and Mt. Falterona) and rivers (the Mugnone and Arno), evoking Cosimo I de' Medici's territories or spheres of influence. The fountain of Florence personified as Venus Anadyomene suggests something similar, but also indicates that this is a pleasure garden.

The second form of representation in the Renaissance garden consisted of the garden's reference to nature itself, to other landscapes. In this, the garden designer's vocabulary of forms might be described as self-reflexive, almost as if it constituted a meta-language, capable of commenting on itself. As Hunt has pointed out, the forms of the garden as third nature were initially extrapolated from first nature (mounts indicated hills or mountains; labyrinths and *bosquets* referred to the apparently disorganized and "wild" natural world; grottoes to naturally occurring caves and pergolas to open paths through woodlands) and second nature (artificial clearings became lawns, ornamental canals invoked drainage ditches, fountains referred to irrigation systems).[19] A labyrinth, *bosco* or *bosquet*, therefore, refers to both the superficial disorder of first nature and wider cultural concepts of nature as, in the sixteenth century, a model to be imitated after its improvement or after its inherent natural (divine) order had been revealed.

To summarize the Renaissance garden was an ambiguous and mutable site. It was also the result of collaboration between the designer's art and his raw material—nature. The relationship between the two may have been weighted differently in individual gardens, but there was always, to a greater or lesser extent, some form of cooperation between, or synthesis of art, the organic and the inorganic. As the most contrived category or version of nature in the tripartite scheme elaborated by Renaissance writers such as Taegio and Bonfadio, the garden often made deliberate reference to first and second nature. In this sense, it was a self-reflexive representational medium, beyond the straightforward representations of statues, automata, inscriptions and other elements. We can now turn to an account of the way(s) in which these concepts contributed to the meaning of the Renaissance garden.

THE TOPOI OF THE RENAISSANCE GARDEN

Form and content were indivisible in the Renaissance garden. Consequently, one or two additional points need to be made here about the fundamental design principle that in Chapter 1 was referred to as "variety and contrast" before the broader meanings of four important gardens of the period—the Villa d'Este, Tivoli, the Villa Lante, Bagnaia, the Hortus Palatinus, Heidelberg, and the Château de Versailles—can be explored.

Most sixteenth-century gardens were laid out as a series of loosely related spaces in which variety and contrast rather than unity and homogeneity were the controlling aesthetic concepts. In following this principle, Renaissance garden designers were subscribing to the idea of the garden articulated in Pliny the Younger's letter describing his Tuscan villa and its landscape environs, an idea that was first revived in the villa gardens of sixteenth-century Tuscany and Lazio.

Pliny's letter was addressed to Domitius Apollinaris and probably written between 100 C.E. and 105 C.E.[20] To the Renaissance, it seemed to offer the most complete account—an *identikit*—of a fine Roman villa and garden.[21] In one of the best-known passages of the letter, Pliny asks his friend to "figure to yourself an immense amphitheatre, such as the hand of nature could alone form" from which extensive views into the surrounding countryside could be had. Pliny's villa was located in the midst of this panorama, on a hillside. The terraced garden *all'antica*, descending the slopes of an incline, which reaches its apogee in Pirro Ligorio's design for the Villa d'Este at Tivoli thus has its origins in Pliny's description.

Pliny also mentions a hippodrome, fountains, topiary designs in the form of geometric figures and animals, fruit trees, and obelisks, all of which became part of the standard repertoire of the Renaissance designer. Versions of Pliny's hippodrome, for example, which contained elaborate topiary designs in box hedge, contrasting with a "naturally" planted area at the center, recur throughout Renaissance garden design. The hippodrome of the Palazzo Pitti in Florence is perhaps the most obvious example, but there were numerous others, such as Francesco da Sangallo's ca. 1525 design for the garden of the Villa Madama, the grounds of the late-sixteenth-century Villa Mattei, and the botanical garden at Padua, where there was one outside the main circular garden.[22] Suffice it to say, therefore, that the influence of Pliny's letter on the Italian garden is more or less beyond dispute.

Elizabeth Blair MacDougall has argued that sixteenth century Italian gardens frequently made use of the same basic mythological themes (topoi), almost all of which were derived from Ovid's *Metamorphoses,* to make differing statements.[23] In fact, it is possible to go further and suggest that the iconographical principle of *topoi* was the direct correlative of the design principle that Pliny originally formulated as harmonious and regular variety, which is to say that the meanings of the Renaissance garden can be said to have sprung directly from the principle underlying its layout or, rather, were governed by the Renaissance designer's objectives.

If, in other words, the Renaissance garden was composed of more or less self-sufficient units, then the "narrative" of the garden was similarly atomized to the point where it bore little resemblance to narrative, conventionally understood. Rather, meaning was derived from familiar (at least by the audience to which the garden was addressed) topoi. The close bond between form and content implies that the Ovidian allusions of the Renaissance garden did not, en masse, add up to a narrative program, despite the best efforts of historians to reconstruct them.[24] In general, Renaissance gardens were narrative-less but no less meaningful as a consequence.

THE VILLA D'ESTE, TIVOLI

Hercules, Venus, Diana, Flora, Ceres, Pomona, Neptune, Silenus, Bacchus, Apollo, the Muses, and Pegasus were the presiding deities of the Renaissance garden, and their stories were told repeatedly at sites all over Europe as the Italian garden style became a European garden style by the late sixteenth century. Yet, despite repetition, the iconography of the Renaissance garden was rarely, if ever, monolithic or programmatic.

The episodic and "open" layout of the Villa d'Este garden at Tivoli, for example, like others of the Renaissance, means that its imagery did not contribute to the development of a sequential narrative but, rather, presented a series of interrelated themes that could be encountered in various orders and sequences.

A good example is provided by the most important latitudinal axis at Tivoli: the Alley of the Hundred Fountains, which is punctuated at regular intervals by grotesque heads, eagles, boats, obelisks, d'Este fleurs-de-lis, and scenes from Ovid's *Metamorphoses.* On the far left of the alley is the Fountain of Tivoli (now known as the Oval Fountain), the main feature of which is a colossal statue of the Tiburtine Sibyl, representing Tivoli itself, above a waterfall. On the hillside above the Sibyl, the familiar figure of Pegasus appears, indicating that Tivoli and the cardinal's garden comprise a new Parnassus.

The garden as a "new Parnassus" is one of the most common topoi of the sixteenth century. It is usually expressed by the mount and/or figure of Pegasus. Symbolically, the mount is associated with Parnassus, the dwelling place of Apollo and the muses. In 1517, for example, the Mons Vaticanus in the Vatican gardens was described as a new Parnassus. Mount Parnassus subsequently became closely linked with Mt Helicon, the source of the inspirational Hippocrene spring, brought forth by Pegasus.[25] Although the mount had been a standard feature of the medieval garden, it had lacked the classical significance that, characteristically, the Renaissance attributed to it. Artificial mounts, often planted with laurel, the emblem of Apollo, and decorated with Pegasus fountains as well as statues of the muses, could be found at most major sixteenth-century gardens.

At the Sacro Bosco, Bomarzo, for example, which Vicino Orsini laid out from the early 1560s, there was a Pegasus fountain. The visitor to the garden passed through the so-called Grove of the Muses before arriving at a circular fountain around the edge of which were placed figures of the nine muses. At the center was Pegasus. Known as the Fountain of Hippocrene, the topos suggested that the Sacro Bosco was a place of literary and artistic inspiration.

The d'Este version of the theme alludes to Cardinal Ippolito II d'Este's patronage of the arts and the hill town of Tivoli itself as a new Parnassus adorned by the scholars and poets of the d'Este circle. An artificial Parnassus was also constructed at Pratolino (depicted by Utens in his lunette), which perhaps out of rivalry with the d'Este garden, as Montaigne claimed, included hydraulic-powered musical effects seemingly issuing from the Muses' instruments.

The ubiquity of the topos of Mount Parnassus and Helicon, Apollo and the Muses, and the Hippocrene spring is indicative of the revival of interest in these themes among Renaissance humanists. It is also worth noting that in the poems of the fifteenth and sixteenth centuries, Mt. Parnassus, Apollo, the Muses, and the Hippocrene spring were closely connected with praise for the ruler as patron and protector of the arts and literature: Isabella d'Este was, for example, described as the tenth Muse and her court at Mantua as Parnassus. Later in the sixteenth century the same themes were used in royal or princely triumphal entries, which characterized the ruler as Apollo.

At the other end of the d'Este Alley of the Hundred Fountains is the Rometta, a miniature representation of ancient Rome, which is in turn dominated by a large personification of the city. Tivoli and Rome thus interact across the axis, implying the contribution of the former to the latter's prosperity (in the form of building materials and water). In addition, as Claudia Lazzaro suggests, "the polarities of country and city, nature and art on the extreme sides of the garden also reflect Ippolito d'Este's own life, lived between the ecclesiastical center of power in Rome and his retreat in Tivoli."[26]

Most Italian Renaissance gardens likewise included multiple allusions to, and representations of, the area in which they were themselves located. At Castello, for example, there were personifications of Florence, the Arno and Mugnone rivers as well as the Apennine mountains. The last two also appeared at Pratolino. This local and regional imagery served to make the generic themes of the Renaissance garden—Pegasus releasing the inspirational spring of Hippocrene for example—more specific. The allusion is to *this* place as a new Parnassus, not to some generalized concept of a garden, any garden, as a new Parnassus.

In the d'Este garden, the relationship between Tivoli and Rome is less a story or narrative than an association that, like the boats depicted floating toward one or the other place in the Alley of the Hundred Fountains, flows in both directions. There is, in other words, no necessary sequence or order in which the two miniature cities must be experienced. In short, the basic principle behind the structure and communication of meaning in the d'Este garden is one of topoi, not narrative, but topoi that are nonetheless inflected with local or personal significance. The same motifs and conventions recur over and again in other gardens of the period, such as, for example, the Villa Lante, Bagnaia.

THE VILLA LANTE, BAGNAIA

Giacomo Lauro's depiction of Vignola's design for the Villa Lante shows that the estate was composed of a park (or *bosco*) and an elaborate garden. There is a clear distinction between the two, recalling the gradated hierarchy of nature embodied in the concept of the three natures. In the image, the fountains and other motifs are scattered throughout the park and could be approached from varying directions depending on the choice of the visitor. Once again, therefore, there is no sequential narrative so, by implication, no sequential development of meaning (as in a linear narrative). There is, however, a thematic consistency to the imagery of the whole: a series of topoi that can be identified and related to one another.

The first is focused on the Fountain of the Muses at the entrance to the *bosco*. The Fons Parnasi (as it is called in Lauro's plan) was installed with—as at Pratolino—busts of the nine Muses placed around a large oval basin containing a figure of Pegasus. The park and garden was thus associated with Mount Parnassus. The jet of water that spurted up in front of the figure of Pegasus represented the Spring of Hippocrene that the winged horse created

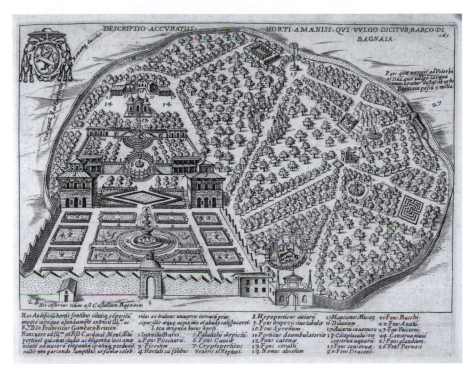

FIGURE 5.1: Giacomo Lauro, Villa Lante, Bagnaia, from *Antiquae urbis splendor,* Rome, 1612–28. Courtesy of Dumbarton Oaks, Trustees for Harvard University.

through striking the mount of Parnassus with his hoof. As Lazzaro put it, "[t]he Fountain of Parnassus at the entrance to the park identifies the whole villa as a place of contemplation under the inspiration of nature, and also as the ideal realm, the earthly paradise which Parnassus is as well. Its placement in the park further underlines the fact that it is *nature* that inspires the arts."[27]

In Ovid's *Metamorphoses,* which was once again the source of the garden's imagery, the Golden Age is described as a period in which men and women coexisted peacefully with nature, subsisting only on acorns and honey (in a reminiscence, though a more positive one, of Philostratus). There is a probable allusion to this in the no longer extant Fountain of the Acorns located, appropriately, in the *bosco* rather than the third nature of the terraced garden. Already then, we have two basic concepts or topoi. On one hand, the whole estate was conceived of as a modern Parnassus, while on the other, the *bosco* was a representation of first nature or the Ovidian Golden Age.

Just as in Genesis, men and women become increasingly sinful until, in retribution, God causes the Deluge so too do the innocent inhabitants of the Golden Age grow increasingly evil until Jupiter decides to destroy them altogether by means of a catastrophic flood. Ovid describes this deluge as pouring down from between the twin peaks of Mount Parnassus. Thus, at the uppermost level of the garden, there is a Fountain of the Deluge (Diluvium). To either side of the fountain are the so-called Houses of the Muses (Mansiones Musarum), the walls of which were lined with water jets that could spray a fine mist over the forecourt of the grotto (signifying the deluge). The two houses most likely symbolized the two peaks of Mt. Parnassus where the human survivors—Deucalion and Pyrrha—escaped the flood. Here, then, quite obviously, there is a repetition of the earlier conceit or topos adumbrated by the Fountain of the Muses—the Villa Lante is a new Parnassus.

The essence of Ovid's story is one of contrast. In the postdiluvial age (the Age of Jupiter), men and women were forced to cultivate the soil and work the land so as to survive (previously unnecessary due to the abundance and bounty of nature). As a result, civilization develops. If, therefore, the park represents the golden age when people lived in harmony with nature then the formal garden represents the development of civilization in the Age of Jupiter. From the grotto fountain depicting the Deluge, which typically attempts to simulate natural caves, to the highly ordered and regular parterres of the lower garden, nature is increasingly refined through collaboration with art/civilization. The *catena d'acqua* (water chain), which is in the form of an elongated crayfish (with head and claws at the top and a pair of giant legs at the bottom), is a direct allusion to the patron of the garden as a whole—Cardinal Gambara (the Italian word for crayfish is *gambaro*)—implying that it is through Gambara that art is made to collaborate with nature, culminating in the geometrical parterres of the lower garden.

The leitmotif of the Villa Lante, the most important topos, is the interchange, collaboration, and *paragone* of nature and art: all of the garden's compartments, grottoes, fountains, and other features can be related to this basic idea. The garden thus generates meaning based on a principle of contrast—between nature and art, the Golden Age and the Age of Jupiter—rather than on the model of linear narrative. In this sense, form and content are again revealed to be closely bonded to one another: as at Tivoli, meaning was generated in a fragmentary, episodic way that corresponds to the Plinian ideal of the garden, revived in the Renaissance, as a site of harmonious and regular variety.

THE RENAISSANCE GARDEN NORTH OF THE ALPS

The extent to which the design principle and concomitant concept of "*topoi, not narrative*" influenced landscape design outside of Italy is indicated by Salomon de Caus's garden design for the Protestant Elector Palatine Frederick V's *Hortus Palatinus* at Heidelberg. There are some particularly striking similarities between Pliny's description of his Tuscan villa garden and the *Hortus Palatinus,* as can be seen in Figure 1.6. In his letter, for example, Pliny notes that,

> Having passed through these manifold winding alleys, the path resumes
> a straight course, and at the same time divides into several tracks, sepa-
> rated by box hedges. In one place you have a little meadow; in another
> the box is interposed in groups, and cut into a thousand different forms;
> sometimes into letters, expressing the name of the master, or again that
> of the artificer: whilst here and there little obelisks rise intermixed alter-
> nately with fruit trees . . . [28]

It is difficult to resist the possibility that de Caus knew this passage at first hand. For example, the beds of the Embroidered Parterre are dominated by sinuous interlacing *broderies,* probably made of colored gravel and sand, incorporating crowns. Running along the base of each of the crowns is a band of rosettes followed by another band containing parts of an inscription, which reads FRIDERICUS V. COMES PAL ELD. BA. 1619 (Frederick V. Count Palatine, Elector, Duke in Bavaria, 1619). This is an allusion to the Elector Palatine Frederick V, who commissioned de Caus to design the *Hortus Palatinus* shortly after his marriage to the English princess Elizabeth, daughter of James I. It can thus hardly fail to recall Pliny's comments on the inscriptions that appeared in his own garden expressing the name of the master.

Like his Italian predecessors to whom he owed so much, de Caus's organization of the *Hortus Palatinus* also aims for maximum variety (and contrast), for heterogeneity instead of homogeneity. His brief commentary on the design and organization of the garden, in the published *Hortus Palatinus* (1620), like Pliny's description, evokes a complex garden of discrete spaces. In both cases, the principle of organization—variety and contrast—requires no conceptual justification or implicit narrative program, hermetic, Neoplatonic or otherwise, that resolves what may appear to us (but not to Pliny's or de Caus's contemporaries) as the problem of the gardens' disunity and their failure to cohere into a unified whole. This realization has important implications for the content of the *Hortus Palatinus* or the ways in which it can be said to communicate meaning.

The *Hortus Palatinus* manifestly exploits the sixteenth-century Italian repertoire of iconographical themes and motifs. The garden's figurative elements include statues of Neptune, Venus, Ceres, Pomona, and the Muses. There is an attic frieze depicting the labors of Hercules and a Parnassian mount. All of these elements were conventional and even standardized. They belong to what was to become a de facto European style, which de Caus was instrumental in disseminating throughout Europe. As at Tivoli and Bagnaia, these Ovidian allusions do not, en masse, add up to a narrative program. Rather, the meanings of the *Hortus Palatinus* derive from the widely understood topoi of the Italian Renaissance garden.

To claim that de Caus's garden does not possess a narrative is not to say that it has no meaning. It is worth restating that the topoi of the Renaissance garden provided a flexible and adaptable lexicon of ideas and images, generic and familiar themes no doubt, but ones that could be given more specific meanings. In the *Hortus Palatinus*, for example, Frederick and Elisabeth are identified with Vertumnus and Pomona. Frederick dedicated the garden to Vertumnus, as the Latin inscription on the niche containing a statue of Neptune proclaims and a statue of Pomona appears in the garden, on the lowest terrace.[29] The rustic columnar order of the *Hortus Palatinus*—tree trunks entwined with vines— alludes to Vertumnus's comparison of marriage to a tree that supports a vine in Ovid's text.[30]

The principle of "topoi, not narrative" was not restricted to Italian Renaissance gardens and their Italianate derivatives elsewhere in Europe, such as the *Hortus Palatinus* or Fontainebleau and St. Germaine-en-Laye in France. The point is equally valid for the Le Nôtrean garden, despite its radically different scale and the changing concept of the relationship between art and nature that it embodies.[31] The various contemporary descriptions and itineraries of Louis XIV's gardens at Versailles reveal that, contrary to expectation perhaps, there was no single, standardized route, in which the garden revealed its meaning(s). In his *Description sommaire du château de Versailles* (1674), for example, André Félibien states that

> Having considered the Château itself, one may view the Gardens and all that is contained within the Petit Parc. However, since there is a multitude of objects which attract the eyes in every direction, and since one is often perplexed as to which way one should go, it is best to follow the order which I shall indicate, so that everything may be seen in order, more conveniently, and without fatigue.[32]

The point here is not that Félibien's route is the only one that enables the visitor to make sense of the garden's narrative. It is, rather, one that enables the visitor to see as much as possible with the least amount of exhaustion. Notably, his itinerary progresses in the opposite direction to Louis XIV's, one of which in the king's own handwriting has survived.[33]

Although the tone of Louis's itinerary is authoritarian, even gruff, there is remarkably little reference to his garden's meaning, less in fact than in Vasari's much earlier description of the garden of the Villa Medici, Castello. Section 5 is typical: "Go down the flight of steps on the north side [of Latona] to reach the view-point. You must consider the steps, the vases, the statues, the lizards, Latona, the Château; and on the other side, the Royal *Allée,* Apollo, the Canal, the tall jets in the *bosquets,* Flora, Saturn, and Ceres on the right, Bacchus to the left."[34] There is no suggestion here, or anywhere else, that these various elements together add up to a narrative: they are, as in the Italian garden, topoi, mostly derived from Ovid, but here inflected with Louis's identification with Apollo, a conceit so obvious that it hardly needs explication, let alone the support of an elaborate narrative program.

During the sixteenth and seventeenth centuries, the garden remains a fairly stable cultural object, at least on the level of meaning. The change in the significance of geometrical design (from revelation to imposition), and the dramatic expansion in scale that are the distinctive features of the later French garden certainly differentiate it from its Italian predecessors. Arguably, however, the reception and experience of gardens—their legibility—did not undergo any fundamental changes. In both Italy and France, the principle of "topoi, not narrative" determined the meanings of garden design and reflected the ways in which gardens were designed during the period. It may, finally, be suggested that the principle is applicable, in one form or another, to all gardens, not just Renaissance gardens.

CHAPTER SIX

Verbal Representations

MICHAEL LESLIE

The circumstances of the making of both literature and gardens change radically in the early modern period. The coming of printing with moveable type affects every aspect of writing and reading, even of those works published and circulated predominantly or solely in manuscript. Printing changed access to works of the past, particularly the classics that became available as never before. New genres appeared as writers and readers excitedly recognized opportunities hitherto unknown. New audiences provided a market for translations and imitations. Changed forms of education shaped writers and readers. And all of this had a profound impact on cultural attitudes to the creation and experience of actual gardens, and to the representation of gardens in verbal works.

Printing also disseminated knowledge of architectural theory and practice, of garden-making present and past, and of the social and cultural connotations of gardens and landscapes through time and different cultures. Although traveling widely remained relatively rare, the growing stream of verbal and visual records of places far away both geographically and in time exerted a powerful influence, even if these accounts and images were frequently inaccurate. Throughout this chapter, attention inevitably shifts between the representation of the garden in literature and the garden's response to the written; often, the direction of influence is ambiguous or double.

Given the near obsession with classical antiquity in this period, response to ancient literature is a major topic. However, the notion that this period saw an abrupt break with the immediate past is as outdated in this context as in others. Readers, writers, and garden makers were conscious of their medieval inheritance and conscious too that their predecessors had knowledge of the ancient world to which they had responded; interpretation of the works of their immediate, medieval predecessors was also part of the early modern expressive palette.

Settling on a single definition of the terms of the relationship between gardens and literature in this period would be factitious, though it is obvious that the central topic, felt behind almost every actual or fictional garden, is the complex of myths composed of the biblical Eden and the classical Golden Age, and the literary tradition of paradise and the *locus amoenus,* ideal places composed from our aspirations to and yearnings for perfection, but shot through with the guilty consciousness of transgression, exile, decline, and loss. But beyond that, no simple scheme will be satisfactory, and it is impossible to disentangle intimate and public, political and sexual, human and divine in gardens and their literary representation; that associative and multidirectional richness is surely one of the principal reasons for the garden's ubiquity in the literary imagination of this period.

This period displays fascination with connections between the natural and the artificial, paralleling the collections of rarities in cabinets of curiosities; the garden in its essence embodied both *naturalia et artificialia* in ever-shifting and ambiguous relationship.[1] Distinct not only from the indisputably constructed realms of buildings, towns, and cities, but also from the apparently unmediated realm of the pastoral landscape, gardens are both of the world and separate, exceptional spaces of unstable character. Literary texts respond by showing the presiding deities, personified Nature and the classical gods of the garden, as themselves chronically ambivalent: Spenser's Venus nurtures her foster-daughter in her garden of love ("a second paradise to ghesse") but also colludes in Amoret's kidnapping (rape?).[2] Andrew Marvell's speaker complacently celebrates the garden as a womblike shelter in "The Garden" ("Two Paradises 'twere in one / To live in Paradise alone)," but the same poet's speaker in "The Mower Against Gardens" denounces the garden as an alien, corrupting environment.[3] Perdita's furious repudiation of grafting in *The Winter's Tale* asserts that the rhetoric of innocent activity conceals corruption, violence, and exploitation.[4]

The garden is often a place of recreation (in several senses), of leisure, retirement, and recuperation, as in the opening of Sir Philip Sidney's *Countess of Pembroke's Arcadia,* Book 1, chapter 3,[5] but posed against that sunny view is the garden as a place demanding unremitting and wary labor: physical, mental, and moral, as in the emblematic Gardeners' Scene in *Richard II* (3.4) and, paradoxically, later in the same chapter of *The Arcadia*. With the emphasis on physical boundaries, entrances and exits, enclosure, exclusion, and differentiation from the world beyond, the structure of the garden lends itself to the development of narratives of transition, change, transformation and metamorphosis, and judgment.

The essential ambiguity of the garden—natural and cultivated—is frequently combined with awareness of its mutability, a compelling topic in this period, and the garden is used to represent the meaning of changefulness in all aspects of human life. It can be an image of human and divine creativity, all things growing toward their perfection: the gardener's work shapes nature and cultivates self, soul, and society. Alternatively, the ever-changing garden can represent the tendency of all things to decay from an original purity to corruption and ultimately death, both physical and spiritual.

One cannot read far in the literature of gardens in any period, but most of all this, without confronting sexuality as both metaphor and meaning. In the early modern period, human sexuality is frequently imaged in terms of the garden and is itself near pervasive as a figuration of everything the mind encounters, from politics to cosmology. This chapter ends with the garden of love that concludes Luís Vaz de Camões's epic poem, *The Lusiads* [*Os Lusíadas*] (1572). In that troubling vision many of the interconnected themes of this essay come into sharp focus: the implications of expressing the ideal in the image of the garden; the deeper meaning of the human impulse to order and manipulate nature; the relationship between the retired self of the garden and the life of action beyond its boundaries; and the underlying attitudes encoded in the figuration of the garden as female, subject to appropriation by the male explorer. The epic romances of the early modern period are all concerned with the politics of domination, the long conflict of Christian and Islamic cultures, and the quest for empire. Though representation of the garden may seem distant from such themes, the reverse is true. And the garden is central to considerations of two great engines of nationalism and imperialism, language and the book.

"THIS BOOKES THE GARDEN": LANGUAGE, RHETORIC, BOOK, EPIGRAM, INSCRIPTION

Language

The garden is frequently invoked as a metaphor for language and literature, *ut hortus poesis,* with both positive and negative implications. Both language and the garden are products of nature and art; their hybridity is often seen as morally ambiguous.

We have to wait for nineteenth-century historical linguistics to see a positive figuration of language as organic, its change and variations seen as signs of vigor and growth, but garden analogies begin to appear in the early modern period, as at the beginning of Joachim du Bellay's *La Deffence et illustration de la langue Francoyse* (1549), where complex comparisons are made between language, the ruinous architecture of the Tower of Babel, and the greater wholesomeness of plant life:

> This diversity and confusion [of languages] can rightly be called the Tower of Babel. For languages are not born of themselves in the same way as grasses, roots, and trees: some weak and debilitated in their kind, others healthy and robust, and more apt to carry the results of human thought; but all their strength is born in the world by the will and judgement of mortals.[6]

But even here, the contrasts result in no simple endorsement: Du Bellay wonders whether Nature is the nurturing mother of language or the "maratre," its step- or harsh mother.[7] Is Nature a protector or one who deceives to achieve only her own ends, like Spenser's goddess at the Temple of Venus?

Rhetoric

Despite ambivalence, the figuration of language as plantlike became increasingly prominent. Like plants, language was also recognized as possessing mysterious power, for good or ill, and the places of language cultivation were therefore seen as requiring wary control, all the more so since the language arts, in particular rhetoric, assumed remarkable prominence in this period. When rhetoric was conceptualized, the image of the garden was never far away. Henry Peacham nowhere gives a full explanation for the metaphor of the title to his 1577 treatise *The Garden of Eloquence*, but it is clear from the outset that he associates rhetoric with fruitfulness, colorfulness, and growth; and its cultivation with activities of gathering, sampling, ordering, and what we would now call scientific description (Peacham was surely aware of the new botanical gardens in Europe, such as those at Pisa and Leiden, with their carefully ordered plant beds and collections, and their catalogues). In The Netherlands, the competing "chambers of rhetoric" often had plant nicknames, the Leiden chamber known as "De witte Acoleyen" publishing their best pieces as *Den Lust-hof van Rethorica* (1596).[8]

Language acquisition as the cultivation of foreign plants is imaged in Peter Erondell's *The French Garden for English Ladies and Gentlewomen* (1605). Gardens and the art of rhetoric constitute spaces in which differences are carefully identified, and where what is learnt is both delightful and useful. The undercurrent of concern is still present, however: one collects things in a botanical garden to facilitate study, but also to enclose in the hope of controlling the use to which potentially dangerous materials are put. Language, like nature, has power; it must be cultivated, but carefully and in special, enclosed spaces. George Gascoigne warns of the perils of unguided reading: "the venemous spider wil sucke poison out of the most holesome herbe."[9] In Peacham's "Epistle Dedicatory" to Sir John Puckering in the 1593 edition of *The Garden of Eloquence* many of these associations appear:

> which figures or formes of speech, I have disposed into orders, described by their properties, distinguished by their differe[n]ces, noted their singular uses, & added certain Cautions to compasse them for feare of abuse.[10]

As will be seen later, literary gardens are often places of seduction through intoxicating delights; the frequent imaging of the language arts in garden terms itself suggests associations with pleasure, power, danger, and abuse.

The Book

Closely associated with rhetoric is the image of the book as a garden. This is often most evident in titles and other paratextual elements that control and condition interpretation. Garden associations are particularly invoked for collections, anthologies, and miscellanies. The connection is obvious in the names: *florilegia,* and anthology, from the Greek for flower and collection, respectively. These genres resemble contemporary cabinets of curiosities, *Wunderkammer,* and encyclopedism. In 1501 Antoine Vérard published *Le Jardin de plaisance et fleurs de Rhétorique,* a poetic anthology of courtly verse republished six times in forty years, in which each of the poems is represented as being recited in a Garden of Delights; in illustrations the speakers are shown addressing each other in an aristocratic garden setting, serving to reassure less socially elevated purchasers that, though printed, this product had the status of a manuscript collection.[11] Reading this book, it is implied, is equivalent to gaining access to a privy garden, to an exclusive space: "One day . . . az the Gardin door waz open, & her highnes a hunting by licens of my good friend Adrian [The Gardiner], I cam in at a bek . . . ".[12]

The anthology as possessing garden-like order stands in necessary contrast to collections without dominant organization: *sylvae,* deriving from Statius's *Sylvae* (ca. CE 89–95), all the more powerful an example given that so many of its poems praise the villa gardens of Statius's friends, a counterpart to Horace's poems. *Sylva* means "a wood" (as in John Evelyn's use for his *Sylva, or Discourse on Forest Trees* [1664]), with the suggestion that such collections are wild, but *sylva* can also mean "raw material," implying that the poems within the volume are hurriedly produced, not yet shaped (the meaning Statius himself gives in the Dedicatory Epistle to Book One: "little pieces, which streamed from my pen in the heat of the moment").[13] The two meanings are combined by Ben Jonson ("the ancients called that kind of body *sylva* . . . in which there were works of diverse nature and matter congested, as the multitude call timber-trees, promiscuously growing, a wood or forest; so am I bold to entitle these lesser poems of later growth by this of *Underwood*").[14] In the fifteenth century, the genre had been explored and his poems imitated by Statius's editor, Poliziano and by Lorenzo de' Medici; Ronsard's *Le bocage* (1554) continues this in French in the sixteenth, and its influence perhaps reaches its zenith in the collection *Las Soledades* (1613) by Luis de Góngora, roughly contemporary with Jonson's *Works* (1616), though the latter's *Underwoods* were not published until 1640. Unusually, Góngora's *silvae* have a characteristic metrical form, but are certainly composed within the Statian tradition.

The *sylva* stands in deliberate contrast to the prevailing associations of the garden: control, pruning, and selection. Timothy Kendall in his *Flowers of Epigrammes* (1577) hastens to assure the reader: "Marrie this I must let thee understand, that . . . I have left the lewde, I have chosen the chaste: I have weeded away all wanton and woorthlesse woordes: I have pared away all pernicious patches: I have chipt & chopt of all beastly boughes and branches, all filthy and fulsome phrases."[15] Similarly, translation and imitation can be presented as grafting and transference of cuttings, as by George Gascoigne in the full title of his *Hundreth Sundry Flowers:* the volume contains works "Gathered partely (by translation) in the fyne outlandish Gardins of Euripedes, Ovid, Petrarke, Ariosto, and others: and partly by invention, out of our owne fruitefull Orchardes in Englande: Yelding sundrie sweete savours of Tragical, Comical, and Morall Discourses, bothe pleasaunt and profitable to the well smellyng noses of learned Readers"; or in William Basse's *A Helpe to memory and discourse* (1620),[16] where the book's collected wisdom is compared to "a ground, / Set with rich grafts and plants but rarely found."[17]

Books, divided into sections and chapters, could be imagined as gardens with partitions, compartments, beds, and arbors: Lawrence Anderton exhorts his reader to behave like "a man comming into a curious Garden, [who] layeth not hold of every flower, which first presenteth it selfe to his sight, but will gather here and there such, as are most pleasing to the eye, & smell"[18] The writer is the creator of the garden, but—as both in the experience of actual gardens and in the literary representation of garden visiting—the reader has striking autonomy if he chooses to exercise it, to resist the garden's agenda and create his own. The reader can determine what to do in the book, what paths to take, what flowers to pluck, and what to reject. "W. Lort," in his prefatory poem "In praise of the Worke, and the Author" to William Basse's *A Helpe to memory and discourse* (1620), says the book will

> leade [the reader] a long
> To the choice Arbors, where a fragraunt throung
> Of savors delicate, seemes to invite him
> And mutually agree, all to delight em.
> This bookes the Garden, and since thou art in,
> Walke through each Arbor, whilst alone unseen.
> Thou contemplate the beauties that be there,
> Planted to fill, thy pleasure every where;[19]

The reader is solitary, unseen, voyeuristic, transforming vegetable pleasures into spiritual medicines.

The Epigram

Lyric poetry was itself conceived of as an enclosed space and its boundedness made the connection with the garden almost inevitable. Forcefully influenced by the rediscovery of classical literary texts, not least the *Greek Anthology* (the Planudean text first printed in 1494, the Palatine text in 1616), such forms as the epigram flourished in early modern literary culture; and garden reference is frequent in titles: Kendall's *Flowers of Epigrammes*; Lucas D'Heere's *Den Hof en Boomgaerd der Poësien* (1565); John Florio's collection of proverbial phrases *The Gardine of Recreations* (1591); and more allusively in Robert Herrick's *Hesperides* (1648), a volume of epigrams, anacreontics, and other short forms, or in the popular French handbook, François des Rues's *Les Marguerites françoises; ou, Thresor des fleurs du bien dire* (1595). Stemming from Seneca's "Moral Epistle" 84, the image of the ideal mind as a bee darting among flowers, distilling the accumulated inspiration as honey, became commonplace, as in Richard Taverner's *The Garden of Wysdom* (1539). Erasmus's version of Seneca's advice was crucial to this popularization: "So the student like the diligent bee will fly through all the authors' gardens, leaping on to every little flower, from all sides collecting honey for the hive."[20] Seneca and Erasmus's metaphor is invoked with recognizable English curmudgeonliness by Thomas Jordan in his *Poeticall Varieties* (1637), to declare the native independence of his plain poetry: "I have not rob'd the Hive of any mans endeavours, or exhausted his hony treasurie to enrich my barren labours, but from the native flower suck'd I my sweetenesse, if there bee ought that may content thy wealthy pallat, it is thine owne, the Cooke prepar'd it for thee."[21] Within such volumes, the individual poems are the flowers, to be gathered for transfer into the reader's commonplace book, in the manner of cuttings.

Garden Inscriptions

The transfer could also be from the book as metaphorical garden directly into the actual garden: the epigram was perfectly suited to the fashion for garden inscriptions, which in the best examples became essential to a complex, mixed art form composed of garden, image, literary texts, and theatre. Etymologically, *epigram* means "written upon," and though used more broadly, the epigram had this real use, being inscribed on and in gardens. The early-sixteenth-century Lake Garda garden of the Veronese humanist Agostino Brenzoni at San Vigilio looked across to sites associated with the Roman poet Catullus, as well as having associations with Virgil; progress through the gardens was shaped and punctuated by a series of inscriptions, texts probably by Brenzoni himself. He evoked not only the ancients but also his fellow humanist Petrarch, whose story of desire, frustration, and transcendence in the *Rime sparsi* influenced attitudes to love, literature, and landscape throughout Europe. An account of the garden, possibly by Brenzoni himself, represents the experience in terms of myth, inherited culture, literature, and garden forms. The "Garden of Apollo" is dominated by a statue of the god of the arts, who is addressed by the bust of Petrarch:

> O may thy glance inspire the spring
> Of this our love, as now my tears
> On hidden roots such blessings bring
> That Earth all sweet and green appears.[22]

Poetry, landscape, water, flowers and trees, art and desire, the gods of antiquity and the gods of contemporary European culture: all combine here, in a rich and allusive stew. Brenzoni also participates in the tradition of inscribing the laws of the gardens, the *lex hortorum,* another kind of pithy, epigrammatic utterance, at the entrance, thereby constructing the visitor's frame of mind before entering, with a combination of wry, often cryptic exhortations and clearer practical prohibitions:[23]

> 2. Leave your troubles in the town.
> 4. Keep your servants' hands off the garden.
>   . . .
> 6. Drink the cup that will quench your thirst.
> 12. Let the honour of the place be its noblest law.

The same serious playfulness, *serio ludens,* is found in such sixteenth-century English gardens as Nonsuch. As at San Vigilio, the inscriptions use ambiguous, cryptic utterance to vivify the visitor's sense of uncertainty, appearing to pierce through to hidden desires and fears, the epigrammatic inscriptions suggesting an unseen but all-seeing mind at home in the garden as the reader is not. A late sixteenth-century visitor recorded the inscriptions that confronted the walking visitor at liminal points: "Nil impudicum pudicitia Dea, nil turpe suadet, sceleris vindicta, sed mala mens, mala animus" (The temptation to impurity does not come from the chaste goddess, who is chastity itself, but from an evil mind, an evil spirit); "Impuri fons impuri rivuli; / Ingratae mentis impuri oculi" (Impure spring, impure waters; / From a graceless mind, impure sight); "Aestuanti umbra, languenti sedes. Noli in umbra umbrantilis esse, nec sint sedenti serpentis oculi" (Shade from the summer heat, a seat for the weary. In the shade, become not shady, nor resting become serpent eyed). Confronted with the representation of Actaeon being torn apart by his own hounds, the visitor reads

> Ictus piscator sapit: sed infelix Actaeon semper praeceps. Casta virgo facile miseretur: sed potens Diana scelus ulciscitur. Praeda canibus, exemplum juvenibus, suis dedecus pereat Actaeon.
>
> (The fisherman who has been wounded learns, though late, to beware; but unfortunate Actaeon always presses on. The chaste virgin easily sympathized, but potent Diana revenges the injury. A prey to his dogs, an example to young men, a disgrace to his people, may Actaeon fall.)

This is comprehensively Ovidian, refracted through the literary and gardenist use of the *Metamporphoses* over centuries. The educated visitor would immediately have recognized the myths, genres, and allusions.[24]

The inscriptions in both these gardens are encountered at points of entry and transition: crossing thresholds implies decision and choice, rendered vivid by the invocation of classical myth and the Ovidian fictions of the garden. Although there are no inscriptions in Spenser's most famous fictional garden, the Bower of Bliss, inscription occurs through the poem's *ekphrases* of the reliefs above its gates:

> All this, and more might in that goodly gate
> Be red;[25]

Division and the typical *compartment* structure facilitated the imagery of a journey with significant stages. Spenser's questing knight and his guide, who venture into and eventually destroy the Bower, participate in a moralized equivalent of the allegorical pilgrimage, such as the spiritual journey of Guillaume de Digulleville (1295–1358?) in *La Pèlerinage de vie humaine* and the secular love journey through a garden of the *Romance of the Rose*. But they also play on the association of gardens with fundamental characteristics of the human experience of language, whether in the form of the book, as persuasive speech, or incised into the frame of a garden gate.

LITERATURE

Judgment

The garden as a space in which the careful gardener trims, trains, and chooses makes it an obvious metaphor for the exercise or otherwise of judgment. So in the scene from *Richard II* already mentioned, the chief gardener, "old Adam's likeness," makes no attempt to conceal his application of the lessons of horticulture to the king's duty to manage family and state:

> Go, bind thou up yon dangling apricocks,
> Which, like unruly children, make their sire
> Stoop with oppression of their prodigal weight:
> Give some supportance to the bending twigs.
> Go thou, and like an executioner,
> Cut off the heads of too fast growing sprays,

That look too lofty in our commonwealth:
All must be even in our government.
You thus employ'd, I will go root away
The noisome weeds, which without profit suck
The soil's fertility from wholesome flowers.

(Act 3, Scene 4)

The soul must be governed as the state, of course: Thomas Jenner's *The soules solace, or Thirtie and one spirituall emblems* (1626) combines the two: "The danger of *wicked men* abiding in the Church" has an image showing a railed garden being tended by an assiduous gardener. Here God is the gardener who "roots . . . out" the "*weeds, or thistles*" of hypocrisy, banishing the sinner to "Goe live with *Turkes,* and *Heathens,* from the pale / Of *Christian people*."[26] Another emblem, "12. A remedy against *spirituall* pride," uses the metaphor of the garden to assert the mind's responsibility to control impassioned response to the senses, exactly the point made by God as he judges Adam for resigning his will to Eve, the "fairest unsupported flower" of the Garden of Eden (*Paradise Lost,* 9.432):

Adorned

She was indeed, and lovely to attract
Thy love, not thy subjection, and her gifts
Were such as under government well seemed,
Unseemly to bear rule, which was thy part
And person, hadst thou known thyself aright.

(10.151–156)[27]

In the emblem, Christians confident they have received salvific grace are in particular peril, because, looking down, they complacently compare themselves with the rest of creation. The gardener's joy "is such / He thinkes one well could live by these," but he needs to gain perspective by gazing at the sun, even if it leads to temporary blindness. The sun's brilliance exceeds the pleasures of the garden even as Jesus does the things of this world. As in so many emblems, the relationship here between verse (the "word") and image is ambiguous (not only because the image is printed upside down in the first publication). A figure stands gazing sunwards within a railed compartment containing straggly vegetation, separated by a path from a second compartment, this one filled with tall, flowering plants, each in a rectangular bed.

Is the implication that the flourishing compartment needs no intermediary between it and the sun? Or that, having once gazed at incomparable, blinding glory, the Christian gardener devotes no further attention to ephemeral vanities?

Henry Peacham, author of *The Garden of Eloquence,* uses the figure of the garden in yet another way in his book of emblems, *Minerva Britanna or A garden of heroical devises* (1612). As well as invoking the "choice collection" meaning in the title, Peacham's emblem "*Unum, et semel*" ("One, and once") shows a disembodied hand plucking a flower at a garden's centre. Again, the emblem is shot through with ambiguities. The world may be spacious, but the garden of the image is tightly bounded by pergolas; the verse stresses free choice, but the image suggests that prudent choice is limited to a single flower. The visitor has God's leave to "walke" (line 2) but must be careful not to "erre" (*errare,* to wander). Closely allied to the literary epigram and the garden inscription, such emblems play on the sense of irrevocable choices, unspecified guilt, treacherous beauty, and the prospect of "ruine ever after."[28]

"OUR BODIES ARE OUR GARDENS": THE GARDEN, THE BODY, AND THE FEMALE

"Our bodies are our gardens, to the which our wills are gardeners." So says Shakespeare's Iago (*Othello*, 1.3.317–318). Here, Iago's usually fetid sexuality seems abstract, even clichéd; and indeed his allegory is perhaps derived immediately from Pierre de la Primaudaye's *The French Academy,* a collection of philosophical and moral knowledge and advice, all of which Primaudaye called "a Platonicall garden or orchard."[29] La Primaudaye's garden metaphor distils much early modern thinking:

> Even so doth nature, or rather the prince thereof worke in a *mans body,* which is as it were *a garden* that hath a soule. Wherein the Creator of this whole frame sheweth himselfe no lesse wonderfull, nay rather much more then in this great *garden of the whole earth, & of the great world.* (pt. 2, ch. 64)

Man as a garden with a soul, created by God but governed by will. The garden, plants, and human body are morally neutral; but the gardener, imaging the infected will of Lactantian and Augustinian tradition, renders the garden either sterile or fertile. But as he proceeds Iago abandons his initial nonjudgmental stance, and instead intensifies anxiety and suggests the ineradicable evil of some of the materials nature provides: "so that if we will plant nettles or sow lettuce, set hyssop and weed up thyme, supply it with one gender of herbs or distract it with many, either to have it sterile with idleness or manured with industry, why, the power and corrigible authority of this lies in our wills" (318–322). John Erskine Hankins pointed out that *Romeo and Juliet*'s setting of scenes concerning the control of youthful sexuality in Friar Lawrence's garden of simples suggests a more pervasive distrust of the natural elements of man's sexual nature and the need for forceful government.[30]

Most surviving poetry of the early modern period is by men and it comes as no surprise that the image of the garden is often used for the female body and, particularly, for the female genitalia (individual plants are often used: the fig often represents the vagina, the raisin standing for the penis). Writers found this usage authorized in *The Greek Anthology* in poems by the pungent soldier-poet Archilochus. The image of the female body as garden and virginity as a garden flower to be plucked underlies the carpe diem tradition, so beloved of early modern poets, stemming principally from Horace's example; poets such as Poliziano bring many of these metaphors and themes together in their works. Another stream is the tradition of the poetic blazon of the female body, developed by Clément Marot in *Les Blasons anatomiques du corps féminin* (1536), the topographical hints of which are developed in obvious landscape terms in the collection *La Puce de Madame des-Roches* (1582), inspired and collected by Catherine Des Roches.

The most powerful instance, however, is in the lyric poetry of Pierre de Ronsard, influential throughout Europe. In his study of imitation in sixteenth-century poetry, and particularly in the lyric tradition from Petrarch, Thomas M. Greene notes that there is almost a fetishisation of the landscape, and that this becomes overwhelmingly intense in Ronsard's *Amours*: "[the] woman's body [tends] to become a landscape and conversely, [the] landscape to become her body,"[31] as in this lyric:

> Ha, seigneur dieu, que de graces écloses
> Dans le jardin de ce sein verdelet,
> Enflent le rond de deus gazons de lait,
> Où des Amours les fléches sont encloses!

> (Oh, lord God, how many graces disclose themselves
> In the garden of this beautiful green breast?
> Swelling the spheres of two green swards of milk
> Where love's arrows are enclosed!)

(Les Amours, 1–4)

As Michael Riffaterre notes, Ronsard's image invokes the *blazon anatomique* only to embark on a series of giddying associations and vertiginous imaginative extensions that defy non-poetic logic, departing from the *blason*'s conventions, converting the *pome acerbe* of youthful female beauty and the conventional milky white of the beloved's breasts into green lawns, echoing and extrapolating from not only the poetry of antiquity but also responses to antiquity in, among others, Petrarch and Ariosto, particularly the paradox of Alcina's breasts (*Orlando furioso,* 7.14), "green yet ivory," both natural and artificial, organic and inorganic like the garden itself, and paralleled in the outrageous pun of Ronsard's *verdelet / vert de lait*.[32] Characteristically, Ronsard throws himself into this meditation on body, garden, and lyric as all being equivalent exceptional spaces and he does this knowing that in daring the reader to follow him he invites imaginative participation in the erotic experience: "C'est toi qui tâtes sa hanche / Sa gréve et sa cuisse blanche, / Et son [. . .], qui ne fait encore / Que se frizer de fils d'or" (It's you who touch her hips, her loin, her white thigh, and her [. . .] which only just frizzes with filaments of gold) (*Ode à la Fontaine Belerie,* ll. 80–83).[33] Almost inevitably, Ronsard moves directly to Ovidian reference that unites both the resources of poetry and the resources of actual garden decoration, lover and reader transformed by an intense erotic experience which is also a garden experience: "Je me transforme en cent metamorfoses" (I transform myself in a hundred metamorphoses) when her beautiful body is seen, including the desire to be changed into a flea by day to perch on her breasts; ". . . mais la nuit je voudroi / Que rechanger en homme je me pusse" (but at night I would wish / To be changed back into a man, if I could).

Ronsard is surely conscious of the garden experience of the lover in the *Romance of the Rose,* and he is certainly responding to and reacting against the landscape metaphors of Petrarch's *Rime*. But it is striking that Ronsard combines the figurative uses of the garden and the Petrarchan landscape with the intense garden-centred poetry of the carpe diem tradition. The moral judgments found in the epic romance and earthly paradises of Renaissance literature (see the following sections) fall away: lyric's focus and its capacity to represent intensity dissolve externally–derived rules of conduct. Instead, Ronsard gives the reader a highly theatrical sense of overhearing a private and often obsessive response to the beloved that is characteristic of early modern love lyric and in particular of the sonnet. Later in his career, the carpe diem tradition and the image of the female body as a garden return as he laments the untimely death of a different beloved:

"Sur La Mort de Marie: IV"

As in May month, on its stem we see the rose
In its sweet youthfulness, in its freshest flower,
Making the heavens jealous with living colour,
Dawn sprinkles it with tears in the morning glow:
Grace lies in all its petals, and love, I know,
Scenting the trees and scenting the garden's bower,
But, assaulted by scorching heat or a shower,
Languishing, it dies, and petals on petals flow.

So in your freshness, so in all your first newness,
When earth and heaven both honoured your loveliness,
The Fates destroyed you, and you are but dust below.

Accept my tears and my sorrow for obsequies,
This bowl of milk, this basket of flowers from me,
So living and dead your body will still be rose.

THE GARDEN AND THE CONSUMMATION OF DESIRE

Passion, physical sexuality, death, and the garden appear again in Thomas Kyd's seminal Elizabethan play, *The Spanish Tragedy*, in which Bel-Imperia and Horatio meet to consummate their relationship at night in his father's garden, only to be surprised by her brother and Horatio's rival who murder him and string his body up in the bower in which they had been making love. As he stabs, her brother comments with heavy horticultural irony, "these are the fruits of love!" The image of Horatio hung in the bower formed the frontispiece of the 1615 printed edition of the play (and all subsequent editions before the Civil War), a rare instance of staging and scenery being represented, suggesting how compelling and famous this garden scene was; it perhaps stands behind Friar Lawrence's garden of simples in *Romeo and Juliet*, staged a few years later.

The associations of the garden, sexuality unsanctioned by marriage, and death is particularly powerful in two works printed in 1499, both anonymous: the scandalous and immensely popular Spanish work *The Tragicomedy of Calisto and Melibea*,[34] better known as the *Celestina*, and the strange combination of Petrarchan love allegory and architectural treatise, the *Hypnerotomachia*

Polifili.[35] The *Celestina,* largely prose but presented in dialogue form, circulated widely throughout Europe (it was translated and adapted as a play by
John Rastell, *A new comedy in English,* as early as 1525). There are no explicit
allusions, but the fatal bower scene in Kyd's *The Spanish Tragedy* may owe
something to the notorious sexual looseness of the garden scenes in *Celestina.*
The *Hypnerotomachia* also travels quickly from Venice, where it was printed
by Aldus Manutius, to France in 1546 as the *Songe de Poliphile,* and reaching
England in partial translation in 1592.

Although with many radical dissimilarities, both works centre on desire
and sexuality set in the gardens that dominate each. The *Hypnerotomachia* is
famously beautiful as a physical object, superb in its printing and mise-en-page
and containing fascinating and teasing illustrations. This book has long been
adduced rather vaguely as an influence on landscape design, but the pace has
quickened since the quincentenary of its publication, and in particular, Hervé
Brunot has published in the new, aptly named journal *Polia* a suggestive article
proposing links between the *Hypnerotomachia* and sixteenth-century Italian
gardens.[36]

The *Hypnerotomachia*'s narrative is conventionally Petrarchan, however
idiosyncratic it is in other respects: the title roughly translates as "Poliphilus's
love battle in a dream" (*The Strife of Love in a Dream,* in the 1592 translation). Poliphilus begins in the middle of a Dantean *selva oscura,* then wanders
through a landscape of bizarre monuments and structures in search of Polia.
Meeting her, the pair travel to the island of Venus, the heart of the book,
with its marvelous circular organization, its topiary and friezes, its fountains
and statues: a veritable garden of love. And there, after more mild mishaps,
Poliphilus and Polia are united, though the story ends unhappily with Polia's
death, as such a Dantean and Petrarchan work should.

However, the unhappiness is not an expression of moral condemnation,
even though the author is generally supposed to have been a friar. Poliphilus's ultimate disappointment renders the summit of Petrarchan desire beyond
consummation, in unattainability and exquisite grief, seemingly without any
reflection on the morality of physical sexuality; the ordered beauties of the
garden express an untroubled exaltation of love's fulfillment.

There is nothing sacred about sex in the *Celestina,* this nickname belonging to the most vivid and pungent character, a bawd, brothel-keeper wise-
woman, and maybe witch. The *Celestina* is utterly surprising: Calisto erupts
with desire for a young woman, Melibea; she refuses his urgent advances
(perhaps just as a test), so on the recommendation of his servants he turns to
the wise woman. Celestina visits Melibea in her father's townhouse garden

and is successful in gaining access for Calisto. The story then careens off completely unexpectedly: Calisto richly rewards the bawd with a golden chain; the servants demand a share of the payment, which she refuses, so they murder her. Calisto enjoys a night of uninhibited sex in the garden, Melibea's only complaint being the brevity of the act. Meanwhile, the two servants are arrested and publicly executed for murder, and their lovers seek revenge on Calisto and Melibea. The next night, Calisto returns to the garden with two more servants, but once inside hears the noise of a fracas in the street. He climbs back over the wall to intervene, but falls and dies. Melibea climbs to the top of her father's house and, after a despairing monologue, throws herself to her death.

The garden dominates the image world of the *Celestina*. Unlike the *Hypnerotomachia,* there is remarkably little description (hard to do convincingly in a dialogue form); nonetheless, the reader constantly imagines the spaces of the tale, above all Melibea's garden. It is a town garden with high walls, perhaps responding to medieval imaginings of paradise as a garden in a city, as Jacque Le Goff and others have pointed out. The characters talk about this garden as a *locus amoenus,* though the reader gets little detail: there are trees, a water source, and grass. What we get instead is remarkable: the garden is a paradise but of the frankest, physically sexual kind: Melibea's servant Lucrecia finds the presence of the lover and the atmosphere of the garden so intoxicating that she lunges at Calisto and has to be told by her mistress Melibea to desist:

> What is the matter, Lucrecia? Have you gone mad with pleasure? Let him alone. Don't tear him to pieces. Don't burden his body with your heavy embraces. Let me enjoy what's mine. Don't disturb my pleasure. (Act 19)

The expression of physical desire goes uncondemned on moral grounds. And the praise of her garden as a locale for sexual pleasure is what has proven so irresistible for Lucrecia:

> The whole garden rejoices that you have come. Look at the moon, how clearly she has shown her face! Look at the clouds scudding by. Listen to the water flowing from this little spring. How much softer it sounds, and how much more liquid in the fresh grass! Listen to the tall cypresses, how peacefully their branches kiss, driven to it by a little warm breeze that sways them. Look at their quiet shadows. How dark they are and ready to conceal our joys! (Act 19)[37]

The maid sings a garden song:

> If I owned this garden
>> And all its bounteous flowers
> I would pluck your kisses
>> In the morning hours.
>
> The lilies and the roses
>> Would make their colours new.
> They would revive their odours
>> Each day as I walked through.
>
> Welcome is the fountain
>> To one whose throat is dry
> But pleasanter is Calisto's face
>> To Melibea's eye.
>
> For though the night be dark
>> She will enjoy the sight
> Of her love leaping o'er the wall
>> And kiss him with delight.
>
> The wolf leaps with pleasure
>> When he sees the lambs;
> The little goats leap to the teat,
>> And she leaps to his arms.
>
> Never did lady welcome
>> Her love with more delight
> Never did garden witness love
>> More tireless any night.[38]

Her mistress joins her in a duet, and then Melibea ends the song alone:

> The midnight hour has struck
>> And still he does not come.
> Ask if he has another love
>> Who keeps him in her room.[39]

Melibea sings exhilaratingly of a paradoxical freedom in the garden: walled but open verticality as she looks up through the tree's branches and into the night sky, shining with stars:

And O you stars, shine out,
    Pole star and star of day!
Why find you not my sleeping joy
    And rouse him with your ray?

This has all the physical, erotic charge of the Song of Songs, and the sexual assertiveness of the women is reminiscent of the Beloved's lines in the Biblical text. Lucrecia images Melibea, the female, as a male predatory animal in her desire for Calisto: "the wolf leaps with pleasure / When he sees the lambs". And as in the Song of Songs, the detail (if it can be called that) of the garden seems everywhere symbolic—the flowers, the colors, the odors, the fountain, the spring, the wall, the trees.

Although Melibea commits suicide in her grief for Calisto's death, her account of the affair is long on its pleasures and perfunctory in the application of conventional morality, which seems peripheral at best in this text, as it is in the *Hypnerotomachia*. The energy of both books is desire for physical consummation and the garden is both the setting and the metaphor for its triumph.

THE EARTHLY PARADISE AND THE EPIC ROMANCE

The most famous literary gardens of the early modern period are those of the epic romances, principally Boiardo's *Orlando innamorato* (1495), Ariosto's *Orlando furioso* (1516; 1532), Trissino's *L'Italia liberata dai Goti* (1547–1548), Tasso's *Gerusalemme liberata* (1581), and Spenser's *The Faerie Queene* (1590; 1596), with a final, but very different reflection in Milton's *Paradise Lost* (1667). In each of these the work of art reaches a climax in a version of the *locus amoenus,* usually in a crucial scene wherein the moral and cultural questions that are at the heart of the poem come into sharp focus. Here, morality is anything but peripheral.

As modern terms, *paradise, Eden,* and *earthly paradise* may seem interchangeable, but this was not so in the sixteenth century. In particular, the term *earthly paradise* suggested the myth of a terrestrial perfection characteristic of Islam: a world of unreproved physical and sexual pleasure for the devout male. Conversely, Christian myths of paradise could not be disentangled from ideas of the Fall and original sin, which Augustine had glossed as concupiscence. Norman Daniel writes, "it was the Islamic Paradise, which, more than any other theme, summed up the Christian notion of Islam,"[40] and Dorothee Metlitzki confirms the importance of the contrast: "To the Western public the Muslim garden of delight was the antitype par excellence of the Christian paradise."[41]

In early modern Europe, the clash of civilizations itself can be seen as a clash of imagined gardens, of paradises. In *The Faerie Queene,* the evil enchantress of the Bower of Bliss is Muslim; in Ariosto's *Orlando furioso,* Alcina's Saracen garden of delights is contrasted with Logistilla's garden of virtue. The contrast is inherited from earlier writers, particularly Fidenzio of Padua, Ramon Llull, and the authors of the *Romance of the Rose.* The gardens of the romance epics are invariably the property of and inhabited by female seducers, destroyers ultimately revealed as monstrous and Muslim. Tasso allows his witch to convert to Christianity: Armida and her garden survive, but are radically diminished. Spenser's hero Sir Guyon utterly destroys Acrasia's paradise. The contrast between Christian and Islamic paradises was not merely between virtue and vice. The Christian paradise, inherited from the Middle Ages, was essentially a figuration of a spiritual state in which the believer apprehended God in a vision reminiscent of the rose of Dante's *Paradiso.* But "[the Islamic paradise] was always thought to prove the contention that this was no spiritual religion."[42] In *The Faerie Queene* the enchantress liquefies and sucks out her captive's soul.

In a Protestant twist, John Earle in 1620 praised his Oxford college's gardens in contrast to the "godless gardens which in vain / Th'Italians for their heaven feign," continuing a common English association of Islam and the papacy, both judged godless.[43] The absence of what he deems visual trickery characterizes the wholesome English Protestant garden; strikingly, the gardens inhabited by the Muslim seductresses of the romance epics are radically different, entrapping even the most resilient of heroes. These writers are surely drawing on a contemporary fascination: Islamic gardens encountered before 1500 were more sophisticated in horticulture and technology than those of the Christian West. Where the gardens of the epic romances have boundaries, these are designed to imprison the corrupted Christian rather than secure a virtuous realm from invasion. In France, Bernard Palissy imagines another Protestant garden offering secure retreat from modern evils, where one could "flee the iniquities and maliciousness of men, in order to serve God . . . [a garden welcoming] Christians exiled in a time of persecution into a hilly *locus amoenus* filled with shady grottoes protecting one from the heat of the sun. In this circular garden animals would wander freely and the sayings of divine wisdom would be expressed in the letters of leaves and the scrolls of branches."[44]

In the epic romances, the garden has become the special place in which the inextricably interlocking themes of beauty and art, aspiration and desire, identity and heroism, sexuality, and moral choice are represented with aching beauty and driven to frequently uncomfortable resolutions. The earthly paradise is the exceptional and primary space in which personal, cultural, almost cosmic decisions are encountered and faced. It is no surprise that at the centre of virtually every *locus amoenus* of the period, we find an example of the carpe diem poem, explicitly challenging the reader's Christian perspective on time, present pleasure, and future judgment:

> So passes in the passing of a day,
> The life of man, the fruit, the leaf, the flower;
> Spring may return, but these will pass away;
> The green will fade, and youth will lose its power.
> Gather the rose in the fresh of dawn today,
> For this sweet time will only last an hour;
> Gather the rose of love as lovers do,
> And love while you yourself can be loved too.[45]

Even in the virtuous antitype to the Bower of Bliss in Spenser's *The Faerie Queene*, "Great enemy to it, and to all the rest, / That in the *Garden* of *Adonis* springs, / Is wicked *Time*" (3.6).

THE ISLAND OF LOVE IN *THE LUSIADS* (1572)

In the culminating episode of Camões's poem, many of these themes are restated, but with a surprising perspective. Like other early modern epic-romances, *The Lusiads* takes the Virgilian theme of the heroic definition of the nation, this time that of Portugal through the voyages of Vasco da Gama. The hero and his sailors embody the destined triumph of Western, Christian civilization, having fulfilled a cultural quest, reaching the farthest and most valuable parts of the world. Thereby they achieve two stunning objectives: the promotion of Portugal to the rank of empire and the defeat of Saracen and Moor, whose threat to Christendom was the point of origin of so many early modern epics.

Quest completed, the hero is permitted a vision on Venus's Island of Love, a *locus amoenus* of intense fertility and beauty, but while there, da Gama and his sailors also engage in an orgy with the island's nymphs, an orgy that seems a necessary precondition to knowledge of the purposes of providence. Camões describes this anonymous sexual gratification in sometimes startlingly graphic detail, without a hint of moral condemnation. The females of the island, itself represented as an intensely desirable female body, are eager to please and be pleased; far from being Muslim temptresses and enchanters, free access to their bodies is the reward for overcoming Islam and the Christian victors experience the benefits of the Muslim "earthly paradise." In *The Lusiads,* exhilaration at the prospect of empire seems to generate an ideal garden experience in which all that had hitherto been signs of virtue or vice are inverted, all boundaries crossed, all restraint abandoned. The world domination revealed to da Gama is imaged in possession of the Island's paradise garden and the bodies of its female inhabitants. After the orgy, he is graced with sight of the *máquina do mundo*. The poem celebrates masculine, Christian power, but the reward is close to metamorphosis into the feared opposite. Camões's poem seems unaware that trouble awaits that triumphant imperial man at the end of this garden's path.

CHAPTER SEVEN

Visual Representations

MAŁGORZATA SZAFRAŃSKA

THE ROYAL CASTLE IN WARSAW

During his journeys throughout Europe, Michel de Montaigne visited the Villa d'Este in Tivoli. On arriving there, he took out his journal so that he could continue with his descriptions of beautiful and interesting places. He hesitated. Should he describe the Villa d'Este? Or, perhaps, paint it? This master of words may have felt less skilled in the art of *disegno*, because he quickly found an excuse to content himself with writing a description. "I would try here to paint [all these things], but there are books about them and well-known images."[1] During the Renaissance period, gardens were a sight to be marveled at. Texts written in classical antiquity showed that works of art created by human hands—even if not related to a religious cult—could become objects of admiration, the subject of a description, a point of reference for making comparisons, a cause of rivalry. It is, therefore, no surprise that gardens and indeed various features in the garden—fountains in particular—were included in sixteenth-century guides, travel journals, and letters. These descriptions appeared alongside drawings (paintings, engravings) and they complemented each other. In this way, Giovanni Guidiccioni became interested in one of the new Roman fountains and asked his friend, the humanist Annibale Caro, to "either describe it or draw it." Caro replied that he was in Naples and could, therefore, only write a description of it, which he would endeavor to do as best he could, but, as to the drawing, he would ask his brother in Rome, "who had already asked an artist, who is a friend of mine if he would make [a drawing]." The image of the fountain was to be of a documentary nature and include all the necessary details. Caro wrote that if his description (which devoted a lot of attention to the workings of the fountain) was unclear, then he should "get a drawing to help."[2] These words were combined with a picture when a woodcut engraving depicting the garden with all its various features was included in Francesco de' Vieri's work on Pratolino.[3] The image is somewhat schematic, and the fact that it was added to the second edition of the work would seem to suggest that it was intended primarily to help the reader understand this labyrinthine poem. A popular drawing depicting the Villa d'Este in Tivoli (and one that Montaigne may have known) is a combination of a view, axonometric projections, and maps of the garden, to show off the greatest number of attractions. The artist who entered the garden with his sketchbook made personal drawings, which were fragmentary. The fountains in Pratolino drawn by Giovanni Guerra were intended to help him record the complicated and astounding way in which they worked.[4] Heinrich Schickhardt's sketch drawings also record many of the *meravigliose opere* in Pratolino and nowadays constitute invaluable documentary material.[5] The drawing of the Villa Lante in Bagnaia, which Giovanni Guerra based on a drawing by T. Ligustri (1596), in order to sketch "tutto il contenuto del Giardino di Bagnaia"[6] provides a good opportunity for taking a brief look at the Renaissance tourist-cum-artist. He may have been unable to purchase the drawing, so he hurriedly made a copy "in ristretto." How many times have we ourselves done just this when traveling!

It was, therefore, the travelers (tourists) and artists who immortalized the gardens because they already knew that they had returned to the realms of *res mirabiles,* as in ancient times. At the beginning of the seventeenth century, drawings which depicted contemporary Roman gardens devoted to *aedifici et ruinae Romae* began to appear. The garden was no longer simply a work worthy of admiration on the same scale as the architecture, but also a form of contemporary art comparable to the achievements of antiquity. The written word dominated Renaissance culture, and descriptions were written before paintings were made. A description was usually sufficient and was broader in scope. It was only later that illustrations began to be included—rather warily—in the treatises and manuals on how to create a garden.

The appearance of Jacques Androuet Du Cerceau's major work, and particularly, Johann Vredeman de Vries's pattern book certainly changed people's awareness about the design of the new garden. These depictions of gardens put

an end to a superficial knowledge about Renaissance designs in countries north
of the Alps. The twenty-eight engravings in the pattern book contained no text,
and Vredeman de Vries presents an explicit scheme for making use of the space
in the Renaissance garden. His small book, which found its way to a market
which already knew him rather well as the author of popular architectural
and ornamental pattern books, received favorable response; later, new editions
were published which inspired more than one imitator. When we examine the
many gardens in the paintings or panoramas of towns and cities, which seem
to be taken straight out of Vredeman de Vries's book, we ask ourselves if quite
so many gardens in this style were indeed created in Europe under the influence
of his pattern book or whether Vries in fact inspired the visual imagination of
the period? Did his engravings travel back and forth between the workshops of
painters and graphic artists, and did they find their way to the garden designers? They could probably be found in the hands of both, and in both instances
could provide a model for the late Renaissance garden, the influence of which
lasted until the middle of the seventeenth century.

FIGURE 7.1: View of a garden. From Johann Vredeman de Vries, *Hortorum viridari-
orumquae elegantes et multiplicis formae* (Antverpiae, 1583). Courtesy of National
Library at Warsaw.

In the fifteenth and sixteenth centuries, the garden acquired a new status in society. This status did not result simply from an interest in garden art, visiting and immortalizing the features, the awareness that these gardens sometimes cost a fortune and therefore could be a symbol of the owner's wealth or the affluence of the town. Another important change was the fact that the architects themselves began to take an interest in gardens. The formal Renaissance garden, which gradually developed a closer architectonic relationship with the residence itself, began to come within the domain of architects and engineers—the masters of *architecturae militaris*. The account of the Medici's Villa Castello contains the only garden description in Giorgio Vasari's *Le Vite*. This in-depth text, which appears under the life of the architect Tribolo, is evidence of how highly the ability to create gardens was rated and how these skills were attributed to architects. In the Middle Ages, pattern books, manuals and architectural treatises were already being illustrated. The fact that gardens began to fall within the sphere of interest of the architects led to a natural correlation arising between practical experience in designing and the need for explanatory illustrations.

Architects influenced the Renaissance garden in yet another way. Not only did the garden have a regular form; it also had perspective. Linear (geometric) perspective, called *costruzione legittima,* was discovered in Italy at the beginning of the fifteenth century when artists and architects began to work together. It was an academic technique used for presenting three-dimensional space and solid mass on a two-dimensional surface and was to become a crucial tool when representing the world as seen. The new type of geometrical garden, made up of box-boxlike interiors, was an ideal subject for depicting in linear perspective. It was also an ideal model for demonstrating the principles of perspective, which is why until the eighteenth century, gardens often appeared in textbooks on perspective and geometry. The gardens skillfully depicted by Androuet du Cerceau and Vredeman de Vries with the masterly use of perspective, constitute an illustrated annex to their works on the theory and technique of perspective, and Hendrick Hondius included some views of gardens in the *Institutio artis perspectivae* (1622).

The Renaissance nobleman not only knew about art and spent time collecting it, but he also decorated his home with works of art. It would seem that the ability to draw landscapes and gardens—a skill which flourished among eighteenth-century enthusiasts of traveling—was not a rare occurrence in the Renaissance period. Otherwise, Olivier de Serres would not have written about it in his popular treatise, as a skill recommended to every owner of a country residence, to help relieve his boredom. To fill the hours of solitude—he writes—the following skills come in handy: "arithmetic, geometry, architecture, perspective and drawing, in order to be able to depict fortresses, towns, castles, landscapes worthy of the notice of the nobleman; a knowledge of these arts enables him to draw a plan of fortresses, private houses, to arrange the buildings of his residence, garden, trees and to plan other elements skilfully and with favourable results."[7] In the privacy of a room, by the fireside, during the long winter evenings, amateur designs for gardens thus came into existence, in many variations, in part inspired by engravings, the illustrations in the manuals, and personal drawings made during travels. The connoisseur of gardens—John Evelyn—left behind drawings which were used to modernize his gardens and those of his brother.[8] Although Evelyn was not just an average amateur gardener, but a thoroughly educated lover and theoretician of garden design, it can be assumed that other "country gentlemen" just as easily took up a pen and began to draw gardens. During the Renaissance period, miniature models were widely used in the discussions between the garden designer and commissioner, so drawings—which were easier to execute—must have been used during the realization of the garden, in order to set down new ideas and requirements.

The depictions of gardens which the *pater familiae*—bored during the winter months in his *praedium rusticum*—would pull out from his collection to peruse confirmed his visual reception of the garden and indicated what features should be admired in the garden. Two impressive volumes by Jacques Androuet du Cerceau *Les plus excellents Bastiments de France* (1576 and 1579) show a bird's-eye view of a garden residence, an axiometric view, a plan, also taking into consideration some of the smaller details.[9] These two volumes emphasized the significance of garden art, and the significance of the garden in increasing the residence's value both formally and materially. The drawings which appeared at the same time as the engravings and which were earmarked—according to Françoise Boudon—for giving as luxury gifts, included a more sophisticated layout of the beds than was depicted in the engravings. This surprising fact says much about how fashionable gardens were becoming and the popularity of graphic images, which appealed not only to the educated artistic élite, but also to a wider circle of recipients with more traditional requirements. Not for the first time do we consider these depictions ambiguous. Even in a drawing crafted with characteristic cartographic precision, the Renaissance garden was depicted as it looked, or as it would look, or as it could have looked, and nowadays, it is often difficult to establish in all certainty which of these representations was the one which was being shown.

One hundred years after the publications of du Cerceau's work, Giovanni Battista Falda published several series of views of Rome and its neighboring

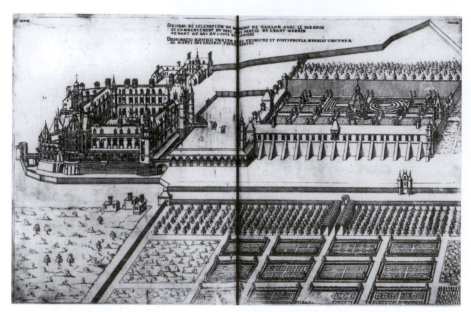

FIGURE 7.2: View of the castle with gardens and parc at Gaillon. From Jacques Androuet du Cerceau, *Le premier volume des plus excellents Bastiments de France* (Paris, 1576). Courtesy of Wroclaw University Library.

gardens, architecture and, above all, fountains. These were connected with the emergence of the new crucial, long-awaited water network in Rome. His very beautiful engravings, which were extremely popular (and which nowadays can be found in nearly every large library), popularized a clear and irresistibly simple model of the Renaissance garden throughout Europe at the turn of the seventeenth century. At this time, the new French style was already in fashion, making use of complex optical illusions, where the space was designed like a stage set, with the use of painterly perspective (gradation of colors). Meanwhile, Falda depicted a traditional, albeit striking, garden in which its modernity could be limited to the new ornaments for the parterres, and its splendor resting—as the people presented in it indicated—on magnificent fountains, cascades, vantage points on terraces. The people presented in the engraving show how the garden can be received, where to stand, from what angle the water theater, for example, should be looked at, and from which terrace of it the setting sun should be admired (a view from one of the fountains at the Villa Ludovisi in Frascati!).

The views of the gardens described previously were looked at in intimate settings: by one or several spectators discussing their journeys, getting bored in the country during rainy weather, designing changes in their residences. There were also depictions of gardens that were intended to be viewed by a wider

PRIMA FONTANA AVANTI IL PALAZZO DEL GIARDINO LVDOVISI À FRASCATI.

FIGURE 7.3: *The first fountain in front of the Ludovisi Garden palace at Frascati*. From Giovanni Battista Falda, *Le Fontane delle ville di Frascati*, part II (Rome, 1680). Courtesy of National Library at Warsaw.

public. These depictions were symbols of ownership, wealth, power—paintings or frescoes situated in interiors visited by many people.

Recording views of one's property for posterity became a widespread fashion during the Renaissance period. In the sixteenth century, two basic models of the residence were created: the house of the citizen, and the splendid ceremonial "court of the Duke," and this model had an influence on many cultural codes in Europe of the seventeenth and eighteenth centuries. The duke had to display his capabilities to his court, which accounted for, among others, the ever more and more magnificent interiors covered in frescoes and tapestries, and filled with sculptures and other works of art. He could boast of owning other residences by hanging pictures of them on his walls. Unequivocal proof of the fact that gardens could be regarded as a symbol of high social rank and affluence are the portraits depicting gardens as a background—often appearing above shoulder height of the portrayed person. On the whole, they depict specific gardens. Roy Strong collected and analyzed a large number of English portraits of this type. The collection begins with *The Family of Henry VIII* (ca. 1545) with their invaluable portrayals of the Whitehall Palace gardens.[10]

The presence of a garden in a portrait could be used to emphasize the intellectual or spiritual abilities of the portrayed person, such values being associated with the concept of cultivation (raising and caring for) or to give the portrait symbolic content. These gardens are depicted as an enclosed expanse of luxury, accessible to but a few people: the owner, members of his household and selected guests. When we look at the portrait of Alathea Talbot, countess of Arundel, by Daniel Mytens (1618), in which a view of the garden adjoining the house can be seen in the background in perspective, at the end of a gallery, or at the portrait of Thomas Howard, Earl of Arundel, attributed to the same artist (ca. 1627), with its garden full of antique sculptures—we are reminded of seventeenth-century Dutch paintings, in which the views of the interior with its collection of paintings, for example, included a bouquet of flowers standing on a table. A garden full of rare plants, imaginatively cut hedges—based on ancient forms—and elaborate fountains was the obvious complement to the collections of *artificialia et naturalia* that were becoming popular in the sixteenth and seventeenth centuries.

An interest in geography and cartography, combined with a desire to portray one's own residence, was characteristic of the Renaissance period and gave the hypothetical Duke the possibility of demonstrating "his own place within the context of *orbis terrarum*."[11] On the walls of the Palazzo Farnese in Caprarola, the family's estates and a view of the villa and gardens were depicted as if they were an "economic network of latifundia and part of a polycentric system." The residences of other owners were also portrayed, as in the splendid Palazzina Gambara gallery, decorated with frescoes and adorned with views of the newly emerging and "most fashionable" gardens of the Palaces in the Lazio region: the Villa d'Este in Tivoli, the Farnese in Capodimonte, and the Caprarola palaces and the villa in Bagnaia (the gallery was built between 1566 and 1578). These frescoes are evidence of the keen artistic awareness among the Italian elite, and the fact that the members of this elite compared their achievements in the sphere of patronage and in the sphere of designing gardens.

Gardens could also be presented as seen by the courtiers and guests during formal celebrations. Thus, the gardens of the Tuileries and Fontainebleau were transformed into a festival ground when receiving the Polish ambassadors who presented the Polish crown to the brother of the French king. These festivities were captured in the drawings of Antoine Caron (1573)[12] and in an unusually striking cycle of tapestries.[13] These tapestries froze this ephemeral spectacle in time, showing the significance of the fleeting decorations and effects that were one of the tools used to manipulate the sensibilities of the onlookers. Members of the Royal family were shown in the gardens and the land they ruled over. In this instance, the celebrations in the royal garden fired the imagination and were a symbol of power and political allegories.

A visit to the Museo Storico-Topografico Firenze com'era today is certainly as unforgettable an experience as was a visit four hundred years ago to the Tuscan Villa Artimino. We have before us fourteen views depicting the Medici villas, arranged like a virtual journey through a closed microcosmos—in an integrated Tuscan landscape. Giusto Utens (1599)—the Flemish author of these tempera landscapes (of which there were two others)—chose a high horizon line/vantage point (as they were to be presented in the lunettes), combining a normal view with a bird's-eye view. He, therefore, achieved cartographic precision. However, we can look at the façades of the villas and (although in very small numbers) discern people who are hunting or arriving at the residences. Daniela Mignani analyzes the inconsistency in the use of perspective in the works of Utens, which was due to him wanting to show all the features of the property, even those which, in reality, could not have been encompassed within a simple glance.[14] At the close of the Renaissance, in these depictions (which illustrated the estates owned by the family, and which were displayed in the villa, which was the center of the estate) perspective is no longer used as it was in the fifteenth century. That is, it is no longer an academic technique, but a tool for shaping reality.

Views of the garden in Wrocław belonging to the humanist Laurentius Scholz, and also of the graphic representations of, for example, the Villa d'Este in Tivoli, the Villa Lante in Bagnaia, the royal residences in Saint Germain-en-Laye and Fontainebleau of 1614, Neugebäude in Vienna, the gardens of Rome,[15] and the Jardin des Plantes Médicinales in Paris,[16] have keys to decode the letters which appear on various elements of the paintings. The gardens are rather too large to be quickly described and easily understood or taken in in just one glance. Gardens in the Middle Ages could be very extensive, but they were comprised of smaller, autonomous units. During the sixteenth century, however, the Renaissance garden grew from its boxlike interior—the parterre adjoining the residence—into a huge organism with a multi-thematic spatial structure, which included architecture, sculptures, water and flora. A person walking through it already needed help to see and understand everything, and not to miss anything. He was therefore provided with an engraving containing a view and explanations. So far, this sufficed. In the second half of the seventeenth century a guide would also be required.

Renaissance gardens were usually portrayed from an elevated vantage point. It was as if the onlooker was looking at it from a high terrace or floor of the villa; it was often a birds-eye view, at that time embracing a vista wider than just that of the residence. In the époque of the geometrical garden and the birth of the ornamental parterre and conviction that beauty depended on proportion and *symmetry,* it was self-evident that a view should be executed from an elevated vantage point. These attributes were only visible from an elevated position thus leading to the development of various kinds of galleries, logia, terraces, and elevated alleyways, which all served to help people admire the garden. The scale of views depicted from above did not often enable people to be shown in the garden. In time, views of individual features began to appear, such as the beautiful series of six views of Pratolino by Stefano della Bella (ca. 1658). These etchings portraying fragments of the garden almost at the eye level of the stroller, depict people walking, talking, marveling at the features in the garden, avoiding the water traps, sitting, and even sleeping on garden walls. Similarly to Falda, we not only can see the different ways in which a garden was experienced: walking along one of the axis or making an expressive gesture during a discussion in front of a sculpture or a fountain, but we can also see ordinary people, that is, those who do not necessarily belong to high society, just being in a garden. On leafing through subsequent pages of Falda's album, as we climb up to the higher terraces of the Villa Aldobrandini in Frascati, we notice that we are gradually leaving behind us refined society accustomed to its comforts. And what is typical of Italian gardens is that we, from time to time, come across men sitting on the grass in the company of bottles and baskets of victuals. At the end of the sixteenth century, given the considerable vastness of the gardens, figures of people were introduced into the views in order—we can only ascertain—to emphasize particular spots and to draw attention to all the possibilities for taking advantage of the attractions. Francesco Mingucci's drawing depicting a view of the *Parchetto* in Pesaro, is a good example of this.[17] The owner—Francesco Maria della Rovere—is shown in the foreground; thus, it depicts his estate. Many human figures were included where the owner and the designer of the garden wanted to emphasize a particular feature: near every building, on all the stairs, ramps, terraces, balconies of the villa, near the fountains, the benches, under the shady portico, and finally at the edges of the highest terrace, from where one of the figures is pointing to the surrounding mountainous landscape with an outstretched hand (and the engraver wrote the name of each mountain above the summit of each one). This is a way "of leading by the hand" the potential recipient of the garden who, for the moment, is only looking at a picture of it. Thus, with the help of human figures, the way in which the garden was received could be introduced into a visual depiction of it. By contrast to the paintings and frescos, which were formal portraits of the estates, engravings, which were becoming more and more popular at the beginning of the seventeenth century, provided information about famous works of garden art or an aid for those setting out on a journey. This was also why the human figures located in key spots around the garden played such an important role. The extended use of artistic models resulted in an increase of new ways of spending time in the garden.

When views showing specific details in a garden began to appear alongside panoramic views, series of representations of the very same garden could be produced, preceded by an overall view and plan with a description enabling the depicted fragments to be found on the plan. The first such cycle to be systemically produced was Salomon de Caus's *Hortus Palatinus* (1620). These thirty engravings depicting the garden of Frederick V's (the elector of the Palatinate's) residence in Heidelberg are a mine of valuable information. On examining these detailed fragments, created by the designer of the garden, and trying to find them on the overall view of the residence, which encompasses a landscape of somewhat cosmic proportions, the most interesting issue seems to be that some of these fragments were never actually realized. Which fragments were realized, and when, is not altogether clear.[18] De Caus executed a complete set of views when it appeared the huge garden was under threat of not being completed. The elector took up the Czech throne and left Heidelberg. The garden designer, therefore, executed these engravings mainly (according to the preface to the collection), in order to encourage Frederick to continue the work. Another reason could have been his desire to show other potential patrons what he was capable of achieving. It could also have been an attempt by the artist, who saw that his work of art would never be completed—to produce at least a "virtual" vision of his oeuvre in the form of a series of engravings. To us, this is good evidence of how misleading iconographical documents can turn out to be when we want to use them as historical evidence. However, they do not fail us when we use them to study people's awareness and visualization of gardens.

Gardens were portrayed in order to ennoble their owners. In the Renaissance period, having a garden became a social prerequisite, a sign of refinement and of belonging to a world of people with high aspirations. Not only could the owners boast of their gardens, but so could the town also. In the sixteenth century views and panoramas of towns frequently contained overly ostentatious depictions of gardens. The wealth of the town's inhabitants, which was based on commerce, can be discerned in the depictions of gardens painted in the style of J. Vredeman de Vries, which Anton Möller put in his *Allegory of Wealth* and which forms part of the triptych *Model of the world and society of Gdańsk* (beginning of the seventeenth century)[19]. Humanists ranked gardens very highly among the works of man, as they testified to his skills, inventiveness, wealth, and predilection for collecting. All these elements can be discerned in the fairytale portrayal of the Palace Gardens in Jerusalem in the painting titled *King David and Bathsheba* by the Polish artist Bartłomiej Strobel (1630).[20] The artist, who was at that time influenced by the Mannerist art of the imperial court in Prague, perceived this biblical scene according to the conventions of the ancient East. In the foreground is an exotic "jungle" with fashionable plants in vases and a fountain with a celestial globe and astrological symbols, similar to the one which was actually built in Prague in ca. 1600. In the background, as if in a dream, we can see a visionary panorama of Jerusalem with the garden of King David in front of it. This was quintessentially what the garden had become in the Renaissance period. It combined the concepts of artistic culture with splendour, *inventio,* affluence, and the important concept of *mirabilium.* Sixteenth-century gardens were a land of surprises and "miracles." They contained elements of entertainment that palaces and cloisters did not. They were amusing, surprising, and, at times, even dangerous. This is why Strobel imagined part of the garden like an exotic thicket with an ostrich and, at the same time, painters such as Roelandt Saverij and Gillis Claesz d'Hondecoeter painted paradisiacal gardens devoid of any geometry whatsoever, without any artificiality about them, close to John Milton's poetic vision. It is rather puzzling that at the beginning of the seventeenth century, during the triumph of the formal garden, painters seemed to be certain that Adam and Eve's Garden of Eden was a wilderness, despite the fact that in the Bible it was called a garden and was sometimes depicted as such in medieval miniatures.

Strobel's painting are classed among the depictions of imaginary gardens which emerged alongside the paintings, engravings and drawings mentioned above, and which—according to Strong's formulae—were portraits of places. Gardens which did not exist in reality included the model gardens, intended to be specimens for designers, and gardens which were allegorical elements. The former appeared in manuals that, in the sixteenth century, were still very poorly illustrated. The *Hypnerotomachia Poliphili,* with its richly and interestingly illustrated woodcut engravings from the circle of Andrea Mantegna, was not a manual, although it was used as one. Comprehensive views of gardens were only included in the book by Thomas Hill[21] and in some editions of *Opus ruralium commodorum* by Pietro de' Crescenzi[22]—although these illustrations have more of an informative than artistic value. The engravings with suggestions for garden design contained in the treatises by Joseph Futternbach (who was primarily a master of the theater) skillfully transform the Renaissance garden into something verging on the Baroque style. The drawings for

FIGURE 7.4: Bartłomiej Strobel, *David and Bathsheba*, 1630. Courtesy of Státní Zámek at Mnichovo Hradiště.

the engravings were executed by either Furttembach himself or others. Johann Jacop Campanus produced designs for mazes, one of which—with its parallel avenues of trees and innumerable gates—gives one the impression of being totally lost.[23]

Although such depictions were included in manuals that served a practical purpose, they are also an introduction to the graphics that developed in the seventeenth and eighteenth centuries and that contained an element of entertainment. These were both secular and religious, political, moralizing, often based on a riddle, a play on words, a rebus, and calligrams, which formed geometric patterns out of words. Gardens appeared in emblematic collections and symbolic graphics, usually due to their association with the joy of life (which was either well or badly assessed) and the virtues inherent in the gardener's work—such as patience and protectiveness—with both moral and physical cleanliness, as an attribute of the Virgin Mary or a symbol of the church looking after its flock. Because they were so perfect in their symmetry, they could symbolize the world of art, particularly architecture and music, due to their having a similar

mathematical structure. The presence of allegories of gardens from the fifteenth
century onward in the writings of the alchemists resulted in graphic depictions
of gardens sometimes appearing in these hermetic works. The garden's perfect,
latticed, closed form illustrated the concept of perfection in the alchemist's
opus, which was compared with the laborious, patient work of the gardener or
the farmer who helped plants undergo their transformation.[24]

Paintings that showed gardeners actually at work had a specifically moral
undertone. The medieval calendars included in the *Books of Hours,* portray
gardens full of gardeners in the spring months. These "encyclopedic" representations show the successive stages of the work undertaken on the estate
and the *exemplum* of diligence, which brought to mind the benefits this work
entailed. In Renaissance variations on this theme, the proprietor (or propri-
etress) or both of them were also portrayed, linking in this way the subject of
helping to carry out some of the spring tasks whilst out taking a stroll in the
garden. The garden was but one, albeit the most important, element of the
residence. As in the famous drawing by Pieter Brueghel the Elder—which,
thanks to an engraving by Pieter van der Heyden (1570), had an influence on
other artists[25]—apart from the work carried out in the garden, other work that
took place in the spring was also depicted, that is, relating to the farm animals,
ponds, meadows, the farmland, preparing the "May Tree," and so on. In these
compositions, the garden's appeal lay in its geometrical form, which was very
suitable for producing perspective views and when depicting rare plants, sometimes cut, sometimes in pots and baskets next to the prepared beds waiting to
be planted.

The months of the year were depicted allegorically. In March, the garden is
usually abuzz with work. In April, there is less work, however there are more
people walking and playing. Brueghel's composition—mentioned earlier—
contained motifs of games next to the theme of work. As in Medieval poetry,
the gardens and meadows are full of dancing and flirting couples. In a gouache
in the Czartoryski Museum in Kraków, Hans Bol portrayed nature in its various stages of maturity: on the left side of the painting, the trees are without
leaves, but they gradually develop toward the right side of the painting, as
they become covered in foliage. Likewise, the naked earth becomes covered
with grass, the heavens slowly clear, and the people's tasks in the garden also
change: to the left of the picture, they are working hard in the beds, but to the
right, they are simply dancing, and feasting in the bowers. This is an allegory of
Spring. Proof of the fact that we are also dealing with a depiction of the passing
of time can be found in an engraving titled *Spring* by Johannes Sadeler, based
on another of Bol's drawings. Above a similar depiction showing the changing

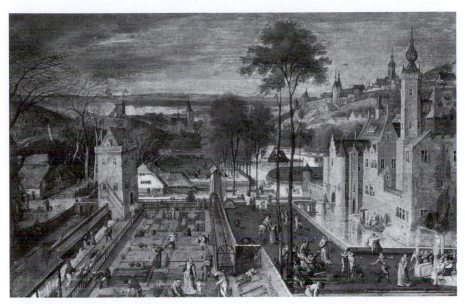

FIGURE 7.5: Hans Bol, *Spring in the Castle Garden*, 1584. Courtesy of Fundacja XX Czartoryskich, Cracow.

phases of nature, the weather, and people at work, the artist has included the three successive signs of the Zodiac denoting Spring: Aries, Taurus, and Gemini. Under Gemini, which is the sign for May, we can see people at play around a ritual tree, symbolizing the rebirth of Spring and the start of the season for young people's outdoor games.[26]

Depicting work in the garden in a more or less successive manner indicates that the garden was popular for showing allegories of Spring. It is a place in which nature is revived on an annual basis, a place of beauty and joy, and it became an allegorical landscape of love. The frescos in the Palazzo Schifanoia in Ferrara allegorically depicted April as the *Triumph of Venus*. The goddess, dressed in the fashion of the court, belongs to the world of the Early Renaissance *trionfi,* and the flirting couples are posing in gardens filled with rabbits, reminiscent of the concise allegorical nature of the lovers' retreat of the late Middle Ages. Admittedly, love is not governed by the calendar, nor is it only professed in gardens; however, the archetype of the *paradisus terrestris* resulted in the fact that the garden—both in poetry and in art—permanently and clearly, became a temple of love. In the imagination of artists and poets, it kept on reappearing as a special place, which gives us eternal youth. The miniature in the manuscript *De Sphaera,* attributed to Gregorio and Lorenzo Dati (fifteenth century), portrays a garden with "a fountain of youth," in which people are bathing, raising glasses, and are as happy as those who are seated around the fountain caressing each other and listening to music, close to a table laden with food.[27] The medieval meadow, strewn with flowers and surrounded by a wall, for some time still served the painters of the Renaissance as a preconceived reference to a "Paradise on Earth." This is the case, for example, in Lukas Cranach the Elder's painting titled *The Golden Age* (ca. 1530), in which the ancient myth merged with the biblical and the nakedness of the frolicking figures was supposed to be proof of their regained innocence.

The medieval tradition of the "Garden of Love" was continued in the Renaissance period and resulted in enamored couples beginning to be specific features of the pleasure garden, just like the flowers, birds and fountains. The illustration to a work by Crescentiis, which was translated into Polish, and in particular to the fragment which speaks of the large gardens (viridarium) of wealthy owners, was also used by printers in other books as a stereotype of a painting of a garden or Paradise. Renaissance art continued representing the Garden of Love, giving it a moralizing nature and showing the various stages of amatory pursuits. Symbols of amatory pursuits included a journey by boat, or a walk in the maze, a feature often found in Renaissance gardens

FIGURE 7.6: View of a garden. From P. de Crescentiis, *Księgi o gospodarstwie* (Kraków, 1549). Courtesy of National Library at Warsaw.

FIGURE 7.7: Benedetto Caliari (attributed to), *Garden of a Venetian villa*, 1555–1575. Courtesy of Accademia Carrara at Bergamo.

and in images of them, particularly from the end of the sixteenth century. In the first half of the seventeenth century in Italy and the Netherlands, numerous paintings also appeared depicting banquets held in gardens. In Dutch art, these include games played in groves as well as in the meadows adjoining the residences (*buitenpartijen*). These magnificent scenes depicting love and games, also popularized by artists such as David Vinckboons, Louis de Caulery, Esaias van de Velde, Willem Buytewech, and Dirk Hals were without doubt gardens of love with a moral significance and full of grand pictures of nouveau riche pastimes[28]. Often, the feasts at the table are accompanied by dances, couples strolling toward a far corner of the garden, pastimes on the grass, and tender and heated scenes. It is difficult, therefore, to distinguish between the garden of love in its pure form and the outdoor pleasures of refined company. The painting *Conversatie à la mode* by Peter Paul Rubens (1632–1633)[29] is an original and personal artistic vision and one in which the artist himself introduces the recently married and young Helena Fourment into the world of love and marriage. This is a garden of love based on personal experience, but it also shows various aspects of the relationship between men and women.

During garden parties, music often resounded and was accompanied by people at play, and this is reflected in paintings. Musical ensembles played for dancing couples or close to the bowers where the feasts were held; the participants also take up instruments and notes. In scenes which are explicitly amorous, the music of the playing and singing couples testifies to the harmony of their feelings. Music is the theme of a painting by Ludevic Toeputa (Pozzoserrato) titled *Concert in the garden* (ca. 1590). When looking at the lady sitting at the virginals in the foreground of the painting, we are reminded of the virginals from Antwerp, which were beautifully painted with scenes of gardens and couples at play.[30] The painting *Venus and Cupid with an organ player* by Titian showed, very succinctly, the similarity between music and the geometrical art of a garden within the context of the play between proportion and harmony of numbers, which was so important during the Renaissance period.[31] Etienne Delaune's drawing, which is an allegory of music (ca. 1570),[32] has a parterre with a particularly captivating polyphonic structure: a rhythmically captured balustrade behind which a labyrinth created from herbs intertwines harmoniously with a polyphony of circles and rectangles. A silver Limoges platter ornamented with enamel based on two other compositions by Delaune is devoted to an allegory of May.[33] We can see the garden divided into quarters with a meadow decorated with flowers; the music "resounds" in both these spaces: in the meadow, a lute is being played by a girl, and in the garden bower, a powerful sounding madrigal is being sung by five men bent over the notes.

Spring is love; love, as every humanist/Neoplatonist would tell us, is harmony, and therefore, Spring is music.

In the depictions of gardens of love, in particular in German and Dutch paintings, what is so striking is the presence of medieval elements in the form of adjoining meadows decorated for entertainments which appear right next to the geometric parterre.[34] It was here that the pavilion for the banquet was set up. Baths and huge fountains with bathing pools were set up here in the vicinity of the pergolas and bowers used for changing and resting. In Renaissance paintings, these bathing retreats located in the garden were attractive settings for the biblical tales of *Susannah and the Elders* and of *Bethsheba and King David*. Italian artists combined the theme of nudity with the garden, thus emphasizing its significance as a secret place, a place of sensual pleasure, *hortus conclusus* and a garden of love. In ancient poetry, the woman's body was compared to a garden—the quintessential example of this tradition was the *Canticum canticorum,* a work which exerted so much influence on the religious and erotic imagination of the Middle Ages—and discernible in the paintings of Benedetto Cagliari, Jacopo Tintoretto, and Baldassare Croce, in

FIGURE 7.8: Jan van Londerseel, after David Vinckboons, *Susanna and the Elders*, before 1624. Courtesy of The Metropolitan Museum of Art, New York, The Elisha Whittelsey Collection, The Elisha Whittelsey Fund, 1949 (49.95.2272).

which dazzling bodies, compete with the cold white of the fountain jets, and everything is surrounded by a luxuriant garden in full bloom. The surprised women seem to be more like models posing in the nude, representing beauty and fertility, similarly to the gardens that surround them. Northern artists such as Albrecht Altdorfer, Lukas van Gassel, and David Vinckboons visualized the theme rather differently. For them, it was not the female nude that was important, but the garden, and the biblical scene was only a pretext for the painting. Van Gassel placed small figures of Bethsheba and her companions in the background of the painting, amid a complex of several gardens. King David, who appears in the foreground—thus near the viewer—is gazing afar, in search of the heroine of the tale, thus leading the eye of the viewer in discovery of the architectural expanse of the gardens, which are skillfully depicted in perspective.[35] Similarly, but much later, the foreground theme of the engraving of *Susannah and the Elders* by Jan van Londerseel, according to Vinckboons was a *wilderness,* accompanied by a Renaissance parterre, full of garden animals, with a decorative fountain in a bathing pool.

In allegorical depictions, the garden was often only an attractive setting for an event. It was, however, at times also an autonomous symbol, as in religious themes: the Annunciation, the Madonna and Child, the Prayer on the Mount of Olives, *Noli me tangere.* In these instances, the garden emerges in all its artistic symbolism, set apart, described and popularized by theological writings, literature and poetry. Both fifteenth-century Flemish paintings and Italian paintings of the Quattrocento make use of Late Mediaeval iconographic traditions, combining the Mary of the *hortus conclusus* with the meadow with its symbolic flowers,[36] the fountain in the garden and the bush of roses. Early scenes of the Annunciation, including the most beautiful of these by Leonardo da Vinci in the Uffizi Gallery in Florence, delight us with their "medieval" meadows combined with marble benches, walls, and vases in the purest Renaissance style. This combination of the traditional meadow in which new architectural and sculptural details were added also appear in graphics in books, for example, German ones dating from the beginning of the sixteenth century, and therefore, we can probably believe that such gardens existed in reality. The garden in depictions of Christ's prayer on the Mount of Olives is reduced to a mere sign. In paintings such as Andrea Mantegna's the *Agony in the Garden* (ca. 1450) or Giovanni Bellini's,[37] "garden" is designated by a simple fence around the hills, a sacred boundary dividing the space where mystic events took place. The artists who painted these well-known stories from the Gospels could refer to people's knowledge of the basic significance of the garden and introduce it into the composition simply as a sign: a tree, a fragment of a fence, a carpet of flowers under the feet of the figures.

Art strengthened the association between the garden and the concept of abundance, gifts of nature, fullness, and prosperity. Garden skills, such as the cultivation of rare plants, importing and cultivating plants from overseas, the art of cultivating fruits trees and vines, were expressed in the allegories of Flora, Pomona, Spring, and the senses of Taste and Smell.[38] The figures in Sandro Botticelli's *Primavera* (1478) are stepping through a meadow amid an orange grove. This garden is a very natural one and not artificial. This changes in the later period. Representations of this allegory become a glorification of the garden as a place in which the artistry and ingeniousness of man can be seen. The main female figure is often placed in the foreground, surrounded by flowers and garden implements, an elegant garden behind her, in the background. Jan Massys's *Flora* with a view of Genoa and gardens (after 1550) provides additional documentary value for these kinds of depictions.[39] Both in this painting, and, for example, on the faience platter in the composition *La Belle Jardinière* (second half of the sixteenth century) by Bernard Palissy,[40] the master of ceramics, grottos and gardens—we can see the characteristic way in which flowers were displayed in allegories of the garden in the period 1550–1650. They are not only discernible in gardens, growing from the ground in rows and in vases, but they also appear in baskets (which was how they were taken into the house to be arranged into bouquets) or in decorative vases already arranged in a typical bouquet for the house, even though the scene is taking place outdoors. At this time, plant portraits began to develop, and it signaled the birth of the painted bouquets that flourished in the seventeenth century and melded permanently with the notion of Baroque culture. These Kingdoms of Flora—painted on many occasions by Jan Brueghel the Elder and his imitators[41]—also depict the garden as an *atelier* for decorating the interiors. When looking at the cupids filling baskets with flowers in Brueghel's garden, we look, in spite of ourselves, for a house or palace whose interiors will be filled with the bouquets arranged from these flowers. This stylistic device emphasized the significance of the garden for the collector and the value of its botanical resources.

Pomona is often portrayed in the company of Vertumnus—the god of transformation who seduced her. Jan van Kessel St. (*Vertumnus and Pomona*, mid-seventeenth century) made use of the pattern used in "Flora's garden," substituting the profusion of flowers with the richness of fruits and vegetables. A cycle of large tapestries, which Philip II commissioned from Wilhelm Pannemaker,[42] shows the subsequent stages of the young god's attempts to conquer the goddess of orchards and gardens, and they meet in front of a garden, which is remarkably like the description in the *Hypnerotomachia Poliphili*.[43]

It has long been known that metamorphosis takes place in the garden. This not only pertains to its cyclical nature. Ariosto, Tasso made the garden the seat of fairies, who changed the shape of reality. The developing skills of the gardener, the creation of new varieties of plants, the development of the orangery and *ars topiaria*, in which—contrary to Ovid's *Metamorphosis*—plants are shown as people, animals and objects caused the garden to be seen as a temple of magic and transgressions. This was one of the reasons why the garden began to be of interest to the theater. In the Renaissance, mannerist, and baroque periods, the garden came to be one of the basic conventional forms of stage decoration. The development of perspective painting and attempts to recreate the ancient theatre contributed to the creation of "box" scenes in Italian theater. The geometrical garden was a suitable medium for re-creating such theater. In the early modern era, garden scenery was among the most popular type of scenery— together with urban, pastoral, and sea scenery. Fantastic gardens were usually the seat of wizards, deities of love, temples of happiness and bliss, and places full of magical surprises. In the French baroque theater at court, a huge number of gardens were built on stage. Elements of the garden, for example, Mount Parnas, were built during festivals, *trionfi, cavallerie,* and tournaments.[44] The theater, on the other hand, also went out into the garden, where it was staged in a natural setting or was supplemented with garden scenery, certainly no later than from the staging of Niccolò Macchiavelli's *Mondragone*. Bernardo Buontalenti and his continuator Alfonso Parigi created magnificent gardens on the stages in Florence and these gardens inspired the imagination, for example, of Inigo Jones, the master of Stuart court masques;[45] and Joseph Furttenbach, who published designs for garden scenery; and the Polish prince Ladislaus Vasa, who, in the first half of the seventeenth century in Warsaw, created one of the most modern European theaters in which, of course, gardens also featured on the stage.

Gardens became increasingly popular in the theatre from the end of the sixteenth century. This popularity was due to the most important characteristics and representations of gardens in the fifteenth and sixteenth centuries, which included above all their relation to reality, perspective as a means of reproducing reality, the use of numbers as a basis for aesthetic expression and—at the end of the period—plants and their metamorphosis symbolizing the richness of nature, which overstepped the boundaries of the world as Man knows it and Man's abilities. Linear perspective—one of the great discoveries of the Renaissance period, which Leonardo da Vinci compared to philosophy, since it deals with the "movement" of increasing and decreasing forms[46]—found its main models in gardens and in architecture. Artists and enthusiasts derived great pleasure from depicting the main part of the garden (the parterre) and—what was more difficult—the tunnel arbors. Perspective had an impact on how gardens were presented and the choice of which areas were to be portrayed. It certainly also influenced how the garden was received, because the visual arts emphasized the significance of the parterre from the point of view of the perspective lines.

The way in which Neoplatonists and Neo-Pythagoreans evaluated reality, and the idea that beauty was based on numbers and *symmetria,* favored the development of geometrical forms in garden art. In his allegory *Pallas expelling the Vices from the Garden of Virtue* (1497), Andrea Mantegna—the master of stereo-metric views of objects and space—linked virtue and understanding to shapes cut into the garden, whereas vices are portrayed among natural forms, that are not created by man.[47] This painting is a representation of the garden of the Quattrocento—that is, the first phase of the Renaissance period, when the art of the geometrical garden had been mastered and had won popular acclaim. These gardens with their plants cut neatly in various forms were shown

FIGURE 7.9: Andrea Mantegna, *Pallas expelling the Vices from the Garden of Virtue,* 1497. Courtesy of Musée du Louvre, Paris.

FIGURE 7.10: A scene at a garden. From *Journeys and adventures of Charles the Great*, 1571. Courtesy of Bibliothèque Nationale de France, Paris, ms. Ad.134 Res.

in stark contrast to the freedom of nature. The reason for this kind of representation was ideological, but these representations seemed to turn a blind eye to the fact that in the real Renaissance garden, there were many widespread natural areas. One of these areas was the natural meadow, where games and feasts were held, and later it did not seem to get in the way when displaying the geometrical beauty of the parterre, which was shown in linear perspective. In contrast to a medieval one, the Renaissance garden represented a new form, a new type of space. This is also why visual reception of the garden dominated all the other senses—a feature emphasized in the visual arts. Artists often elected to portray the main part of the garden, making use of the opportunity to show off the art of linear perspective,[48] which at that time was one of the basic skills required of the painter.[49] Because fantasy and imagination were often subject matter for purely recreational art, the question has to be asked was whether the Renaissance garden was also, in all probability, a kind of three-dimensional game in which the viewer/connoisseur could find the effects of perspective and art, because the garden itself became like a painting—a work of art.

The introduction of the garden in the sixteenth century into the realms of the theater and the increasing number of decorative theater sets with a garden theme, which appeared at the beginning of the seventeenth century was a sign that the garden was evolving toward the baroque. It evolved from the visual to the dramatic:

from a depiction to a spectacle—from simply looking at it to surrendering oneself to illusions. The Renaissance garden, as depicted in art, does not exude a fragrance. It remains within the domain of sight. It was only in the second half of the sixteenth century that artists began to paint flowers in all their profusion—under the pretext of allegories of Spring or Flora—as if they had not existed in gardens before then. This was yet another step toward the Baroque and its search for illusion.

The discourse between gardens and the paintings in which they are depicted was beneficial both for art and for the garden. As far as the visual arts were concerned, gardens were an excellent subject for showing off the use of perspective. The art of designing gardens popularized the new styles and stereotypes of its reception and reinforced the symbolic meanings of gardens, in what they can tell us, or in the awareness of the educated strollers. The virtual Renaissance garden, created by the visual arts, reappears from time to time, recalled by artists. Italian games and boat trips, which were widely developed in Dutch art, inspired the paintings of Antoine Watteau and many of his imitators. The Pre-Raphaelite period saw the return of the quiet nooks found in the Renaissance gardens, the fountains, and the *Hypnerotomachia Poliphili*. Contemporary photographs, which can be found in the albums and manuals of garden historians, show the same preferences as those of the Renaissance artists. Views of the parterre, or other interesting details—either a fountain or a cascade—also predominate. The incomplete nature of the artistic medium used is one of art's faults as well as attractions. However, we can always leave the art gallery and go for a walk in a Renaissance garden, sit among the scented plants in it, in an accidental place, far away from the axis, far away from the parterre.

Translated by Anne-Marie Fabianowska

CHAPTER EIGHT

Gardens and the Larger Landscape

MIRKA BENEŠ

For people of the early modern period, known in Western societies as the Renaissance and the baroque period, the larger landscape was, in one way or another, an integral element in the making of gardens. The garden was a bounded property of limited extension, surrounded by some kind of wall, and what was not contained inside belonged, by definition, to the larger landscape outside—be it wild, agricultural, or urban. But inclusion and exclusion operated on a spectrum of many gradations. At one end of the spectrum, even a totally enclosing perimeter wall acknowledged the presence of the larger landscape by excluding it.[1] In the middle of the spectrum, a garden could both exclude the larger landscape by means of a surrounding parapet and yet also incorporate views of it, for example in the small terrace garden of the Palazzo Piccolomini at Pienza (1459–62), with its *theatrum* of superimposed loggias that afforded magnificent views over both the garden itself and the countryside extending into the distance. At the other end of the spectrum, a garden could appear coextensive with the larger landscape, to the point of being nearly indistinguishable from it, as in the cases of some seventeenth-century villa parks in Rome and of later seventeenth-century English landscape gardens, for example, the many illustrated in Johannes Kip's *Nouveau Theatre*

FIGURE 8.1: Garden of the Palazzo Piccolomini, Pienza, built 1459–62. Photograph by the author.

de la Grande Bretagne (London, 1713–16), and, of course, eighteenth-century ones such as Rousham Garden (1737–43). Peoples of early modern societies were quite clear about the many and complex relationships between the two spheres, as we shall see from several of their garden designs and from their written and visual documents.

Garden historians have only recently begun to pay attention to these relationships between garden and larger landscape.[2] Traditionally trained as art historians with an emphasis on the art object, they had tended to excerpt and isolate the gardens from their larger physical contexts. Only very recently have they tried to recover these original contexts, with important contributions made by geographers, social historians, and practicing landscape architects, raising awareness of the larger geographical, natural, and social systems in which gardens are embedded.[3]

In this chapter, I propose that what was greatly prized in many cultures was not so much the separateness of designed garden and larger landscape, but what I call here the *tension between* the two. The tension was structured by the degrees of separation and by the various forms of inviting in the larger landscape, or representing it, or projecting the garden out into the landscape, and the resulting formal configurations were in turn embedded with social, cultural, and economic values that varied according to each society and its culture. Factors such as climate and security were, of course, broad determinants of the tension and its cultural values: harsh climates and poor security led to sharper distinctions between garden and larger landscape, whereas amenable climates and better security enabled a greater merging of the two. In the case of many Persian gardens, usually set in arid and desertic environments, the relationship was one of either/or, either the garden or the larger landscape. In the case of many Italian and French gardens, it was one of both/and, both the garden *and* the larger landscape, and even the garden *as* the larger landscape.

In what form or by what means was the larger landscape made to participate in the tension garden/landscape in the Europe of 1400–1700? There are many ways in which a synthetic look at this phenomenon could be structured, but I choose to treat it here by focusing on one paradigmatic culture of garden design, that of Italy (specifically Rome), reviewing its major design developments and the cultural lenses through which these operated. This allows for specificity and a close look at how the larger landscape was engaged. In the conclusion to the chapter, I attempt to contextualize the Roman situation and to raise some of its broader implications for gardens in sixteenth- and seventeenth-century France.

Overall, in the period 1400–1700, particularly in Europe, the larger landscape was increasingly brought into the design of gardens, far more than previously. Several political and cultural developments over the three centuries in question help explain this heightened attention to the larger landscape. One was the steady increase in the political control by Renaissance princes over sovereign states and thus over natural resources and the landscape. Another was the increase in economic and symbolic values of landowning and land uses for the elite classes. Still another was the renewed study of geography and topography from the Renaissance on, deriving content and authority from the classical authors of the ancient world, but also driven by the practical needs of trade and colonization in new worlds, the Americas and Asia.[4] The political confidence of early Renaissance princes, in their homelands, was decisive in engaging the larger landscape materially, but soon each development was feeding the other, and their relationship was dialectical across the period we investigate. The princes and the elites became very adept at enlisting geographical culture as part of political and ideological strategies to organize their states and lands. Sixteenth-century Medici villas, such as the ones at Castello and Pratolino, were used to represent these strategies in garden forms. In this way, they can be called garden representations of state or national territories. So can the later Vaux-le-Vicomte and Versailles in France.

These political and cultural developments affected garden design not only by generating increased attention to the larger landscape but also by shaping the character of that landscape, hence the kind of role it played in garden design. For example, in early modern France, the sovereign financial investment in and control of infrastructure and natural resources—roads, fortifications, ports, river systems, transportation canals, forestry management, and so forth—were progressively reflected and embedded in the design of the gardens, particularly between 1550 and 1700. In Rome and the Papal States, by contrast, such infrastructural investment was more limited and sporadic, and so was its presence in garden design. While, already in the 1400s, the northern Italian states of Lombardy and the Venetian Republic sponsored the building of irrigation and transportation systems, still in the 1700s the absence of such systems in the Papal States and southern Italy led travelers, especially those from northern Europe, to be astounded at their lack. Gilbert Burnet, traveling in the 1680s, was struck by the relationship between northern Italian governmental strategies and their beneficial stewardship of the larger landscape, as he left the carefully cultivated lands of the Veneto and entered the abandoned farmlands of the papal state of Ferrara, crossing "the Po [River], which divides the territory of the republic from the Ferrarese, which is now the Pope's country; and here one sees what a difference a good and bad government makes in a country; for tho' the soil is the same on both sides of the river, . . . [in] Ferrara: I could not but ask all [whom] I saw, how it came, that so rich a soil was so strangely abandoned?"[5]

The political and material interest in larger landscapes in this period intersected with long-standing concerns with landscape in arts such as poetry, painting, and garden design, which could thus mediate between the political forces and garden design; these were often structured by notions of the pastoral, a theme to which we shall return. The tension "garden/landscape" had long pre-existed the Renaissance period: because of the great importance of geography, topography, and landscape in ancient classical culture—in rhetoric (the *artes dicendi* used landscape types for a hierarchy of expressions), literary genres, visual arts, history, and political writings—the Renaissance and Baroque ages de facto inherited or recovered a large lexicon of antique literary and visual representations of both larger landscapes and of gardens, often placed in dialectical tension. Ancient Roman frescoes of topographical and larger landscape scenes, frequently integrated with garden elements, were known in Renaissance and Baroque Rome, for example the rocky landscape with cave, waterfall, shrines and garden structures in an ancient wall painting discovered by the Barberini family in Rome in 1627 and copied several times, including in paintings of the

FIGURE 8.2: Pietro Santi Bartoli, "Barberini Landscape," engraving based on painting ca. 1635. From P.S. Bartoli et al., *Picturae antiquae cryptarum Romanarum et Sepulcri Nasonum delineatae* (Rome, 1750). Private collection, photograph by the author.

1630s, a drawing of 1661 by Claude Lorrain, and prints.[6] Through the Roman Renaissance and Baroque examples, European gardens shared this revival of classical landscape, and above all through landscape themes drawn from ancient literature; in Italy, that return to the antique was also strengthened by absorption and reinvention of what could be gleaned from ancient Roman landscape architecture on the ground.

BEL-VEDERE: THE GARDEN AND THE VIEW IN ITALY

From the early 1400s on, one of the most privileged aspects of the garden/landscape relationship was the view. The Alpine and Appennine mountain ranges that structured the Italian peninsula's topography afforded a hilly landscape with natural terracing and overlooks, as well as many cliff-like coastal areas. The beauty of the peninsula's natural and cultivated landscapes had been celebrated since the ancient poetry of Virgil, Horace, Ovid, Statius, and others, who however made clear that there were both good and bad landscapes, safe and dangerous ones, beautiful and desolate ones, each with their societal and emotional meanings. As in most Mediterranean countries, in Italy, the garden as a distinct type could be found in locations that ranged from within city walls to suburban or peri-urban areas to rural countryside, and even in areas of semi-wilderness, each of these locations bringing the garden into juxtaposition with urban, rural, or wild scenery. When it was in suburban or countryside landscapes, the garden was almost always part of a villa, whether it was more vernacular in character or dignified by the design of an architect. Leon Battista Alberti, preparing his *De Re Aedificatoria* in the 1440s, deemed the gentleman's or nobleman's villa (not the farmer's house) as both the viewing box and the object of a view: "Moreover, I would prefer to locate the house of a gentleman somewhere dignified, . . . where it could enjoy all the benefit and delight of breeze, sun, and view. It should have easy access to the fields, . . . ; it should be in view, and have itself a view of some city, town, stretch of coast, or plain, or it should have within sight the peaks of some notable hills or mountains, delightful gardens, and attractive haunts for fishing and hunting."[7] In all parts of Italy, the denomination "bel-vedere" cropped up in countless villas, concomitant with the growing significance of the view. This was not a new phenomenon, but rather one that received a new emphasis in Renaissance culture; it was a *continuatio* from ancient Italy that had never really been broken, and as new princes secured their sovereign territories and security increased, the opportunities for viewing the landscape increased too.[8] For centuries preceding, viewing the cityscape or the larger landscape outside the city had been part of the design of palaces, villas, and even monasteries. The examples can range from the Villa Rufolo ca. 1200, a palace-villa complex at Ravello on the Amalfi coast with one of its loggias facing the sea and the hilltop garden terraces; to Giotto's frescoes of the town of Assisi painted ca. 1300 in the Upper Basilica of San Francesco, showing belvederes built on the tops of houses to catch the views; to the hilltop Carthusian Monastery of Ema at Galluzzo just south of Florence, founded ca. 1340, where each cell has not only an enclosed garden but also a loggia on an upper story looking out over the landscape.

It is against this tradition that the Renaissance predilection for the loggia in the villa building and also next to the garden can be seen, whether it remained as representation, as with the castle-with-loggia high on the hill and facing a vast landscape below in Benozzo Gozzoli's fresco of *The Procession of the Magi* (1459–60) in the family chapel of the Palazzo Medici (later Riccardi), Florence, or was actually built into the main house. The loggia was frequently used as the mediating device between palace and garden, and if the garden faced a landscape, the loggia could allow for a rich set of views over both garden and landscape, or each singly. This was the case with the stunning views southward at Pienza over the small garden of the Palazzo Piccolomini and farther out to the vast landscape beyond on the border between Tuscany and Latium. Three superimposed loggias rise the whole height of the palace's rear façade and constitute a viewing theater to the landscape, an innovative concept that would be repeated variously thereafter, for example at the Villa Aldobrandini at Frascati near Rome, built ca. 1600, where superimposed loggias provide viewing boxes onto the rear hillside gardens. Pius II Piccolomini, writing eloquently in his *Commentarii* of the views that had been literally constructed for him at Pienza, practiced the ancient art of describing the larger landscape: "[t]he view from the three porticoes to the south is bounded . . . by towering and wooded Mt. Amiata. You look down on the valley of the Orcia . . . and fruited fields and vineyards, towns and citadels and precipitous cliffs . . . "[9] But his landscape viewing was not only steeped in the classics of Greco-Roman Antiquity, it also took place in the present, facing south toward Rome, the seat of the papacy and of his power. And it was connected to this humanist's expanding interest in ancient and modern geography.[10] At Pienza, the larger landscape is greatly emphasized, and it was even more so in the garden's original state with a lower parapet, but it does not touch the garden's design, except for its position, and the garden remains separate and self-referential: garden and larger landscape are two separate worlds.

Alberti's precepts about the villa's views and Pienza's example were elaborated on for centuries thereafter in Italian villa garden design and in French gardens. Most travelers to Italy and many native inhabitants who frequented the villa gardens praise implicitly or explicitly the juxtaposition of garden and larger landscape through the device of the view.[11] The examples are so numerous, from the time of the Villa Medici at Poggio a Caiano (near Florence) on, that just one classic instance can be recounted here, namely that of the Villa Madama at Rome, built ca. 1518–25 by Raphael. Before his early death in 1520, Raphael had composed a letter giving a tour of the villa, in the style of Pliny the Younger's two letters on his own villas, in which the complex itself was described as on "a high point, in a dominant position in the landscape" and the views from the main palace gave onto "the beautiful countryside, the Tiber and Rome," while the villa itself was surrounded by gardens, "the grounds of the villa abound with trees, as is fitting for such a building, . . . "[12] Andrea Palladio would take this approach, when possible, to his villa sites in the Veneto, placing the Villa Capra (La Rotonda) "sopra un monticello" (on a little hill) outside Vicenza, and he and his successor, Vincenzo Scamozzi, would emphasize in their architectural treatises the siting of villas for their views.[13] Later visitors experienced the same tension between garden and larger landscape. In April 1661, Balthasar Grangier de Liverdis, a French visitor to Rome, toured the Villa Madama and contrasted in juxtaposed sentences the refreshing interior delights of the garden's groves, covered walks, and water jets with the view to the exterior landscape, seen from the basin-shaped site itself, wide open like an amphitheater, providing panoramic views of the city of Rome, its surrounding fields, and even the distant hill towns such as Frascati and Tivoli.[14] In the century and a half between Raphael and the French visitor at the Villa Madama, visitors and natives alike in Rome and other parts of Italy would often use the view with its binary contrasts of garden/landscape to express their experiences of villa gardens, basing their phrasing on that of Pliny the Younger in his letter about his Tusculan villa and its amphitheatrical larger landscape.[15]

The larger landscape and its structures were always present in the minds of visitors, who, when they were literate and educated, had training in a kind of "geographical thinking," as I call it, from reading the classical geographers, historians, and poets, which structured for them the situation of a city or a villa garden in its larger site. Nicolas Audebert, for one, took in the broad geographical siting of the town of Tivoli and the Villa d'Este on the mountainside, and wrote in his journal in 1576: "[t]he siting of Tivoli is on the slope of the mountain that traverses all Italy in its length, named Mount Appennine,

FIGURE 8.3: Villa Barbaro, Maser, built ca. 1550–59. Photograph by the author.

which is very high . . . The countryside is lovely and pleasant, the air very good and healthful, and the lands very fertile."[16] Devoting several pages to the abundant natural waters of the site, Audebert quotes from Virgil's *Aeneid,* Book VII, about the cold water of the Aniene River, *"gelidumque Anienem."*[17]

FIGURE 8.4: View of the villas at Frascati, near Rome, engraving, ca. 1660. Private collection, photograph by the author.

The views created from Italian villa gardens, and towards them, had not only aesthetic roles but also major political and symbolic ones, for example, those of the possessive or lordly view over both villa gardens and landholdings held by the villa owner—as it was for Pius II at Pienza and the Medici at their villas in Tuscany. Recently, Marcello Fagiolo has demonstrated the importance of striking physical, visual, and symbolic axes that were forged by the deliberate orientation of villa buildings in the larger urban and suburban landscapes of Rome; he has also shown this for villas and ancient sacred sites in the countryside of Latium. Roads and vistas linked villas to important antique monuments, other villas, and urban centers. Margherita Azzi Visentini has focused on the siting of villas and gardens in the larger landscape for both the Veneto and the Latium. David Coffin, Claudia Lazzaro, and, most recently, Denis Ribouillault have shown for such key gardens as the Villa d'Este the roles that painted portraits of the gardens played in the visitor's experience of the latter through views, movement and memory; for example, Ribouillault has pointed to the Villa d'Este's symbolic connections to specific mountains and structures in the surrounding larger landscape.[18]

Axial views were aligned with approach roads and were used to focus attention in the larger landscape directly on the villa and its entrance, its façade or face to the landscape. The Villa Madama, according to Raphael's letter, was located at the center of four such approach roads, including ones coming over the Monte Mario towards Rome. The Villa Giulia (1550–55) too was given grand axial approach roads from the Tiber to the main façade. The Villa Farnese at Caprarola has on its main façade a loggia from which one can see along a grand axis cut willfully from the palace through the old town, beyond it and, as the view dramatically widens outward, across the sweep of the Roman countryside for some fifty miles beyond. The use of the view at Caprarola represents a highly charged symbolic gesture, conveying the *signoria* or seigneurial ownership of the Farnese over their fief and its subject lands. The tradition of such views and axes was strong in the Roman countryside, where nobles organized their palaces and villas along a dominant axis from palace to countryside, expressing lordly rule, for example at Fraicati. Palladio and other Veneto architects situated their villas in the fields in relation to axial approaches, older or newly created ones; a dominant axis led from palace and gardens through the estate and into the countryside. In many instances, the tree-lined avenue was the modus operandi, the trees serving not only to break the wind and to provide shade but also for their visual and iconographic significance as extensions of the order of the garden into the larger landscape and as expressions of the power of the owner who could afford to plant them.

The axial domination of the larger landscape by the aristocratic country residence was adapted, partly on the Italian model, partly on one of the French château garden—Vaux-le-Vicomte, Chantilly, Meudon, and Versailles are key examples—in indigenous traditions all over Europe, from Spain and England to Poland and Scandinavia. It was used in Italy from the later seventeenth century on, from the Venaria Reale complex (1660–72) near Turin, capital of the Savoy Duchy, to the palace, gardens, and forest of Caserta (1750s) near Naples. The central role of these axes connecting the garden and the larger landscape was as power axes, expressing the rule of the lord over the land, but they also articulated the tension between the order of the garden and farmlands and the uncultivated forms of nature further distant.

FOUR WAYS TO DESIGN WITH THE LARGER LANDSCAPE

More could be said about the view, especially about the design strategies used to manipulate it, but in the interest of brevity, I turn to highlight four other approaches by which a *tension between* garden and larger landscape was set up in Italian gardens. Although the view works essentially by connecting or juxtaposing the garden and the larger landscape, the "here" and the "there," these four approaches operate by transposing some qualities of the landscape into the garden, or vice versa. After briefly highlighting these four approaches, I then elaborate on two of them that are particularly important in the Roman context.

First, we can consider garden forms that came to define the identity of Italian gardens, such as podiums, terraces, ramps, and staircases. These are hybrid forms, architectural in their geometries, vocabulary, and techniques, yet used to shape and contain landscape elements such as earth and water. When used at large, topographical scale—the scale of hills and valleys—they amount to a parallel, *constructed architectural landscape,* emulating inside the garden the scale and disposition of the larger landscape outside, in imitation of how this had been done in Roman Antiquity with the merging of infrastructure and landscape. Ancient Roman designers had architecturalized the landscape by following contour lines of topography, reinforcing them and building on them: Hadrian's Villa and the ancient Sanctuary of Fortuna Primigenia on the mountainside at Praeneste (modern Palestrina) are striking examples of this practice. The Villa d'Este displays this approach with the monumental terraces that structure the slope of the hill, and with the fishponds that structure the valley at the bottom of the hill: both hill and valley are architecturalized. This approach was, of course, particularly widespread in Rome and Latium, where many large-scale ancient sites survived and where villas were often sited right atop their ruins, for example, from the 1550s the Farnese Gardens on the Palatine Hill and the Villa Medici on the Pincian Hill in Rome, many villas at Frascati, and later, the Villa Barberini at Castelgandolfo in the Alban Hills, built in the 1630s on top of the immense terraces of Domitian's imperial villa named Albanum.

Second, the larger landscape was evoked by being *represented* in or *incorporated in* the garden at much smaller scale than the natural forms of that landscape, that is, through designed metaphors and allegories. Geographical and poetical thinking, based on ancient texts and on the discovery of actual ancient artifacts, including villas and garden sculptures, led to artificial representations of larger natural systems such as caves, springs, rivers, hills, and mountains in the form of grottoes, fountains, and sculptures—as seen from early in the sixteenth century in Rome, at the Vigna Cesi, Vigna Carpi, and Villa Giulia, and as noted by Audebert on his visit to the Villa d'Este in 1576: "And at the end of this platform [of the Rometta], there is a old bearded man, lying on his side, which is only of stone and represents the Tiber."[19] Not only sculptures and water, but also plantings, were used representationally and metaphorically.[20] The planting of regular groves (*boschetti*) of trees was deployed to stand for cultivated, agrarian landscapes and an ordered, idealized version of them, imparting ideas and emotions of order and harmony; less regular, more naturalistic groves, as would be found in a woodland in the larger landscape, were planted to represent forests (*boschi*), with implicit associations of the *orrido* (fearsome) and the wild.[21] Allegory and metaphor, used to evoke larger geographies and their features, are particularly evident in many of the sixteenth-century Medici villa gardens, both in Florence and in the countryside. The colossal Appennine statues that, along with river god statues and Appennine fir groves, consorted to represent the geography and dominion over nature of the Tuscan ducal realm in the Villas Medici at Castello (1540s) and Pratolino (1560s) were among the most famous of this type in their day. This very important aspect of the relationships between Central Italian gardens and their larger landscapes, mediated through metaphorical and figurative representation of natural systems and topography, has been investigated in key studies over several decades, in particular those by David R. Coffin, Elizabeth B. MacDougall, John Dixon Hunt, and Claudia Lazzaro, so I do not dwell on it here, but raise it contextually as called for by the discussion. The issue is one of representation, and it is striking to see how natural it was in Audebert's day and at the just-built Villa d'Este to speak of "representation" in this way—including his use of the words *fort bien representez*.[22]

The third approach is in many ways closely related to the second, because it operates by bringing in and *incorporating* into the garden certain features

FIGURE 8.5: Fountain of the River Gods, the Tiber and Arno, Villa Lante, Bagnaia, built 1570s. Photograph by the author.

usually found in larger landscapes. However, what is brought into the garden is a living replica or enhancement of natural features—in the configurations, scales and forms that would actually be found in the wider landscape, rather than just sculptures or fountains or groves representing that landscape metaphorically or allegorically. It appears to be unmediated nature, yet it is consciously reproduced and laden with symbolic meanings. In other words, instead of stone river gods and Colossi one would find streams, meadows, forests, or tree groves, rocks, lakes, hills, and valleys, re-creating the configurative environment of a natural setting and its sensory experiences. When reconstructed at *landscape scale,* these larger incorporations usually changed the concept of the garden to become something else, namely, the park.[23] Several villa parks in this category are examined more closely further on.

In the fourth approach, the garden was *connected* or *extended to,* or *projected into* the larger landscape by means of means of dominating axes, often tree-lined avenues, as we saw earlier, and by the gardening of that landscape outside the garden limits, making it into a coextensive park-like, managed environment, in which cultivated or even semi-wild areas were graced with garden elements, such as avenues of trees, orderly groves, and fountains; at times, they contained streams, ponds, artificial lakes, seating, and small buildings for rest, dining, and leisure. Garden and larger landscape shared an overall connection of gardening, but the garden proper was a separate enclosed unit whereas the larger landscape was not necessarily bounded by estate walls. Among the simpler forms of this approach were the villas, along with their irrigation and planting infrastructure, built by Andrea Palladio on the Veneto terra ferma.[24] More complex in their design of the larger landscape were the sixteenth-century Medici villas in grand-ducal Tuscany. The seventeen principal ones were portrayed in a cycle of lunettes painted for the grand hall of the Villa Medici at Artimino in 1599 by Justus Utens, and many of them show this approach to gardening the larger landscape beyond the walls of enclosed pleasure gardens or estate compounds. Just as in the case of the Veneto villas by Palladio, so the gardening of the landscape be-yond the Medici villas had much to do with the exploitation and preservation of natural resources. Documents for their construction confirm this for the Villas Medici at Collemignoli, built 1568–72 in the mountainous area of the Vallom-brosa, east of Florence, and at Serravezza, built 1562–68 in the hilly area north of Pisa, close to the sea, both for Cosimo I de' Medici.[25] In fact, Suzanne B. But-ters recently compared Collemignoli and Serravezza, with their hunting lodges, lakes, and vast fir plantations, to English landscape gardens:

> [At Collemignoli] New plantations of fir-trees formed a visual bridge to the surrounding forests and artificial lake, unbroken by an enclosing wall. This must have produced an impression of blended woodland contiguity, similar to the effect created for agricultural landscapes by eighteenth-century Eng-lish ha-has. So it had also been at Cosimo's Seravezza, with its mountain backdrop of thousands of newly planted fir-trees and "selva dei castagni."[26]

The next sections of this chapter focus on Roman villa gardens and are devoted to a closer examination of two of the approaches just outlined: that of creating parallel constructed architectural landscapes at topographical scale in garden design since 1500 and that of incorporating the larger landscape in villa parks from 1550 to the late seventeenth century. Both are specific to the Roman situation—to Roman topography, to a keen interest in antiquity, and to the sociopolitical conditions of the papacy in the early modern period.

THE ANTIQUE LANGUAGE OF CONSTRUCTED ARCHITECTURAL LANDSCAPES

The first approach that I will examine more closely, the creation of archi-tecturalized landscapes through terracing and similar devices carried out at a topographical scale, was inaugurated by Bramante at the Belvedere Court

(1501–04), then repeated by Raphael at the Villa Madama (1516–20), by Girolamo Genga at the Villa Imperiale at Pesaro along the Adriatic coast (1525–35), later by Pirro Ligorio at the Villa d'Este (1560–72) and by Nanni di Baccio Bigio at the Villa Medici in Rome (1560s–80s), and it would shape countless gardens over two centuries, constituting either the whole garden (as at the Villa d'Este) or the formal core of a much-larger estate (as at the Villa Pamphili, Rome, almost a century later). This design approach was explicitly inspired by the example of ancient Rome, relevant not only because of the ubiquitous presence of its ruins but also, especially, because recent historical developments had conferred a new powerful political relevance to it. The design and construction of the Belvedere Court for Pope Julius II took place within a political and ideological program of urban and architectural *renovatio* of ancient imperial scope, both within the Vatican compound with the huge-scale rebuilding of the old Saint Peter's, and in the city of Rome with the new straight streets, Via Giulia and Via Lungara—all of them, church and streets, conceptualized at the scale of the landscape. The Church in Rome was reasserting its global—imperial—image, especially in the face of the recent fall of Constantinople to the Ottoman Turks in 1453, which marked at once a new threat to the Christian West and a restored prominence of Rome as its sole center, now that the Byzantine church had lost its own imperial seat of Constantinople. Indeed, in its overall imagery, the 1,000-foot-long Belvedere Court can be seen as a Roman Catholic version of Constantine's hippodrome and palace complex in what had now become Istanbul. Besides this overarching reference, other ancient models in Rome itself played a role. One was the ancient Sanctuary of Fortuna Primigenia on the mountainside at Praeneste twenty miles east of Rome, where the sanctuary's ramps and terraces recast the mountain in architectural form. Another was the Palatine hill in Rome, with its imperial palaces and the sunken stadium court next to the palace of Domitian. Yet another was the topographical scale of many buildings and walkways linking palaces and gardens of Hadrian's Villa at Tivoli, which also inspired Raphael at the Villa Madama (fig. 8.6). And the flat terraces that crowned the two symmetrical and immense multistory sides of the Belvedere Court were like ancient viaducts: in fact, Julius II had placed the bronze letters of a dedicatory inscription over the main outer portal to the Court, later called the Porta Sant'Anna, which read . . . IVLIVS II . . . VIAM HANC . . . (this road). All of these sites also shared the quality of hybridity.

By creating garden platforms and terraces that were at the scale of the pre-existing hill or valley, Bramante, Raphael, and Ligorio left behind the self-referential quality—the *hortus conclusus*—of the Quattrocento gardens of Pienza and even the Villa Medici at Fiesole. And they did this despite the fact

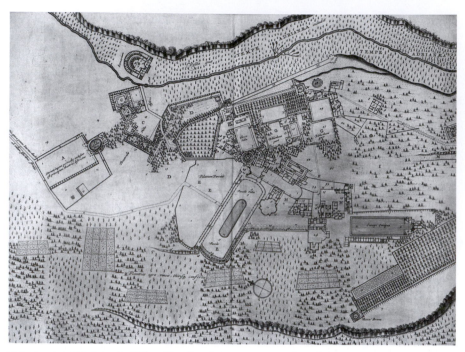

FIGURE 8.6: Hadrian's Villa, Tivoli, plan, engraving based on a survey drawing of
1634–36. From Athanasius Kircher, *Latium Id Est Nova, & parallela Latii tum veteris,
tum novi descriptio* (Rome, 1669). Private collection, photograph by the author.

that these huge artificial landscapes of the period 1500–50 were essentially
enclosed spaces with or without views of the larger landscapes outside. The
tension between garden and larger landscape established by these complexes
resides in the garden itself, more than in physical or visual continuity between
garden and landscape—it resides in the ambiguous hybridity of the design
forms themselves. At the Villa d'Este the slope of the main hill is structured
by nine very long, horizontal cross-avenues that are like terraces, the *xysti*
so praised by Raphael in his letter on his Villa Madama: traversing the entire
breadth of the hill slope of the garden, these avenues are at the scale of the hill,
not of the palace.[27] Taken together, they *are* an architectural hill on a par with
those outside the garden, while the fishponds below *are* a valley at the bottom of two converging slopes. The huge platform of the Villa Medici is not a
construction on top of the Pincian hill; it *is* the hill. Much as in the ancient examples that inspired them, the gardens at the Villas d'Este and Medici are garden and larger landscape all at once. In the next century, a key example is the
formal core of the Villa Pamphili, built 1645–70 on the Janiculum Hill. Set on
a ridge of the hill, it consisted of a sequence of three huge terraced platforms,

FIGURE 8.7: Villa Pamphili, built 1645–48, etched view of south facade by Dominique Barrière. From *Villa Pamphilia eiusque Palatium, . . .* (Rome, ca. 1670). Private collection, photograph by the author.

upon which stood a cubic block (the villa palace) surmounted by a smaller cubic belvedere and originally meant to be flanked by two wings terminating in small pavilions: wings, palace, and belvedere were all topped by terraces. Seen from the lower platform, the whole amounted to a five-stepped complex of terraces, one organic composition all unified by architectural orders progressing from Doric on the lower retaining wall to Composite at the roof level of the belvedere; the running of continuous parapets on all the levels crystallized this unity. Much as in Domitian's palace on the Palatine Hill, palace, garden, and hill were one and the same.

It was this hybridity of the Italian garden's engagement with the larger landscape, one that drew its inspiration and meaning from Roman antiquity in situ, that would be taken up by the designers of French gardens in the mid-sixteenth century, notably Philibert Delorme at the château of Anet, memory of his studies of Hadrian's Villa at Tivoli during his Roman sojourns in 1532–1536 and 1553–1560.[28] More than any specific forms or arrangements, the lessons of this hybridity—the ability of architectural garden forms to become elements in the larger landscape and the ability to transition seamlessly from architecture to garden to larger landscape—helped garden architects such as de l'Orme and

Le Nôtre to unlock totally new possibilities in a situation very different from Italy, entailing different landscapes, different typologies such as the moated château and the fortified bastion, and different political aims and social practices. I briefly return to this in the concluding section of this chapter.

INCORPORATING THE ROMAN LANDSCAPE

I turn now to the other approach that, like the constructed architectural landscape, articulated the tension between garden and larger landscape through topographical elements of the garden, in this case natural forms of the larger landscape incorporated *at landscape scale,* rather than through allegorical representation in statues or fountains. This approach can be found in the Roman villa parks from 1550 to the late seventeenth century, built for new families of the top Roman elite, namely the popes who were not Roman, their families, and cardinals with papal ambitions; these newcomers to Rome invented a new typology. It involved a tenfold jump in size from earlier villas and the incorporation of landscape forms such as forests and meadows, hills and valleys, streams and lakes, into the confines of the garden—the whole entity set in a location, immediately within or outside the city walls, where Romans were used to seeing small vernacular gardens and vineyards, called the *vigne.* The Villa Giulia, built 1550–55 for Pope Julius III Ciocchi del Monte, inaugurated the new type.[29] Its territory straddled the Via Flaminia a half mile outside the Porta del Popolo at the northern edge of the city. It was assembled by acquiring several *vigne* from other owners, encompassing a great variety of terrain and landscape features, such as the meadows, agrarian lands, and orchards of the incorporated *vigne,* thus reconstituting a beautiful native Roman topography formed of rough high cliffs toward the east around the valley where its main palace lay, and a riverfront on the Tiber to the west.[30] The designers retained part of that agrarian *vigna* landscape and replaced part with formal tree gardens. Elegant pavilions with loggias were made out of the older vernacular buildings that had stood on the *vigne* acquired for the villa, transforming them from agrarian to aristocratic. Ancient sculptures and new benches with tables were laid out along tree-lined avenues in the hillsides. At the center of the valley was placed a palace with large formal gardens. What had been a patchwork of small *vigne* was now a park with a circumference of three to four miles, although its areas were not unified as one design, it appears, but simply connected by avenues and paths, and the villa likely remained articulated in several parts that corresponded to the broad borders of the acquired *vigne.* The aesthetic structure of the whole imitated that of ancient estates: it was designed to provide surprising contrasts and great variety—a highly adorned palace with a portico, wings, courts on different levels, loggias, and enclosed formal gardens—and a huge area of gardens and park, within which formality contrasted with irregularity and naturalism.[31]

The newly planted trees came from many different sites and donors—the big farming estates (*casali*) in the Roman Campagna, the coastal areas (the "marina"), other parts of Latium, Naples, and so on. They ranged from poplar, elm, and chestnut trees to peach and other fruit trees, and were subdivided into productive, ornamental, and semi-wild areas, the latter containing *arbori selvatichi*, which Alberta Campitelli identifies as the Mediterranean *macchia* or maquis.[32] A letter of 1555 by one of the architects, Bartolomeo Ammannati, describes the scale of this sea of greenery, at 36,000 newly planted trees, which must have strongly contrasted with the surrounding landscape of little *vigna* properties.[33]

In sum, the Villa Giulia was a park in which high-style and vernacular cultures and cultivations were contrasted by means of transposing into the estate larger landscapes from varied origins: on one hand, agrarian, with productive

FIGURE 8.8: Villa Giulia and its park, built 1550–55, engraved view. From Charles Percier and P.F.L. Fontaine, *Choix des plus célèbres maisons de plaisance de Rome et de ses environs* (Paris, 1809). Private collection, photograph by the author.

areas of fruit trees and vineyards, and on the other, aristocratic, with many kinds of trees that denoted grandeur and magnificence.[34] If one were to visualize what it looked like from the 1550s to 1600, one might imagine it as a combination of Tuscan (i.e., Medici) and Roman approaches to designing a parkland—the Villa Medici at Castello; the Boboli Gardens in Florence that Ammannati designed after 1550 (he and Vasari, both architects at Villa Giulia, surely applied Tuscan ideas here), with large swaths of *boschetti* covering the hill slopes; a more informal park like that of the later Villa Lante at Bagnaia crisscrossed by very long avenues (built 1570s); and incorporation of Rome's *vigne* and Campagna landscapes. The patron of the Villa Giulia, Pope Julius III, was a Tuscan, and the construction of his Roman villa park may have been done with a competitive eye to the new Medici park at the Boboli Gardens, which was, notably, also in a suburban location with respect to Florence. And, with its neo-antique palatial courts, its pavilions in the park, and its celebration of undulating topography, the Villa Giulia could recall the meandering layout of Hadrian's Villa to erudite visitors, who might have known about Ligorio's excavations there from the 1540s on; its stadium-shaped courts with freestanding walls, marking the passage of the Aqua Virgo aqueduct, may well have appeared like a recreated Canopus Canal set amidst the greenery of the antique villa with its topographical variety.[35] In a synthetic way, it evoked both ancient Roman precedents and modern Medici parks.

After the Villa Giulia, a series of new villa parks was built within or near the city walls of Rome, similarly incorporating the larger landscape. It included the Villas Montalto-Peretti (1576–90, revised 1620s), Borghese (1606–33), Ludovisi (1621–23), and Pamphili (1645–70). Each was commissioned by a reigning pope or by the key representative of a papal family.[36] Each elaborated on this new tradition of incorporation, creating variations on the genre, and the early-seventeenth-century examples form a coherent group, formally and socially: indeed, one of the papal patrons, Paul V Borghese, saw the Villa Giulia as such an important new model to follow that he tried, unsuccessfully, to buy it in 1608 for his family and to expand it by adding his small adjacent *vigne* on the Pincian Hill.[37] Very large, at 150 to 300 acres apiece, and with perimeter walls two to five miles long, these villa parks stood out at five to ten times the size of their Renaissance predecessors such as the Villa Medici on the Pincian Hill. Like the Villa Giulia, each had a formal core of palace and gardens richly decorated with antique sculptural reliefs, in turn surrounded by vast tracts of enclosed land, largely unleveled but often replanted with huge groves of trees since their acquisition. The formal area did not govern the design of the remainder of the estate, but was simply connected to it by long avenues for

promenading and carriage riding, extending the axes into huge tree plantations and, at the Villas Borghese and Pamphilj, a hunting park that contained
groves, cow pastures, and a lake with ducks and other waterfowl. At both the
Villas Borghese and Pamphilj, the design of the parks was more coherent than
what we can surmise for the Villa Giulia: these two parks were unified through
continuous tree plantings that tied together the formal and the informal areas,
relying on the unity provided by a limited range of trees species. For example,
in both parks, tall umbrella pines, fir trees, holm oaks, and laurels predomi-
nated, planted in clear and massive groupings. Also, both hunting parks contained very large open areas with meadows treated naturalistically, as if they
were untouched pieces of the open Campagna farther away from Rome: perceptually graspable in a single glance because of their openness, and conceptu-
ally referring to a single comprehensive category—the grazing landscape—they
provided a higher level of coherence than the plantings predominant at the
Villa Giulia. Yet, even so, all of these parks relied on the juxtaposition of several distinct components (formal garden, *boschetti,* meadows, etc.) in homage
to an ancient aesthetic of contrast and surprise.[38] The larger landscape was one
element, not the whole narrative.

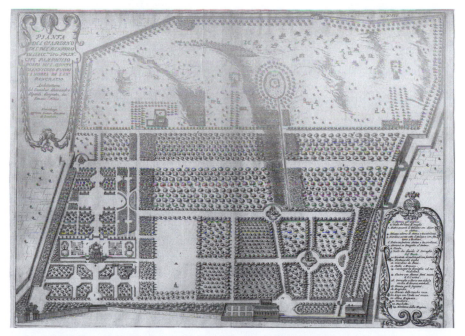

FIGURE 8.9: Park of the Villa Pamphili, built 1645–70, bird's-eye view. From Giovanni
Battista Falda, *Li Giardini di Roma,* reedition by Joachim von Sandrart (Nüremberg,
ca.1685). Private collection, photograph by the author.

FIGURE 8.10: Park of the Villa Pamphili with the lake in mid-ground. Photograph by the author.

In all of these villas, from the Villa Giulia to the Villa Pamphilj, the tension between garden and larger landscape operated at two intertwined levels. On one hand, there was the matter of location—the transposition of certain landscape forms from their native location in the larger landscape to a new location, in the garden. On the other hand, there was the matter of character—specifically the pastoral character associated with some of the transposed landscape forms.

The matter of location was essential in defining the meanings of this group of estate villas, or villa parks. While great parks with vast tree plantations had long existed in the Roman territory, they were usually found far from the city, some forty to fifty miles out, in the forested fieflands of the old Roman nobility, the barons, which lay in the hills and mountainous areas at the outer edge of the Roman countryside; most of these parks were of medieval origin and served as enclosed hunting parks. It must have been a shock to Romans to see a great park of fine trees or a lake so close to Rome's city center. Here, the designers of these villas deployed a concept that can be called the displacing or transposing of native landscapes.[39] Transpositions of landscape elements were enacted by incorporation of landscapes, agrarian and forested, that were typical of territorial zones other than the local one of vineyards and occasional formal gardens in which the villa itself lay. These landscapes and their elements were "transposed" within a recognized territorial network of landscapes and their languages of design. Romans could appreciate this concept of transposition, because they had what I call a mental map by which they interpreted the landscape around their city and its territory, a map that combined social and geographical categories. One aspect of this mental map was that they thought of the land around Rome in terms of three concentric rings around the city proper. Each ring corresponded to a category of rural property: the ring nearest Rome contained the small agrarian properties called vineyards by the Romans (*vigne*), the next huge farming estates (*casali*), and the third fief towns and their surrounding lands (*feudi*), which had been fortified settlements (*castra*) in the early medieval period. All of the estate villas were located within the inner ring of *vigne,* near its periphery. Their designers achieved a surprising modification of commonly expected categories by transposing into the villa—at both conceptual and material levels—farming landscapes (the meadows and *arbori selvatichi*) from the nearby *casali* in the Campagna and vast tree plantations from the baronial fiefs. With these transpositions came also the social meanings of those original locations, including the pastoral nature of the meadowlands and the aristocratic nature of the baronial tree forests, and the power relationships among the elite families, reflected in the ownership of farms and baronial fiefs, which was then undergoing a big shift from families of ancient lineage to new families made rich by the papacy and curial success.[40]

The play on transposed locations that I have pointed out for the estate villas from the Villa Giulia to the Villa Pamphilj derived authority and content from ancient Rome. One aspect of this play was the location of the parks very close to the city center, on the model of the ancient *horti* or great estates that arose, particularly in the period 30 B.C.E. to 70 C.E., on the borderland between the city and the *suburbium*—and of the "primus inter pares" of those estates, the Golden House of the Emperor Nero, built 64–68 C.E. and described by Suetonius and Tacitus.[41] With its woods, fields and lake, it extended from the base of the Palatine hill to the Esquiline; and yet, it lay at the very center of the city. The ancient poets, for example, Martial, had expressed this as *rus in urbe,* the country brought into the city. Another aspect indebted to antiquity was the arrangement of landscape scenery inside a park to evoke specific landscape configurations from elsewhere—not just lakes, for example, but a particular lake.[42]

These two intertwined aspects of antique incorporation were particularly explicit at the Villas Borghese and Pamphilj. On one hand, these two villa parks were envisioned by their patrons as contemporary versions of ancient *horti,* and specifically the Golden House, with their vineyards, pastures, woods, animals, and lakes. The guardian of the Villa Borghese, Jacopo Manilli, made this clear when he invoked parity with ancient Roman *horti* in his guidebook to the villa.[43] Antiquarians since Flavio Biondo in the 1440s had used Tacitus and Suetonius to describe the Golden House's reversal of expected categories. Tacitus had described the marvel and the shock of seeing "fields and lakes and the air of solitude given by wooded grounds alternating with clear tracts and open landscapes" in the Golden House.[44] Manilli's words for the hunting park at the Villa Borghese ring with the evocation of Tacitus's, when he writes, "this enclosure . . . contains in its spaciousness valleys, hills, plains, woods, houses, and gardens." The parks at the Villas Borghese and Pamphilj were constituted precisely by such landscapes and, by their location and their contents, they reinterpreted in modern configurations the ancient topographical conceit of the Golden House, including the lakes echoing the Neronian one over which the Colosseum had been built.

After this extended discussion of transposed location in the Roman villa parks, I now turn to a closely related theme, pastoralism. For the elites who owned or visited these parks, the transpositions of scenery were mediated not only through their mental map (social and geographical) of the three rings of properties in the contemporary Roman territory, or through the antique associations evoked by such transpositions, as seen with the Golden House. They were also mediated through an elite cultural form, well loved in the early modern period, that of the pastoral.[45] With the pastoral, we return to the theme that has structured this essay from the start, namely, "the tension between" garden and larger landscape, now experienced in terms of human activity and culture rather than location. Recovered from antiquity, specifically the poetry of Theocritus and Virgil, the pastoral genre spread from the late 1400s in both poetic and painterly forms, also in musical and theatrical ones, becoming most renowned through the publication of Jacopo Sannazaro's *Arcadia* ("Libro pastorale nominato Arcadio," written 1480s; published Naples, 1504), which saw some seventy editions in the sixteenth century alone. Its themes of shepherds singing and playing pipes, nostalgic and lovelorn, while their flocks peacefully grazed in an idyllic and naturally lush landscape, articulated the human experience of dialectical relationships between civilization and nature, between city and country, conflict and harmony, equating civilization with artifice and nature with simplicity, reverie, and emotional freedom. These themes had been frequent in ancient Roman gardens and poetry, populated by nymphs and satyrs, and ancient statues of them were recovered in Renaissance Rome and set up anew in villa gardens such as the Villas Giulia and d'Este. The Villa Giulia itself may have been the site of outdoor performances of pastoral plays, in which the settings of garden courtyards, murmuring fountains, and woodland glades on the hills would have been real protagonists.[46] The Roman villa parks, from the Villa Giulia on, articulated precisely such pastoral dialectics between urbane architecture (with its formal groves) and naturalistic park, as articulated in the opening lines of Sannazaro's *Arcadia:* "More often than not the tall and spreading trees brought forth by nature on the shaggy mountains are wont to bring greater pleasure to those who view them than are the cultivated trees pruned and thinned by cunning hands in ornamented gardens."[47]

The pastoral mode, in three dimensions, was at play in the Villas Borghese and Pamphilj. A view of the Villa Pamphilj about 1675 shows the dairy farm overlooking the lake and its grazing meadows in the hunting park where deer roam. As on the Campagna farms, the villa meadowland here and at the Villa Borghese was mown twice a year for hay; livestock was brought in from the Campagna, with herders to guard it; and noblemen and cardinals came here, the way they went to their *casali,* for sports such as netting birds, hunting, fishing, and walking. In his guidebook to the Villa Borghese, the villa's guardian constantly referred to this pastoral area of the Villa Borghese as "its countrysides" (*le sue campagne*). At both the Villas Borghese and Pamphilj, the pastoral landscapes and activities of the Roman Campagna formed the conceptual basis for their design. A good part of these pastoral pleasures lay in the mix of aristocratic and rural delights within walking distance of the city and in the unexpected context of an aristocratic park instead of the standard *casale* many miles farther out.[48]

The themes expressed in pastoral poetry and in these pastoral parks were timeless ones of human existence. At a more concrete level, the pastoralist motif could also evoke, for the Roman elites of the early modern period, far more immediate concerns in the present, notably the long-term shift in the economy of the Campagna from agriculture to livestock, a shift that increased after 1600, and the shifting fortunes of both landowners and laborers that followed. Well beyond the pleasures of nobles strolling among sheep, pastoralism could mediate between present reality and existential meaning, sublimating the former into the latter. The painter Claude Lorrain, working in Rome all his career, more than most captured this tension in his landscape paintings, at once so mythical and so specific in their depiction of the grazing landscapes of the Roman Campagna, so carefree and yet so full of foreboding. He also used the dialectical structure of transposition by lifting grand palaces and temples from their urban settings and inserting them into the Campagna, where they were like apparitions. Romans and foreigners alike, especially the French, patronized his scenes of the larger landscape, and the English would use them as part of their conceptualization of landscape gardens.

WIDER IMPLICATIONS AND CONCLUSIONS

In this chapter, my approach to the garden and the larger landscape has been to structure it in terms of the tension between the two in a given culture, by exploring how contemporaries formulated that tension and by focusing on the design approaches they used in setting it up. Both approaches to garden design—giving landscape and topographical qualification to a man-made architectural element like a terrace and giving garden qualification to a natural landscape element like a meadow or a hillock—conveyed meanings at two levels. One had to do with the here and now, the current earthly concerns of Roman society whether material or symbolic; the other had to do with more timeless philosophical and existential resonances that operated at an emotional level. It is from this universal or transcendent quality that they draw their emotional power and their durability in the history of garden design, as heirs to the ancient Roman garden traditions, as exported styles beyond Italy, and at a deeper structural level.

In contextualizing the Roman situation, one can note that both approaches, architectural landscapes and villa parks, arose very specifically in moments in which the culture of antiquarian studies of ancient Roman sites was particularly strong and was harnessed ideologically to the revival of ancient imperial Roman imagery for papal political interests. In the first half of the sixteenth century in Rome, architects such as Bramante, Raphael, and Ligorio were drawn to the study of the ancient Roman ruins, and, for landscape projects, particularly to those sites such as Praeneste and Hadrian's Villa in which the Romans had merged architectural and landscape forms, creating hybridity and ambiguity by architecturalizing topography and by using the scale of landscape. In the second half of the sixteenth century in Rome, under the influence of the Counter-Reformational cultural tenor that demanded severity and sobriety of style, this imperial dimension was absent or at least less prominent, in part replaced by Counter-Reformational interest in early Christian archaeology. It surged again in the early to mid-seventeenth century in Rome, between the Villa Aldobrandini and the Villa Pamphilj. The Villa Aldobrandini's water theater drew its architecturalized landscape forms from both the antique and the modern, its exedra set piece from the Canopus Canal at Hadrian's Villa's Canopus[49] and its wings with roof terraces from Michelangelo's Capitoline palaces; it is the hill become building. Antiquarian research on ancient Roman sites, too, surged again in the 1620s to 1650s in Rome. Architects drew and antiquarians such as Cassiano Dal Pozzo collected drawings (Cassiano in his Musaeum Chartaceum, 1620s to 57) of sites that were particularly rich in the hybridity of their landscape architectural forms, for example, Praeneste once again, Domitian's Villa Albanum at Castel Gandolfo, Pliny's Laurentine Villa near Ostia, and Hadrian's Villa. The 1630s saw the first complete survey drawing made of Hadrian's Villa, which recovered the extensive landscape features and architecturalized topography of the site. Ancient Roman topography and geography in Latium were studied to a degree not done before, with a strong emphasis on landscape features, as in the drawings and antiquarian research of the geographer Lucas Holstenius.[50] Antiquarians and geographers were particularly interested in the emperor Nero's prodigious, hybridic works that brought the larger landscape into the city, as at the Golden House, or that merged the architectural and the natural in landscape settings such as his villa at Sublacqueum (Subicao) with its three dammed ponds in a riverine gorge.

The villa parks arose as a genre at the same moment, ca. 1600, as did landscape painting in Rome, along with a growing interest in land, geography, and topography. Painters who made painting the larger landscape a specialization, such as Nicolas Poussin and Claude Lorrain, were immersed in this world of antiquarian research on ancient topography, in books and on-site. Poussin and Claude, in particular, focused in their paintings on hybridic forms of architecture at landscape scale and on the bringing in of the larger landscape as primary subject; following the antiquarians, they conceptualized buildings as hills and nature as ambiguously tectonic and organic at once. The topical interest of both Poussin and Claude in landscape as a genre not only reflected the growing economic importance of landholding and its symbolic value as status for Roman aristocrats, and for their foreign patrons as well, but also, and especially, classical Antiquity's love of the larger landscape and its hybridic, ambiguous approach to the natural and the man-made.

The transcendent dimension that I have pointed out in the Roman sites discussed earlier—a quality that translated well—made their essences eminently exportable to other European garden cultures, even while the latter had their own autonomous developments. In other Italian states, France, the Netherlands, England, the German principalities, and the Austro-Habsburg Empire, the Roman model of the architecturalized landscape was absorbed into local idiom and translated into local meanings. One need only think of the immense infrastructure of the Escorial in Spain (1563–84), of Saint-Germain-en-Laye (1594–1600)—echoing both Praeneste and the Villa D'Este—and of the Hortus Palatinus of Heidelberg Castle (1614–19). Recent studies of Dutch gardens have pointed to their owners' interest for the cultural associations and design of Italian gardens. John Dixon Hunt has eloquently described the "Englishing" of Italian garden forms between 1600 to 1750[51], and he has shown how the rustic and agricultural elements of the Roman villa parks, both near the city and out in the countryside, such as the Villas Borghese (Rome) and Aldobrandini (Frascati), helped English visitors ca. 1700 conceptualize the gardening of rural landscape estates, once they were back in England.[52] As an example of this translation, I look briefly at the case of France, and see that the Roman exports operated at a deeper structural level than mere imitation, enabling important moments of the largely autonomous development of French gardens.

French gardens developed primarily as château gardens, which meant that they were part of a domain or vast estate located deep in the countryside, in which the center was the unit of castle, moat, and gardens, at some distance from a forest or woods, but conceptualized in functional and symbolic relationship to it.[53] Jean Guillaume has synthetically traced the historical evolution of the relationship between château and garden from the early 1500s to Le Nôtre's day: the garden, which first lay as a separate walled unit at the side of the castle, gradually develops to envelop the building on two or even three sides; the château building, moated with towers and closed around a court at first, becomes a type of pavilion, open on all sides to gardens as at Vaux-le-Vicomte (1656–61).[54] Gradually the gardens, too, become tightly axed on the château itself, even when they consist of multiple platforms, as can be seen in many examples by the 1570s, published in Jacques Androuet Du Cerceau's *Les Plus Excellents Bastiments de France* (1576–79). The overriding development is that of a single, unitary composition, focused along a single view, which projects the château and gardens visually out into the larger landscape of the estate, often by means of avenues cutting through the woods and fields.[55] The multiple platforms on which the garden parterres lie become, by the time of Vaux-le-Vicomte, one unitary composition, articulated into several platforms, architectural but also merging with ground until *it is ground*.

The merging of architecture and ground, at the scale of the landscape, enters the French development early on at the château of Anet (1547–52), built by Philibert Delorme for the mistress of King Henri II, Diane de Poitiers. The fortified perimeter includes both château and garden, with everything within subject to its overall rectangular order, unlike anything seen in France to that date. Hybridity and unity both reign here. The entrance pavilion is part triumphal arch and part terraced garden; the traditional sentinel walkways have become balustraded roof gardens with groves of trees; the garden proper behind the château, sunken and surrounded by a portico and cryptoporticus, is like an ancient peristyle, that ultimate hybrid typology, but at the scale of the whole site. Building has become topography. The important connection to the larger landscape at Anet resides both in its layout as a comprehensive site at topographical scale, not building scale, and in the ambiguity of its elements— raised grounds, sunken garden, buildings that are also terraces, gardens, and miniaturized fortifications. This remarkable innovation by Delorme appears to have coalesced with the input of his Roman experiences.

At Vaux-le-Vicomte, built for Nicolas Fouquet a century after Anet, the ground of the entire designed part of the domain, what can be called the gardens, is conceived as a vast open, articulated surface that projects from the grand entrance to the end of the gardens, and beyond the canal that cuts transversally across them. On it unfolds one seamless transition from the slightly sloping ground of the entrance court to the château's platform, to the platforms of the parterre gardens and to the ground beyond the canal, and from the canal to the larger landscape that it implies. Essential to this seamlessness is the hybrid quality of the platforms in the garden: they are clearly artificial, yet their sequence closely hugs the slight natural slope, almost merging with the ground. They do so not only in the longitudinal, projecting direction as we would expect, articulating a nearly imperceptible staircase from château to canal, but they also articulate that slope in a transversal direction, in three slight steps from right down to left. [56] Here, too, as at Anet earlier, the hybridity of Roman architecturalized landscapes likely played a key role in coalescing the innovative concept of

projected ground in a unitary composition. Between Anet and Vaux, French garden architects would repeatedly work with this concept. Once Delorme introduced a new paradigm in French architecture, including this hybridity, it became
part of French design tradition. At Vaux, Fouquet's direct contacts with Rome
and the painter Poussin may have enabled this coalescence. Following Vaux-le-
Vicomte, Le Nôtre would work with ground in a similar way at Meudon, Versailles, and Chantilly, among other sites. In all of these, he would use hybridity
at two levels, at the level of ambiguity between architecture and ground, and at
the level of alluding to fortifications, roads, canals, and infrastructure; expressing royal political control; and reflecting royal and national systems to fortify
France's borders and improve river and road systems. The larger landscapes,
both natural and artificial, were brought in and represented in these gardens.[57]

   This chapter has taken us on an itinerary exploring the forms and meanings that designing gardens in relationship to the larger landscape could have
in early modern Europe. I have posited that one mental framework that contemporaries had in conceptualizing the pairing of garden and landscape was
as a dialectical tension between the two. I have focused primarily on Italy and
Rome, but also followed some of the implications that the Roman approaches
had for other European garden cultures, such as France. The emphasis has
been on understanding the synthetic relationship between design and the web
of cultural meanings that articulated these approaches. Hybridity and transposition, each with an ancient Roman heritage, were not just two conceptual
modes in which designers engaged the larger landscape. They were also cultural, transmitted culturally from antiquity to the early modern period, and
not just as visual effects or literary motifs but at the level of structures. By this,
I mean the level at which a given society conceptualizes something and medi-
ates that society's economic, social, and cultural concerns with it in artistic
forms. For hybridity, this meant transmission from Praeneste to Raphael to
Delorme and to Le Nôtre, for transposition, from Ovid to Claude Lorrain to
English landscape gardens such as Blenheim and Castle Howard. Because they
were transmitted as structures, they were capable of assuming cultural specificity in different geographies—from imperial revival under Pope Julius II to
political control of infrastructure under Louis XIV and from the three rings of
land around Rome to the English Enclosure Acts.

NOTES

Introduction

1. G. Pico della Mirandola, *Oration on the Dignity of Man,* trans. A. R. Caponigri with introduction by R. Kirk (Chicago: Regnery Edition, 1956), 8.

2. See M. C. Horowitz, *Seeds of Virtue and Knowledge* (Princeton, NJ: Princeton University Press, 1998); and R. W. Bushnell, *A Culture of Teaching: Early Modern Humanism in Theory and Practice* (Ithaca, NY: Cornell University Press, 1996) for discussions of the allegory.

3. S. Greenblatt, *Renaissance Self-Fashioning: From More to Shakespeare* (Chicago: University of Chicago Press, 1980).

4. For a review of recent literature and the state of the debate, see W. Caferro, *Contesting the Renaissance* (Oxford: Wiley-Blackwell, 2011).

5. M. Baxandall, *Painting and Experience in Fifteenth-Century Italy: A Primer in the Social History of Pictorial Style* (Oxford: Oxford University Press, 1988).

6. See for example, A. Giusti and W. Koeppe, eds., *Art of the Royal Court: Treasures in Pietre Dure from the Palaces of Europe* (New York: Metropolitan Museum of Art, 2008).

7. J. D. Hunt, *Greater Perfections: The Practice of Garden Theory* (London: Thames and Hudson, 2000), 32–34.

8. T. Mariage, *The World of André Le Nôtre,* trans. G. Larkin with foreword by J. D. Hunt (Philadelphia: University of Pennsylvania Press, 1999).

9. L. Jardine, *Worldly Goods: A New History of the Renaissance* (New York: W. W. Norton, 1998).

10. For an analysis of the growth of European attempts to know their own flora, see A. Cooper, *Inventing the Indigenous: Local Knowledge and Natural History in Early Modern Europe* (Cambridge: Cambridge University Press, 2010).

11. For an authoritative analysis of the Dutch tulip mania, see A. Goldgar, *Tulipmania: Money, Honor, and Knowledge in the Dutch Golden Age* (Chicago: Chicago University Press, 2008).

12. E. de Jong, "Of Plants and Gardeners, Prints and Books: Reception and Exchange in Northern European Garden Culture 1648–1725," in *Baroque Garden Cultures: Emulation, Sublimation, Subversion,* ed. M. Conan (Washington, D.C.: Dumbarton Oaks Research Library and Collection, 2005), 37–84.

13. For a new analysis of the role of the peasantry in the evolution of the garden, see M. Ambrosoli, "From the Italian Countryside to the Italianate Landscape: Peasants as Gardeners and Foreign Observers in Italy, 1500–1850," in *Clio in the Italian Garden: Twenty-First-Century Studies in Historical Methods and Theoretical Perspectives,* ed. M. Beneš and M. G. Lee (Washington, D.C.: Dumbarton Oaks Research Library and Collection, 2011), 145–68.

14. There was a commercial impetus, as well, for the higher the demand for rare plants, the higher their economic value and the greater the need to know for what one was paying.

15. See M. Baridon, *A History of the Gardens of Versailles,* chap. 7 "Hydraulics and Physics: Water and Air," tr. A. Mason (Philadelphia: University of Pennsylvania Press, 2008), 98–107.

16. A. Goldgar, *Impolite Learning: Conduct and Community in the Republic of Letters, 1680–1750* (New Haven, CT: Yale University, 1995); and P. Miller, *Peiresc's Europe: Learning and Virtue in the Seventeenth Century* (New Haven, CT: Yale University Press, 2000).

17. R. F. Giannetto, *Medici Gardens: From Making to Design* (Philadelphia: University of Pennsylvania Press, 2008), 161–78.

18. F. Colonna, *Hypnerotomachia Poliphili* (Venice: Aldus Manutius, 1499); O. de Serres, *Le Théâtre d'agriculture et mesnage des champs,* 3rd ed. (Paris: Abr. Saugrain, 1600); and A. Mollet, *Le jardin de plaisir* (Stockholm: Henry Kayser, 1651).

19. P. Vallet, *Le jardin du roy tres chrestien Henri IV* (Paris: n.p., 1608).

20. G. B. Ferrari, *De florum cultura* (Roma: Stephanus Paulinus, 1633) and *Flora overo cultura di fiori* (Rome: Pier.' Ant. Facciotti, 1638).

21. F.L.D.T.R., *Secrets pour teindre la fleur d'immortelle en diverses couleurs, avec la maniere de la cultiver. Pour faire des pastes de differentes odeurs fort agreables. Et pour contrefaire du marbre au naturel propre pour toutes sorte d'ouvrages figurez* (Paris: Charles de Sercy, 1690).

22. N. V., *Connoissance et culture parfaite des tulippes rares, des anemones extraordinaires, des oeillets fins, et des belles oreilles d'ours panachées* (Paris: Laurent d'Houry, 1688), "Avertissement," n.p. "Quel goût y a-t'il en comparaison dans d'autres curiositez plus à la mode, dans les Tableaux, les Medailles & les Porcelaines. Regardez-les tant qu'il vous plaira, vous verrez toujours la même chose. La varieté & ce jeu annuel des Fleurs sont bien plus satisfaisans. Toutes les beautez de l'Art de la Peinture sont dans le dessein, l'execution & le coloris. Je défie l'Academie de Peinture entière d'imaginer en Fleur aussi à propos que le naturel, d'exécuter dans la dernière perfection ce qu'il nous montre, & d'approcher jamais du coloris des Fleurs. Un tableau est toujours un, un oignon se multiplie. On donne à son amy une rare Fleur, & on l'a à soy; ce sont plusieurs originaux aussi se communiquement, l'art ne va point là. Une Medaille toute usée, dont ce défaut fait en partie le merite, quel-qu'ancienne qu'elle soit, est toujours moderne à l'égard des Fleurs; elles sont

de la création du monde. S'il plaisoit aux Sçavans de raisonne sur elles, comme sur une Medaille qui ne prouve jamais rien de tout ce que leur sçavoir leur fait debiter, leur Dissertations plairoient également. Il en est de meme à proportion des Porcelains, & des autres raretez qui sont en vogue, & quand on voudra que la raison se mesle des goûts, les belles Fleurs teindront le premier rang parmy les plaisirs de la veüe."

23. A. Schnapper, *Curieux du Grand Siècle. Oeuvres d'art,* vol. 2. *Collections et collectionneurs dans la France du XVIIe siècle* (Paris: Flammarion, 1994); A. Schnapper, *Le Géant, la licorne, et la tulipe. Histoire et histoire naturelle,* vol. 1. *Collections et collectionneurs dans la France du XVIIe siècle* (Paris: Flammarion, 1988); and K. Pomian, *Collectors and Curiosities: Paris and Venice, 1500–1800,* trans. E. Wiles-Portier (Cambridge, MA: Polity Press, 1990).

24. Antoine Furetière wrote in his 1690 *Dictionnaire universel,* in the entry under *Goust:* "GOUST, se dit figurement en Morale des jugements de l'esprit. Les manieres de cet homme-la sont au *goust* de tout le monde, cet esprit a le *goust* fin. Mr. Blondel a fait un Traitte du bon *goust* dans son livre d'Architecture." He continued: "GOUST, se dit aussi des bastiments, des statues, des tableaux. Le *goust* des Grecs a este le meilleur pour les bastiments. Les uns ont le *goust* des tableux de Poussin, les autres de Rubens. Le bon *goust* consiste a se former une idée des choses la plus parfaite qu'on peut, & a la suivre. On confound quelquefois ce mot avec *maniere;* & l'on dit, Voila un ouvrage de grande *maniere,* pour dire de grand *goust.*" A. Furetière, *Dictionnaire universel des arts et des sciences* (La Haye: n.p., 1690), s.v. "goust."

25. See, for example, M. Beneš, "Villa Pamphilj (1630–1670): Family, Land, and Gardens in Papal Rome," PhD diss, Yale University, 1989; M. Beneš, "Landowning and the Villa in the Social Geography of the Roman Territory: The Location and Landscapes of the Villa Pamphilij, 1645–1670," in *Form, Modernism, and History: Essays in Honor of Eduard F. Sekler,* ed. A. von Hoffmann, 187–209 (Cambridge, MA: Harvard University Graduate School of Design, 1996); and R. F. Giannetto, *Medici Gardens: From Making to Design* (Philadelphia: University of Pennsylvania Press, 2008).

26. See C. Mukerji, *Territorial Ambitions and the Gardens of Versailles* (Cambridge: Cambridge University Press, 1997); and E. Hyde, *Cultivated Power: Flowers, Culture, and Politics in the Reign of Louis XIV* (Philadelphia: University of Pennsylvania Press, 2005).

27. The images were etched by Israel Silvestre and published in Paris by Nicolas Langlois.

28. Furetière, *Dictionnaire universel,* s.v. "paisage." The entries read, "PAISAGE. S.m. Aspect d'un pays, le territoire qui s'estende jusqu'ou la veue peut porter. Les bois, les collines & les rivieres font les beau *paisages.* And "PAISAGE, se dit aussi des tableaux ou font representees quelques veues de maisons, ou de campagnes. Les veues des Maisons Royales font peintres en *paisages* a Fontainebleau & ailleurs."

29. Mariage, *The World of André Le Nôtre,* 44.

30. Furetière, *Dictionnaire universel,* s.v. "Veue." "Veue, se dit aussi de la maniere de regarder les choses. Une veue de face, de profil, de coste (accent). Pour bien voir

les perspectives, il faut ester au point de veue, dans la ligne de veue, qui est a la hauteur de l'oeil qui regarde. On appelle aussi une perspective a veue d'oiseau ou d'hyrondelle, quand le point de veue est si eleve, qui les bastiments, ou autres corps qui sont devant, n'empechent point qu'on ne voye ce qui est derriere . . . ."

31. Furetière, s.v. "Perspective." The entry reads, "PERSPECTIVE. s.f. Tableau du'on met ordinairement dans les jardins, ou au fonds des galleries, qui est fait expres pour tromper la *veue,* en representant la continuation d'une allee, ou du lieu ou elle est posee, ou quelque veue de bastiment ou paysage en lointain."

32. M. Foucault, *The Order of Things: A Archaeology of the Human Sciences* (New York: Vintage Books, 1973), 63.

33. Foucault, *The Order of Things,* 131.

1 Design

1. T. Tasso, *Gerusalemme liberta* (Parma, 1581).

2. L. B. Alberti, *On the Art of Building in Ten Books,* book 4, tr. J. Rykwert et al. (Cambridge, MA: MIT Press, 1988), 196.

3. Alberti, *Art of Building,* book 9, 300.

4. For more on the geometrical design of the botanical garden at Padua, see L. Morgan, "Early Modern Edens: The Landscape and Language of Paradise," *Studies in the History of Gardens and Designed Landscapes* 27, no. 2 (2007): 142–48.

5. R. Wittkower, *Architectural Principles in the Age of Humanism,* 4th ed. (London: Academy Editions, 1973), 7.

6. C. Mukerji has made a similar point about "bourgeois" gardens of the Renaissance in France: "Land control strategies used on a well-ordered estate, according to Estienne and Liebault, were designed to make the property more edenic. The point was to restore the land to the perfection intended in Creation through geometrical measurement and practical action. The spiritual task was aided by geometry, since a perfect geometrical figure, particularly the circle, was itself a symbol of perfection. A well-ordered estate, then, had as its fundamental structure a geometrical form and used geometries to articulate spaces." C. Mukerji, "Bourgeois Culture and French Gardening in the Sixteenth and Seventeenth Centuries," in *Bourgeois and Aristocratic Cultural Encounters in Garden Art, 1550–1850,* ed. M. Conan (Washington, D.C.: Dumbarton Oaks Research Library and Collection), 178–79.

7. C. Acidini Luchinat, ed., *Giardini Medicei: Giardini di Palazzo e di villa nella Firenze del Quattrocento* (Milan: Frederico Motta Editore, 1996).

8. A. Segre, "Untangling the Knot: Garden Design in Francesco Colonnas *Hypnerotomachia Poliphili,*" *Word and Image* 14, nos. 1/2 (1998): 82.

9. Segre, "Untangling the Knot," 82.

10. For an illustration, see Acidini Luchinat, *Giardini Medicei,* 34.

11. D. Coffin, *The Villa in the Life of Renaissance Rome* (Princeton, NJ: Princeton University Press, 1979), vii.

12. See C. Lazzaro, *The Italian Renaissance Garden: From the Conventions of Planting, Design, and Ornament to the Grand Gardens of Sixteenth-Century Central Italy* (New Haven, CT: Yale University, 1990), 2.

13. R. Fabiani Giannetto, "The Medici Gardens of Fifteenth-Century Florence: Conceptionalization and Tradition" (PhD diss., University of Pennsylvania, 2004).

14. Fabiani Giannetto, "The Medici Gardens," 154. See also Mario Gori Sassoli. "Michelozzo e l'architettura di villa nel primo Rinascimento," *Sotira dell'Arte* 23 (1975): 5–51.

15. See Fabiani Giannetto, "Medici Gardens," 19. Thierry Mariage, makes a similar point about the development of the French garden; see *L'univers de Le Nostre et les origins de l'aménagement du territoire* (Brussels: P. Mardaga, 1990; tr. by G. Larkin as *The World of André Le Nôtre* [Philadelphia: University of Philadelphia Press, 1999]).

16. The sketch is reproduced in Fabiani Giannetto, "Medici Gardens," 297.

17. For chronologies of the works at both sites, see Lazzaro, *Renaissance Garden,* 327–28.

18. See B. L. Edelstein, "'Acqua viva e corrente': Private Display and Public Distribution of Fresh Water at the Neapolitan Villa of Poggioreale as a Hydraulic Model for Sixteenth-Century Medici Gardens," in *Artistic Exchange and Cultural Translation in the Italian Renaissance City,* ed. S. J. Campbell and S. J. Milner (Cambridge: Cambridge University Press, 2004), 193.

19. G. Vasari, *The Lives of the Painters, Sculptors and Architects,* rev. ed., tr. A. B. Hinds (London: Dent; New York: Dutton, 1963), vol. 3, 169.

20. Before long Tribolo had begun building a second aqueduct from the nearby Villa Medici at Petraia, to increase still further the water supply to Castello; see Lazzaro, *Renaissance Garden,* 327.

21. Lazzaro, *Renaissance Garden,* 168.

22. Vasari, *The Lives of the Painters,* 171.

23. As Claudio Pizzorusso has pointed out, "a close reading of Vasari's detailed description shows that he, too, followed exactly this double course." See C. Pizzorusso, "Galileo in the Garden: Observations on the Sculptural Furnishings of Florentine Gardens between the Sixteenth and the Seventeenth Centuries," in *The Medici, Michelangelo, and the Art of Late Florence* (New Haven, CT: Yale University Press, 2002), 114.

24. Alberti, *On Painting,* 75.

25. For a useful general account of the early seventeenth-century preference for variety, see V. S. Ogden, "The Principles of Variety and Contrast in Seventeenth-Century Aesthetics and Milton's Poetry," *Journal of the History of Ideas* 10, no. 2 (April 1949): 159–82. For the principles of variety and contrast in the Italian Renaissance garden, see J. D. Hunt, *Garden and Grove: The Italian Renaissance Garden in the English Imagination 1600–1750* (London: J. M. Dent & Sons, 1986), 83–89.

26. See Pliny the Younger, *Letters,* book 5, letter 6, tr. W. Melmoth (London: William Heinemann; New York: Macmillan, 1927).

27. Note also the perceived medicinal benefits of variety. See D. R. Edward Wright, "Some Medici Gardens of the Florentine Renaissance: An Essay in Post-Aesthetic Interpretation," in *The Italian Garden: Art, Design, and Culture,* ed. J. D. Hunt (Cambridge: Cambridge University Press, 1996), 41–42.

28. For a discussion of these sources, see Fabiani Giannetto, "Medici Gardens."

29. Vasari, *The Lives of the Painters,* 170.
30. Vasari, *The Lives of the Painters,* 172.
31. The fountain is now at the Villa Medici, Petraia.
32. See, among other publications, J. D. Hunt, "*Paragone* in Paradise: Translating the Garden," *Comparative Criticism* 18 (1996): 55–70.
33. Vasari, *The Lives of the Painters,* 172.
34. Alberti, *Art of Building,* book IX, 300.
35. E. B. MacDougall, "Imitation and Invention: Language and Decoration in Roman Renaissance Gardens," in *Fountains, Statues and Flowers: Studies in Italian Gardens of the Sixteenth and Seventeenth Centuries* (Washington, D.C.: Dumbarton Oaks Research Collection, 1994), 113–26.
36. Vasari, *The Lives of the Painters,* 168.
37. Edelstein has made this point: "The Castello program, with its intended completion in the provision of water to the Duke's Florentine subjects at a public outlet, was subsequently given humorous treatment in the garden of his son, Francesco I, at Pratolino." See "Acqua viva e corrente," 195.
38. Quoted in Lazzaro, *Renaissance Garden,* 161.
39. As Lazzaro puts it, "The pissing boy provided yet another source of water, a witty counterpart to Jupiter at the head of the garden, and together the boy and the laundress present an ironic commentary on the grandiose imagery at the top of the hill, contrasting the water's supernatural origins with its mundane destination"; see *Renaissance Garden,* 165. In his comments on garden design, Alberti approved of "comic statues . . . provided they are not obscene" and, indeed, the garden is the first major site in which genre or "low-life" sculptures begin to appear during the Renaissance (Alberti, *Art of Building,* book 9, 300). The rustic figures by Nanni di Stocco and Valerio Cioli, and others for the Boboli Gardens in Florence, most of which are now installed around or near the Isolotto, provide other examples in addition to those at Pratolino. See L. M. Medri, ed., *Il giardino di Boboli* (Milan: Silvana Editoriale, 2003), 195ff. In fact, Nanni di Stocco's *Peasant Emptying a Cask* of ca. 1556 (after Baccio Bandinelli) for the Boboli gardens is the first known example of genre sculpture in the rustic mode, a sculptural type that would soon proliferate in European gardens. See Edelstein "Acqua viva e corrente," 201; and A. Brook, "Sixteenth-Century 'Genre' Statuary in Medici Gardens and Giambologna's Fontana del Villano," in *Boboli 90: Atti del convegno internazionale di studi per la salvaguardia e la valorizzazione del giardino,* ed. C. Acidini Luchinat and E. Garbero Zorzi, 2 vols. (Florence: EDIFIR, 1991), 122.
40. M. de Montaigne, *Montaigne's Travel Journal,* tr. D. M. Frame (San Francisco, CA: North Point Press, 1983), 99.
41. Montaigne, *Montaigne's Travel Journal,* 98.
42. See Lazzaro, *Renaissance Garden,* 92.
43. On the new aqueduct, see Lazzaro, *Renaissance Garden,* 215.
44. Lazzaro, *Renaissance Garden,* 223.
45. See I. Barisi, "The Design of the Garden and its Botanic Architecture," in *Villa d'Este,* ed. I. Barisi, M. Fagiolo, and M. L. Madonna (Rome: De Luca Editori d'Arte, 2003), 62.

46. Quoted in Pizzorusso, "Galileo in the Garden," 115.

47. See Lazzaro, *Renaissance Garden,* 221, for these details.

48. Quoted in Barisi, "The Design of the Garden," 65.

49. D. Dernie, *The Villa d'Este at Tivoli* (London: Academy Editions, 1996).

50. For Audebert's response to the Villa d'Este, see R. W. Lightbown, "Nicolas Aude-bert and the Villa d'Este," *Journal of the Warburg and Courtauld Institutes* 27 (1985): 169; for Testi's, see Lazzaro, *Renaissance Garden,* 217.

51. P. Fortini Brown, *Venice and Antiquity: The Venetian Sense of the Past* (New Haven, CT: Yale University Press, 1996), 214.

52. L. White Jr., "The Flavor of Early Renaissance Technology," in *Developments in the Early Renaissance,* ed. B. S. Levy (Albany: State University of New York Press, 1972), 41.

53. See the recent book by C. Pagnini, *Costantino de' Servi, architetto-scenografo fiorentino alla corte d'Inghilterra (1611–1615)* (Florence: Societá Editrice Fioren-tina, 2006).

54. R. Strong, *Henry, Prince of Wales and England's Lost Renaissance* (New Haven, CT: Yale University Press, 1986), 68.

55. The garden at Saint-Germain-en-Laye, which was terraced on the model of the Villa d'Este provides a good example. For an account of the design, see K. Wood-bridge, *Princely Gardens. The Origins and Development of the French Formal Garden* (New York: Rizzoli, 1986), 129–33.

56. Mariage, *André Le Nôtre,* 42.

57. The translation is from Woodbridge, *Princely Gardens,* 179.

58. Woodbridge, *Princely Gardens,* 202.

59. Mariage, *André Le Nôtre,* 46.

60. Mariage, *André Le Nôtre,* 46.

61. See E. Panofsky, "The Ideological Antecedents of the Rolls-Royce Radiator," in *Three Essays on Style,* ed. I. Lavin (Cambridge, MA: MIT Press, 1995), 131.

62. "Jardins de voyage" is Mariage's phrase. See his *André Le Nôtre,* 44.

63. Quoted in Mariage, *André Le Nôtre,* 91.

64. This point is made by Woodbridge in *Princely Gardens,* 202.

65. See A. Marie, *Naissance de Versailles* (Pairs: Vincent, Fréal et Cie, 1968) for a com-prehensive history of the bosquets.

66. See Woodbridge, *Princely Gardens,* 201, for more detail.

67. For an account of trompe l'oeil painting in French gardens and courtyards, see L. Morgan, "The Early Modern Trompe L'Oeil Garden," *Garden History* 33, no. 2 (2007): 142–48.

68. P.-A. Lablaude, *The Gardens of Versailles* (London: Zwemmer, 1995), 36.

69. Quoted in Mariage, *André Le Nôtre,* 86.

2 Types of Gardens

1. G. C. Argan, *Progetto e destino* (Milan: Casa Editrice Il Saggiatore, 1965), 76–77.

2. This idea was first expressed by French architects Jacques-François Blondel, in the second volume of his Cours d'architecture of 1772, and Quatremère de Quincy in

the first volume of his *Encyclopédie méthodique: Architecture* of 1788. See Anthony Vidler, *The Writing of the Walls: Architectural Theory in the Late Enlightenment* (Princeton, NJ: Princeton University Press, 1987), 154ff.

3. Q. de Quincy, "Type" in *Encyclopédie méthodique* (Paris: Agasse, 1825), quoted in Vidler, *The Writing of the Walls*, 152.

4. My understanding of type and typology is indebted to Giulio Carlo Argan's elaboration of the concept in his chapter "Sul concetto di tipologia architettonica." See Argan, *Progetto e destino*, 75–81.

5. Argan, *Progetto e destino*, 77.

6. For an extensive account of French château gardens, see K. Woodbridge, *Princely Gardens: The Origins and Development of the French Formal Garden* (New York: Rizzoli, 1986). See also J. Guillaume, ed., *Architecture, jardin, paysage: l'environnement du château et de la villa aux XVe et XVIe siècles: actes du colloque tenu à Tours du 1er au 4 juin 1992* (Paris: Picard, 1999). The essays in Guillaume's book tend to minimize the influence of Italian garden architecture on French formal gardens. With regard to the formal garden of England and to the English recreation of the Italian villa experience see J. D. Hunt, *Garden and Grove: The Italian Renaissance Garden in the English Imagination, 1600–1750* (Philadelphia: University of Pennsylvania Press, 1996). Also, see R. C. Strong, *The Renaissance Garden in England* (London: Thames and Hudson, 1979).

7. L. B. Alberti, "Villa," in *Opere Volgari*, vol. 1, ed. C. Grayson (Bari, Italy: G. Laterza, 1960), 359–60.

8. P. Bracciolini, *La vera nobiltá/De Vera Nobilitate* (Rome: Salerno, 1999), 31.

9. M. van der Meulen, "Cardinal Cesi's Antique Sculpture garden: Notes on a Painting by Hendrick Van Cleef III," *The Burlington Magazine* 116, no. 14 (1974): 18.

10. See D. R. Edward Wright, "The Medici Villa at Olmo a Castello: Its History and Iconography" (PhD diss., Princeton University, 1976). See also C. Conforti, "L'invenzione delle allegorie territoriali e dinastinche nel giardino di Castello a Firenze," in *Il giardino come labirinto della storia: convegno internazionale, Palermo 14–17 aprile 1984: Raccolta degli atti*, ed. J. Abel and E. Mauro (Palermo: Centro studi di storia e arte dei giardini), 190–97.

11. D. R. Coffin, *The Villa in the Life of Renaissance Rome* (Princeton, NJ: Princeton University Press, 1979), 151.

12. Coffin, *The Villa in the Life of Renaissance Rome*, 167.

13. M. Beneš, "The Social Significance of Transforming the Landscape at the Villa Borghese, 1606–30: Territory, Trees, and Agriculture in the Design of the First Roman Baroque Park," in *Gardens in the Time of the Great Muslim Empires: Theory and Design*, ed. A. Petruccioli (Leiden: Brill, 1997), 4.

14. A garden subdivided into three units is mentioned by Pietro Bembo in *Gli Asolani*. Here the author describes the garden of Caterina Cornaro at Asolo as composed of compartments with a cross pergola, a *pratello* or meadow, and a *selvatico* of laurels. See C. Lazzaro, *The Italian Renaissance Garden: From the Conventions of Planting, Design, and Ornament to the Grand Gardens of Sixteenth-Century Central Italy* (New Haven, CT: Yale University Press, 1990), 87.

15. For a more complete description of Castello, see R. Fabiani Giannetto, *Medici Gardens: From Making to Design* (Philadelphia: University of Pennsylvania, 2008).

16. On the practical functions of the gardens at Castello, see D. R. Edward Wright, "Some Medici Gardens of the Florentine Renaissance: An Essay in Post-Aesthetic Interpretation," in *The Italian Garden: Art, Design, and Culture,* ed. J. D. Hunt (Cambridge: Cambridge University Press, 1996), 40–43.

17. Tribolo did not live long enough to see the amphitheater completed, and his project was carried on by Bartolomeo Ammannati, whose contribution is still visible in the plan of Florence drawn by Buonsignori in 1584, and in the lunette painted by Giusto Utens in 1599.

18. Beneš, "The Social Significance of Transforming the Landscape at the Villa Borghese," 9.

19. Coffin, *The Villa in the Life of Renaissance Rome,* 325.

20. Beneš, "The Social Significance of Transforming the Landscape at the Villa Borghese," 3.

21. C. Wilkinson Zerner, "European Convergences: Philip II and the Landscape at Aranjuez," in *Architecture, jardin, paysage: l'environnement du château et de la villa aux XVe et XVIe siècles,* ed. J. Guillaume (Paris: Picard, 1999), 243.

22. J. Ackerman, *The Villa: Form and Ideology of Country Houses* (Princeton, NJ: Princeton University Press, 1990), 14.

23. Ackerman, *The Villa,* 14.

24. Wilkinson Zerner, "European Convergences," 248.

25. Wilkinson Zerner, "European Convergences," 245.

26. Wilkinson Zerner, "European Convergences," 246.

27. Ackerman, *The Villa,* 26.

28. Hunt, *Garden and Grove,* 11.

29. D. Fairchild Ruggles, *Gardens, Landscapes, and Vision in the Palaces of Islamic Spain* (University Park: Pennsylvania State University Press, 2000), 17.

30. The site in Via Santa Maria is traditionally considered the third that the botanical garden occupied in Pisa, and the garden is thought to have served the university and its students in all three locations, the preceding two sites being the Medici Arsenal and a site near the church of Santa Viviana. See, for example, F. Garbari et al., *Giardino dei semplici = Garden of Simples* (Pisa: Edizioni Plus, 2002). This view has convincingly been put into question by Anatole Tchikine. He argues that the first and second ducal gardens, while growing simples and exotic plants, were not, in fact, created for exclusive use of the university. They were private gardens owned by the Medicis, although records show that permission may have been granted to the Medici herbalists, first Luca Ghini and later Andrea Cesalpino, who were also professors of *materia medica,* to open the gardens to their students. I am grateful to Anatole Tchikine for allowing me to read his manuscript before publication. See A. Tchikine, "Gardens of Mistaken Identity: The Giardino delle Stalle in Florence and the Giardino dell'Arsenale in Pisa," *Studies in the History of Gardens and Designed Landscapes* 33, no. 1 (2013): 1–13.

31. The botanical garden replaced the *Giardino delle stalle* founded by Cosimo I in 1545. At that time the duke rented from the nuns of San Domenico del Maglio a piece of land situated between the ducal stables—whence the name of the garden, which was retained afterwards—and the nuns' monastery, for the purpose of constructing a pleasure garden. See Tchikine, "Gardens of Mistaken Identity," 2.

32. A. del Riccio, *Agricoltura sperimentale* (Florence: Biblioteca Nazionale Centrale di Firenze) (Targioni Tozzetti, 56, I, fol. 168r, and II, fol. 365r). See D. Heikamp, "Agostino del Riccio. Del giardino di un re," in *Il giardino storico italiano: problemi di indagine, fonti letterarie e storiche: atti del convegno di studi, Siena-San Quirico d'Orcia, 6–8 ottobre 1978,* ed. G. Ragionieri (Florence: Olschki, 1981), 75n12.

33. A. Targioni Tozzetti, *Cenni storici sulla introduzione di varie piante nell'agricoltura ed orticoltura Toscana* (Florence: Tipografia Galileiana, 1853), 122.

34. I am grateful to Anatole Tchikine for this information.

35. See Tchikine, "Gardens of Mistaken Identity," 6. A plan of the garden (ca. 1587) probably executed by Casabona is conserved at Pisa, Biblioteca Universitaria, Ms. 464, fol. 60r (59r old pagination).

36. Archivio di Stato di Firenze, *Spedale di San Paolo dei Convalescenti, 653.*

37. M. Azzi Visentini, *L'orto botanico di Padova* (Milan: Il Polifilo, 1984), 117.

38. Garbari et al., *Giardino dei semplici,* 211.

39. F. Hopper, "Clusius' World: The Meeting of Science and Art," in *The Authentic Garden: A Symposium on Gardens,* ed. L. Tjon Sie Fat et al. (Leiden, the Netherlands: Clusius Foundation, 1991), 15.

40. A. del Riccio, *Agricoltura sperimentale* (Florence: Biblioteca Nazionale Centrale di Firenze) (Targioni Tozzetti, 56, I, fol. 74v.).

41. J. M. Prest, *The Garden of Eden: The Botanic Garden and the Re-Creation of Paradise* (New Haven, CT: Yale University Press, 1981), 44.

42. E. de Jong, "Nature and Art. The Leiden Hortus as 'Musaeum,'" in *The Authentic Garden: A Symposium on Gardens,* ed. L. Tjon Sie Fat et al. (Leiden: Clusius Foundation, 1991), 47.

43. Prest, *The Garden of Eden,* 54.

44. Prest, *The Garden of Eden,* 47.

45. B. Castiglione, *Il libro del cortegiano* (Milan: Biblioteca Universale Rizzoli, 1998), 77.

46. H. Brunon, "La chasse et l'organisation du paysage dans la Toscane des Médicis," in *Chasses princières dans l'Europe de la Renaissance. Actes du colloque de Chambord (1er et 2 octobre 2004),* ed. C. d'Anthenaise and M. Chatenet (Arles: Actes Sud, 2007), 219.

47. Brunon, "La chasse et l'organisation du paysage dans la Toscane des Médicis," 224. See also P. Galloni, *Storia e cultura della caccia: dalla preistoria a oggi* (Rome: Laterza, 2000), 142.

48. The damage done to farms by the upper classes' hunting or by the animals in the game preserves across Europe caused the lower classes' frequent complaints. In 1560, for example, the commoners of France complained directly to the king about "the carelessness of the gentleman's hunting habits, particularly his invasion of fields that had recently been planted or which contained vineyards"; see W. L. Wiley, *The Gentleman of Renaissance France* (Cambridge, MA: Harvard University Press, 1954), 133. In 1543, in an effort to restore the moral and legal order of Castilian society, Pedro Núñez de Avendaño published his *Auiso de caçadores y de caça,* a book dedicated to the secular lords of his day, in which he declared that the right to chase belonged to every individual so long as he conformed to a proper

manner of hunting, one respectful of others' property and rights; see J. B. Owens, "Diana at the Bar: Hunting, Aristocrats and the Law in Renaissance Castile," *The Sixteenth Century Journal* 8 (1977): 17–36.

49. M. Azzi Visentini, "La chasse dans le duché de Milan a l'époque des Visconti et des Sforza: Les parcs de Pavie et de Milan," in *Chasses princières dans l'Europe de la Renaissance: actes du colloque de Chambord, 1er et 2 octobre 2004,* ed. C. d'Anthenaise and M. Chatenet (Arles: Actes Sud, 2007), 190.

50. J.-M. Derex, "Les Parcs de Vincennes et de Boulogne au XVIe siècle," in *Chasses princières dans l'Europe de la Renaissance: actes du colloque de Chambord, 1er et 2 octobre 2004,* ed. C. d'Anthenaise and M. Chatenet (Arles: Actes Sud, 2007), 258–59.

51. Owens, "Diana at the Bar: Hunting, Aristocrats and the Law in Renaissance Castile," 31.

52. Galloni, *Storia e cultura della caccia,* 144–45.

53. Azzi Visentini, "La chasse dans le duché de Milan a l'époque des Visconti et des Sforza: Les parcs de Pavie et de Milan," 209n30.

54. Azzi Visentini, "La chasse dans le duché de Milan a l'époque des Visconti et des Sforza: Les parcs de Pavie et de Milan," 188.

55. The Visconti also possessed a *barco ducale* at Milan, which dates from the beginning of the fifteenth century and was destroyed by the Milanese Republic after the death of Filippo Maria, the last descendent of the Visconti. A new park and castle were built by Francesco Sforza after his entry into the city in 1450; Azzi Visentini, "La chasse dans le duché de Milan a l'époque des Visconti et des Sforza: Les parcs de Pavie et de Milan," 192–93. The Sforza also built the villa called Sforzesca, a farm south of Vigevano that was completed by 1486. The villa included a *barco* and a labyrinth of trees. According to Antonio Colbertaldo, biographer of Caterina Cornaro, Pietro Bembo suggested to the queen the use of the name *barco,* which was also approved by her brother Giorgio, who had seen one such type "essere vicino a Pavia altre volte fabricato da Giovan Galeazzo Visconte duca di Milano cosidetto." See T. Marson et al., *Il barco di Altivole: contributi per la conoscenza* (Treviso, Italy: Canova, 2000), 27. Although it is possible that Giorgio Cornaro had visited the Visconti's *barco* at Pavia, the ties between the Republic of Venice and the duchy of Milan are also confirmed by an inscription found at Sforzesca and attributed to the humanist Ermolao Barbaro, the Venetian ambassador at Milan, according to whom Ludovico Sforza had transformed the land from "*vilis gleba*" into "*ditissima tellus.*"

56. The earliest representation of the three walls is in a map from 1546 conserved at the Biblioteca Comunale di Treviso in G. Battista Malimpensa, *Territorio del Trivigiano tra il Livenza ed il Marzenigo,* ms. 1398. See T. Marson et al., *Il barco di Altivole,* 50n6.

57. M. Azzi Visentini, *L'Arte dei giardini. Scritti teorici e practici dal XIV al XIX secolo* (Milan: Edizioni Il Polifilo, 1999), 74–77.

58. I.W.U. Chase, *Horace Walpole: Gardenist; An Edition of Walpole's* The History of the Modern Taste in Gardening, *with an Estimate of Walpole's Contribution to Landscape Architecture* (Princeton, NJ: Princeton University Press, 1943), 13–14.

See also T. Williamson, *Suffolk's Gardens and Parks: Designed Landscapes from the Tudors to the Victorians* (Cheshire, UK: Windgather Press, 2000), 19–29, 84. I thank John Dixon Hunt for these references.

59. Derex, "Les Parcs de Vincennes et de Boulogne au XVIe siècle," 252.

60. Derex, "Les Parcs de Vincennes," 253–54.

61. Derex, "Les Parcs de Vincennes," 265n18.

62. The Medicis were not the only Tuscan family to own several *bandite*. Toward the seventeenth century, in fact, the grand duke began to assign newly created feuds to some of the wealthiest families of Tuscany, such as the Guicciardini. The purpose was to create a new social class whose nobility would be based on the possession of land, more than on commerce as was often the case in Florence. The creation of the feuds had also the objective to help develop the grand duchy into a cohesive state. Although the *bandite* did not always coincide with feuds, they always marked land that was owned by wealthy courtiers, such as the Salviati. See L. Zangheri, *Storia del giardino e del paesaggio: il verde nella cultura occidentale* (Florence: Olschki, 2003), 122–24.

63. Brunon, "La chasse et l'organisation du paysage dans la Toscane des Médicis," 226–27.

64. L. Zangheri, "Il disegno del parco venatorio in età barocca," in *Giardini, contesto, paesaggio: sistemi di giardini e architetture vegetali nel paesaggio: metodi di studio, valutazione, tutela,* ed. L. S. Pelissetti et al. (Florence: Olshcki, 2005), 580.

65. Brunon, "La chasse et l'organisation du paysage dans la Toscane des Médicis," 237.

66. Brunon, "La chasse et l'organisation du paysage dans la Toscane des Médicis," 240.

67. On the meaning of *paretaio*, or *frasconaia*, and *boschetto da tordi*, see Brunon, "La chasse et l'organisation du paysage dans la Toscane des Médicis," 229.

68. The site of the Villa Lante was indeed a hunting park when Cardinal Raffaele Riario owned the land. The park included a hunting lodge and was enclosed in 1514. Later in the century, when Cardinal Gambara commissioned the Villa Lante, the wooded area was emptied of its animals and remained as a foil to the formal gardens of the villa.

69. Coffin, *The Villa in the Life of Renaissance Rome,* 141.

70. Owens, "Diana at the Bar," 32.

71. Williamson, *Suffolk's Gardens and Parks,* 27.

72. See note 3, above.

3 Plantings

1. A. del Riccio, *Agricoltura sperimentale e teorica* (Florence: Biblioteca Nazionale Centrale di Firenze) (ms. Targioni Tozzetti 56, passim).

2. It can be found in largely widespread works such as C. Estienne—J. Liebault, *Maison rustique* (Paris, 1564), and its many following editions, as well as in locally rooted ones like G. Saminiati, "Trattato di agricoltura," in *L'arte dei giardini,* ed. M. Azzi Visentini (Milan: Il Polifilo, 1999), 387ff.

3. M. Pozzana, *Il giardino dei frutti: frutteti, orti, pomari nel giardino e nel paesaggio toscano* (Florence: Ponte alle Grazie, 1990).

4. G. Galletti, "Fortune e sfortune del bosso nei giardini italiani dal Rinascimento al Novecento," in *Topiaria. Architetture e sculture vegetali nel giardino occidentale dall'antichitá ad oggi*, ed. M. Azzi Visentini (Treviso: Fondazione Benetton Studi e Ricerche, 2004), 93–103.

5. For an ample excursus on the Renaissance garden, see Claudia Lazzaro, *The Italian Renaissance Garden, From the Conventions of Planting, Design and Ornament to the Grand Gardens of Sixteenth-Century Central Italy* (New Haven, CT: Yale University Press, 1990).

6. M. Pozzana, "Il giardino del Trebbio," in *Giardini Medicei: Giardini di palazzo e di villa nella Firenze del Quattrocento*, ed. C. Acidini Luchinat (Milan: Federico Motta Editore, 1996), 148–52.

7. It is not within the scope of this essay to discuss this topic. See, for example, M. Levi d'Ancona, *The Garden of the Renaissance. Botanical Symbolism in Italian Painting* (Florence: Olschki, 1977).

8. See on this subject, C. Acidini Luchinat, "Il giardino fiorentino nello specchio delle arti figurative," 17.

9. M. Pozzana, "Agricoltura e orticoltura nella Toscana del Quattrocento," in *Giardini Medicei*, 120–37.

10. "12 quadri tutti con spalliere di lontaggine drento à ciascun quadro v'è otto alberi fruttiferi diversi . . . ," ". . . una muraglia coperta di diversi frutti, cioè prugni, nespole, et granati, et cotogni . . . un viale grande con una spalliera di vite con legnami, et un filo di fichi," "un boschetto d'olive con una spalliera di rose," "una fonte chiamata la Tazza con un bollore in mezo circondata d'olivo con suo sedere di sopra acanto il conservone c'è un boschetto di fichi. A mano manca di detta fonte c'è un viale con varie sorti di frutti, . . .": Inventarium bonorum Palatii Bagnaniae et illius barchi, 29 marzo 1588, ms. Archivio di Stato, Rome, in *L'Arte dei Giardini*, 379–384.

11. M. Tanaglia, *De agricultura*, written around 1489 and published in 1953 by Aurelio Roncaglia (Bologna: Libreria Palmaverde). See also S. Zaninelli, ed., *Scritti teorici e tecnici di agricoltura* (Milan: Il Polifilo, 1995).

12. M. Azzi Visentini, ed., *Topiaria. Architetture e sculture vegetali nel giardino occidentale dall'antichità ad oggi* (Treviso: Fondazione Benetton Studi e Ricerche, 2004).

13. M. Azzi Visentini, "Architetture e sculture vegetali nei giardini italiani tra Trecento e Settecento. Fonti iconografiche e letterarie," in *Topiaria*, 81–92.

14. See R. Wittkower's classic text, *Architectural Principles in the Age of Humanism*, 2nd ed. (London: Tiranti, 1952).

15. L. Battaglia Ricci, "Gardens in Italian Literature during the Thirteenth and Fourteenth Centuries," in *The Italian Garden: Art, Design and Culture*, ed. J. D. Hunt (Cambridge: Cambridge University Press, 1996), 6–33.

16. E. Panofsky, "Artista scienziato genio: appunti sulla 'Renaissance-Dämmerung,'" in *Annali dell'Istituto storico italo-germanico di Trento*, III (City, Publisher, 1977), 278–320; and L. Tongiorgi Tomasi, "L'immagine naturalistica: tecnica e invenzione," in *Natura-Cultura. L'interpretazione del Mondo Fisico nei Testi e nelle Immagini*, Atti del Convegno Internazionale di Studi, ed. G. Olmi, L. Tongiorgi Tomasi, and A. Zanca (Florence: Olschki, 2000), 137–38.

17. Cf. J. Prest, *The Garden of Eden: The Botanical Garden and the Re-Creation of Paradise* (New Haven, CT: Yale University Press, 1981). L. Tongiorgi Tomasi, "'Extra' e 'Intus': progettualità degli orti botanici e collezionismo eclettico tra il XVI e XVII secolo," in *Il giardino come labirinto della storia,* proceedings of an international meeting (Palermo: XX, n.d.), 48–53; and "Gli orti botanici nei secoli XVI e XVII," in *L'architettura dei giardini d'Occidente. Dal Rinascimento al Novecento,* ed. M. Mosser and G. Teyssot (Milan: Electa, 1990), 77–79.

18. See the study by L. Tongiorgi Tomasi, "Projects for Botanical and Other Gardens: A 16th Century Manual," *Journal of Garden History* 3, no. 1 (1983): 1–34, which is still extremely current and full of stimulating points for reflection.

19. On the botanical garden of Padua, see G. Porro, *L'horto de i semplici di Padova* (Venezia, 1591); M. Azzi Visentini, "Il giardino dei semplici di Padova: un prodotto della cultura del Rinascimento," *Comunità* 182 (1980): 259–338; and M. Azzi Visentini, *L'Orto botanico di Padova* (Milan: The publisher is II Polifilo Publisher, 1984). L. Tongiorgi Tomasi, "Gli orti botanici." On the botanical garden of Pisa, see L. Tongiorgi Tomasi, *Giardino dei Semplici* (Pisa: Pacini, 1991), and in particular the discussion of Ms. 464 (conserved in Pisa, Biblioteca Universitaria), which contains several designs for flowerbeds; and L. Tongiorgi Tomasi, "Projects." Finally, on the garden of Leiden, see L. Tjon Sie Fat, "Clusius' Garden: A Reconstruction," in *The Authentic Garden. A Symposium on Gardens,* ed. L. Tjon Sie Fat and E. de Jong (Leiden: Clusius Foundation, 1991), 3–12.

20. For a useful survey of the botanical collections of the Medici and the importance of this phenomenon in sixteenth century Italy, see the authoritative work by L. Tongiorgi Tomasi, "The Flowering of Florence: Botanical Art for the Medici," in *The Flowering of Florence: Botanical Art for the Medici,* exhibition catalogue ed. L. Tongiorgi Tomasi and G. A. Hirschauer (London: Lund Humphries, 2002), 15–57.

21. L. Tongiorgi Tomasi, "The Flowering of Florence."

22. See above and L. Tongiorgi Tomasi, "The Flowering of Florence," 52.

23. A. del Riccio, *Agricoltura sperimentale e teorica,* see note 1. This work has never been published and survives in the form of a somewhat disorganized manuscript.

24. They include the Salviati, the Soderini, the da Sommaia, the Gaddi, the Filicaia, the Acciaiuoli, and the Strozzi. A. del Riccio, "Del giardino di un re," in *Il giardino storico italiano. Problemi di indagine e fonti letterarie,* proceedings of a scholarly meeting, ed. G. Ragionieri (Florence: Olschki, 1981), 59–123. On del Riccio, see also *Istoria delle Pietre,* ed. P. Barocchi (Florence: SPES, 1979).

25. M. Zalum Cardon, *Passione e cultura dei fiori tra Firenze e Roma nel XVI e XVII secolo* (Florence: Olschki, 2008), 18–97.

26. W. Blunt, *Tulipomania* (Harmondsworth: Penguin Books, 1950).

27. *Musaeum Tradescantianum; or, A Collection of Rarities preserved at South Lambeth, near London* (London: John Grismond, 1656). The collection of plants was by far the largest part of the museum, and included many varieties of garlic, lettuces, artichokes, and even nettles.

28. H. Vredeman de Vries, *Hortorum viridariorumque elegantes et multiplices formae, ad architectonicae artis normam* (Antwerp, 1583).

29. A. Gallo, *Le dieci giornate della vera agricoltura, e piaceri della villa* (Venezia: Domenico Farri, 1565); and *Trattato di agricoltura di Giovanvettorio Soderini ora per la prima volta pubblicato* (Firenze: Stamperia del Giglio, 1811).

30. I have used the following edition: *L'agriculture, et Maison rustique de mm. Charles Estienne, & Jean Liebault, docteurs en médecine,* edition dernière, reueue & augmentée . . . , (Lyon: Jaques du Puis, 1578).

31. G. B. Della Porta, Villae (Frankfurt: A. Wechel, 1592).

32. A. Segre, "Le retour de Flore: Naissance et évolution des jardins de fleurs de 1550 à 1650," in *L'Empire de Flore: Histoire et représentation des fleurs en Europe du XVIe au XIXe siècle* ed. S. van Sprang (Brussels: Renaissance du livre, 1996), where these sixteenth-century treatises are also cited.

33. With regard to the planting of bulbs in Italian gardens, see the very interesting study by A. Maiorino, M. Minelli, A. L. Monti, B. Negroni, and A. Segre, "L'uso dei bulbi da fiore nei giardini del Rinascimento. Il caso di Boboli," in *Boboli 90,* ed. C. Acidini Luchinat and E. Garbero Zorzi (Florence: Edifir, 1991), 277–89.

34. Florence, Biblioteca Medicea Laurenziana, Ms. Ashburnam 380. This is a manuscript of about one hundred pages, with two sets of page numbers, that contains an incomplete version of the poem *Sileno,* many poetic fragments, a collection of epigraphic inscriptions relating to the Roman emperors, and other miscellaneous material. See M. Azzi Visentini, "Il governo del giardino storico: l'apporto delle fonti," in *Il Giardino e il tempo. Conservazione e manutenzione delle architetture vegetali,* ed. M. Boriani and L. Scazzosi (Milan: Guerini e associati, 1992), 83–90; and M. Zalum Cardon, *Passione e cultura,* 180–82.

35. P. Vallet, *Le Jardin du roy très Chrestien Henri IV* (Paris: n.p., 1608).

36. B. Besler, *Hortus Eistettensis* (Nuremberg, 1614). On the history of the florilegium, see L. Tongiorgi Tomasi, *An Oak Spring Flora: Flower Illustration from the 15th Century to the Present Time* (Upperville, VA: Oak Spring Garden Library, 1997), 52–57 (with further bibliography); and *Fiori, cinque secoli di pittura floreale,* ed. F. Solinas (Rome: Campisano Editore, 2004), 105–39.

37. E. van Gelder, *Tussen hof en keizerskroon: Carolus Clusius en de ontwikkeling van de botanie aan Midden-Europese hoven (1573–1593)* (Leiden: Leiden University Press, 2011).

38. A part of Caccini's correspondence is now conserved in the Bibliothèque Royale Albert I in Brussels (hereafter cited as BAB): M. Zalum Cardon, *Passione e cultura.* On the culture of exchange and its relevance for the development of natural history, see F. Egmond, P. Hoftijzer, and R. Visser, eds., *Carolus Clusius: Towards a Cultural History of a Renaissance Naturalist* (Amsterdam: Koninklijke Nederlandse Akademie van Wetenschappen, 2007); and F. Egmond, *The World of Carolus Clusius: Natural History in the Making, 1550–1610* (London: Pickering and Chatto, 2010).

39. This was the case, for example, with the "Narciso di Cipro," a plant described by Matthias de L'Obel that Caccini was very eager to acquire. Arembergh wrote in person to L'Obel in England and asked if he might have a specimen; see BAB, 3.893.2, letters no. 107, 109 and 120. Arembergh also sent Caccini an anemone "di velluto" from his own garden after having sought and failed to find another specimen: "Intratanto mando qui un pezeto del anemone de veluto che mi è stato

dato per gran presente non avendone retenuta cossa [In the meantime I send you a piece of the velvet (plush) anemone that was presented to me as a gift, not having kept any for myself]"; cf. letters no. 107 and 112. See also G. Masson, "Italian Flower Collectors' Gardens," in *The Italian Garden,* ed. D. Coffin (Washington, D.C.: Dumbarton Oaks, 1972), 75.

40. The ties between Arembergh and Clusius are documented in some letters now kept in the archives of the Capuchin monastery in Enghien (A. Roeykens, "Charles, prince-comte d'Arembergh: Restaurateur du parc d'Enghien au début di XVIIe siècle," *Annales du Cercle d'Archéologique d'Enghien,* 15 [1967–69]: 211–45, where one may also find some information on Enghien), as well as in letters sent by Clusius to Caccini, in which the prince-count is often mentioned (P. Ginori Conti, *Lettere inedite di Charles de l'Escluse [Carolus Clusius] a Matteo Caccini floricoltore fiorentino. Contributo alla storia della botanica* [Florence: Olschki, 1939]). See also Egmond, Hoftijzer, and Visser, *Carlous Clusius,* and Egmond, *The world of Carolus Clusius.*

41. G. Masson, "Italian Flower Collectors' Gardens," 66.

42. "[The anemones] adornano assay un Jardino quando li bulbose anno finito il suo Corso che di ordinario la Major parte è a fin de Junio si no sono le anemone che si a trovato inventione di averli tuti li mesi del anno et per esser vero ne ho Adesso che stanno con le fiori et per questo prego a V.S. mandarmi de puy sorti": BAB, 3.893.2, letter no. 107.

43. Cf. BAB, 3.893.2, letter dated 5 March 1609, no. 108.

44. BAB, 3.893.2, letter no. 183.

45. BAB, 3.893.2, letter no. 184.

46. On the theme of metamorphosis and the culture of gardening at the beginning of the seventeenth century, see A. Segre, "La metamorfosi e il giardino italiano nel Seicento," in *Il Giardino delle Muse. Arti e artifici nel barocco europeo,* atti del IV Colloquio Internazionale, ed. M. A. Giusti and A. Tagliolini (Firenze, Edifir, 1995), 97–126.

47. "cosa da Principe il dar leggi, sì come agli uomini, così anche ai fiori": G. B. Ferrari, *Flora overo cultura di fiori* (Roma, 1638), 9.

48. BAB, 3.893.2, letter no. 128.

49. Rome, Archivio Fondazione Caetani (AFC), letter dated December 11, 1621; G. P. Bellori, *Nota delli Musei, Librerie, Gallerie & ornamenti di statue, e pitture, né Palazzi, nelle Case, e né Giardini di Roma* (Roma, 1664), 54. On conventual apothecaries in Rome, see M. Breccia Fratadocchi and S. Buttò, eds., *Erbe e speziali. I laboratori della salute,* exhibition cat. (Rome: Aboca Museum, 2007).

50. Roma, Biblioteca Corsiniana (hereafter cited as BC), Archivio della Pia Casa degli Orfani di Santa Maria in Aquiro, Fondo Faber, vol. 419, f. 659, cited in I. Baldriga, *L'occhio della lince. I primi lincei tra arte, scienza e collezionismo (1603–1630)* (Rome: Accademia Nazionale dei Lincei, 2002), 197–98, 199. For some documents on Faber's activities as an intermediary between collectors, see p. 202. Cardinal Pio's garden will become famous for a new type of pergola designed for citrus plants, which is described in G. B. Ferrari's treatise, *Hesperides sive de malorum aureorum cultura* (Roma, 1646), 145; see A. Campitelli, "I cocchi di agrumi nelle ville romane," in *Il giardino delle Esperidi. Gli agrumi nella storia, nella letteratura*

e nell'arte, ed. A. Tagliolini and M. Azzi Visentini (Florence: Edifir, 1996), 175–96. Faber's manuscript catalogue of Rondanini's plants is mentioned in G. Gabrieli, *Contributi alla storia dell'Accademia dei Lincei* (Rome: Accademia Nazionale dei Lincei, 1989), 1179, 1280–81; and by I. Baldriga, *L'occhio della lince,* 206. It is conserved in BC, Fondo Faber, vol. 413, c. 752–56.

51. See respectively, I. Baldriga, *L'occhio della lince,* 211–12; and G. P. Bellori, *Nota delli Musei,* 21.

52. A. Campitelli, "Gli 'Horti di Flora.' I giardini di Roma ai tempi di Giovan Battista Ferrari," in G. B. Ferrari, *Flora overo cultura di fiori,* reproduction in facsimile edited with an introduction by L. Tongiorgi Tomasi (Florence: Olschki, 2001), 27–42.

53. E. Sweerts, *Florilegium tractans de variis floribus, at aliis indicis plantis ad vivum delineatum in duabus partibus* (Frankfurt, 1612–14).

54. L. Ramón-Laca, "The Additions by the Count of Aremberg," in *Drawn after Nature: The Complete Botanical Watercolours of the 16th-Century* Libri Picturati, ed. J. de Koning, G. van Uffelen, A. Zemanek, and B. Zemanek (Zeist, the Netherlands: KNNV Publishing, 2008), 29–31. Van Coxcie is not the only artist to take up the cultivation of flowers: Schnapper cites the case of the French painter Roch Voisin (whose works today are either lost or unknown), who is an assiduous collector of tulips; see A. Schnapper, "'Curieux fleuristes'. Collectionneurs de fleurs dans la France du XVIe siècle," *Commentaire,* n. 21 (1983): 178; Idem, *Introduction* to G. Aymonin's D. Rabel, *Cent fleurs et insects,* ed. G. Aymonin (Arcueil: Anthèse, 1991) 11. It appears that Jacques de Gheyn II, who is one of the first artists in the Low Countries to specialize in the new genre of flower painting, possessed a large collection of bulbous plants; see C. Swan, *Art, Science and Witchcraft in Early Modern Holland: Jacques de Gheyn II (1565–1629)* (Cambridge: Cambridge University Press, 2005), passim.

55. E. Hyde, "The Cultivation of a King, or the Flower Gardens of Louis XIV," in *Tradition and Innovation in French Garden Art. Chapters of a New History,* ed. J. D. Hunt and M. Conan (Philadelphia: University of Pennsylvania Press, 2002), 1–21; and E. Hyde, "Flowers of Distinction: Taste, Class and Floriculture in Seventeenth Century France," in *Bourgeois and Aristocratic Cultural Encounters in Garden Art, 1550–1850,* Colloquium in the History of Landscape Architecture 23, ed. M. Conan (Washington, D.C.: Dumbarton Oaks, 2002), 77–100.

56. A. Schnapper, *Le Géant, la licorne et la tulipe. Collections et collectionneurs dans la France du XVIIe siècle,* vol. 1—*Histoire et histoire naturelle* (Paris: Flammarion, 1988), 228–31.

57. R. W. Lightbown, "Some Notes on Spanish Baroque Collectors," in *The Origins of Museums. The Cabinet of Curiosities in Sixteenth- and Seventeenth-Century Europe,* ed. O. Impey and A. MacGregor (Oxford: Clarendon Press, 1985), 136–46. See also S. Gómez López, "Natural collections in the Spanish Renaissance," in *From Private to Public: Natural Collections and Museums,* ed. M. Beretta (Sagamore Beach, MA: Science History Publications, 2005), 13–40.

58. T. Aldini, *Exactissima descriptio rariorum quarundam plantarum quæ continentur Romæ in Horto Farnesiano* (Roma, 1625). For a detailed description of the Farnese gardens, see the important collection of studies, M. Serio, ed., *Gli Orti Farnesiani sul Palatino,* proceedings of an international meeting (Rome: Ecole française de Rome-Soprintendenza Archeologica 1990).

59. F. Colonna, *Minus cognitarum stirpium aliquot, ac etiam rariorum nostro coelo orientium ekphrasis* (Rome: apud Guilielmum Facciottum, 1606).

60. Montpellier, Bibliothèque de l'Ecole de Médècine, Ms. H 170, c. 94r. The same text can be found in a manuscript in the Biblioteca Apostolica Vaticana (hereafter cited as BAV), Ms. Barb. lat. 4282, c. 17v; cf. L. Tongiorgi Tomasi, "Francesco Mingucci 'giardiniere' e pittore naturalista: un aspetto della committenza barberiniana nella Roma seicentesca," in *Atti del Convegno celebrativo del IV centenario della nascita di Federico Cesi,* (Rome: Accademia Nazionale dei Lincei, 1986), 277–306, in particular 290.

61. A. Alessandrini, *Cimeli lincei a Montpellier* (Rome: Accademia Nazionale dei Lincei, 1978), 246.

62. Montpellier, Bibliothèque de l'École del Médècine, Ms. H 502. The work by Romauli can also be found in BAV, Ms. Barb. lat. 4278. It was published by L. Tongiorgi Tomasi, "Francesco Mingucci"; subsequently, the work was correctly attributed to Romauli by L. Tongiorgi Tomasi, "L'arte ingenua e ingegnosa di coltivare i fiori. Note su *Flora overo cultura di fiori* di Giovan Battista Ferrari," in G. B. Ferrari, *Flora ovvero cultura di fiori,* reproduction in facsimile edited with an introduction by L. Tongiorgi Tomasi (Florence: Olschki, 2001), 15. See also D. Freedberg, "Cassiano, Ferrari and Other Drawings of Citrus Fruits," in *Citrus Fruits. The Paper Museum of Cassiano dal Pozzo: A Catalogue Raisonné,* ed. D. Freedberg and E. Baldini (London: Harvey Miller, 1997), 45.

63. BAV, Barb. lat. 4283; see L. Tongiorgi Tomasi, "Francesco Mingucci," 287.

64. L. Tongiorgi Tomasi, "Geometric Schemes for Plant Beds and Gardens: A Contribution to the History of the Garden in the Sixteenth and Seventeenth Centuries," in *World Art. Themes of Unity in Diversity,* Acts of the 26th International Congress on the History of Art, ed. I. Lavin (University Park: Penn State University Press, 1989), 213; C. Swan, *Art, Science.*

65. On this process of change see F. Egmond, "Clusius and Friends: Cultures of Exchange in the Circle of European Naturalists," in *Carolus Clusius,* 23–24.

66. See Flora, *short title,* passim.

67. On his gift of an African antelope, see F. Solinas, "The Oryx," in *Il Museo cartaceo di Cassiano Dal Pozzo. Cassiano naturalista, Quaderni puteani* 1, (Milan: Olivetti, 1989), 48–51. Peiresc also sends to Cardinal Francesco (through Cassiano dal Pozzo) the "gelsomino giallo indiano odoratissimo" to be introduced in the Barberini gardens (Ferrari, *Flora overo,* 389).

68. G. B. Ferrari, *De florum cultura* (Roma: Stephanus Paulinus, 1633); *Flora overo;* and *Hesperides.*

69. On Aldrovandi and his profound ties with the culture of the past, see G. Olmi, *L'inventario del mondo: catalogazione della natura e luoghi del sapere nella prima età moderna* (Bologna: Il Mulino, 1992), 32–33.

70. On Cassiano dal Pozzo and his monumental project to catalogue all of perceptible reality, see F. Solinas, ed., *Cassiano Dal Pozzo,* proceedings of an international seminar (Rome: De Luca, 1989); *Quaderni puteani,* published by Olivetti between 1989 and 1993; and finally F. Solinas, ed., *I segreti di un collezionista,* exhibition catalogue (Rome: De Luca, 2000).

71. See P. Rosemberg and L.A. Prat, eds., *Nicolas Poussin,* exhibition catalogue (Paris: Reunion des Musee Nationaux, 1994), 146–49, 203–5.

72. G. P. Bellori, *Le vite de' pittori, scultori ed architetti moderni* (Roma, 1672), 441–42.

4 Use and Reception

1. Built between 1569 and 1581 by Bernardo Buontalenti, they were still under construction when Montaigne arrived.

2. M. de Montaigne, *The Complete Works: Essays, Travel Journal, Letters,* tr. D. M. Frame with an introduction by Stuart Hampshire (New York: Everyman's Library, Alfred K. Knopf, 2003), 1132.

3. Montaigne, *Complete Works,* 1132.

4. J. Evelyn, *The Diary of John Evelyn,* vol. 2, ed. E. S. de Beer (Oxford: Oxford University Press, 1955), 418.

5. For all six images, see M. Becattini, *Parco Mediceo di Pratolino: Villa Demidoff. Una storia per immagini,* with preface by L. Zangheri (Firenze, Italy: Edizioni Polistampa, 2005), 31–36. See also A. de Vesme, *Stefano Della Bella: Catalogue Raisonné,* with introduction and additions by P. D. Massar (New York: Collectors Editions, 1971), 129–30. See also S. W. Reed and R. Wallace, *Italian Etchers of the Renaissance & Baroque* (Boston: Museum of Fine Arts, 1989), 239–40.

6. Hunt has argued that Italian humanists Bartolomeo Taegio and Jacopo Bonfadio, each by invoking the notion of a third nature to describe the formal garden, alluded to Cicero's *De natura deorum,* in which Cicero described human agricultural intervention on the landscape as a second nature. J. D. Hunt, *Greater Perfections: The Practice of Garden Theory* (London: Thames and Hudson, 2000), 32–34.

7. N. de Bonnefons, *Le Jardinier François, qui enseigne à cultiver les arbres et herbes potagers; avec la maniere de conserver les fruicts, & faire toutes sortes de confitures, conserves & massepans. Dédié aux dames* (Paris: Chez Pierre Des-Hayes, 1651).

8. For a bibliographical analysis of books published on fruits in the Renaissance and early modern period, see S. Raphael, *An Oak Spring Pomona: A Selection of the Rare Books on Fruit in the Oak Spring Garden Library* (Upperville, VA: Oak Spring Garden Library, 1990).

9. J. de la Quintinie, *Instruction pour les Jardins Fruitiers et Potagers, avec un Traité des Orangers, suivy de quelques Réflexions sur l'Agriculture, par feu Mr de la Quintinye, Directeur de tous les Jardins Fruitiers et Potagers du Roy* (Paris: Claude Barbin, 1690).

10. O. de Serres, *Le Théâtre d'agriculture et mesnage des champs* (Paris: Paris: Abr. Saugrain, 1600; repr. 1605).

11. J. Evelyn, *Sylva; or, A Discourse of Forest-Trees, and the Propagation of Timber in His Majesties Dominions* (London: Jo. Martyn and Ja. Allestry, 1664). For a discussion of the book, see Raphael, *An Oak Spring Pomona,* 95–97.

12. For a discussion of the nursery system at Versailles, see E. Hyde, *Cultivated Power: Flowers, Culture, and Politics in the Reign of Louis XIV* (Philadelphia: University of Pennsylvania Press, 2005).

13. For a discussion of the gendered division of labor in gardening, see E. Hyde, *Cultivated Power: Flowers, Culture, and Politics in the Reign of Louis XIV* (Philadelphia: University of Pennsylvania Press, 2005), 19–26.

14. *La Culture des fleurs, ou il est traitté generalement de la maniere de semer, planter, transplanter & conserver toutes sortes de fleurs & d'arbres, ou arbrisseaux à fleurs,*

connus in France. Et de douze maximes generales desquelles il est necessaire d'être instruit our pratiquer utilement cette sort d'agriculture (Bourge en Bresse: Joseph Ravoux, 1692), preface, n.p.

15. H. Memling, *Annunciation,* c. 1465–75. Metropolitan Museum of Art, 17.190.7.

16. G. Rucellai, *Le Api* (1539); and L. Alamanni, *La Coltivatione* (Paris: Robert Estienne, 1546). For discussion of Renaissance interest in Virgil, see L. P. Wilkinson's introduction in Virgil, *The Georgics,* tr. L. P. Wilkinson (London: Cambridge University Press, 1969), 47.

17. R. Rapinus, *Of Gardens. Four Books. First written in Latine Verse by Renatus Rapinus,* tr. J. Evelyn (London: T.R. & N.T., 1673), preface, n.p.

18. Rapinus, *Of Gardens,* preface, n.p.

19. Rapinus, *Of Gardens,* preface, n.p.

20. A. Félibien, *La Description du château de Versailles* (Paris: Antoine Vilette, 1694), 84–85.

21. Quoted in P.-A. Lablaude, *Gardens of Versailles* (Paris: Editions Scala France, 2006), 104.

22. J. B. Colbert, *Lettres, instructions, et mémoires de Colbert,* vol. 5 (Paris: Imprimerie Impériale, 1861–1882), quoted in A. Marie, *Naissance de Versailles,* vol. 2 (Paris: Vincent, Fréal et Cie, 1968), 225.

23. R. W. Berger and T. F. Hedin, *Diplomatic Tours in the Gardens of Versailles under Louis XIV* (Philadelphia: University of Pennsylvania Press, 2008), 15.

24. Pieter Brueghel the Elder, *Spring,* ca. 1570. National Museum of Art of Romania, Bucharest.

25. Montaigne, *Complete Works,* 1132.

26. See, for example, *The Mystical Marriage of St. Catherine,* c. 1490, Museu nacional de art antiga, Lisbon, reproduced in S. Landsberg, *The Medieval Garden* (Toronto: University of Toronto Press), 14.

27. R. Fabiani Giannetto, *Medici Gardens: From Making to Design* (Philadelphia: University of Pennsylvania Press, 2008), 50–53.

28. M. Conan, "Friendship and Imagination in French Baroque Gardens before 1661," in *Baroque Garden Cultures: Emulation, Sublimation, Subversion,* ed. M. Conan (Washington, D.C.: Dumbarton Oaks Research Library and Collection, 2005), 323–84.

29. For a discussion of the garden's iconography, see L. Impelluso, *Gardens in Art,* trans. S. Sartarelli (Los Angeles: J. Paul Getty Museum, 2007), 49.

30. See P. Carpeggiani, "Labyrinths in the Gardens of the Renaissance," in *The Architecture of Western Gardens,* ed. M. Mosser and G. Teyssot (Cambridge, MA: MIT Press, 1991), 84.

31. Carpeggiani, "Labyrinths," 84.

32. C. Mollet, *Théâtre des plans et jardinages* (Paris: Charles de Sercy, 1652).

33. M. Baridon, *A History of the Gardens of Versailles,* trans. A. Mason (Philadelphia: University of Pennsylvania Press, 2008), 184–89. See also M. Conan, "The Conundrum of Le Nôtre's Labyrinthe," in *Garden History: Issues, Approaches, Methods,* ed. J. D. Hunt (Washington, D.C.: Dumbarton Oaks Research Library and Collection, 1992): 119–50.

34. E. B. MacDougall, *Fountains, Statues, and Flowers: Studies in Italian Gardens of the Sixteenth and Seventeenth Centuries* (Washington, D.C.: Dumbarton Oaks Research Library and Collection, 1994), 25.

35. J. Evelyn, *The Diary of John Evelyn,* vol. 2, ed. E. S. de Beer (Oxford: Oxford University Press, 1955), 132–33.

36. J. D. Hunt, "Curiosities to Adorn Cabinets and Gardens," in *The Origins of Museums: The Cabinet of Curiosities in Sixteenth- and Seventeenth-Century Europe,* ed. by O. Impey and A. MacGregor (Oxford: Clarendon Press, 1985), 193–203.

37. E. B. MacDougall, "A Cardinal's Bulb Garden: A *Giardino Segreto* at the Palazzo Barberini in Rome," in *Fountains, Statues, and Flowers,* 219–347.

38. Hyde, *Cultivated Power,* 155–57.

39. L. Tongiorgi Tomasi, "Botanical Gardens of the Sixteenth and Seventeenth Centuries," in *The Architecture of Western Gardens,* ed. M. Mosser and G. Teyssot (Cambridge, MA: MIT Press, 1991), 81.

40. L. Tongiorgi Tomasi, "Gardens of Knowledge and the *République des Gens de Sciences,*" in *Baroque Garden Cultures: Emulation, Sublimation, and Subversion,* ed. M. Conan (Washington, D.C.: Dumbarton Oaks Research Library and Collection, 2005), 88–89, 108–109.

41. P. Taylor, ed., "Paris, Jardin des Plantes," in *The Oxford Companion to the Garden* (Oxford: Oxford University Press, 2009), 364.

42. E. C. Spary, *Utopia's Garden: French Natural History from Old Regime to Revolution* (Chicago: University of Chicago Press, 2000).

43. The botanist Carolus Clusius had obtained his tulip bulbs from Ogier Ghiselin de Busbecq, the imperial ambassador to Constantinople. For the best account of the Dutch tulip mania, see A. Goldgar, *Tulipmania: Money, Honor, and Knowledge in the Dutch Golden Age* (Chicago: University of Chicago Press, 2008).

44. See E. Magne, *Le Château de Marly, d'après des documents inédits* (Paris: Calmann-Lévy, 1934), 157–60.

45. N. Valnay, *Connoissance et culture parfaite des tulippes rares, des anemones extraordinaires, des oeillets fins, et des belles oreilles d'ours panachées* (Paris: Laurent d'Houry, 1688), 55.

46. See Matteo Valleriani, "Pratolino: The History of Science in a Garden," http://pratolino.mpiwg-berlin.mpg.de/ (accessed February 4, 2013). The treatise was written by Greek mathematician Hero of Alexandria in the first century CE. It was translated into Latin in 1575 by Federico Commandino.

47. A. Ramelli, *Le diverse et artificiose machine del capitano Agostino Ramelli . . . Nellequali si contengono uarij et industriosi mouimenti, degni digrandissima speculatione, per cauarne beneficio infinito in ogni sorte d'operatione; composte in lingua italiana et francese* (Paris, 1588); and S. de Caus, *Les raisons des forces mouuantes, auec diuerses machines tant vtilles que plaisantes: aus quelles sont adioints plusieurs desseings de grotes et fontaines* (Frankfurt: En la boutique de Ian Norton, 1615).

48. A. Grafton, *Worlds Made by Words: Scholarship and Community in the Modern West* (Cambridge, MA: Harvard University Press, 2009), 90–97.

49. See Valleriani, "Pratolino"; L. Morgan, *Nature as Model: Salomon de Caus and Early Seventeenth-Century Landscape Design* (Philadelphia: University of

Pennsylvania Press, 2007); and M. Baridon, *A History of the Gardens of Versailles,* trans. A. Mason (Philadelphia: University of Pennsylvania Press, 2008).

50. K. Woodbridge, *Princely Gardens: The Origins and Development of the French Formal Style* (New York: Rizzoli, 1986), 61.

51. See Morgan, *Nature as Model.*

52. Morgan, *Nature as Model,* 64.

53. Berger and Hedin, *Diplomatic Tours,* 15, 17.

54. Baridon, *A History of the Gardens of Versailles,* 103–5.

55. See B. Saule, ed., *Catalogue de la Exposition Sciences et Curiosités à la cour de Versailles* (Versailles: RMN éditions and Etablissement public du château, du musée et du domaine national de Versailles, 2010).

56. For the most complete discussion of this thesis, see C. Mukerji, *Territorial Ambitions and the Gardens of Versailles* (Cambridge: Cambridge University Press, 1997).

57. For discussion of this image, see S. W. Reed, *French Prints from the Age of the Musketeers* (Boston: Museum of Fine Arts, 1998), 134.

58. O. de Serres, *Le Théâtre d'agriculture et mesnage des champs,* 3rd ed. (Paris: Abr. Saugrain, 1605), 500–501.

59. For an overview of the royal taste for hunting in the seventeenth and eighteenth centuries, see T. Blanning, *The Pursuit of Glory: The Five Revolutions that Made Modern Europe, 1648–1815* (New York: Penguin Books, 2008), 393–422.

60. For a description, see B. Adorni, "The Villa Lante at Bagnaia," in *The Architecture of Western Gardens,* 91–95.

61. See Jacques de Celloles, *Archery Contest,* ca. 1480, Bibliothèque Nationale de France, Paris; and *The Game of Blindman's Bluff,* miniature in collection of French love poems by Peirra Sala, British Library, London, both reproduced in Lucia Impelluso, *Gardens into Art,* 264–65.

62. *Nouveau traité de la civilité qui se pratique en France parmi les honnêtes-gens. Nouvelle Edition revuë, corrigée, & de beaucoup augmentée par l'Auteur* (Paris: Chez Louis Josse and Charles Robustez, 1728), 159.

63. For a description, see P. Hobhouse, "Vatican Gardens," *The Oxford Companion to the Garden,* ed. P. Taylor (Oxford.: Oxford University Press, 2006), 492–93.

64. R. Fabiani Giannetto, *Medici Gardens: From Making to Design* (Philadelphia: University of Pennsylvania Press, 2008), 155–61.

65. Woodbridge, *Princely Gardens,* 81–83.

66. Writes Woodbridge, "The structures made for these theatrical occasions were becoming permanent features in gardens, where utility gave way to, or at times mingled with, symbolism and allegory." See Woodbridge, *Princely Gardens,* 83.

67. Baridon, *A History of the Gardens of Versailles,* 182–84.

68. Morgan, *Nature as Model,* 179–80.

69. On the Medici gardens, see T. Comito, "The Humanist Garden," in *The Architecture of Western Gardens,* 40; for an exploration of the use of the Virgilian Golden Age by Louis XIV and his iconographers, see Hyde, *Cultivated Power.*

70. M. R. Delalande, "Du Palais de Flore dansé à Trianon devant Sa Majesté le 5 janvier 1689," in *Recueil des sujets paroles d'une partie des ballets, dansez devant sa Majesté* (Paris: Christophe Ballard, 1709), 7.

71. Berger and Hedin, *Diplomatic Tours.*

72. Berger and Hedin, *Diplomatic Tours,* 17.

73. *Mercure Galant,* 1686.

74. *Tapisseries du Roi, où sont représentés les quatre éléments et les quatre saisons* (Paris: Imp. Royale, 1670).

75. J. U. Krauss, *Tapisseries du roy, où sont representez les quatre élémens et les quatre saisons, avec les devises qui les accompagnent et leur explication. Königliche französische Tapezereyen, oder überaus schöne Sinn-Bilder, in welchen die vier Element samt den vier Jahr-Zeiten . . . an den Tag gegeben und verlegt durch Johann Ulrich Krauss* (Augsburg, Germany: gedruckt daselbst durch J. Koppmayer, 1687).

76. See M. Martin, *Dairy Queens: The Politics of Pastoral Architecture from Catherine de'Medici to Marie-Antoinette* (Cambridge, MA: Harvard University Press, 2011).

77. E. de Jong, "Of Plants and Gardeners, Prints and Books: Reception and Exchange in Northern European Garden Culture 1648–1725," in *Baroque Garden Cultures: Emulation, Sublimation, Subversion,* ed. M. Conan (Washington, D.C.: Dumbarton Oaks Research Library and Collection, 2005), 37–84.

78. Montaigne, *Complete Works,* 1135–36.

5 Meaning

1. U. Eco, *A Theory of Semiotics* (Bloomington: Indiana University Press, 1976), 275.

2. See M. Francis and R. T. Hester Jr., eds., *Meaning of Gardens: Ideas, Place and Action* (Cambridge, MA: MIT Press, 1990), 4. Michel Foucault argued that gardens were heterotopias or "counter-sites, a kind of effectively enacted utopia in which the real sites, all the other real sites that can be found within the culture, are simultaneously represented, contested and inverted." See M. Foucault, "Of Other Spaces," *Diacritics* 16, no. 3 (1986): 24.

3. J. Elkins, "On the Conceptual Analysis of Gardens," 189.

4. G. Vasari, *The Lives of the Painters, Sculptors and Architects,* rev. ed., tr. A. B. Hinds (London: Dent; New York: Dutton, 1963), 174.

5. M. de Montaigne, *Montaigne's Travel Journal,* tr. D. M. Frame (San Francisco, CA: North Point Press, 1983).

6. R. Barthes, "From Work to Text," in *Image Music Text,* tr. S. Heath (London: Fontana Press, 1977), 159.

7. Hunt makes this point in *Garden and Grove: The Italian Renaissance Garden in the English Imagination, 1600–1750* (London: J. M. Dent & Sons, 2000), 42.

8. The almost complete absence of Christian imagery and symbolism in the Renaissance garden still seems surprising, especially given the importance of the Garden of Eden in the Judeo-Christian tradition, not to mention water, the operative element of entry into the church, or baptism, and without extensive supplies of which the construction of no garden of the early modern period would have been contemplated.

9. It is worth noting, however, that both L. B. Alberti, writing in the mid-fifteenth century, and P. Ligorio, writing in the second half of the sixteenth, object to the inclusion of "obscene" or "lascivious" fountains in gardens, on moral grounds. See Alberti, *On the Art of Building in Ten Books,* tr. J. Rykwert et al. (Cambridge,

MA: MIT Press, 1988), book 9, 300; and D. Coffin, "Pirro Ligorio on the Nobility of the Arts," *Journal of the Warburg and Courtauld Institutes* 27 (1964): 200.

10. See L. B. Alberti, *Art of Building,* book 4, 196; and S. de Caus, *La Perspective, avec le raison des ombres et miroirs* (London, J. Norton, 1611), fols. 30–31. See also Chapter 1 in this volume.

11. The classical literary ideal of the *locus amoenus* (pleasant place) is familiar from the works of Homer, Theocritus, and Virgil. The notion became a standard topos of Renaissance evocations of real and ideal gardens, much used, for example, by Bartolomeo Taegio in his *La villa. Un dialogo* (1559). For an account of the revival and subsequent fortunes of the idea in Italian literature prior to the Renaissance, see L. B. Ricci, "Gardens in Italian Literature during the Thirteenth and Fourteenth Centuries," in *The Italian Garden: Art, Design and Culture,* ed. J. H. Dixon (Cambridge: Cambridge University Press, 1996), 6–33; and R. Fabiani Giannetto, "Writing the Garden in the Age of Humanism: Petrarch and Boccaccio," *Studies in the History of Gardens and Designed Landscapes* 23, no. 3 (2003): 213–57. For *La Villa,* see B Taegio, *La Villa,* ed. and tr. T. E. Beck (Philadelphia: University of Pennsylvania, 2011).

12. For Basil's view, see J. M. Prest, *Garden of Eden: The Botanic Garden and the Re-Creation of Paradise* (New Haven, CT: Yale University Press, 1981), 18; for Polybius and Philostratus, see E. Panofsky, "*Et in Arcadia Ego:* Poussin and the Elegiac Tradition," in *Meaning in the Visual Arts* (Hammondsworth: Penguin, 1970), 343.

13. For Bacon's 1625 essay "Of Gardens," see J. D. Hunt and P. Willis, eds., *Genius of the Place: The English Landscape Garden 1620–1820* (London: Elek, 1975), 51–56.

14. R. Williams, *Keywords: A Vocabulary of Culture and Society* (London: Fontana, 1976), 219.

15. See, among other publications, J. D. Hunt, "*Paragone* in Paradise: Translating the Garden," *Comparative Criticism* 18 (1996): 55–70.

16. See C. Lazzaro, *The Italian Renaissance Garden: From the Conventions of Planting, Design, and Ornament to the Grand Gardens of Sixteenth-Century Central Italy* (New Haven, CT: Yale University Press, 1990), 61.

17. Lazzaro, *Renaissance Garden,* 27.

18. Hunt, "*Paragone* in Paradise," 59. On the general subject of representation, see also J. D. Hunt, *Greater Perfections: The Practice of Garden Theory* (Philadelphia: University of Pennsylvania Press, 2000), 76–115.

19. Hunt, *Greater Perfections,* 84–85.

20. Pliny the Younger, *Letters,* tr. W. Melmoth (London: William Heinemann; New York: Macmillan, 1927), letter 6, book 5.

21. See Hunt, *Garden and Grove,* 12.

22. See Lazzaro, *Renaissance Garden,* 79, for details of hippodromes. For a detailed study, see L. Cellauro, "Classical Paradigms: Pliny the Younger's Hippodrome at his Tuscan Villa and Renaissance Gardens," *Gartenkunst* 17, no.1 (2005): 73–89.

23. E. B. MacDougall, "Imitation and Invention: language and Decoration in Roman Renaissance Gardens," in *Fountains, Statues and Flowers: Studies in Italian Gardens of the Sixteenth and Seventeenth Centuries* (Washington, D.C.: Dumbarton Oaks Research Collection and Library, 1994), 57–87.

24. For a more detailed discussion of garden "narratives," see L. Morgan, *Nature as Model: Salomon de Caus and Early Seventeenth-Century Landscape Design* (Philadelphia: University of Pennsylvania Press, 2007), 152–55.

25. My comments are indebted to Louis Cellauro's "Iconographical Aspects of the Renaissance Villa and Garden: Mount Parassus, Pegasus and the Muses," *Studies in the History of Gardens and Designed Landscapes* 23, no. 1 (January–March 2003): 42–57.

26. Lazzaro, *Renaissance Garden,* 236.

27. C. Lazzaro, "The Villa Lante at Bagnaia: An Allegory of Art and Nature," *Art Bulletin* 4, no. 59 (1977): 555.

28. Pliny, *Letters,* letter 6, book 5.

29. "Frederick, King of Bohemia, Count of the Rhine and Elector Palatine, after he had toppled the peaks of the mountains into the valleys, consecrated this place, once holy to Diana, to Vertumnus. He decorated it with water pipes, grottos, statues, plants, flowers and extremely tall trees, transplanted very artfully from the suburban garden, and he completed this work to this point in the year of our Lord 1619." For a discussion of this inscription, see R. Zimmermann, "Iconography in German and Austrian Renaissance Gardens," in *Garden History: Issues, Approaches, Methods,* ed. J. D. Hunt (Washington, D.C.: Dumbarton Oaks Research Library and Collection, 1992), 98.

30. For the long history of the motif, see P. Demetz, "The Elm and the Vine: Notes toward the History of a Marriage Topos," *PMLA: Publications of the Modern Language Association of America* 73, no. 5 (1958): 521.

31. See Chapter 1 of this volume.

32. Quoted in C. Thacker, "'Manière de montrer les jardins de Versaille': by Louis XIV and Others," *Garden History* 1, no. 1 (1972): 50.

33. See Thacker, "Maniére de montrer," 49–69, for transcriptions and translations into English of Louis XIV's itinerary and other related ones.

34. Thacker, "Maniére de montrer," 66.

6 *Verbal Representations*

1. See J. Kenseth, ed., *The Age of the Marvelous: Catalog of an Exhibition Held at the Hood Museum of Art, Dartmouth College, Sept. 21–Nov. 24, 1991* (Hanover, NH: Hood Museum of Art, Dartmouth College, 1991).

2. E. Spenser, *The Faerie Queene,* ed. A. C. Hamilton (London: Longman, 1977), 4.10.20–29.

3. A. Marvell, *Poems,* rev. ed., ed. N. Smith (Harlow: Pearson Education, 2007), LL., 63–64.

4. S. Greenblatt et al., eds., *The Norton Shakespeare: Based on the Oxford Edition,* 2nd ed. (New York: W. W. Norton, 2008), 4.4.79–104.

5. P. Sidney, *The Countess of Pembroke's Arcadia (The Old Arcadia),* ed. K. Duncan-Jones (Oxford: Oxford University Press, 1994).

6. J. du Bellay, *La Deffence et illustration de la langue Francoyse,* ed. Henri Chamard (Paris: Didier, 1970), 12: "Laquéle diversité & confusion se peut à bon droict

appeller le Tour de Babel. Donques les Langues ne soit nées d'elles mesmes en façon d'herbes, raciness & arbres: les unes infirmes & debiles en leurs espéces: les autres saines & robustes, & plus aptes à porter le faiz des conceptions humaines: mais toute leur vertu est née au monde du vouloir & arbiter des mortelz."

7. du Belly, *La Deffence,* 11–12.

8. W. Waterschoot, "Marot or Ronsard? New French Poetics among Dutch Rhetoricians in the Second Half of the 16th Century" in *Rhetoric = Rhetoriqueurs = Rederijkers,* ed. J. Koopmans (Amsterdam: North Holland Publishing, 1995), 141–56, 151.

9. P. Erondell, *The French Garden for English Ladies and Gentlewomen to alke in. Or A sommer days labour: Being an instruction for the attaining vnto the knowledge of the French tongue: wherein for the practice thereof, are framed thirteen dialogues in French and English, concerning diuers matters from the rising in the morning till bed-time. Also the historie of the centurion mencioned in the Gospell: in French verses. Which is easier and shorter method than hath beene yet set forth, to bring the lowers of the French tongue to the perfection of the same* (London: [By E. Allde] for Edward White, 1605), *Hundreth Sundry Flowers* [1573], A2^{r-v}.

10. H. Peacham, *The Garden of Eloquence: conteyning the figures of grammer and rhetoric, from whence maye bee gathered all manner of flowers, coulors, ornaments, exornations, forms and fashions of speech, very profitablefor all those that be studious of eloquence, and that reade most eloquent poets and orators, and also helpeth much for the better vnderstanding of the holy Scriptures* (1577), "Espistle Dedicatory," A.B.iv^r.

11. S. R. Kovacs, "Staging Lyric Performances in Early Printing Culture: *Le Jardin de Plaisance et Fleur de Rethorique* (c. 1501–02)," *French Studies* 55 (2001): 1–24.

12. [R. Laneham], *A letter whearin part of the entertainment vntoo the Queenz Maiesty at Killingwoorth Castl in Warwik sheer in this soomerz progress 1575 is signified / from a freend officer attendant in coourt vntoo hiz freend a citizen and merchaunt of London* (1575), 70.

13. F. De Bruyn, "The Classical Silva and the Generic Development of Scientific Writing in Seventeenth-Century England," *New Literary History* 32 (2001): 347–73.

14. G. Parfitt, ed., "To the Reader," in *Ben Jonson: The Complete Poems* (Harmondsworth: Penguin, 1975), 122.

15. T. Kendall, *Flovvers of epigrammes, out of sundrie the moste singular authours selected, as well auncient as late writers. Pleasant and profitable to the expert readers of quicke capacitie* (1577), A5^r.

16. W. Basse, *A Helpe to memory and discourse with table- talke as musicke to a banquet of wine: being a compendium of witty, and vsefull propositions, problemes, and sentences / extracted from the larger volumes of physicians, philosophers, orators and poets, distilled in their assiduous and learned obseruations, and which for method, manner, and referent handling may be fitly tearmed, A Second misselany, or helpe to discourse* (London: Barnard Alsop for Leonard Becket, 1620). The garden metaphors of the paratext are further developed in the second edition of 1630.

17. Basse, *A Helpe,* "Ad Lectorem," A3^v.

18. L. Anderton, *Miscellania; or, A Treatise Contayning Two Hundred Controversiall Animadversions* (1640), A3^v.

19. Basse, *A Helpe,* "In praise of the Worke, and the Author," A2ᵛ.

20. "Itaque studiosus ille velut apicula diligens, per omnes au[c]torum hortos volitabit, flosculis omnibus adsultabit, vndique succi non nihil colligens, quod in suum de ferat aluearium." *De Copia* (1512), T5ʳ.

21. T. Jordan, *Poeticall varieties; or, Varietie of fancie. By Tho. Iordan Gent* (1637), A3ᵛ.

22. See M. Azzi Visentini, "The Gardens of Villas in the Veneto from the Fifteenth to the Eighteenth Centuries" in *The Italian Garden: Art, Design and Culture,* ed. J. D. Hunt (Cambridge: Cambridge University Press, 2007), 93–126, esp. 124–26; and M. Azzi Visentini, "A Model Humanist Garden: Villa Brenzone at Punta San Virgilio" in *The History of Garden Design: The Western Tradition from the Renaissance to the Present Day,* ed. M. Mosser and G. Teyssot (London: Thames and Hudson, 1991), 106–8.

23. See D. Coffin, "The 'Lex Hortorum' and Access to Gardens of Latium during the Renaissance," *Journal of Garden History* 2 (1982): 201–32.

24. G. W. Groos, ed. and tr., *The Diary of Baron Waldstein: A Traveller in Elizabethan England* (London: Thames and Hudson, 1981), 155–63.

25. Spenser, *Faerie Queen,* 2.12.44–46.

26. T. Jenner, *The soules solace, or Thirtie and one spirituall emblems* (1626), Emblem 26 (Plate 1).

27. J. Milton, *Paradise Lost,* 2nd ed., ed. A. Fowler (London: Longman, 1998), 547

28. H. Peacham, *Minerva Britanna or A garden of heroical devises* (1612), "*Unum, et semel,*" line 12.

29. J. E. Hankins, *Shakespeare's Derived Imagery* (Lawrence: Kansas University Press, 1953), 81–83 and chapter 14: "The Unweeded Garden," esp. 189; and P. de la Primaudaye, *The French academie wherein is discoursed the institution of manners, and whatsoever else concerneth the good and happie life of all estates and callings, by precepts of doctrine, and examples of the lives of ancient sages and famous men: by Peter de la Primaudaye Esquire, Lord of the said place, and of Barree, one of the ordinarie gentlemen of the Kings Chamber: dedicated to the most Christian King Henrie the third, and newly translated to English by T. B.* (1614), pt. 1, chap. 16; pt. 2, chap. 64. The architectural title page of *The French academie,* with its vines curling around pillars and strapwork, itself evokes a garden gate.

30. Hankins, *Shakespeare's Derived Imagery,* 82.

31. T. Greene, *The Light in Troy: Imitation and Discovery in Renaissance Poetry* (New Haven, CT: Yale University Press, 1982), 205.

32. M. Riffaterre, *Semiotics of Poetry* (Bloomington: University of Indiana Press, 1978), 82–83 and note 4.

33. See M. M. McGowan, *Ideal Forms in the Age of Ronsard* (Berkeley: University of California Press, 1985), 192–207, esp. 204–5.

34. The *Celestina* has a complex publication history, appearing early in two forms: *Comedia de Calisto y Melibea* (1499), with 16 "acts" or chapters; *Tragicomedia de Calisto y Melibea* (1502), with 21 acts.

35. [F. Colonna], *Hypnerotomachia Poliphili, ubi humana omnia non nisi somnium esse docet, atque obiter plurima scitu sane quam digna commemorat* (Venice: Aldus Manutius, 1499).

36. H. Brunot, "Du *Songe de Poliphile* à la Grande Grotte de Boboli: la dualité dramatique du paysage," *Polia: Revue de l'art des jardins* 2 (2004): 7–26.

37. F. de Rojas, *La Celestina: The Spanish Bawd,* tr. J. M. Cohen (New York: New York University Press, 1996), 231.

38. de Rojas, *La Celestina,* 229–30.

39. de Rojas, *La Celestina,* 230.

40. N. Daniel, *Islam and the West: The Making of an Image* (Oxford: Oneworld, 1960; rev. ed., 1993).

41. D. Metlitzki, *Matter of Araby in Medieval England* (New Haven, CT: Yale University Press, 1977), 210–11.

42. Daniel, *Islam and the West,* 148.

43. D. Chambers, "'Hortus Mertonensis': John Earle's Garden Poem of 1620" *Journal of Garden History* 2 (1982): 117–32.

44. Bernard Palissy, *Recepte veritable, par laquelle tous les homes de la France pourront apprendre a multiplier et augmenter leurs thresors. Item, ceux qui n'ont jamais eu cognoissance des letters, pourront apprendere une philosophie necessaire à tous les habitans de la terre. Item, en ce livre est contenu le dessein d'un jardin autant delectable & d'utile invention, qu'il en fut onques veu. Item, le dessein & ordonnance d'une ille de forteresse, la plus impregnable qu'homme ouyt jamais parler* (1563).

45. T. Tasso, *Gerusalemme liberate* (1581), 16, lines 14–15.

7 Visual Representations

1. M. de Montaigne, *Journal de voyage en Italie, par la Suisse et l'Allemagne, en 1580 et 1581,* in *Oeuvres complètes*(Paris: Éditions du Seuil, 1967), 501.

2. A. Caro, "Lettera a Monsignor Guidiccione, a Lucca (13 luglio 1538)," in *L'Arte dei giardini. Scritti teorici e pratici dal XIV al XIX secolo,* vol. 1, ed. M. Azzi Visentini (Milano: Edizioni Il Polifilo, 1999), 230, 232.

3. F. de' Vieri, *Discorsi delle maravigliose opere di Pratolino,* 2nd ed. (Firenze: Giorgio Marescotti, 1587).

4. End of the sixteenth century, Vienna, Albertina. John Dixon Hunt drew attention to the fact that Guerra's drawings of Italian gardens not only document the artistic form as seen by the artist but also "how they struck him"; J. D. Hunt, *The Afterlife of Gardens* (Philadelphia: University of Pennsylvania Press, 2004), 57.

5. The iconography of *l'Appennino* in Pratolino in "H-Keutner, *Note interno all' Appennino del Giambologna. L'Appennino del Giambologna. Anatomia e identità del gigante,* ed. A. Vezzosi. (Firenze: Alinea Editrice, 1990), 18–27. Compare also the model, in-depth monograph by L. Zangheri, *Pratolino. Il giardino delle meraviglie,* 2 vols. (Firenze: Gonnelli, 1979).

6. M. Azzi Visentini, *La villa in Italia. Quattrocento e Cinquecento* (Milano: Electa, 1995), 197.

7. O. de Serres, *Le Théâtre d'Agriculture et Mesnage des Champs* (1600; repr. Geneva: Matthieu Berjou, 1611), 1189.

8. R. Strong, *The Renaissance Garden in England* (London: Thames and Hudson, 1979), 220–22.

9. Françoise Boudon writes, "du Cerceau uses an unusual technique of view taking, unknown in the history of architectural presentation, the equivalent of a filmmaker's zoom lens"; "Illustrations of Gardens in the Sixteenth Century," in *The*

Architecture of Western Gardens, ed. M. Mosser, and G. Teyssot (Cambridge, MA: MIT Press, 1991), 100–102.

10. R. Strong, *The Artist & the Garden* (New Haven, CT: Yale University Press, 2000), chapter 1, "Pride of Possession: Gardens in Portraits," 17–83.

11. M. A. Giusti, "La veduta–documento e le serie 'catastali,'" in *Lo specchio del paradiso. L'immagine del giardino dall'Antico al Novecento,* ed. M. Fagiolo and M. A. Giusti (Milan: Silvana Editoriale, 1996), 45.

12. Saunderstown, collection of Mr. and Mrs. Windslow Arnes.

13. Florence, Galleria degli Uffizi. F. A. Yates, *The Valois Tapestries* (London: The Warburg Institute, 1959); and K. Woodbridge, *Princely Gardens: The Origins and Development of the French Formal Style* (London: Thames and Hudson, 1986), 83.

14. D. Mignani, *Le Ville Medicee di Giusto Utens* (Firenze: Arnaud, 1993), 9–10.

15. M. Greuter, *Vedute e Giardini di Roma* (Roma, 1623).

16. Engraving in G. de La Brosse, *Description du Jardin Royal des Plantes Médicinales* (Paris, 1636).

17. Drawing in the Biblioteca Apostolica Vaticana, in Azzi Visentini, *La villa,* 144–45. On the significance of figures in representations of gardens for becoming acquainted with types of perception, see L. Cabe Halpern, *The Uses of Paintings in Garden History,* in *Garden History: Issues, Approaches, Methods,* Colloquium on the History of Landscape Architecture 13, ed. J. D. Hunt (Washington, D.C.: Dumbarton Oaks, 1992), 196.

18. Strong, *The Artist,* 184–85; and M. Conan, "Postface," in *Le Jardin Palatin* by S. de Caus (Paris: Editions du Moniteur, 1981).

19. Poznań, Muzeum Narodowe, Muzeum Zamek in Gołuchów. Jacek Tylicki attributes the painting to Herman Han; M. Szafrańska, ed., *Ogród. Forma-Symbol-Marzenie* (Garden. Form-Symbol-Dream), catalogue of the exhibition (Warsaw: Arx Regia, 1998), no. 40.

20. T. DaCosta Kaufmann, *L'école de Prague. La peinture à la cour de Rodolphe II* (Paris: Flammarion, 1985), 159. J. Tylicki analyzes the paintings' artistic form and symbolic content in *Bartłomiej Strobel. Malarz epoki wojny trzydziestoletniej* (Toruń: Wydawnictwo Uniwersytetu Mikołaja Kopernika, 2000), vol. 1: 58–71; vol. 2: 31–33.

21. D. Mountain [T. Hill], *The Gardener's Labyrinth* (London, 1577; comp. by J. D. Hunt, New York: Garland, 1982).

22. For example, in Polish translations edited in Cracow 1549 and 1571.

23. J. Furttenbach, *Architectura recreationis* (Augspurg: Johann Schultes, 1640).

24. For example, M. Maier, *Symbola Aurae mensae duodecim nationum* (Frankfurt, 1617) and *Atalanta Fugiens* (Oppenheim, 1618), no. 32. E.g. Marten de Vos, according to a drawing on which the engraving by Nicolaes de Bruyn, *Spring* (end of the sixteenth century) was based; Abel Grimmer, *Spring* in the cycle of four paintings depicting the seasons of the year (1607, Amberes, Koninklijk Museum voor Schone Kunsten).

25. E.g. Marten de Vos, according to a drawing on which the engraving by Nicolaes de Bruyn, *Spring* (end of the sixteenth century) was based; Abel Grimmer, *Spring* in the cycle of four paintings depicting the seasons of the year (1607, Koninklijk Museum voor Schone Kunsten, Amberes).

26. *Felipe II. El rey íntimo. Jardín y Naturaleza en el siglo XVI,* catalogue of the exhibition, Palacio del Real Sitio de Aranjuez, 23 de septiembre–23 de noviembre

1998, no. 48. Kahren Jones Hellerstedt considers that in Flemish painting the allegory of Spring evolved from depictions of work in the garden to scenes of refined entertainments (*Gardens of Earthly Delight. Sixteenth and Seventeenth-Century Netherlandish Gardens,* catalogue of the exhibition [Pittsburgh, PA: The Frick Art Museum, 1986], 14).

27. Modena, Biblioteca Extense. Antonio Vivarini painted the *Fons salutatis* in a garden securely enclosed within a hedge of roses, surrounded by young and exquisitely dressed people, with movements and costumes that are still characteristic of late medieval frequenters of gardens (Melbourne National Gallery of Victoria).

28. K. J. Hellerstedt considers the possibilities behind the symbolic significance of these depictions in *Gardens of Earthly Delight,* Chapter 5, "Garden Parties."

29. Madrid, Museo Nacional del Prado. A. Glang-Süberkrüb, *Der Liebesgarten. Eine Untersuchung über die Bedeutung der Konfiguration für das Bildthema im Spätwerk des Peter Paul Rubens* (Bern: Lang, 1975).

30. Painting in Treviso, Museo Civico; virginals: Hans Ruckert the Elder, Antwerp 1581, New York, The Metropolitan Museum of Art and Martin van der Biest, Antwerp 1580, Nuremberg, Germanisches Nationalmuseum.

31. Michel Baridon gives expression to this problem based on the example of L. B. Alberti in *Les jardins. Paysagistes–Jardiniers–Poètes* (Paris: Robert Laffont, 1998), 598–99. See also M. A. Giusti, "Vita in giardino," in *Lo specchio del paradiso L'immagine del giardino dall'Antico al Novecento,* ed. M. Fagiolo and M. A. Giusti (Milano: Silvana Editoriale, 1996), 67–69.

32. Paris, Musée du Louvre.

33. Ca. 1570, Baltimore, Walters Art Gallery.

34. Szafranska attempts to describe this enigmatic phenomenon in an article titled *Łąka ze źródłem, czyli o problemach periodyzacji historii ogrodów* (The Meadow with a Spring. The Problematic Periodization of Gardens History), in *Sztuka około 1500* (Warsaw: Arx Regia, 1997), 343–55.

35. *David and Bethsheba,* ca. 1540, Hartford, The Wadsworth Atheneum.

36. An in-depth analysis of the symbolism of plants in Renaissance paintings is made by Mirella Levi d'Ancona in *The Garden of the Renaissance* (Firenze: Olschki, 1977) and in *Botticelli's Primavera. A Botanical Interpretation including Astrology, Alchemy and the Medici* (Firenze: Leo S. Olschi Editore, 1983).

37. Both paintings in The National Gallery, London.

38. L. Tongiorgi Tomasi and A. Tosi, *Flora e Pomona. L'orticoltura nei disegni e nelle incisioni dei secoli XVI-XIX* (Firenze: Leo S. Olschki, 1990).

39. Stockholm, Nationalmuseum. To date a fragment exists of the splendid fountain shown centrally; M. Fagiolo, "Il giardino del mito," in *Lo specchio del paradiso,* 176.

40. Musée du Louvre, Paris.

41. For example, *Allegory of Fragrance,* Madrid, Museo Nacional del Prado; Ludger Fon Ring de Jong, *Garden with lilies and Irises,* beginning of the seventeenth century, Münster, Westfalischer Kunstrerein; Juan ven der Hamen y León, *Sacrifice for Flora,* 1627, Madrid, Museo Nacional del Prado. L. Tongiorgi Tomasi, *Il Giardino*

di Flora: natura e simbolo nell'immagine dei fiori, ed. M. Gallo Cataldi and E. Simonetti (Geneva: Sagep Editrice, 1986).

42. According to cartoons by Jan Cornelisz Vermeyen, ca. 1564, Madrid, Patrimonio Nacional, Palacio Real; *Felipe II,* 110–11.

43. More about this allegory in Fagiolo, "Il giardino del mito," 177–79.

44. A. Pietrogrande, "La teatralizzazione della natura e i suoi elementi. Giardini e luogo scenico tra Rinascimento e Barocco," in *Les Éléments et les metamorphoses de la nature. Imaginaire symbolique des arts dans la culture européenne du XVIe au XVIIIe siècle,* Actes du colloque, septembre 1997 (Paris: William Blake/Art & Arts, 2004), 201–12.

45. S. Orgel and R. Strong, *The Theatre of the Stuart Court* (London: Sotheby Park Bernet; Los Angeles: University of California Press, 1973).

46. *Trattato della Pittura,* I, 9.

47. Musée du Louvre, Paris.

48. L. Cabe Halpern emphasizes the artist's conscious choice of characteristic features of the garden that is portrayed; "The Uses of Paintings," 184. Similarly, in a wider context: J. D. Hunt, *Greater Perfections: The Practice of Garden Theory* (London: Thames and Hudson, 2000), 153.

49. This subject was written about by the following artists: Jacopo Carucci da Pontormo in a letter to Benedetto Varchi (1548) and Paolo Pino in *Dialogo di Pittura* (Venezia, 1548).

8 Gardens and the Larger Landscape

All translations are the author's, unless otherwise noted.

1. For perceptive essays on gardens as enclosures, see C. Acidini Luchinat et al., eds., *Il giardino e le mura: ai confini fra natura e storia. Atti del convegno di studi, San Miniato Alto (Pisa) 23–24 giugno 1995* (Florence: Edifir, 1997); and J. D. Hunt, *Greater Perfections: The Practice of Garden Theory* (London: Thames and Hudson, 2000), 14–29, esp. 23–24.

2. Already in 1972, Eugenio Battisti, a historian of Renaissance art who studied Italian gardens, referring to V. J. Scully, *The Earth, the Temple and the Gods: Greek Sacred Architecture* (New Haven, CT: Yale University Press, 1962), lamented this paradox: "Although many visitors, and even specialists, such as [Luigi] Dami, are convinced of the importance of the surrounding landscape to the Italian garden, we are actually in the situation of critical indifference similar to that regretted by Scully for Greek temples"; E. Battisti, "*Natura Artificiosa* to *Natura Artificialis,*" in *The Italian Garden,* ed. D. R. Coffin (Washington, D.C.: Dumbarton Oaks, 1972), 24. See more recently, J. Dixon Hunt, *Greater Perfections,* 34; and D. Fairchild Ruggles, *Islamic Gardens and Landscapes* (Philadelphia: University of Pennsylvania Press, 2008), ix, xi.

3. See, as examples, A. Petruccioli, ed., *Il giardino islamico. Architettura, natura, paesaggio* (Milan: Electa, 1994); D. Cosgrove and S. Daniels, eds., *The Iconography of Landscape: Essays on the Symbolic Representation, Design, and the Use of Past Environments* (Cambridge: Cambridge University Press, 1988); D. Cosgrove, *The Palladian Landscape: Geographical Change and Its Cultural Representations in*

Sixteenth-Century Italy (Leicester: University of Leicester Press, 1993); M. Ambrosoli, *The Wild and the Sown: Botany and Agriculture in Western Europe, 1350–1850,* tr. M. McCann Salvatorelli (Cambridge: Cambridge University Press, 1997); M. Ambrosoli, "From the Italian Countryside to the Italianate Landscape: Peasants as Gardeners and Foreign Observers in Italy, 1500–1850," in *Clio in the Italian Garden: Twenty-First-Century Studies in Historical Methods and Theoretical perspectives,* ed. M. Beneš and M. G. Lee (Washington, D.C.: Dumbarton Oaks Research Library and Collection, 2011), 145–68; C. Pieri, ed., *Le Nôtre, Un Inconnu Illustre?* (Paris: Centre des Monuments Nationaux/MONUM and Éditions du Patrimoine, 2003); G. Farhat, ed., *André Le Nôtre. Fragments d'un paysage culturel. Institutions, arts, sciences, & techniques* (Sceaux: Musée de l'Île-de-France, Domaine de Sceaux, 2006); G. Guerci, L. S. Pelissetti, and L. Scazzosi, eds., *Oltre il giardino. Le architetture vegetali e il paesaggio* (Florence: Olschki, 2003); and L. S. Pelissetti and L. Scazzosi, eds., *Giardini, contesto, paesaggio: sistemi di giardini e architetture vegetali nel paesaggio. Metodi di studio, valutazione, tutela* (Florence: Olschki, 2005). Such methodological changes are discussed in M. Beneš, "Introduction. Italian and French Gardens, A Century of Historical Study (1900–2000)," in *Villas and Gardens in Early Modern Italy and France,* ed. M. Beneš and D. Harris (Cambridge: Cambridge University Press, 2001), 1–16; H. Brunon, "L'essor artistique et la fabrique culturelle du paysage à la Renaissance. Réflexions à propos de recherches récentes," *Studiolo. Revue d'Histoire de l'Art de l'Académie de France à Rome* 4 (2006): 261–90; H. Brunon, "Questions et Méthodes de l'Histoire des Jardins en France," in *Giardini storici. A 25 anni dalle Carte di Firenze: esperienze e prospettive,* vol. 1, ed. L. S. Pelissetti and L. Scazzosi (Florence: Olschki, 2009), 31–46; and M. Beneš, "Methodological Changes in the Study of Italian Gardens from the 1970s to the 1990s: A Personal Itinerary," in *Clio in the Italian Garden: Twenty-First-Century Studies in Historical Methods and Theoretical Perspectives,* ed. M. Beneš and M. G. Lee (Washington, D.C.: Dumbarton Oaks Research Library and Collection, 2011), 17–54.

4. See, for example, F. de Dainville, *La géographie des humanistes* (Paris: Beauchesne, 1940); L. B. Cormack, *Charting an Empire. Geography at the English Universities, 1580–1620* (Chicago: University of Chicago Press, 1997); D. Buisseret, *The Mapmaker's Quest: Depicting New Worlds in Renaissance Europe* (Oxford: Oxford University Press, 2003); and studies by J.-M. Besse, including *Les grandeurs de la terre. Aspects du savoir géographique à la Renaissance* (Lyon: ENS, 2003).

5. G. Burnet, *Some Letters containing an account of what seemed most Remarkable in Travelling through . . . Italy . . . in the years 1685 and 1686* (Rotterdam, 1686).

6. See, for example, E. B. MacDougall, "The Villa Mattei and the Development of the Roman Garden Style" (PhD diss., Harvard University, 1970), 94–95; H. Whitehouse, *Ancient Mosaics and Wallpaintings: Paper Museum of Cassiano dal Pozzo. Series A, Antiquities and Architecture,* pt. 1 (London: Harvey Miller, 2001), for the ancient, so-called Barberini landscape wallpainting, see esp. 202–8, 409–12; and also L. Holstenius, *Vetus pictura nymphaeum referens commentariolo explicata a Luca Holstenio. Accedunt alia quaedam eiusdem auctoris* (Rome: Typis Barberinis, execudebat Michael Hercules, 1676); D. Ribouillault, "Landscape *all'antica* and

Topographical Anachronism in Roman Fresco Painting of the Sixteenth Century," *Journal of the Warburg and Courtauld Institutes* 71 (2008): 211–37; D. Duport, *Les Jardins qui sentent le sauvage. Ronsard et la poétique du paysage* (Geneva: Droz, 2000); and D. Duport, *Le Jardin et la nature. Ordre et variété dans la literature de la Renaissance* (Geneva: Droz, 2002). For the ancient works themselves, Sir Archibald Geikie, *The Love of Nature among the Romans during the Later Decades of the Republic and the First Century of the Empire* (London: John Murray, 1912); E. W. Leach, *The Rhetoric of Space: Literary and Artistic Representations of Landscape in Republican and Augustan Rome* (Princeton, NJ: Princeton University Press, 1988); E. La Rocca, *Lo Spazio negato. La pittura di paesaggio nella cultura artistica greca e romana* (Milan: Mondadori Electa, 2008); and J.-M. Croisille, *Paysages dans la peinture romaine. Aux origins d'un genre pictural* (Paris: Picard, 2010).

7. L. B. Alberti, *On the Art of Building in Ten Books,* tr. J. Rykwert et al. (Cambridge, MA: MIT Press, 1988), 145.

8. N. Purcell, "Town in Country and Country in Town," in *Ancient Roman Villa Gardens,* ed. E. B. MacDougall (Washington, D.C.: Dumbarton Oaks Library and Research Collection, 1987), 194–97; B. Bergmann, "Painted Perspectives of a Villa Visit," in *Roman Art in the Private Sphere,* ed. E. Gazda (Ann Arbor: University of Michigan Press, 1991), 49–70; and H. Maguire, "Gardens and Parks in Constantinople," *Dumbarton Oaks Papers* 54 (2000), 262.

9. C. R. Mack, *Pienza: The Creation of a Renaissance City* (Ithaca, NY: Cornell University Press, 1987), 60.

10. Eugenio Battisti notes the political character of such landscape views: "In Pienza contemplation of the landscape is also associated with pride in feudal possessions. Pius II looks at this dominion like Christ viewing the cities of the world . . . "; Battisti, "*Natura Artificiosa* to *Natura Artificialis,*" 26–27. See also M. Warnke, *Politische Landschaft: zur Kunstgeschichte der Natur* (Munich: C. Hamer, 1992; published in English as *Political landscape: The Art History of Nature* [London: Reaktion, 1994]). For humanist geographical studies, see A. Scafi, "Pio II e la cartografia: un papa e un mappamondo tra Medioevo e Rinascimento," in *Enea Silvio Piccolomini Pius Secundus. Poeta Laureatus Pontifex Maximus,* ed. M. Sodi and A. Antoniutti (Rome: Associazione Culturale Shakespeare and Libreria Editrice Vaticana, 2007), 239–64; C. Benocci, "Pio II paesaggista e gli Sforza: il rinnovamento del monte Amiata e di Santa Fiora dopo il viaggio papale," in *Enea Silvio Piccolomini Pius Secundus. Poeta Laureatus Pontifex Maximus,* ed. M. Sodi and A. Antoniutti (Rome: Associazione Culturale Shakespeare and Libreria Editrice Vaticana, 2007), 341–58; and D. Ribouillault, "Les paysages urbains de la loggia du Belvédère d'Innocent VIII au Vatican: nostalgie de l'antique, géographie et croisades à la fin du XVe siècle," *Studiolo. Revue d'Histoire de l'Art de l'Académie de France à Rome* 8 (2010): 139–67.

11. On travelers' perceptions, J. D. Hunt, *Garden and Grove. The Italian Renaissance Garden in the English Imagination: 1600–1750* (Princeton, NJ: Princeton University Press, 1986), 86, 88–89, and passim. On framing landscape views, G. Crandell, *Nature Pictorialized: The "View" in Landscape History* (Baltimore: Johns

Hopkins University Press, 1993); R. Dubbini, *Geografie dello sguardo: visione e paesaggio in età moderna* (Turin: G. Einaudi, 1994; tr. L. G. Cochrane, *Geography of the Gaze: Urban and Rural Vision in Early Modern Europe* [Chicago: University of Chicago Press, 2002]); E. Casey, *Representing Place: Landscape Painting and Maps* (Minneapolis: University of Minnesota Press, 2002); D. Harris, *The Nature of Authority: Villa Culture, Landscape, and Representation in Eighteenth-Century Lombardy* (University Park: Pennsylvania State University Press, 2003); D. Harris and D. Fairchild Ruggles, eds., *Sites Unseen: Landscape and Vision* (Pittsburgh, PA: University of Pittsburgh Press, 2007); and Ribouillault, "Toward an Archaeology of the Gaze: The Perception and Function of Garden Views in Italian Renaissance Villas," In *Clio in the Italian Garden: Twenty-First -Century Studies in Historical Methods and Theoretical Perspectives,* ed. M. Beneš and M. G. Lee (Washington, D.C.: Dumbarton Oaks Research Library and Collection, 2011), 203–32.

12. R. Jones and N. Penny, *Raphael* (New Haven, CT: Yale University Press, 1983), 247–48.

13. A. Palladio, *I quattro libri dell'architettura* (Venice, 1570), book 2, 18, 45–78; V. Scamozzi, *L'idea della architettura universale,* 2 vols. (Venice, 1615), vol. 1, book 3: 266–349. Also V. Scamozzi, *The Idea of a Universal Architecture. III: Villas and Country Estates* (Amsterdam: Architecture & Natura Press, 2003), 124; and L. De Benedetti, "Giardino, paesaggio, territorio," in *Il giardino Veneto dal tardo medioevo al novecento,* ed. M. Azzi Visentini (Milan: Electa, 1988), 281–301.

14. B. Grangier de Liverdis, *Journal d'un voyage de France et d'Italie fait par un gentilhomme François. Commencé le quartorzième septembre 1660 & achevé le trentunième May 1661* (Paris: Michel Vaugon, 1667), 628–29: "Elle [Villa Madama] est fort diversifiée dans ses allées couvertes, . . . : plusieurs jets d'eau ui y sont, luy donnent vn merveilleux agréément: . . . Mais encor ce que j'admiray & consideray par dessus toutes choses en cette charmante & agreable maison, fut la situation, laquelle est en forme d'Amphitheatre à l'égard du païs circonvoisin: L'on y void le Tybre, & les gra[n]des prairies au deça & au delà de ce fleuve, se presentent à l'oeil & luy font vn objet agreable . . . . vous découvrirez d'vn côté Castel-Gandolphe, & de l'autre Frescati & Tivoli . . . "

15. Pliny the Younger, *Letters,* tr. W. Melmoth (London: William Heinemann; New York: Macmillan, 1927), book 5, letter VI.

16. N. Audebert, *Voyage d'Italie,* critical ed. by A. Olivero, 2 vols. (Rome: Luciano Lucarini, 1983), vol. 2: 65.

17. Audebert, *Voyage d'Italie,* vol. 2: 67.

18. In the early twentieth century, when Italian gardens began to be studied by art historians, German scholars such as Heinrich Wölfflin, Albert E. Brinckmann, and Carlludwig Franck emphasized the relationship between the view and the dominant axis that connected garden and larger landscape. See now M. Fagiolo, "Da Villa Madama a Villa Giulia e al Gianicolo: Gli Assi delle memoria storica," in *Roma-il verde e la città. Giardini e spazi verdi nella construzione della forma urbana,* ed. R. Cassetti and M. Fagiolo (Rome: Gangemi Editore, 2002), 31–47; M. Fagiolo, "Systems of Gardens in Italy: Princely Residences and Villas in Rome and Latium, Savoy Piedmont, Royal Bourbon Naples, and Bagheria, Sicily," in

Clio in the Italian Garden: Twenty-First-Century Studies in Historical Methods and Theoretical Perspectives, ed. M. Beneš and M. G. Lee (Washington, D.C.: Dumbarton Oaks Research Library and Collection, 2011), 81–114, esp. 84–91; M. Azzi Visentini, "The Gardens of Villas in the Veneto from the Fifteenth to the Eighteenth Centuries," in *The Italian Garden: Art, Design and Culture,* ed. J. D. Hunt (Cambridge: Cambridge University Press, 1996); and M. Azzi Visentini, "Alle origini dell'architettura del paesaggio: Considerazioni in margine al rapporto tra gli edifici, i giardini e il sito nelle ville laziali del Cinquecento," in *Villa Lante a Bagnaia,* ed. S. Frommel (Milan: Electa, 2005), 190–205. For the visitor's imagined connections between garden and larger landscape, see C. Lazzaro, "The Sixteenth-Century Central Italian Villa and the Cultural Landscape," in *Architecture, Jardin, Paysage. L'Environnement du Château et de la Villa aux XVe et XVIe siècles,* ed. J. Guillaume (Paris: Picard, 1999), 29–44, esp. 29; and Ribouillault, "Toward an Archaeology of the Gaze," esp. 205. Also on view and dominant axis, see M. Conan, ed., "Garden Displays of Majestic Will," in *The Triumph of the Baroque. Architecture in Europe 1600–1750, ed.* H. A. Millon (Milan: Bompiani, 1999), 279–313; and Hunt, *Greater Perfections,* 34–40.

19. Audebert, *Voyage d'Italie,* vol. 2: 73.
20. On this well-studied topic, see D. R. Coffin, *The Villa D'Este at Tivoli* (Princeton, NJ: Princeton University Press, 1960); E. Battisti, *L'antirinascimento. Con un'appendice di testi inediti,* 2 vols. (Milan: Feltrinelli, 1962; enlarged ed., 2 vols., Milan: Garzanti, 1989); Battisti," *Natura Artificiosa to Natura Artificialis*"; MacDougall, "The Villa Mattei"; E. B. MacDougall, "*Ars Hortulorum:* Sixteenth Century Garden Iconography and Literary Theory in Italy," in *The Italian Garden,* ed. D. R. Coffin (Washington, D.C.: Dumbarton Oaks Research Library and Collection, 1972), 37–59; E. B. MacDougall, *Fountains, Statues, and Flowers: Studies in Italian Gardens of the Sixteenth and Seventeenth Centuries* (Washington, D.C.: Dumbarton Oaks Research Library and Collection, 1994); D. R. Coffin, *The Villa in the Life of Renaissance Rome* (Princeton, NJ: Princeton University Press, 1979); D.R. Coffin, *Gardens and Gardening in Papal Rome* (Princeton, NJ: Princeton University Press, 1991); L. Zangheri, *Pratolino: il giardino delle meraviglie,* 2 vols. (Florence: Gonnelli, 1979); M. Fagiolo, ed., *La città effimera e l'universo artificiale del giardino: la Firenze dei Medici e l'Italia del '500* (Rome: Edizioni Officina, 1980); M. Fagiolo, ed., *Natura e artificio: l'ordine rustico, le fontane, gli autonomi nella cultura del Manierismo europeo* (Rome: Edizioni Officina, 1981); Hunt, *Garden and Grove,* esp. 42–58; C. Lazzaro, *The Italian Renaissance Garden: From the Conventions of Planting, Design, and Ornament to the Grand Gardens of Sixteenth-Century Central Italy* (New Haven, CT: Yale University Press, 1990); and H. Brunon, "Pratolino: art des jardins et imaginaire de la nature dans l'Italie de la seconde moitié du XVIe siècle," doctoral thesis, 5 vols., Université de Paris-I Panthéon-Sorbonne, 2001).
21. On the emotional associations of garden and the wider landscape, including wilderness, see Battisti, "*Natura Artificiosa to Natura Artificialis,*" esp. 24–36; MacDougall, "*Ars Hortulorum,*" esp. 47–53; A. Venturi, "*Picta poësis:* ricerche sulla poesia e il giardino dalle origini al Seicento," in *Storia d'Italia. Annali 5: Il paesaggio,*

ed. C. De Seta (Turin: Giulio Einaudi editore, 1982); and A. Venturi, "La selva e il giardino. Tasso e il paesaggio," in *Archivi dello sguardo. Origini e momenti di pittura di paesaggio in Italia. Atti del Convegno, Ferrara, Castello Estense, 22–23 ottobre 2004,* ed. F. Cappelletti (Florence: Casa Editrice Le Lettere, 2006), 75–96. On agriculture and the gardenlike quality of Italy's landscapes, see E. Sereni, *Storia del paesaggio agrario italiano* (Bari, Italy: Laterza, 1961; tr. with introduction by R. Burr Litchfield, *History of the Italian Agricultural Landscape* [Princeton, NJ: Princeton University Press, 1996]); Hunt, *Garden and Grove,* 30–40; Lazzaro, *The Italian Renaissance Garden,* passim; A. Saltini and M. Sframeli, *L'agricoltura e il paesaggio italiano nella pittura dal Trecento all'Ottocento* (Florence: Franco Cantini, 1995); Hunt, *Greater Perfections,* 68–70; C. Lazzaro, "Italy Is a Garden: The Idea of Italy and the Italian Garden Tradition," in *Villas and Gardens in Early Modern Italy and France,* ed. M. Beneš and D. Harris (Cambridge: Cambridge University Press, 2001), 29–60, esp. 42–46; T. L. Ehrlich, *Landscape and Identity in Early Modern Rome: Villa Culture at Frascati in the Borghese Era* (Cambridge: Cambridge University Press, 2002), esp. 242–64; and Ambrosoli, "From the Italian Countryside." In general, for Italy, see L. Puppi, "L'ambiente, il paesaggio e il territorio," in *Materiali e problemi: Ricerche spaziali e tecnologiche (Storia dell'arte italiana I:IV),* ed. G. Previtali (Turin, Italy: Giulio Einaudi editore, 1980), 41–100.

22. Audebert, *Voyage d'Italie,* vol. 2, 73. See the works by Coffin, MacDougall, and Lazzaro, cited previously; also, Hunt, *Greater Perfections,* esp. chap. 3, 32–75, and chap. 4, 76–11, "Representation."

23. In the Roman setting of the period 1500–1700, the park—called *barco* (for hunting and leisure) or *parco* (usually for leisure only)—was a fairly ambiguous term, not well-defined, and it was something different from parks in the other Italian states. For *parco* and *barco,* Lazzaro, *The Italian Renaissance Garden,* 109–30; S. Varoli Piazza, "Giardino, Barchetto e Barco della Rocca Ruspoli a Vignanello," in *La dimensione europea dei Farnese [Bulletin de l'Institut Historique Belge de Rome,* LXIII], ed. B. De Groof and E. Galdieri (Turnhout, Belgium: Brepols, 1994), 421–29; M. Beneš, "The Social Significance of Transforming the Landscape of the Villa Borghese, 1606–1630: Territory, Trees, and Agriculture in the design of the First Roman Baroque Park," in *Gardens in the Time of the Great Muslim Empires: Theory and Design,* ed. A. Petruccioli (Cambridge: Brill, 1997), 1–31; H. Brunon, "Dalle 'fiere non rapaci' ai 'fruttiferi e pomati arbori' Villa Lante a Bagnaia e l'evoluzione del barco nel Rinascimento," in *Villa Lante a Bagnaia,* ed. S. Frommel (Milan: Electa, 2005), 31–43.

24. See G. Beltramini and H. Burns, eds., *Andrea Palladio e la villa veneta da Petrarca a Carlo Scarpa* (Venice: Marsilio, 2005).

25. See S. B. Butters, "Cosimo I's Collemignoli. A Forgotten Medici Villa, Lake and Landscape on the Pratomagno," in *"Some Degree of Happiness": Studi di storia dell'architettura in onore di Howard Burns,* ed. M. Beltramini and C. Elam (Pisa: Scuola Normale Superiore, Edizioni della Normale, 2010), 407–45; H. Brunon, "La chasse et l'organisation du paysage dans la Toscane des Médicis," in *Chasses princières dans l'Europe de la Renaissance. Actes du colloque de Chambord (1er et*

2 octobre 2004), 219–46. Also see V. F. Pardo and G. Casali, *I Medici nel contado fiorentino: ville e possedimenti agricoli tra Quattrocento e Cinquecento* (Florence: Cooperative Editrice Universitaria, 1978); C. Barni, *Villa La Magia: Una dimora signorile nel contado pistolese (secc. XIV–XIX)* (Florence: Edam, 1999); S. B. Butters, "Pressed Labor and Pratolino. Social Imagery and Social Reality at a Medici Garden," in *Villas and Gardens in Early Modern Italy and France,* ed. M. Beneš and D. Harris (Cambridge: Cambridge University Press, 2001), 61–87.

26. Butters, "Cosimo I's Collemignoli," 428–29.

27. Coffin, *The Villa D'Este at Tivoli,* 22–34, for the long cross-axial avenues, called *viali.*

28. For Delorme's dates in Italy and his study of Hadrian's Villa, see W. L. MacDonald and J. A. Pinto, *Hadrian's Villa and Its Legacy* (New Haven, CT: Yale University Press, 1995), 214–15.

29. From about 1500 until the Villa Giulia, Roman villa gardens consisted of formal gardens (usually low-lying, regular planting beds near the main house or casino, laid out in grids and open to encompassing views) and tree gardens, called *boschetti* or groves, literally "little woods." A third element was often combined, rustic elements from the typically Roman *vigna* property, which was an agrarian plot that could contain vineyards, vegetable gardens, and orchards. *Boschetti* could be arranged as regularly planted stands of trees, or else naturalistically in relation to ancient sculptures, imitating what ancient Roman gardens were thought to look like, based on literary evidence. The turning point to this less-formal approach to planting took place during the 1540s and 1550s, when groves and statuary, both freestanding and in fountains, were introduced in Roman gardens. The Roman use of *boschetti* had northern Italian and Tuscan origins. For this Roman garden practice, see MacDougall, "The Villa Mattei," 26–66, and esp. 50–51, for the northern importation of *boschetti*; MacDougall, "*Ars Hortulorum*"; Hunt, *Garden and Grove,* 30–42; Lazzaro, *The Italian Renaissance Garden,* 20–45; and Coffin, *Gardens and Gardening in Papal Rome.*

30. On the Villa Giulia, see J. Coolidge, "The Villa Giulia. A Study of Central Italian Architecture in the Mid-Sixteenth Century," *The Art Bulletin* 25 (1943): 177–225; M. Bafile, *Villa Giulia. L'Architettura. Il Giardino* (Rome: Istituto Poligrafico dello Stato, 1948); MacDougall, "The Villa Mattei," 40–51; Coffin, *The Villa in the Life,* 150–74, with earlier key literature. For a modern plan reconstructing the estate of the villa about 1555, including the borders of the acquired vigne, see Bafile, *Villa Giulia,* plate 10. On the Villa Giulia as a significant prototype for the new typology: M. Beneš, "The Villa Pamphilj (1630–1670): Family Land, and Gardens in Papal Rome" (PhD diss., 3 vols., Yale University, 1989), 501–17, esp. 501–3; Beneš, "Social Significance," 4. Alberta Campitelli's new interpretation of the planting documents clarifies that the Villa Giulia initiated the series of villa parks: Campitelli, "Committenti e giardini nella Roma della prima metà del Cinquecento. Alcuni documenti e un'ipotesi per Villa Giulia," in *Delizie in Villa. Il Giardino Rinascimentale e i Suoi Committenti,* ed. G. Venturi and F. Ceccarelli (Florence: Olschki, 2008), 119–28. See also S. Varoli Piazza, "Territorio, ambiente

e paesaggio del Parco dei Musei, Valle Giulia e Villa Borghese," in *Villa Borghese. Storia e gestione. Atti del convegno (Roma, 2003),* ed. A. Campitelli (Milan: Skira, 2005): 79–92. Denis Ribouillault has forthcoming an important interpretative study of the relationship of the Villa Giulia to the antique, a draft of which the author very graciously shared with me in 2009, and I thank him warmly here. His treatment of the topic far supersedes my brief one here, but we make a few similar points, especially with regard to the Villa Giulia's similarity to an ancient Roman estate. I have yet to see the published essay: D. Ribouillault, "La Villa Giulia et le champs de Mars augustéen. Jardins et topographie antique dans la Rome de Jules III del Monte (1550–1550)," in *Le miroir et l'espace du prince dans l'art italien de la Renaissance,* ed. P. Morel (Tours: Presses Universitaires François-Rabelais de Tours, 2012).

31. On the Villa Giulia and ancient Roman gardens, see MacDougall, "The Villa Mattei," 86, 93; as an ancient estate like the Golden House of Nero, see Beneš, "The Villa Pamphilj," 504–5. On variety as an aesthetic principle in Italian gardens, see Hunt, *Garden and Grove,* 83–89.

32. Campitelli, "Committenti e giardini," 215, 218–19.

33. Ammannati refers to the planting layout as an "Agricoltura" and describes "lovely gardens adorned with hedges and very beautiful avenues," at least one area "commodious for all sorts of animals," and groves and thickets for hunting birds. Ammannati, quoted in Bafile, *Villa Giulia,* 32; MacDougall, "Villa Mattei," 185, 195–96. To visualize the 36,000 trees on the ground, one needs to add the 400 pines, the 1,000 firs, and the 600 holm oaks that were planted by the 1630s in the first two enclosures flanking the main palace of the Villa Borghese, and multiply the surface covered by those 2,000 trees some tenfold to grasp just how large an estate the Villa Giulia was—of the 36,000 trees, many appear to have been small or wild shrubs, hence taking less space than the tree gardens at the Villa Borghese. Beneš, "Social Significance," 6–7; Campitelli, "Committenti e giardini," 119–28.

34. For the aristocratic associations of grand trees, for example, the *pinus pinea,* and ancient literary sources for this, such as Martial, see Beneš, "The Villa Pamphilj," 487–89; Ehrlich, *Landscape and Identity,* 245–46.

35. "Et questa parte alta, soprastante alla vallata, fu edificato tutto, tanto sottoterra come sopra terra, di alberghi, di giardini, di selvette, di piazze, di portiche . . ."; P. Ligorio, *Libro dell'antica città di Tivoli e di alcune famose ville,* ed. A. Ten (Rome: De Luca, 2005), 50. Ligorio and other antiquarians describe the buildings at Hadrian's Villa as surrounded by gardens.

36. On the formal and social coherence of the group, Beneš," Villa Pamphilj," 501–17; M. Beneš, "Landowning and the Villa in the Social Geography of the Roman Territory: The location and landscapes of the Vila Pamphilj, 1645–70," in *Modernism, and History: Essays in Honor of Eduard F. Sekler,* ed. A. von Hoffman (Cambridge, MA: Harvard University Graduate School of Design, 1996), 187–209; and Beneš, "Social Significance." On the Villas Montalto, Borghese, Ludovisi, and Pamphilj, see M. Quast, *Die Villa Montalto in Rom: Entstehung und Gestaltung im Cinquecento* (Munich: Tuduv, 1991); A. Campitelli, *Villa Borghese. Da Giardino del Principe A Parco Dei Romani* (Rome: Istituto Poligrafico e Zecca dello Stato,

Libreria dello Stato, 2003); A. Campitelli, ed., *Villa Borghese. Storia e gestione* (Milan: Skira editore, 2005); C. Benocci, *Villa Doria Pamphilj* (Rome: Editalia, 1996); C. Benocci, ed., *Villa Doria Pamphilj* (Rome: Art Color Printing srl, Archivio Storico Culturale del Municipio Roma XVI, 2005); and C. Benocci, *Villa Ludovisi* (Rome: Istituto Poligrafico e Zecca dello Stato, 2010).

37. The *avviso* (newsletter) of February 16, 1608, reporting Paul V's intentions for the Villa Giulia is in J.A.F. Orbaan, *Documenti sul barocco in Roma,* 2 vols. (Rome: Società Romana di Storia Patria, alla Biblioteca Vallicelliana, 1920), vol. 1: 97: the Pope ordered that "si risarcisse la vigna nel modo che stava, quando era vivo il Papa autore di essa, havendo dato assegnamento per la spesa l'utile, che si cava dalla vigna medesima . . . In ogni modo si vede, che Nostro Signore voglia comprarla per li fratelli et unirla con le altre, che ha là vicino." In the end, Paul V was able to buy only a tiny part of the Villa Giulia. Alberta Campitelli has identified a pavilion still extant in the Villa Borghese, the Casino del Graziano, as an original part of the Villa Giulia. Campitelli, "Committenti e giardini," 221–28; she does not mention this *avviso.*

38. The reader may have noticed how difficult it is to define these Roman parks, which here I call "villa parks" and have previously called "estate villas." Beneš, "Landowning and the Villa." Contemporaries also had difficulties; for example, Giovanni Baglione, the art critic and painter, grew frustrated in trying to describe the Villa Borghese: "Outside the Porta Pinciana, the pope built a beautiful palace in a Vigna of his, or Garden, or Villa, or whatever we want to call it, . . . " ("Fuori di porta Pinciana fece edificare vn bel palazzo in vna sua Vigna, o Giardino, o Villa, che vogliamo chiamarla, . . . "); G. Baglione, *Le Vite de' Pittori, Scultori et Architetti. Dal Pontificato di Gregorio XIII fino a tutto quello d'Urbano VIII,* 2nd ed. (Rome: Menelfo Manelfi, 1649), 96.

39. On this issue, see Beneš, "Villa Pamphilj," 539–69; Beneš, "Landowning"; and Beneš, "Social Significance"; on the concept of transposition, see M. Beneš, "Pastoralism in the Roman Baroque Villa and in Claude Lorrain: Myths and Realities of the Roman Campagna," in *Villas and Gardens in Early Modern Italy and France,* ed. M. Beneš and D. Harris (Cambridge: Cambridge University Press, 2001), 88–113.

40. The Roman villa parks near the city of Rome were not the only designed parks to be built in the Roman territory from the 1550s on; they were also not the only ones to use the concept of incorporation of the larger landscape. For example, villa parks were built with large tree plantations in the precincts of the Sacro Bosco of Bomarzo (c. 1550–70s), the Farnese palace at Caprarola (c. 1555–85), the Villa Lante at Bagnaia (1570s), the Villa Colonna at Marino (1580s), the Villa Aldobrandini at Frascati (1598–1605), the Villa Mondragone-Borghese at Frascati (1613–33), and the Villa Giustiniani at Bassano di Sutri (1595–1638). But, location mattered. These villa parks lay far from the city, in the hill towns of Latium, and, once in the countryside, incorporating rustic landscapes and forest trees from the immediate surroundings did not have the same values as in urban settings. The same can be said for many parks built elsewhere in Italy during the sixteenth and seventeenth centuries, for example, those of the Medici villas in Tuscany.

41. Suetonius, *The Lives of the Caesars,* vol. 2, tr. J.C. Rolfe, Loeb classical library edition (London: W. Heinemann; New York: Macmillan, 1914), book 6, "Nero," chapter 31, 135–37: "He made a palace extending all the way from the Palatine to the Esquiline, . . . the Golden House . . . was so extensive that it had a triple colonnade a mile long. There was a pond too, like a sea, surrounded with buildings to represent cities, besides tracts of country, varied by tilled fields, vineyards, pastures and woods, with great numbers of wild and domestic animals." For the *horti,* such as those of Maecenas, Lucullus, and Sallust, and the Golden House, see E. Champlin, "The Suburbium of Rome," *American Journal of Ancient History* 7, no. 2 (1982): 97–107; Purcell, "Town in Country and Country in Town," esp. 203; M. Cima and E. La Rocca, eds., *Horti Romani* (Rome: L'Suna di Bretschneider 1998). For the villa parks of 1550 to 1670, based on the ancient estates and the Golden House, see Beneš, "The Villa Pamphilj (1630–1670)," 504–6, 566, 584–86; Beneš, "The Social Significance," 3–4,10–11,15, 31; for the Villa Pamphilj and the Golden House, see M. Beneš, "Disegni e Stampe per il Casino di Villa Pamphilj," in *Alessandro Algardi. L'altra faccia del barocco,* exhibit catalogue, ed. J. Montagu (Rome: De Luca, 1999), 316–18.

42. For an example from the 1620s, the lake at the Villa Borghese, see Beneš, "The Social Significance," 10–11. For replication and reversing categories of landscapes and the natural order in ancient Roman literature and gardens, see Purcell, "Town in Country and Country in Town," 187–203, esp. 198–200; B. Andreae, *'Am Birnbaum.' Gärten und Parks im antiken Rom, in den Vesuvstädten und in Ostia* (Mainz: von Zabern, 1996), 9–16 on Martial's concept of *rus in urbe,* esp. 15 for Martial, *Epigrams,* Book 12; 17–20 on the Golden House.

43. J. Manilli, *Villa Borghese Fuori di Porta Pinciana Descritta Da Iacomo Manilli romano Guardarobba di detta Villa* (Rome: Lodovico Grignani, 1650), 1, referring to "gli antichi Horti." In the Latin preface to D. Barrière, *Villa Pamphilia eiusque Palatium . . .* (Rome: Giovanni Giacomo de Rossi, ca. 1670), the publisher Giovanni Giacomo de Rossi spoke similarly of the contrasts in the Villa Pamphilj's rural landscape park: "In fact, with the countryside [*rus*] divided into three areas, you wished this three-fold lavish expanse of your greatness to endure: perpetual spring in the flower-beds . . . ; in the dense woods a winding course of roads, . . . ; in the thickets designed for . . . prey, you enclose wild beasts . . . "

44. Tacitus, *The Annals,* tr. John Jackson, Loeb edition (London: Harvard University Press, 1937), book 15, 42.

45. On pastoral themes in Roman Renaissance gardens and arts, MacDougall, "The Villa Mattei"; MacDougall, *"Ars Hortulorum"*; MacDougall, *Fountains, Statues, and Flowers,* passim; the essays in J. D. Hunt, ed., *The Pastoral Landscape,* Studies in the History of Art 36 (Washington, D.C.: National Gallery of Art; Hanover, NH: University Press of New England, 1992). On what follows on pastoral in the Roman villa parks, see Beneš, "Pastoralism"; Ehrlich, *Landscape and Identity in Early Modern Rome,* 242–64; and Ehrlich's synthetic essay, "Pastoral Landscape and Social Politics in Baroque Rome," in *Baroque Garden Cultures: Emulation, Sublimation, Subversion,* ed. M. Conan (Washington, D.C.: Dumbarton Oaks

Research Library and Collection, 2005), esp. 132–34, 157–63, 172–73, with earlier literature on the pastoral.

46. On the "teatro" of Villa Giulia's palace and garden courts, see Ammannati's letter of 1555 in Bafile, *Villa Giulia*, 31; MacDougall, "The Villa Mattei," 191: "et il semicircolo del palazzo fa teatro; e quest'altro ch'io Vi descriverò fa scena." As architect of the new Palazzo Pitti and Boboli gardens in the 1550s, Ammannati would have been fully versed in the pastoral entertainments of the Medici court. See I. Fenlon, "Pastoral Pastimes at the Pitti Palace," in *L'arme e gli amori: Ariosto, Tasso and Guarini in Late Renaissance Florence: Acts of an International Conference, Florence, Villa I Tatti, June 27–29, 2001,* ed. M. Rossi and F. G. Superbi (Florence: Olschki, 2004), vol. 2: 199–229.

47. R. Nash, *Jacopo Sannazaro, Arcadia and Piscatorial Eclogues* (Detroit, MI: Wayne State University Press, 1966), 29.

48. The pastoralist villa culture of seventeenth-century Rome is one chapter in the long history of pastoral in European garden design; later examples include the more famous Petit Hameau of Marie-Antoinette at Versailles. The French cases from the sixteenth to the eighteenth century have now been studied by M. S. Martin, *Dairy Queens: The Politics of Pastoral Architecture from Catherine de' Medici to Marie-Antoinette* (Cambridge, MA: Harvard University Press, 2011).

49. Ehrlich, *Landscape and Identity,* 89.

50. See, for example, I. Campbell, *The Paper Museum of Cassiano Dal Pozzo: A Catalogue Raisonné. Series A: Ancient Roman Topography and Architecture,* 3 vols. (London: Harvey Miller/Brepols, 2004); and R. Almagià, *L'opera geografica di Luca Holstenio* (Vatican City: Biblioteca Apostolica Vaticana, 1942).

51. Hunt, *Garden and Grove.*

52. For the Netherlands, see E. A. de Jong, *Nature and Art: Dutch garden and Landscape Architecture, 1650–1740* (Philadelphia: University of Pennsylvania Press, 2000), 11–15, 25, 34, and passim; V. B. Sellers, *Courtly Gardens in Holland 1600–1650: The House of Orange and the Hortus Batavus* (Amsterdam: Architectura & Natura, 2001); and C. Lauterbach, *Gärten der Musen und Grazien: Mensch und Natur im niederländischen Humanistengarten, 1522–1655* (Munich: Deutscher Kunstverlag, 2004). For England, see Hunt, *Garden and Grove,* is key; see E. W. Manwaring, *Italian Landscape in Eighteenth Century England* (New York: Oxford University Press, 1925; repr. London: Russell & Russell, 1965). Also Beneš, "Landowning," 198; Ehrlich, "Pastoral Landscape and Social Politics in Baroque Rome," 180–81.

53. For this discussion of French gardens, key discussions and sources for images are in J.-A. du Cerceau, *Les plus excellents bastiments de France par J.-A. Du Cerceau: présentation et commentaires par David Thomson,* tr. C. Ludet (Paris: Sand & Conti, 1988); H. F. Hazlehurst, *Gardens of Illusion: The Genius of André le Nôtre* (Nashville, TN: Vanderbilt University Press, 1980); K. Woodbridge, *Princely Gardens: The Origins and Development of the French Formal Garden* (New York: Rizzoli, 1986); T. Mariage, *L'univers de Le Nôtre et les origines de l'aménagement du territoire* (Brussels: P. Mardaga, 1990; tr. G. Larkin, *The World of André Le Nôtre* [Philadelphia: University of Pennsylvania Press, 1999]); J.-M. Pérouse de

Montclos, *Vaux-le-Vicomte* (London: Scala, Philip Wilson, 1997); J. Guillaume, "Le jardin mis en ordre. Jardin et château en France du XVe au XVIIe siècle," in *Architecture, Jardin, paysage. L'environnement du Château et de la Villa aux XVe et XVIe siècles,* ed. J. Guillaume (Paris: Picard, 1999), 103–36; J. Guillaume, "Château, jardin, paysage en France du XVe au XVIIe siècle," *Revue de l'art* 124 (1999): 13–32; F. Boudon, "Jardins d'eau et jardins de pente dans la France de la Renaissance," in *Architecture, Jardin, paysage. L'environnement du Château et de la Villa aux XVe et XVIe siècles,* ed. J. Guillaume (Paris: Picard, 1999), 137–84; C. Dupont-Logié, ed., *La Main du Jardinier, l'Oeil du Graveur: Le Nôtre et les Jardins Disparus de son Temps* (Sceaux: Musée de l'Île-de-France, 2000); V. De Ganay and L. Le Bon, eds., *Courances* (Paris: Flamarion, 2003); J. Buridant, "La gestion des forêts de vénerie au XVIIe siècle," *XVIIe siècle [Chasse et forêt au XVIIe siècle]* 226 (2005): 17–28; M. Chatenet, ed., *Maisons des champs dans l'Europe de la Renaissance: Actes des premières Rencontres d'architecture européenne. Château de Maisons 10–13 juin 2003* (Paris: Picard, 2006); G. Farhat, ed., *André Le Nôtre. Fragments d'un paysage culturel. Institutions, arts, sciences & techniques* (Sceaux: Musée de l'Île-de-France, Domaine de Sceaux, 2006); J. Buridant, "La Forêt et la Chasse au XVIe Siècle," in *Chasses princières dans l'Europe de la Renaissance. Actes du colloque de Chambord (1er et 2octobre 2004),* ed. C. d'Anthenaise and M. Chatenet (Arles: Actes Sud, 2007); and F. Boudon and C. Mignot, *Jacques Androuet du Cerceau. Les dessins des plus excellents bâtiments de France* (Paris: Picard and Cité de l'architecture & du patrimoine, 2010).

54. Guillaume, "Le jardin mis en ordre."

55. Guillaume, "Le jardin mis en ordre."

56. Discussing "De l'assiette des Iardins à l'égard du plan de terre" in his treatise of 1638, the garden architect Jacques Boyceau emphasizes this kind of unitary composition: "le Iardin estant veüe de haut, est remarquée & reconnnuüe d'vne seule veüe, ne paroist qu'vn seul parterre . . ."; Boyceau, *Traité du jardinage selon les raisons de la nature et de l'art, divisé en trois livres* (Paris: Michel Van Lochom, 1638), 70.

57. See Mariage, *L'univers de Le Nôstre;* C. Mukerji, *Territorial Ambitions and the Gardens of Versailles* (Cambridge: Cambridge University Press, 1997); the essays in Farhat (ed.), *André Le Nôtre;* and the seminal study by V. J. Scully, *Architecture: The Natural and the Manmade* (New York: St. Martin's Press, 1991), chap. 9, 220–73, and chap. 10, 274–311.

BIBLIOGRAPHY

Acidini Luchinat, C., ed. *Giardini Medicei: Giardini di Palazzo e di villa nella Firenze del Quattrocento*. Milan: Federico Motta Editore, 1996.

Acidini Luchinat, C., et al., eds. *Il giardino e le mura: ai confini fra natura e storia. Atti del convegno di studi, San Miniato Alto (Pisa) 23–24 giugno 1995*. Florence: Edifir, 1997.

Ackerman, J. S. *The Villa: Form and Ideology of Country Houses*. Princeton, NJ: Princeton University Press, 1990.

Alamanni, L. *La Coltivatione*. Paris: Robert Estienne, 1546.

Alberti, L. B. *On Painting*. Rev. ed. Translated by J. R. Spencer. New Haven, CT: Yale University Press, 1966.

Alberti, L. B. *On the Art of Building in Ten Books*. Translated by J. Rykwert et al. Cambridge, MA: MIT Press, 1988.

Alberti, L. B. "Villa." In *Opere Volgari*, vol. 1, ed. Cecil Grayson. Bari: G. Laterza, 1960.

Aldini, T. *Exactissima descriptio rariorum quarundam plantarum quæ continentur Romæ in Horto Farnesiano*, Roma, 1625.

Alessandrini, A. *Cimeli lincei a Montpellier*. Rome: Accademia nazionale dei Lincei, 1978.

Almagià, R. *L'opera geografica di Luca Holstenio*. Vatican City: Biblioteca Apostolica Vaticana, 1942.

Ambrosoli, M. "From the Italian Countryside to the Italianate Landscape: Peasants as Gardeners and Foreign Observers in Italy, 1500–1850." In *Clio in the Italian Garden: Twenty-First-Century Studies in Historical Methods and Theoretical Perspectives,* eds. M. Beneš and M. G. Lee, 145–68. Washington, D.C.: Dumbarton Oaks Research Library and Collection, 2011.

Ambrosoli, M. *Scienzati, contadini e proprietari: Botanica e agricoltura nell'Europa occidentale, 1350–1850*. Turin: Einaudi, 1992.

Ambrosoli, M. *The Wild and the Sown: Botany and Agriculture in Western Europe, 1350–1850*. Translated from the Italian by M. McCann Salvatorelli. Cambridge: Cambridge University Press, 1997.

Andreae, B. *"Am Birnbaum." Gärten und Parks im antiken Rom, in den Vesuvstädten un in Ostia.* Mainz: von Zabern, 1996.

Argan, G. C. *Progetto e destino.* Milan: Casa Editrice Il Saggiatore, 1965.

Ariosto, L. *Orlando Furioso.* Translated by G. Waldman. Oxford: Oxford University Press, 1974.

Audebert, N. *Voyage d'Italie.* Critical edition by A. Olivero, 2 vols. Rome: Luciano Lucarini, 1983.

Bacon, F. *Francis Bacon,* ed. B. Vickers. Oxford: Oxford University Press, 1996.

Bafile, M. *Villa Giulia. L'Architettura. Il Giardino.* Rome: Istituto Poligrafico dello Stato, 1948.

Baglione, G. *Le Vite de' Pittori, Scultori et Architetti: Dal Pontificato di Gregorio XIII fino a tutto quello d'Urbano VIII.* 2nd ed. Rome: Menelfo Manelfi, 1649.

Baldriga, I. *L'occhio della lince: I primi lincei tra arte, scienza e collezionismo (1603–1630).* Rome: Accademia Nazionale dei Lincei, 2002.

Baridon, M. *A History of the Gardens of Versailles.* Translated by A. Mason. Philadelphia: University of Pennsylvania Press, 2008.

Baridon, M. *Les jardins. Paysagistes, Jardiniers, Poètes.* Paris: R. Laffont, 1998.

Barisi, I. "The Design of the Garden and Its Botanic Architecture." In *Villa d'Este,* eds. I. Barisi, M. Fagiolo, and M. L. Madonna, 55–81. Rome: De Luca Editori d'Arte, 2003.

Barni, C. *Villa La Magia: Una dimora signorile nel contado pistolese (secc. XIV–XIX).* Florence: Edam, 1999.

Barthes, R. "From Work to Text." In *Image Music Text,* 155–64. Translated by Stephen Heath. London: Fontana Press, 1977.

Basse, W. *A Helpe to memory and discourse with table- talke as musicke to a banquet of wine: being a compendium of witty, and vsefull propositions, problemes, and sentences / extracted from the larger volumes of physicians, philosophers, orators and poets, distilled in their assiduous and learned obseruations, and which for method, manner, and referent handling may be fitly tearmed, A Second misselany, or helpe to discourse.* London: Barnard Alsop for Leonard Becket, 1620.

Battisti, E. *L'antirinascimento: Con un'appendice di testi inediti,* 2 vols. Milan: Feltrinelli, 1962. Enlarged ed., 2 vols. Milan: Garzanti, 1989.

Battisti, E. *"Natura Artificiosa to Natura Artificialis."* In *The Italian Garden,* ed. D. R. Coffin, 1–36. Washington, D.C.: Dumbarton Oaks, 1972.

Baxandall, M. *Painting and Experience in Fifteenth-Century Italy: A Primer in the Social History of Pictorial Style.* Oxford: Oxford University Press, 1988.

Becattini, M. *Parco Mediceo di Pratolino: Villa Demidoff. Una storia per immagini,* with preface by L. Zangheri. Firenze: Edizioni Polistampa, 2005.

Bellay, J., du. *La Deffence et illustration de la langue Francoyse.* Edited by Henri Chamard. Paris: Didier, 1970.

Bellori, G. P. *Le vite de' pittori, scultori ed architetti moderni.* Rome, 1672.

Beltramini, G., and H. Burns, eds. *Andrea Palladio e la villa veneta da Petrarca a Carlo Scarpa.* Venice: Marsilio, 2005.

Beltramini, M., and C. Elam, eds. *"Some Degree of Happiness": Studi di storia dell'architettura in onore di Howard Burns.* Pisa: Sucola Normale Superiore, Edizioni della Normale, 2010.

Beneš, M. "Introduction. Italian and French Gardens. A Century of Historical Study (1900–2000)." In *Villas and Gardens in Early Modern Italy and France,* ed. M. Beneš and D. Harris, 1–16. Cambridge: Cambridge University Press, 2001.

Beneš, M. "Landowning and the Villa in the Social Geography of the Roman Territory: The Location and Landscapes of the Villa Pamphilj, 1645–70." In *Form, Modernism, and History: Essays in Honor of Eduard F. Sekler,* ed. A. von Hoffmann, 187–209. Cambridge, MA: Harvard University Graduate School of Design, 1996.

Beneš, M. "Methodological Changes in the Study of Italian Gardens from the 1970s to the 1990s: A Personal Itinerary." In *Clio in the Italian Garden: Twenty-First Century Studies in Historical Methods and Theoretical Perspectives,* eds. M. Beneš and M. G. Lee, 17–54. Washington, D.C.: Dumbarton Oaks Research Library and Collection, 2011.

Beneš, M. "Pastoralism in the Roman Baroque Villa and in Claude Lorrain: Myths and Realities of the Roman Campagna." In *Villas and Gardens in Early Modern Italy and France,* eds. M. Beneš and D. Harris, 88–113. Cambridge: Cambridge University Press, 2001.

Beneš, M. "The Social Significance of Transforming the Landscape of the Villa Borghese, 1606–1630: Territory, Trees, and Agriculture in the Design of the First Roman Baroque Park." In *Gardens in the Time of the Great Muslim Empires: Theory and Design,* ed. A. Petruccioli, 1–31. Leiden: Brill, 1997.

Beneš, M. "Villa Pamphilj (1630–1670): Family, Land, and Gardens in Papal Rome." 3 vols. PhD diss., Yale University, 1989.

Beneš, M., and D. Harris, eds. *Villas and Gardens in Early Modern Italy and France.* Cambridge: Cambridge University Press, 2001.

Benocci, C. "Pio II paesaggista e gli Sforza: il rinnovamento del monte Amiata e di Santa Fiora dopo il viaggio papale." In *Enea Silvio Piccolomini Pius Secundus. Poeta Laureatus Pontifex Maximus,* ed. Manlio Sodi and Arianna Antoniutti, 341–58. Rome: Associazione Culturale Shakespeare and Libreria Editrice Vaticana, 2007.

Benocci, C., ed. *Villa Doria Pamphilj.* Rome: Art Color Printing srl, Archivio Storico Culturale del Municipio Roma XVI, 2005.

Benocci, C. *Villa Doria Pamphilj.* Rome: Editalia, 1996.

Benocci, C. *Villa Ludovisi.* Rome: Istituto Poligrafico e Zecca dello Stato, 2010.

Beretta, I. *"The World's a Garden": Garden Poetry of the English Renaissance.* Stockholm, Sweden: Uppsala University Press, 1993.

Berger, R. W., and T. F. Hedin. *Diplomatic Tours in the Gardens of Versailles under Louis XIV.* Philadelphia: University of Pennsylvania Press, 2008.

Bergmann, B. "Painted Perspectives of a Villa Visit." In *Roman Art in the Private Sphere,* ed. E. Gazda, 49–70. Ann Arbor: University of Michigan Press, 1991.

Besler, B. *Hortus Eistettensis.* Nuremberg, 1614.

Besse, J.-M. *Les grandeurs de la terre. Aspects du savoir géographique á la Renaissance.* Lyon: ENS, 2003.

Bevilacqua, M., and M. L. Madonna, eds. *Il sistema delle residenze Nobiliari. Stato Pontificio e Granducato di Toscana. Atlante Tematico del Barocco in Italia. Il sistema delle residenze nobiliari, 1,* directed by M. Fagiolo. Rome: De Luca, 2003.

Blanning, T. *The Pursuit of Glory: The Five Revolutions that Made Modern Europe, 1648–1815.* New York: Penguin Books, 2008.

Blunt, W. *Tulipomania,* Harmondsworth: Penguin Books, 1950.

Boffito, G., et al. *Firenze nelle vedute e piante: studio storico topografico cartografico.* Rome: Bonsignori, 2004.

Boiardo, M. M. *Orlando inamorato.* Venice, 1495.

Bonnefons, N., de. *Le Jardinier François, qui enseigne à cultiver les arbres et herbes potagers; avec la maniere de conserver les fruicts, & faire toutes sortes de confitures, conserves & massepans. Dédié aux dames.* Paris: Chez Pierre Des-Hayes, 1651.

Boudon, F. *"Illustrations of Gardens in the Sixteenth Century."* In *The Architecture of Western Gardens,* ed. M. Mosser and G. Teyssot. Cambridge, MA: MIT University Press, 1991.

Boudon, F. "Jardins d'eau et jardins de pente dans la France de la Renaissance." In *Architecture, Jardin, Paysage: L'environnement du Château et de la Villa aux XVe et XVIe siècles,* ed. J. Guillaume, 137–84. Paris: Picard, 1999.

Boudon, F., and C. Mignot. *Jacques Androuet du Cerceau: Les dessins des plus excellents bâtiments de France.* Paris: Picard and Cité de l'architecture & du patrimoine, 2010.

Boyceau, J. *Traité du jardinage selon les raisons de la nature et de l'art, divisé en trois livres.* Paris: Michel Van Lochom, 1638.

Bracciolini, P. *La vera nobiltà/De Vera Nobilitate.* Rome: Salerno, 1999.

Braham, W. "After Typology: The Suffering of Diagrams." *Architectural Design* 70 (2000): 9–11.

Brook, A. 1991. "Sixteenth-Century 'Genre' Statuary in Medici Gardens and Giambologna's Fontana del Villano." In *Boboli 90: Atti del convegno internazionale di studi per la salvaguardia e la valorizzazione del giardino,* ed. C. Acidini Luchinat and E. G. Zorzi, 2 vols. Florence: EDIFIR, 1991.

Brunon, H. "Dalle 'fiere non rapaci' ai 'fruttiferi e pomati arbori': Villa Lante a Bagnaia e l'evoluzione del barco nel Rinascimento." In *Villa Lante a Bagnaia,* ed. S. Frommel with the collaboration of F. Bardati, 31–43. Milan: Electa, 2005.

Brunon, H. "La chasse et l'organisation du paysage dans la Toscane des Médicis." In *Chasses princières dans l'Europe de la Renaissance. Actes du colloque de Chambord (1er et 2 octobre 2004),* ed. C. d'Anthenaise and M. Chatenet, 219–46. Arles, France: Actes Sud, 2007.

Brunon, H. "L'essor artistique et la fabrique culturelle du paysage à la Renaissance: Réflexions à propos de recherches récentes." *Studiolo: Revue d'Histoire de l'Art de l'Académie de France à Rome* 4 (2006): 261–90.

Brunon, H. "Pratolino: art des jardins et imaginaire de la nature dans l'Italie de la seconde moitié du XVIe siècle." PhD diss., 5 vols., Université de Paris-I Panthéon-Sorbonne, 2001.

Brunon, H. "Questions et Méthodes de l'Histoire des Jardins en France." In *Giardini storici: A 25 anni dalle Carte di Firenze: esperienze e prospettive,* 2 vols., ed. L. S. Pelissetti and L. Scazzosi, vol. 1: 31–46. Florence: Olschki, 2009.

Brunot, H. "Du *Songe de Poliphile* à la Grande Grotte de Boboli: la dualité dramatique du paysage." *Polia: Revue de l'art des jardins* 2 (2004): 7–26.

Bruyn, F., De. "The Classical Silva and the Generic Development of Scientific Writing in Seventeenth-Century England." *New Literary History* 32 (2001): 347–73.

Buisseret, D. *The Mapmaker's Quest: Depicting New Worlds in Renaissance Europe.* Oxford: Oxford University, 2003.

Buridant, J. "La Forêt et la Chasse au XVIe Siècle." In *Chasses princières dans l'Europe de la Renaissance: Actes du colloque de Chambord (1er et 2 octobre 2004),* ed. C. d'Anthenaise and M. Chatenet, 159–77. Arles, France: Actes Sud, 2004.

Buridant, J. "La gestion des forêts de vénerie au XVIIe siècle." *XVIIe siècle* [*Chasse et forêt au XVIIe siècle*] 226 (2005): 17–28.

Burnet, G. *Some Letters containing an account of what seemed most Remarkable in Travelling through . . . Italy . . . in the years 1685 and 1686.* Rotterdam, 1686.

Bushnell, R. W. *A Culture of Teaching: Early Modern Humanism in Theory and Practice.* Ithaca, NY: Cornell University Press, 1996.

Bushnell, R. W. *Green Desire: Imagining Early Modern English Gardens.* Ithaca, NY: Cornell University Press, 2003.

Butters, S. B. "Cosimo I's Collemignoli: A forgotten Medici Villa, Lake and Landscape on the Pratomagno." In *"Some Degree of Happiness": Studi di storia dell'architettura in onore di Howard Burns,* ed. M. Beltramini and C. Elam, 407–45. Pisa: Scuola Normale Superiore, Edizioni della Normale, 2010.

Butters, S. B. "Pressed Labor and Pratolino. Social Imagery and Social Reality at a Medici Garden." In *Villas and Gardens in Early Modern Italy and France,* ed. M. Beneš and D. Harris, 61–87. Cambridge: Cambridge University Press, 2001.

Caferro, W. *Contesting the Renaissance.* Oxford: Wiley-Blackwell, 2011.

Camões, L., Vaz de. *The Lusiads.* Translated by W. C. Atkinson. Harmondsworth: Penguin, 1975.

Camões, L., Vaz de. *Os Lusíadas.* Lisbon, 1572.

Campbell, I. *The Paper Museum of Cassiano Dal Pozzo: A Catalogue Raisonné. Series A: Ancient Roman Topography and Architecture,* 3 vols. London: Harvey Miller-Turnhout; Belgium: Brepols, 2004.

Campitelli, A. "Committenti e giardini nella Roma della prima metà del Cinquecento: Alcuni documenti e un'ipotesi per Villa Giulia." In *Delizie in Villa: Il Giardino Rinascimentale e i Suoi Committenti,* ed. G. Venturi and F. Ceccarelli, 199–228. Florence: Olschki, 2008.

Campitelli, A. "Gli 'Horti di Flora': I giardini di Roma ai tempi di Giovan Battista Ferrari." In G. B. Ferrari, *Flora overo cultura di fiori,* ed. and introduction by L. Tongiorgi Tomasi. Firenze: Leo S. Olschki Editore, 2001.

Campitelli, A. "I cocchi di agrumi nelle ville romane." In *Il giardino delle Esperidi. Gli agrumi nella storia, nella letteratura e nell'arte,* ed. A. Tagliolini and M. Azzi Visentini, 175–96. Florence: Edifir, 1996.

Campitelli, A., ed. *Villa Borghese. Storia e gestione.* Milan: Skira editore, 2005.

Campitelli, A. *Villa Borghese: Da Giardino del Principe A Parco Dei Romani.* Rome: Istituto Poligrafico e Zecca Dello Stato, Libreria dello Stato, 2003.

Caro, A. "Lettera a Monsignor Guidiccione, a Lucca (13 luglio 1538)." In *L'Arte dei giardini: Scritti teorici e practice dal XIV al XIX secolo,* vol. 1, ed. M. Azzi Visentini. Milan: Edizioni Il Polifilo, 1999.

Casey, E. *Representing Place: Landscape Painting and Maps*. Minneapolis: University of Minnesota Press, 2002.

Cassetti, R., and M. Fagiolo, eds. *Roma-il verde e la città: Giardini e spazi verdi nella costruzione della forma urbana*. Rome: Gangemi Editore, 2002.

Castiglione, B. *Il libro del cortegiano*. Milan: Biblioteca Universale Rizzoli, 1998.

Caus, S., de. *La Perspective, avec le raison des ombres et miroirs*. London: J. Norton, 1611.

Caus, S., de. *Les Raisons des forces mouvantes avec diverses machines tant utilles que plaisantes ausquelles sont adjoints plusieurs desseings de grotes et fontaines*. Frankfurt: Jan Norton, 1615.

Ceccarelli, F., and M. Folin, eds. *Delizie estensi: architetture di villa nel Rinascimento italiano ed europeo*. Florence: Olschki, 2009.

Cellauro, L. "Classical Paradigms: Pliny the Younger's Hippodrome at his Tuscan Villa and Renaissance Gardens." *Gartenkunst* 17, no. 1 (2005): 73–89.

Cellauro, L. "Iconographical Aspects of the Renaissance Villa and Garden: Mount Parnassus, Pegasus and the Muses." *Studies in the History of Gardens and Designed Landscapes* 23, no. 1 (January–March 2003): 42–57.

Chambers, D. "'Hortus Mertonensis': John Earle's Garden Poem of 1620." *Journal of Garden History* 2 (1982): 117–32.

Champlin, E. "The Suburbium of Rome." *American Journal of Ancient History* 7, no. 2 (1982): 97–107.

Chase, I.W.U. *Horace Walpole: Gardenist; An Edition of Walpole's The History of the Modern Taste in Gardening, with an Estimate of Walpole's Contribution to Landscape Architecture*. Princeton, NJ: Princeton University Press, 1943.

Chatenet, M., ed. *Maisons des champs dans l'Europe de la Renaissance: Actes des premières Rencontres d'architecture européenne. Château de Maisons 10–13 juin 2003*. Paris: Picard, 2006.

Cima, M., and E. La Rocca, eds. *Horti Romani. Atti del Convegno Internazionale, Roma, 4–6 maggio 1995*. Rome: L'Erma di Bretschneider, 1998.

Coffin, D. "The 'Lex Hortorum' and Access to Gardens of Latium during the Renaissance." *Journal of Garden History* 2 (1982): 201–32.

Coffin, D. "Pirro Ligorio on the Nobility of the Arts." *Journal of the Warburg and Courtauld Institutes* 27 (1964): 191–210.

Coffin, D. R. *Gardens and Gardening in Papal Rome*. Princeton, NJ: Princeton University Press, 1991.

Coffin, D. R., ed. *The Italian Garden*. Washington, D.C.: Dumbarton Oaks Research Library and Collection, 1972.

Coffin, D. R. *The Villa d'Este in Tivoli*. Princeton, NJ: Princeton University Press, 1960.

Coffin, D. R. *The Villa in the Life of Renaissance Rome*. Princeton, NJ: Princeton University Press, 1979.

Colonna, F. *Discours du songe de Poliphile, déduisant comme Amour le combat à l'occasion de Polia. Soubz la fiction de quoy l'auteur monstrant que toutes choses terrestres ne sont que vanité, traicte de plusieurs matières profitables et dignes de mémoire*. Paris, 1554.

Colonna, F. *Hypnerotomachia Poliphili ubi humana omnia non nisi somnium esse docet, atque obiter plurima scitu sane quam digna commemorat.* Venice: Aldus Manutius, 1499.

Colonna, F. *Hypnerotomachia: The Strife of Love in a Dream.* Translated by R[obert] D[allington?]. London, 1592.

Colonna, F. *Minus cognitarum stirpium aliquot, ac etiam rariorum nostro coelo orientium ekphrasis,* Roma: apud Guilielmum Facciottum, 1606.

Comito, T. *The Idea of the Garden in the Renaissance.* New Brunswick, NJ: Rutgers University Press, 1978.

Conan, M., ed. *Baroque Garden Cultures: Emulation, Sublimation, Subversion.* Washington, D.C.: Dumbarton Oaks Research Library and Collection, 2005.

Conan, M. "The Conundrum of Le Nôtre's Labyrinthe." In *Garden History: Issues, Approaches, Methods,* ed. J. D. Hunt, 119–50. Washington, D.C.: Dumbarton Oaks Research Library and Collection, 1992.

Conan, M. "Friendship and Imagination in French Baroque Gardens before 1661." In *Baroque Garden Cultures: Emulation, Sublimation, Subversion,* ed. M. Conan, 323–84. Washington, D.C.: Dumbarton Oaks Research Library and Collection, 2005.

Conan, M. "Garden Displays of Majestic Will." In *The Triumph of the Baroque: Architecture in Europe 1600–1750,* ed. H. A. Millon, 279–313. Milan: Bompiani, 1999.

Conan, M., ed. *Perspectives on Garden Histories.* Washington, D.C.: Dumbarton Oaks Research Library and Collection, 1999.

Conan, M. "Postface." In *Le Jardin Palatin,* ed. S. de Caus. Paris: Editions du Moniteur, 1981.

Conforti, C. "Architettura e giardino: territorio e paesaggio a Firenze in età medicea." In *Villa Lante a Bagnaia,* ed. S. Frommel with the collaboration of F. Bardati, 206–17. Milan: Electa, 2005.

Conforti, C. "L'invenzione delle allegorie territoriali e dinastiche nel giardino di Castello a Firenze." In *Il giardino come labirinto della storia: convegno internazionale, Palermo 14–17 aprile 1984: Raccolta degli atti,* eds. J. Abel et al. Palermo: Centro studi di storia e arte dei giardini, 1984.

Coolidge, J. "The Villa Giulia: A Study of Central Italian Architecture in the Mid-Sixteenth Century." *The Art Bulletin* 25 (1943): 177–225.

Cooper, A. *Inventing the Indigenous: Local Knowledge and Natural History in Early Modern Europe.* Cambridge: Cambridge University Press, 2010.

Cormack, L. B. *Charting an Empire: Georgraphy at the English Universities, 1580–1620.* Chicago: University of Chicago Press, 1997.

Cosgrove, D. *Geography & Vision: Seeing, Imagining and Representing the World.* London: I. B. Tauris, 2008.

Cosgrove, D. *The Palladian Landscape: Geographical Change and Its Cultural Representations in Sixteenth-Century Italy.* Leicester: University of Leicester Press, 1993.

Cosgrove, D. *Social Formation and Symbolic Landscape.* 2nd ed. Madison: University of Wisconsin Press, 1998.

Cosgrove, D., and S. Daniels, eds. *The Iconography of Landscape: Essays on the Symbolic Representation, Design, and Use of Past Environments.* Cambridge: Cambridge University Press, 1988.

Crandell, G. *Nature Pictorialized: The "View" in Landscape History.* Baltimore: Johns Hopkins University Press, 1993.

Crewe, J. "The Garden State." In *Enclosure Acts: Sexuality, Property, and Culture in Early Modern England,* ed. R. Burt and J. M. Archer, 270–89. Ithaca, NY: Cornell University Press, 1994.

Croisille, J.-M. *Paysages dans la peinture romaine: Aux origines d'un genre pictural.* Paris: Picard, 2010.

Curtius, E. R. *European Literature and the Latin Middle Ages.* Translated by W. Trask. Princeton, NJ: Princeton University Press, 1990.

Dainville, F. de. *La géographie des humanists.* Paris: Beauchesne, 1940.

Dami, L. *Il giardino italiano.* Milano: Bestetti, 1924. Translated from the Italian, *The Italian Garden.* New York: Brentano, 1925.

Daniel, N. *Islam and the West: The Making of an Image.* Oxford: Oneworld, 1960; rev. ed., 1993.

d'Anthenaise, C., and M. Chatenet, eds. *Chasses princières dans l'Europe de la Renaissance: Actes du colloque de Chambord (1er et 2 octobre 2004).* Arles, France: Actes Sud, 2007.

De Benedetti, L. "Giardino, paesaggio, territorio." In *Il giardino veneto dal tardo medioevo al novecento,* ed. M. Azzi Visentini, 281–301. Milan: Electa, 1988.

De Ganay, V., and L. Le Bon, eds. *Courances.* Paris: Flamarion, 2003.

Delalande, M. R. "Du Palais de Flore dansé à Trianon devant Sa Majesté le 5 janvier 1689." In *Recueil des sujets paroles d'une partie des ballets, dansez devant sa Majesté.* Paris: Christophe Ballard, 1709.

Demetz, P. "The Elm and the Vine: Notes toward the History of a Marriage Topos." *PMLA* 73, no. 5 (1958): 521.

Den Lust-hof van Rethorica. Leiden: Fransous van Ravelengien, 1596.

Derex, J.-M. "Les Parcs de Vincennes et de Boulogne au XVie siècle." In *Chasses princières dans l'Europe de la Renaissance: actes du colloque de Chambord, 1er et 2 octobre 2004,* ed. C. d'Anthenaise et al. Arles, France: Actes Sud, 2007.

Dernie, D. *The Villa d'Este at Tivoli.* London: Academy Editions, 1996.

De Seta, C., ed. *Storia d'Italia. Annali 5: Il paesaggio.* Turin: Giulio Einaudi editore, 1982.

D'Heere, L. *Den Hof en Boomgaerd der Poësien.* Ghendt: [Drucker:] Ghileyn Manilius, 1565.

Digulleville, G., de. *La Pèlerinage de vie humaine: le songe tre`s chre´tien de l'abbe´ Guillaume de Digulleville,* ed. P. Amblard. Paris: Flammarion, 1998.

Dubbini, R. *Geografie dello sguardo: visione e paesaggio in età moderna* Turin: G. Einaudim 1994. Translated by L. G. Cochrane, *Geography of the Gaze: Urban and Rural Vision in Early Modern Europe.* Chicago: University of Chicago Press, 2002.

Du Cerceau, J.-A. *Les plus excellents bastiments de France par J.-A. Du Cerceau présentation et commentaires par David Thompson.* Translated by C. Ludet. Paris: Sand & Conti, 1988.

Dupont-Logié, C., ed. *La Main du Jardinier, l'Oeil du Graveur: Le Nôtre et les Jardins Disparus de son Temps.* Sceaux: Musée de l'Ile-de-France, 2000.

Duport, D. *Le Jardin et la nature: Ordre et variété dans la littérature de la Renaissance.* Geneva: Droz, 2002.

Duport, D. *Les Jardins qui sentent le sauvage: Ronsard et la poétique du paysage.* Geneva: Droz, 2000.

Eco, U. *The Search for the Perfect Language.* Translated by J. Fentress. Oxford: Blackwell, 1995.

Edelstein, B. L. "'Acqua viva e corrente': Private Display and Public Distribution of Fresh Water at the Neapolitan Villa of Poggioreale as a Hydraulic Model for Sixteenth-Century Medici Gardens." In *Artistic Exchange and Cultural Translation in the Italian Renaissance City,* ed. S. J. Campbell and S. J. Milner, 187–220. Cambridge: Cambridge University Press, 2004.

Egmond, F. "Clusius and Friends: Cultures of Exchange in the Circle of European Naturalists." In *Carolus Clusius: Towards a Cultural History of a Renaissance Naturalist,* ed. F. Egmond, P. Hoftijzer, and R. Visser, 9–48. Amsterdam: Koninklijke Nederlandse Akademie van Wetenschappen, 2007.

Egmond, F. *The World of Carolus Clusius: Natural History in the Making, 1550–1610.* London: Pickering and Chatto, 2010.

Egmond, F., P. Hoftijzer, and R. Visser, eds. *Carolus Clusius: Towards a Cultural History of a Renaissance Naturalist.* Amsterdam: Koninklijke Nederlandse Akademie van Wetenschappen, 2007.

Ehrlich, T. L. *Landscape and Identity in Early Modern Rome: Villa Culture at Frascati in the Borghese Era.* Cambridge: Cambridge University Press, 2002.

Ehrlich, T. L. "Pastoral Landscape and Social Politics in Baroque Rome." In *Baroque Garden Cultures: Emulation, Sublimation, Subversion,* ed. M. Conan, 131–81. Washington, D.C.: Dumbarton Oaks Research Library and Collection, 2005.

Elkins, J. "On the Conceptual Analysis of Gardens." *Journal of Garden History* 13 (1993): 189–98. Republished as "Writing as Reverie," in J. Elkins, *Our Beautiful, Dry, and Distant Texts: Art History as Writing.* University Park: Penn State University Press, 2000.

Erondell, P. *The French garden: for English ladyes and gentlewomen to walke in. Or, A sommer dayes labour: Being an instruction for the attayning vnto the knowledge of the French tongue: wherein for the practise thereof, are framed thirteene dialogues in French and English, concerning diuers matters from the rising in the morning till bed-time. Also the historie of the centurion mencioned in the Gospell: in French verses. Which is an easier and shortter methode then hath beene yet set forth, to bring the louers of the French tongue to the perfection of the same.* London: [By E. Allde] for Edward White, 1605.

Etienne, C., and J. Liebault. *L'agriculture, et Maison rustique de mm. Charles Estienne, & Jean Liebault, docteurs en médecine,* edition dernière, reueue & augmentée . . . Lyon: Jaques du Puis, 1578.

Evelyn, J. *The Diary of John Evelyn,* vol. 2, ed. E. S. de Beer. Oxford: Oxford University Press, 1955.

Evelyn, J. *Sylva; or, A Discourse of Forest-Trees, and the Propagation of Timber in His Majesties Dominions* London: Jo. Martyn and Ja. Allestry, 1664.

Fabiani Giannetto, R. *Medici Gardens: From Making to Design*. Philadelphia: University of Pennsylvania Press, 2008.

Fabiani Giannetto, R. "The Medici Gardens of Fifteenth-Century Florence: Conceptualization and Tradition." PhD diss., University of Pennsylvania, 2004.

Fabiani Giannetto, R. "Writing the Garden in the Age of Humanism: Petrarch and Boccaccio." *Studies in the History of Gardens and Designed Landscapes* 23, no. 3 (2003): 213–57.

Fagiolo, M. "Da Villa Madama a Villa Giulia e al Gianicolo: Gli Assi delle memoria storica." In *Roma-il verde e la città: Giardini e spazi verdi nella costruzione ella forma urbana*, ed. R. Cassetti and M. Fagiolo, 31–47. Rome: Gangemi Editore, 2002.

Fagiolo, M. "Il giardino del mito." In *Lo specchio del paradise L'immagine del giardino dall'Antico al Novecento*, ed. M. Fagiolo and M. A. Giusti. Milan: Silvana Editoriale, 1996.

Fagiolo, M., ed. *La città effimera e l'universo artificiale del giardino: la Firenze dei Medici e l'Italia del '500*. Rome: Edizioni Officina, 1980.

Fagiolo, M., ed. *Natura e artificio: l'ordine rustico, le fontane, gli autonomi nella cultura del Manierismo europeo*. Rome: Edizioni Officina, 1981.

Fagiolo, M. "Systems of Gardens in Italy: Princely Residences and Villas in Rome and Latium, Savoy Piedmont, Royal Bourbon Naples, and Bagheria, Sicily." In *Clio in the Italian Garden: Twenty-First Century Studies in Historical Methods and Theoretical Perspectives*, ed. M. Beneš and M. G. Lee, 81–114. Washington, D.C.: Dumbarton Oaks Research Library and Collection, 2011.

Farhat, G., ed. *André Le Nôtre. Fragments d'un paysage culturel: Institutions, arts, sciences & techniques*. Sceaux: Musée de l'île-de-France, Domaine de Sceaux, 2006.

Fat, L. Tjon Sie, "Clusius' Garden: A Reconstruction." In *The Authentic Garden: A Symposium on Gardens*, ed. L. Tjon Sie Fat and E. de Ljon, 3–12. Leiden: Publisher, 1991.

Fat, L. Tjon Sie et al., eds. *The Authentic Garden: A Symposium on Gardens*. Leiden: Clusius Foundation, 1991.

Félibien, A. *La Description du château de Versailles*. Paris: Antoine Vilette, 1694.

Fenlon, I. "Pastoral Pastimes at the Pitti Palace." In *L'arme e gli amori: Ariosto, Tasso and Guarini in Late Renaissance Florence: Acts of an International Conference, Florence, Villa I Tatti, June 27–29, 2001*, vol. 2, ed. M. Rossi and F. G. Superbi, 199–229. Florence: Olschki, 2004.

Ferrari, G. B. *De florum cultura*. Rome: Stephanus Paulinus, 1633.

Ferrari, G. B. *Flora overo cultura di fiori*. Rome: Facciotti, 1638.

Ferrari, G. B. *Hesperidessive de malorum aureorum cultura*. Rome, 1646.

F.L.D.T.R. *Secrets pour teindre la fleur d'immortelle en diverses couleurs, avec la maniere de la cultiver. Pour faire des pastes de differentes odeurs fort agreables. Et pour contrefaire du marbre au naturel propre pour toutes sorte d'ouvrages figurez*. Paris: Charles de Sercy, 1690.

Florio, J. *Florios second frutes to be gathered of twelue trees, of diuers but delightsome tastes to the tongues of Italians and Englishmen. To which is annexed his Gardine of recreation yeelding six thousand Italian prouerbs*. London, 1591.

Fortini Brown, P. *Venice and Antiquity: The Venetian Sense of the Past.* New Haven, CT: Yale University Press, 1996.

Foucault, M. "Of Other Spaces." *Diacritics* 16, no. 3 (1986): 22–27.

Foucault, M. *The Order of Things: An Archaeology of the Human Sciences.* New York: Vintage Books, 1973.

Franchetti Pardo, V., and G. Casali. *I Medici nel contado fiorentino: ville e possedimenti agricoli tra Quattrocento e Cinquecento.* Florence: Cooperativa Editrice Universitaria, 1978.

Francis, M., and R. T. Hester Jr., eds. *The Meaning of Gardens: Idea, Place and Action.* Cambridge, MA: MIT Press, 1990.

Fratadocchi, M. B., and S. Buttò, eds. *Erbe e speziali. I laboratory della salute.* Exhibition catalogue. Rome: Sansepolcro Aboca Museum, 2007.

Freedberg, D. "Cassiano, Ferrari and other drawings of citrus fruits." In *The Paper Museum of Cassiano dal Pozzo: A Catalogue Raisonné, Part I: Citrus Fruits,* ed. D. Freedberg and E. Baldini. London, Harvey Miller, 1997.

Frommel, S., ed. *Bomarzo: il sacro bosco.* Milan: Electa, 2009.

Frommel, S., ed. *Villa Lante a Bagnaia.* Milan: Electa, 2005.

Furetière, A. *Dictionnaire universel des arts et des sciences.* La Haye, 1690.

Furttenbach, J. *Architectura recreationis.* Augspurg: Johann Schultes, 1640.

Gabrieli, G. *Contributi alla storia dell'Accademia dei Lincei.* Rome: Accademia Nazionale dei Lincei, 1989.

Galletti, G. "Fortune e sfortune del bosso nei giardini italiani dal Rinascimento al Novecento." In *Topiaria. Architetture e sculture vegetali nel giardino occidentale dall'antichità ad oggi,* ed. M. Azzi Visentini, 93–103. Treviso: Fondazione Benetton Studi e Ricerche, 2004.

Gallo. *Le dieci giornate della vera agricoltura, e piaceri della villa.* Venezia: Domenico Farri, 1565.

Galloni, P. *Storia e cultura della caccia: dalla preistoria a oggi.* Rome: Laterza, 2000.

Garbari, F., et al., eds. *Giardino dei semplici = Garden of Simples.* Pisa: Edizioni Plus, 2002.

Gardens of Earthly Delight: Sixteenth and Seventeenth-Century Netherlandish Gardens. Catalogue of the exhibition. Pittsburgh, PA: The Frick Art Museum, 1986.

Gascoigne, G. *A hundreth sundrie flowres bounde vp in one small poesie Gathered partely (by translation) in the fyne outlandish gardins of Euripides, Ouid, Petrarke, Ariosto, and others: and partly by inuention, out of our owne fruitefull orchardes in Englande: yelding sundrie svveete sauours of tragical, comical, and morall discourses.* London, 1573.

Geikie, A. *The Love of Nature among the Romans during the later Decades of the Republic and the First Century of the Empire.* London: John Murray, 1912.

Giamatti, A. B. *The Earthly Paradise and the Renaissance Epic.* Princeton, NJ: Princeton University Press, 1966.

Giusti, A., and W. Koeppe, eds. *Art of the Royal Court: Treasures in Pietre Dure from the Palaces of Europe.* New York: Metropolitan Museum of Art, 2008.

Giusti, M. A. "La veduta–documento e le serie 'catastali.'" In *Lo specchio del paradiso: L'immagine del giardino dall'Antico al Novecento,* ed. M. Fagiolo and M. A. Giusti. Milano: Silvana Editoriale, 1996.

Giusti, M. A. "Vita in giardino." In *Lo specchio del paradise L'immagine del giardino dall'Antico al Novecento,* ed. M. Fagiolo and M. A. Giusti. Milan: Silvana Editoriale, 1996.

Glang-Süberkrüb, A. *Der Liebesgarten: Eine Untersuchung über die Bedeutung der Konfiguration für das Bildthema im Spätwerk des Peter Paul Rubens.* Bern: Lang, 1975.

Goldgar, A. *Impolite Learning: Conduct and Community in the Republic of Letters, 1680–1750.* New Haven, CT: Yale University Press, 1995.

Goldgar, A. *Tulipmania: Money, Honor, and Knowledge in the Dutch Golden Age.* Chicago: Chicago University Press, 2008.

Gómez López, S. "Natural collections in the Spanish Renaissance." In *From Private to Public: Natural Collections and Museums,* ed. M. Beretta. Sagamore Beach, MA: Science History Publications, 2005.

Gothein, M. L. *A History of Garden Art,* ed. W. P. Wright. Translated by Mrs. Archer-Hind. New York: Hacker Art Books, 1966.

Grafton, A. *Worlds Made by Words: Scholarship and Community in the Modern West.* Cambridge, MA: Harvard University Press, 2009.

Grangier de Liverdis, B. *Journal d'un voyage de France et d'Italie fait par un gentilhomme françois: Commencé le quatorzième septembre 1660 & achevé le trentunième May 1661.* Paris: Michel Vaugon, 1667.

Greenblatt, S. *Renaissance Self-Fashioning: From More to Shakespeare.* Chicago: University of Chicago Press, 1980.

Greenblatt, S., et al., eds. *The Norton Shakespeare: Based on the Oxford Edition.* 2nd ed. New York: W. W. Norton, 2008.

Greene, T. M. *The Light in Troy: Imitation and Discovery in Renaissance Poetry.* New Haven, CT: Yale University Press, 1982.

Greuter, M. *Vedute e Giardini di Roma,* Rome, 1623.

Groos, G. W., ed. and tr. *The Diary of Baron Waldstein: A Traveller in Elizabethan England.* London: Thames and Hudson, 1981.

Grove, R. H. *Green Imperialism: Colonial Expansion, Tropical Island Edens, and the Origins of Environmentalism, 1600–1860.* Cambridge: Cambridge University Press, 1995.

Guerci, G., L. Sabrina Pelissetti, and L. Scazzosi, eds. *Oltre il giardino: Le architetture vegetali e il paesaggio.* Florence: Olschki, 2003.

Guillaume, J., ed. *Architecture, Jardin, Paysage: L'environnement du Château et de la Villa aux XVe et XVIe siècles.* Paris: Picard, 1999.

Guillaume, J. "Château, jardin, paysage en France du XVe au XVIIe siècle." *Revue de l'art* 124 (1999): 13–32.

Guillaume, J., ed. *Jacques Androuet du Cerceau: "Un des plus grands architectes qui se soit jamais trouvé en France."* Paris: Picard and Cité de l'architecture & du patrimoine, 2010.

Halpern, L. C. "The Uses of Paintings in Garden History." In *Garden History: Issues, Approaches, Methods,* Colloquium on the History of Landscape Architecture 13, ed. J. D. Hunt. Washington, D.C.: Dumbarton Oaks, 1992.

Hankins, J. E. *Shakespeare's Derived Imagery.* Lawrence: Kansas University Press, 1953.

Harris, D. *The Nature of Authority: Villa Culture, Landscape, and Representation in Eighteenth-Century Lombardy.* University Park: Pennsylvania State University Press, 2003.

Harris, D., and D. Fairchild Ruggles, eds. *Sites Unseen: Landscape and Vision.* Pittsburgh, PA: University of Pittsburgh Press, 2007.

Hazlehurst, H. F. *Gardens of Illusion: The Genius of André Le Nostre.* Nashville, TN: Vanderbilt University Press, 1980.

Heikamp, D. "Agostino del Riccio: Del giardino di un re." In *Il Giardino storico italiano: problemi di indagine, fonti letterarie e storiche: atti del convegno di studi, Siena-San Quirico D'orcia, 6–8 ottobre 1978,* ed. Giovanna Ragionieri. Florence: Olschki, 1981.

Herrick, R. *Hesperides; or, The works both humane & divine of Robert Herrick, Esq.* London, 1648.

Hobhouse, P. "Vatican Gardens." In *The Oxford Companion to the Garden,* ed. P. Taylor, 492–93. Oxford: Oxford University Press, 2006.

Holstenius, L. *Vetus pictura nymphaeum referens commentariolo explicata a Luca Holstenio. Accedunt alia quaedam eiusdem auctoris.* Rome: typis Barberinis, 1676.

Hopper, F. "Clusius' World: The Meeting of Science and Art." In *The Authentic Garden: A Symposium on Gardens,* ed. L. Tjon Sie Fat et al. Leiden: Clusius Foundation, 1991.

Horowitz, M. C. *Seeds of Virtue and Knowledge.* Princeton, NJ: Princeton University Press, 1998.

Hunt, J. D. *The Afterlife of Gardens.* Philadelphia: University of Pennsylvania Press, 2004.

Hunt, J. D. "Curiosities to Adorn Cabinets and Gardens." In *The Origins of Museums: The Cabinet of Curiosities in Sixteenth- and Seventeenth-Century Europe,* ed. O. Impey and A. MacGregor, 193–203. Oxford: Clarendon Press, 1985.

Hunt, J. D. *Garden and Grove: The Italian Renaissance Garden in the English Imagination, 1600–1750.* London: J. M. Dent & Sons, 1986.

Hunt, J. D. *Greater Perfections: The Practice of Garden Theory.* Philadelphia: University of Pennsylvania Press; London: Thames and Hudson, 2000.

Hunt, J. D. "*Paragone* in Paradise: Translating the Garden." *Comparative Criticism* 18 (1996): 55–70.

Hunt, J. D., ed. *The Pastoral Landscape.* Studies in the History of Art 36. Washington, D.C.: National Gallery of Art; Hanover, NH: University Press of New England, 1992.

Hunt, J. D., and P. Willis, eds. *The Genius of the Place: The English Landscape Garden 1620–1820.* London: Elek, 1975.

Hyde, E. *Cultivated Power: Flowers, Culture, and Politics in the Reign of Louis XIV.* Philadelphia: University of Pennsylvania Press, 2005.

Hyde, E. "The Cultivation of a King, or the Flower Fardens of Louis XIV." In *Tradition and Innovation in French Garden Art. Chapters of a New History,* ed. J. D. Hunt and M. Conan. Philadelphia: University of Pennsylvania Press, 2002.

Hyde, E. "Flowers of Distinction: Taste, Class and Floriculture in Seventeenth Century France." In *Bourgeois and Aristocratic Cultural Encounters in Garden Art, 1550–1850,* ed. M. Conan, 77–100. Washington, D.C.: Dumbarton Oaks Research Library and Collection, 2002.

Impelluso, L. *Gardens in Art.* Translated by S. Sartarelli. Los Angeles: J. Paul Getty Museum, 2007.

Jardine, L. *Worldly Goods: A New History of the Renaissance.* New York: W. W. Norton, 1998.

Jenner, T. *The soules solace, or Thirtie and one spirituall emblems.* London, 1626.

Jones, R., and N. Penny. 1983. *Raphael.* New Haven, CT: Yale University Press.

Jong, E., de. "Nature and Art: The Leiden Hortus As 'Museum.'" In *The Authentic Garden: A Symposium on Gardens,* ed. L. Tjon Sie Fat et al. Leiden: Clusius Foundation, 1991.

Jong, E., de. "Of Plants and Gardeners, Prints and Books: Reception and Exchange in Northern European Garden Culture 1648–1725." In *Baroque Garden Cultures: Emulation, Sublimation, Subversion,* ed. M. Conan, 37–84. Washington, D.C.: Dumbarton Oaks Research Library and Collection, 2005.

Jonson, B. *Ben Jonson: The Complete Poems,* ed. G Parfitt. Harmondsworth: Penguin, 1975.

Jordan, T. *Poeticall varieties; or, Varietie of fancies. By Tho. Iordan Gent.* London, 1637.

Kaufmann, T. D. *L'école de Prague: La peinture à la cour de Rodolphe II.* Paris: Flammarion, 1985.

Kendall, T. *Flowers of epigrammes, out of sundrie the moste singular authours selected, as well aunctient as late writers. Pleasant and profitable to the expert readers of quicke capacitie.* London, 1577.

Kenseth, J., ed. *The Age of the Marvelous: Catalog of an Exhibition Held at the Hood Museum of Art, Dartmouth College, Sept. 21–Nov. 24, 1991.* Hanover, NH: Hood Museum of Art, Dartmouth College, 1991.

Kovacs, S. R. "Staging Lyric Performances in Early Printing Culture: *Le Jardin de Plaisance et Fleur de Rethorique* (c. 1501–02)." *French Studies* 55 (2001): 1–24.

Kraus, J. U. *Tapisseries du roy, où sont representez les quatre élémens et les quatre saisons, avec les devises qui les accompagnent et leur explication. Königliche französische Tapezereyen, oder überaus schöne Sinn-Bilder, in welchen die vier Element samt den vier Jahr-Zeiten . . . an den Tag gegeben und verlegt durch Johann Ulrich Krauss.* Augsburg: gedruckt daselbst durch J. Koppmayer, 1687.

Kyd, T. *The Spanish tragedie; or, Hieronimo is mad againe Containing the lamentable end of Don Horatio, and Belimperia; with the pittifull death of Hieronimo.* City, 1592; London, 1615.

Lablaude, P.-A. *Gardens of Versailles.* Paris: Editions Scala France, 2006.

Lablaude, P.-A. *The Gardens of Versailles.* London: Zwemmer, 1995.

La Brosse, G., de. *Description du Jardin Royal des Plantes Médicinales.* Paris, 1636.

La Letteratura e i Giardini: Atti del Convegno Internazionale di Studi di Verona— Garda, 2–5 ottobre 1985. Florence: Olschki, 1987.

Landsberg, S. *The Medieval Garden.* Toronto: University of Toronto Press, 2003.

[Laneham, R.]. *A letter whearin part of the entertainment vntoo the Queenz Maiesty at Killingwoorth Castl in Warwik sheer in this soomerz progress 1575 is signified/ from a freend officer attendant in coourt vntoo hiz freend a citizen and merchaunt of London.* London, 1575.

Langdon, H. "The Imaginative Geographies of Claude Lorrain." In *Transports: Travel, Pleasure, and Imaginative Geography, 1600–1830,* ed. C. Chard and H. Langdon, 151–78. New Haven, CT: Yale University Press, 1996.

L'Appennino del Giambologna: Anatomia e identità del gigante. Firenze: Alinea Editrice, 1990.

La Quintinie, J., de. *Instruction pour les Jardins Fruitiers et Potagers, avec un Traité des Orangers, suivy de quelques Réflexions sur l'Agriculture, par feu Mr de la Quintinye, Directeur de tous les Jardins Fruitiers et Potagers du Roy.* Paris: Claude Barbin, 1690.

La Rocca, E. *Lo spazio negato: La pittura di paesaggio nella cultura artistica greca e romana.* Milan: Mondadori Electa, 2008.

Lauterbach, C. *Gärten der Musen und Grazien: Mensch und Natur im niederländischen Humanistengarten, 1522–1655.* Munich: Deutscher Kunstverlag, 2004.

Lazzaro, C. *The Italian Renaissance Garden: From the Conventions of Planting, Design, and Ornament to the Grand Gardens of Sixteenth-Century Central Italy.* New Haven, CT: Yale University Press, 1990.

Lazzaro, C. "Italy Is a Garden: The Idea of Italy and the Italian Garden Tradition." In *Villas and Gardens in Early Modern Italy and France,* ed. M. Beneš and D. Harris, 29–60. Cambridge: Cambridge University Press, 2001.

Lazzaro, C. "The Sixteenth-Century Central Italian Villa and the Cultural Landscape." In *Architecture, Jardin, Paysage. L'environnement du Château et de la Villa aux XVe et XVIe siècles,* ed. J. Guillaume, 29–44. Paris: Picard, 1999.

Lazzaro-Bruno, C. "The Villa Lante at Bagnaia: An Allegory of Art and Nature." *Art Bulletin* 4, no. 59 (1977): 553–60.

Leach, E. W. *The Rhetoric of Space: Literary and Artistic Representations of Landscape in Republican and Augustan Rome.* Princeton, NJ: Princeton University Press, 1988.

Leslie, M. "Spenser, Sidney, and the Renaissance Garden." *English Literary Renaissance,* 22 (1992): 3–36.

Leslie, M., and T. Raylor, eds. *Culture and Cultivation in Early Modern England: Writing and the Land.* Leicester: Leicester University Press, 1994.

Levi d'Ancona, M. *Botticelli's Primavera: A Botanical Interpretation Including Astrology, Alchemy and the Medici.* Firenze: Leo S. Olschi Editore, 1983.

Levi d'Ancona, M. *The Garden of the Renaissance: Botanical Symbolism in Italian Painting.* Florence: Olschki, 1977.

Lightbown, R. W. "Nicolas Audebert and the Villa d'Este." *Journal of the Warburg and Courtauld Institutes* 27 (1964): 164–90.

Lightbown, R. W. "Some Notes on Spanish Baroque Collectors." In *The Origins of Museums: The Cabinet of Curiosities in Sixteenth- and Seventeenth Century Europe,* ed. O. Impey and A. MacGregor. Oxford: Clarendon Press, 1985.

Ligorio, P. *Libro dell'antica città di Tivoli e di alcune famose ville,* ed. A. Ten. Rome: De Luca, 2005.

Lorris, G., de, and J. de Meun. *Le Roman de la rose,* 3 vols., ed. Félix Lecoy. Paris: Librairie Honoré Champion, 1965–1970.

MacDonald, W. L., and J. A. Pinto. *Hadrian's Villa and Its Legacy.* New Haven, CT: Yale University Press, 1995.

MacDougall, E. B. "*Ars Hortulorum:* Sixteenth Century Garden Iconography and Literary Theory in Italy." In *The Italian Garden,* ed. D. R. Coffin, 37–59. Washington, D.C.: Dumbarton Oaks Research Library and Collection, 1972.

MacDougall, E. B. *Fountains, Statues, and Flowers. Studies in Italian Gardens of the Sixteenth and Seventeenth Centuries.* Washington, D.C.: Dumbarton Oaks Research Library and Collection, 1994.

MacDougall, E. B. "The Villa Mattei and the Development of the Roman Garden Style." PhD diss., Harvard University, 1970.

Mack, C. R. *Pienza: The Creation of a Renaissance City.* Ithaca, NY: Cornell University Press, 1987.

Madden, D. H. *A Chapter of Mediæval History: The Fathers of the Literature of Field Sport and Horses.* London: J. Murray, 1924.

Magne, E. *Le Château de Marly, d'après des documents inédits.* Paris: Calmann-Lévy, 1934.

Maguire, H. "Gardens and Parks in Constantinople." *Dumbarton Oaks Papers* 54 (2000): 251–64.

Maier, M. *Atalanta Fugiens.* Oppenheim, 1618.

Maier, M. *Symbola Aurae mensae duodecim nationum.* Frankfurt, 1617.

Maiorino, A., M. Minelli, A. L. Monti, B. Negroni, and A. Segre. "L'uso dei bulbi da fiore nei giardini del Rinascimento: Il caso di Boboli." In *Boboli 90,* ed. C. Acidini Luchinat and E. Garbero Zorzi, 277–89. Florence: Edifir, 1991.

Malcolmson, C. "The Garden Enclosed/The Woman Enclosed." In *Enclosure Acts: Sexuality, Property, and Culture in Early Modern England,* ed. R. Burt and J. M. Archer, 251–69. Ithaca, NY: Cornell University Press, 1994.

Manilli, J. *Villa Borghese Fuori di Porta Pinciana Descritta Da Iacomo Manilli romano Guardarobba di detta Villa.* Rome: Lodovico Grignani, 1650.

Manwaring, E. W. *Italian Landscape in Eighteenth Century England.* New York: Oxford University Press, 1925; repr. London: Russell & Russell, 1965.

Marchi, P. "Il giardino di boboli e il suo anfiteatro." In *La città effimera e l'universo artificiale del giardino: la Firenze dei Medici e l'Italia del '500,* ed. M. Fagiolo. Rome: Officina, 1980.

Mariage, T. *L'univers de Le Nostre et les origines de l'aménagement du territoire.* Brussels: P. Mardaga, 1990. Translated by G. Larkin, *The World of André Le Nôtre.* Philadelphia: University of Pennsylvania Press, 1999.

Marie, A. *Naissance de Versailles.* Paris: Vincent, Fréal et Cie, 1968.

Marot, C. *Les Blasons anatomiques du corps féminin.* 1536.

Marson, T., et al., eds. *Il barco di Altivole: contributi per la conoscenza.* Treviso: Canova, 2000.

Martin, M. *Dairy Queens: The Politics of Pastoral Architecture from Catherine de'Medici to Marie-Antoinette.* Cambridge, MA: Harvard University Press, 2011.

Marvell, A. *Poems,* rev. ed., ed. N. Smith. Harlow: Pearson Education, 2007.

Masson, G. "Italian Flower Collectors' Gardens." In *The Italian Garden,* ed. D. Coffin. Washington, D.C.: Dumbarton Oaks, 1972.

McGowan, M. M. *Ideal Forms in the Age of Ronsard.* Berkeley: University of California Press, 1985.

Medri, L. M., ed. *Il giardino di Boboli.* Milan: Silvana Editoriale, 2003.

Mercure Galant. Paris: Guillaume de Luynes, 1678–1714.

Metlitzki, D. *Matter of Araby in Medieval England.* New Haven, CT: Yale University Press, 1977.

Meulen, M., van der. "Cardinal Cesi's Antique Sculpture Garden: Notes on a Painting by Hendrick Van Cleef III." *The Burlington Magazine,* 116, no. 14 (1974): 17–24.

Mignani, D. *Le Ville Medicee di Giusto Utens.* Firenze: Arnaud, 1993.

Miller, P. *Peiresc's Europe: Learning and Virtue in the Seventeenth Century.* New Haven, CT: Yale University Press, 2000.

Milton, J. *Paradise Lost,* 2nd ed., ed. A. Fowler. London: Longman, 1998.

Mollet, A. *Le jardin de plaisir.* Stockholm: Henry Kayser, 1651.

Mollet, C. *Théâtre des plans et jardinages.* Paris: Charles de Sercy, 1652.

Montaigne, M., de. *The Complete Works: Essays, Travel Journal, Letters.* Translated by D. M. Frame. New York: Everyman's Library, Alfred K. Knopf, 2003.

Montaigne, M., de. *Journal de voyage en Italie, par la Suisse et l'Allemagne, en 1580 et 1581.* In *Oeuvres complètes.* Paris: Éditions du Seuil, 1967.

Montaigne, M., de. *Montaigne's Travel Journal.* Translated by D. M. Frame. San Francisco, CA: North Point Press, 1983.

Morgan, L. "Early Modern Edens: The Landscape and Language of Paradise." *Studies in the History of Gardens and Designed Landscapes* 27, no. 2 (2007): 142–48.

Morgan, L. "The Early Modern Trompe-L'Oeil Garden." *Garden History* 33, no. 2 (2005): 286–93.

Morgan, L. *Nature as Model: Salomon de Caus and Early Seventeenth-Century Landscape Design.* Philadelphia: University of Pennsylvania Press, 2007.

Mountain, D. [T. Hill]. *The Gardener's Labyrinth.* London: 1577. Compiled by J. D. Hunt. New York: Garland, 1982.

Mukerji, C. "Bourgeois Culture and French Gardening in the Sixteenth and Seventeenth Centuries." In *Bourgeois and Aristocratic Encounters in Garden Art, 1550–1850,* ed. M. Conan, 173–87. Washington, D.C.: Dumbarton Oaks Research Library and Collection, 2002.

Mukerji, C. *Territorial Ambitions and the Gardens of Versailles.* Cambridge: Cambridge University Press, 1997.

Musaeum Tradescantianum; or, A Collection of Rarities preserved at South Lambeth, near London. London: John Grismond, 1656.

Nash, R. *Jacopo Sannazaro, Arcadia and Piscatorial Eclogues.* Detroit, MI: Wayne State University Press, 1966.

Neville, J. "Dance and the Garden: Moving and Static Choreography in Renaissance Europe." *Renaissance Quarterly* 52, no. 3 (1999): 805–36.

Nora, P. "Between Memory and History: *Les Lieux de Mémoire.*" *Representations* 26 (1989): 7–25.

Nouveau traité de la civilité qui se pratique en France parmi les honnêtes-gens. Nouvelle Edition revuë, corrigée, & de beaucoup augmentée par l'Auteur. Paris: Chez Louis Josse and Charles Robustez, 1728.

Oechslin, W. "Premises for the Resumption of the Discussion of Typology." *Assemblage* 1 (1986): 37–53.

Ogden, V. S. "The Principles of Variety and Contrast in Seventeenth-Century Aesthetics and Milton's Poetry." *Journal of the History of Ideas* 10, no. 2 (April 1949): 159–82.

Orbaan, J.A.F. *Documenti sul barocco in Roma,* 2 vols. Rome: Società Romana di Storia Patria, alla Biblioteca Vallicelliana, 1920.

Orgel, S., and R. Strong. *The Theatre of the Stuart Court.* London: Sotheby Park Bernet and University of California Press, 1973.

Ortner, S. B. "Is Female to Male as Nature Is to Culture?" In *Woman, Culture, and Society,* ed. M. Z. Rosaldo and L. Lamphere, 67–87. Stanford, CA: Stanford Unviersity Press, 1974.

Owens, J. B. "Diana at the Bar: Hunting, Aristocrats and the Law in Renaissance Castile." *The Sixteenth Century Journal* 8 (1977): 17–36.

Pagnini, C. *Costantino de' Servi, architetto-scenografo fiorentino alla corte d'Inghilterra (1611–1615).* Florence: Società Editrice Fiorentina, 2006.

Palissy, B. *Recepte veritable, par laquelle tous les hommes de la France pourront apprendre a multiplier et augmenter leurs thresors. Item, ceux qui n'ont jamais eu cognoissance des lettres, pourront apprendre une philosophie necessaire à tous les habitans de la terre. Item, en ce livre est contenu le dessein d'un jardin autant delectable & d'utile invention, qu'il en fut onques veu. Item, le dessein & ordonnance d'une ville de forteresse, la plus imprenable qu'homme ouyt jamais parler.* La Rochelle, 1563.

Palladio, A. *I quattro libri dell'architettura.* Venice, 1570.

Panofsky, E. "Artista scienziato genio: appunti sulla 'Renaissance-Dämmerung.'" *Annali dell'Istituto storico italo-germanico di Trento* 3 (1977): 278–320.

Panofsky, E. "*Et in Arcadia Ego:* Poussin and the Elegiac Tradition." In *Meaning in the Visual Arts,* 340–67. Harmondsworth: Penguin, 1970.

Panofsky, E. "The Ideological Antecedents of the Rolls-Royce Radiator." In *Three Essays on Style,* ed. I. Lavin, 129–66. Cambridge, MA: MIT Press, 1995.

Parfitt, G., ed. "To the Reader." In *Ben Johnson: The Complete Poems,* 122. Harmondsworth: Penguin, 1975.

Peacham, H. *The Garden of Eloquence: conteyning the figures of grammer and rhetorick, from whence maye bee gathered all manner of flowers, coulors, ornaments, exornations, formes and fashions of speech, very profitable for all those that be studious of eloquence, and that reade most eloquent poets and orators, and also helpeth much for the better vnderstanding of the holy Scriptures.* London, 1577.

Peacham, H. *Minerva Britanna or A garden of heroical devises.* London, 1612.

Pelissetti, L. S., and L. Scazzosi, eds. *Giardini, contesto, paesaggio: sistemi di giardini e architetture vegetali nel paesaggio. Metodi di studio, valutazione, tutela.* Florence: Olschki, 2005.

Pelissetti, L. S., and L. Scazzosi, eds. *Giardini storici. A 25 anni dalle Carte di Firenze: esperienze e prospettive,* 2 vols. Florence: Olschki, 2009.

Pérez-Gómez, A. *Polyphilo; or, The Dark Forest Revisited: An Erotic Epiphany of Architecture.* Cambridge, MA: MIT Press, 1992.

Pérouse de Montclos, J.-M. *Vaux-le-Vicomte.* London: Scala, Philip Wilson, 1997.

Petruccioli, A. *Gardens in the Time of the Great Muslim Empires: Theory and Design.* Leiden: Brill, 1997.

Petruccioli, A., ed. *Il giardino islamico. Architettura, natura, paesaggio.* Milan: Electa, 1994.

Pico della Mirandola, G. *Oration on the Dignity of Man.* Translated by A. R. Caponigri. Chicago: Regnery Edition, 1956.

Pieri, C., ed. *Le Nôtre, Un Inconnu Illustre?* Paris: Centre des Monuments Nationaux/ Monum and Éditions du Patrimoine, 2003.

Pietrogrande, A. "La teatralizzazione della natura e i suoi elementi: Giardini e luogo scenico tra Rinascimento e Barocco." In *Les Éléments et les metamorphoses de la nature: Imaginaire symbolique des arts dans la culture européenne du XVIe au XVIIIe siècle, Actes du colloque, septembre 1997*, 201–212. Paris: William Blake/ Art & Arts, 2004.

Pizzorusso, C. "Galileo in the Garden: Observations on the Sculptural Furnishings of Florentine Gardens between the Sixteenth and the Seventeenth Centuries." In *The Medici, Michelangelo, and the Art of Late Renaissance Florence*, ed. C. A. Luchinat, 113–21. New Haven, CT: Yale University Press, 2002.

Pliny the Younger. *Letters.* Translated by W. Melmoth. London: William Heinemann; New York: Macmillan, 1927.

Pomian, K. *Collectors and Curiosities: Paris and Venice, 1500–1800.* Translated by E. Wiles-Portier. Cambridge: Polity Press, 1990.

Porro, G. *L'horto de i semplici di Padova.* Venice, 1591.

Pozzana, M. "Agricoltura e orticoltura nella Toscana del Quattrocento." In *Giardini medicei*, 120–37. Milan: Federico Motta Editore, 1996.

Pozzana, M. *Il giardino dei frutti: frutteti, orti, pomari nel giardino e nel paesaggio toscano*, Florence: Ponte alle Grazie, 1990.

Pozzana, M. "Il giardino del Trebbio." In *Giardini medicei*, 148–52. Milan: Federico Motta Editore, 1996.

Prest, J. M. *The Garden of Eden: The Botanic Garden and the Re-Creation of Paradise*, New Haven, CT: Yale University Press, 1981.

Primaudaye, P., de la. *The French academie wherein is discoursed the institution of manners, and whatsoever else concerneth the good and happie life of all estates and callings, by precepts of doctrine, and examples of the lives of ancient sages and famous men: by Peter de la Primaudaye Esquire, Lord of the said place, and of Barree, one of the ordinarie gentlemen of the Kings Chamber: dedicated to the most Christian King Henrie the third, and newly translated into English by T.B.* London, 1614.

Puppi, L. "L'ambiente, il paesaggio e il territorio." In *Materiali e problemi: Ricerche spaziali e tecnologiche, (Storia dell'arte italiana, I:IV)*, ed. G. Previtali, 41–100. Torino: Giulio Einaudi, 1980.

Purcell, N. "Town in Country and Country in Town." In *Ancient Roman Villa Gardens*, ed. E. B. MacDougall, 187–203. Washington, D.C.: Dumbarton Oaks Library and Research Collection, 1987.

Quast, M. *Die Villa Montalto in Rom: Entstehung und Gestaltung im Cinquecento.* Munich: Tuduv, 1991.

Rabel, D. *Cent fleurs et insects,* ed. G. Aymonin. Arcueil: Anthèse, 1991.

Ragionieri, G., ed. *Il Giardino storico italiano: problemi di indagine, fonti letterarie e storiche: atti del convegno di studi, Siena-San Quirico D'orcia, 6–8 ottobre 1978.* Florence: Olschki, 1981.

Ramelli, A. *Le diverse et artificiose machine del capitano Agostino Ramelli . . . Nelle-quali si contengono uarij et industriosi mouimenti, degni digrandissima specula-tione, per cauarne beneficio infinito in ogni sorte d'operatione; composte in lingua italiana et francese.* Paris, 1588.

Ramón-Laca, L. 2008. "The Additions by the Count of Aremberg." In *Drawn after Nature: The Complete Botanical Watercolurs of the 16th-Century,* ed. J. de Kon-ing, G. van Uffelen, A. Zemanek, and B. Zemanek. Zeist, Germany: KNNV Publishing, 2008.

Raphael, S. *An Oak Spring Pomona: A Selection of the Rare Books on Fruit in the Oak Spring Garden Library.* Upperville, VA: Oak Spring Garden Library, 1990.

Raphael, S. *An Oak Spring Silva: A Selection of the Rare Books on Trees in the Oak Spring Garden Library.* Upperville, VA: Oak Spring Garden Library, 1989.

Rapinus, R. *Of Gardens: Four Books. First Written in Latine Verse by Renatus Rapi-nus.* London: John Evelyn, 1665; tr. London: T.R. & N.T, 1673.

Reed, S. W. *French Prints from the Age of the Musketeers.* Boston: Museum of Fine Arts, 1998.

Reed, S. W., and R. Wallace. *Italian Etchers of the Renaissance & Baroque.* Boston: Museum of Fine Arts, 1989.

Ribouillault, D. "Landscape *all'antica* and Topographical Anachronism in Roman Fresco Painting of the Sixteenth Century." *Journal of the Warburg and Courtauld Institutes* 71 (2008): 211–37.

Ribouillault, D. "Le Salone de la Villa d'Este à Tivoli: un théâtre des jardins et du ter-ritoire." *Studiolo. Revue d'Histoire de l'Art de l'Académie de France à Rome* 3 (2005): 65–94.

Ribouillault, D. "Les paysages urbains de la loggia du Belvédère d'Innocent VIII au Vatican: nostaglie de l'antique, géographie et croisades à la fin du XVe siècle." *Stu-diolo: Revue d'Histoire de l'Art de l'Académie de France à Rome* 8 (2010): 139–67.

Ribouillault, D. "Toward an Archaeology of the Gaze: The Perception and Function of Garden Views in Italian Renaissance Villas." In *Clio in the Italian Garden: Twenty-First Century Studies in Historical Methods and Theoretical Perspectives,* ed. M. Beneš and M. G. Lee, 203–32. Washington, D.C.: Dumbarton Oaks Re-search Library and Collection, 2011.

Ricci, L. B. "Gardens in Italian Literature during the Thirteenth and Fourteenth Cen-turies." In *The Italian Garden: Art, Design and Culture,* ed. J. D. Hunt, 6–33. Cambridge: Cambridge University Press, 1996.

Riccio, A. del. "Del giardino di un re." In *Il giardino storico italiano: Problemi di in-dagine e fonti letterari.* Proceedings of a scholarly meeting, ed. D. Heikamp and G. Ragionieri, 59–123. Florence: Olschki, 1981.

Riffaterre, M., *Semiotics of Poetry.* Bloomington: University of Indiana Press, 1978.

Rinaldi, A. "La costruzione di una cittadella del sapere: l'orto botanico di Firenze." In *La città effimera e l'universo artificiale del giardino: la Firenze dei Medici e l'Italia del '500,* ed. M. Fagiolo. Rome: Officina, 1980.

Roccasecca, P. *Ricerca sul lessico di parchi e giardini.* Rome: Multigrafica, 1990.

Roches, C. Des. *La Puce de Madame des-Roches.* Paris, 1582.

Roeykens, A. "Charles, prince-comte d'Arembergh: Restaurateur du parc d'Enghien au début di XVIIe siècle." *Annales du Cercle d'Archéologique d'Enghien* 15 (1967–69): 211–45.

[Rojas, F. de]. *Comedia de Calisto y Melibea.* Burgos, 1499.

[Rojas, F. de]. *La Celestina: The Spanish Bawd. Being the Tragi-Comedy of Calisto and Melibea.* Translated by J. M. Cohen. London: University of London Press, 1966.

[Rojas, F. de]. *[A new commod]ye in englysh [in] maner [of an enterl]ude ryght elygant & full of craft of rethoryk,] [wherein is shewd & dyscry[byd] as [well the b]ewte & good propertes of wom[e]n, [as theyr] vycys & euyll co[n]dicio[n]s, with a morall [co[n]clusi]on & exhortacyon to vertew.].* London, 1525.

Ronsard, P., de. *Le Bocage de P. de Ronsard Vandomoys, dedié a P. de Paschal, du bas païs de Languedoc.* Paris, 1554.

Ronsard, P., de. *Les Amours de Pierre de Ronsard, Vandomoys [Amours de Cassandre].* Paris, 1552.

Rosenberg, P., and L. A. Prat, eds. *Nicolas Poussin,* exhibition catalogue. Paris: Réunion des musées nationaux, 1994.

Rucellai, G. *Le Api.* 1539.

Rues, F. des. *Les Marguerites françoises; ou, Thresor des fleurs du bien dire.* 1595.

Ruggles, D. F. *Gardens, Landscape, and Vision in the Palaces of Islamic Spain.* University Park: Pennsylvania State University Press, 2000.

Ruggles, D. F. *Islamic Gardens and Landscapes.* Philadelphia: University of Pennsylvania Press, 2008.

Saltini, A., and M. Sframeli. *L'agricoltura e il paesaggio italiano nella pittura dal Trecento all' Ottocento.* Florence: Franco Cantini, 1995.

Saminiati, G. "Trattato di agricoltura." In *L'arte dei giardini,* ed. M. Azzi Visentini. Milan: Il Polifilo, 1999.

Sassoli, M. G. "Michelozzzo e l'architettura di villa nel primo Rinascimento." *Storia dell'Arte* 23 (1975): 5–51.

Saule, B., ed. *Catalogue de la Exposition Sciences et Curiosités à la cour de Versailles.* Versailles: RMN éditions and Etablissement public du château, du musée et du domaine national de Versailles, 2010.

Scafi, A. "Pio II e la cartografia: un papa e un mappamondo tra Medioevo e Rinascimento." In *Enea Silvio Piccolomini Pius Secundus: Poeta Laureatus Pontifex Maximus,* ed. M. Sodi and A. Antoniutti, 239–64. Rome: Associazione Culturale Shakespeare and Libreria Editrice Vaticana, 2007.

Scamozzi, V. *The Idea of a Universal Architecture. III: Villas and Country Estates.* Amsterdam: Architectura & Natura Press, 2003.

Scamozzi, V. *L'idea della architettura universale,* 2 vols. Venice: Vincenzo Scamozzi, 1615.

Schama, S. "Dutch Landscapes: Culture as Foreground." In *Masters of 17th-Century Dutch Landscape Painting,* ed. P. C. Sutton, 64–83. Boston: Museum of Fine Arts, 1987.

Schama, S. *Landscape and Memory.* New York: Alfred A. Knopf, 1995.

Schnapper, A. *Curieux du Grand Siècle. Oeuvres d'art.* Vol. 2. *Collections et collectionneurs dans la France du XVIIe siècle.* Paris: Flammarion, 1994.

Schnapper, A. *Le Géant, la licorne, et la tulipe. Histoire et histoire naturelle.* Vol. 1. *Collections et collectionneurs dans la France du XVIIe siècle.* Paris: Flammarion, 1988.

Scully, V. J. *Architecture: The Natural and the Manmade.* New York: St. Martin's Press, 1991.

Scully, V. J. *The Earth, the Temple and the Gods: Greek Sacred Architecture.* New Haven, CT: Yale University Press, 1962.

Segre, A. "La metamorfosi e il giardino italiano nel Seicento." In *Il Giardino delle Muse. Arti e artifici nel barocco europeo,* atti del IV Colloquio Internazionale, eds. Vincenzo Cazzato, Marcello Fagioli, Maria Adriana Giusti, 97–126. Tagliolini. Firenze: Edifir, 1995.

Segre, A. "Le retour de Flore: Naissance et évolution des jardins de fleurs de 1550 à 1650." In *L'Empire de Flore: Histoire et représentation des fleurs en Europe du XVIe au XIXe siècle,* ed. C. Coppens, S. van Sprang, G. De Brabandere, E. Lauwers Dervaux, et al. Brussels: Renaissance du livre, 1996.

Segre, A. "Untangling the Knot: Garden Design in Francesco Colonna's *Hypnerotomachia Poliphili.*" *Word & Image* 14, nos. 1/2 (1998): 82–108.

Sellers, V. B. *Courtly Gardens in Holland 1600–1650: The House of Orange and the Hortus Batavus.* Amsterdam: Architectura & Natura, 2001.

Sereni, E. *Storia del paesaggio agrario italiano.* Bari, Italy: Laterza, 1961. Translated by R. B. Litchfield, *History of the Italian Agricultural Landscape.* Princeton, NJ: Princeton University Press, 1996.

Serio, M., ed. *Gli Orti Farnesiani sul Palatino.* Proceedings of an international meeting. Rome: Ecole francaise de Rome, Soprientendeiza archeologica, 1990.

Serres, O., de. *Le Théâtre d'agriculture et mesnage des champs.* 3rd ed. Paris: Abr. Saugrain, 1605 [1611].

Sidney, P. *The Countess of Pembroke's Arcadia (The Old Arcadia),* ed. K. Duncan-Jones. Oxford: Oxford University Press, 1994.

Solinas. F., ed. *Cassiano Dal Pozzo,* proceedings of an international seminar. Rome: Du Luca, 1989.

Solinas, F. "The Oryx." In *Il Museo cartaceo di Cassiano Dal Pozzo: Cassiano naturalista, Quaderni puteani* 1. Milan: Olivetti, 1989.

Spary, E. C. *Utopia's Garden: French Natural History from Old Regime to Revolution.* Chicago: University of Chicago Press, 2000.

Spenser, E. *The Faerie Queene,* ed. A. C. Hamilton. London: Longman, 1977.

Strong, R. *The Artist & the Garden.* New Haven, CT: Yale University Press, 2000.

Strong, R. *Henry, Prince of Wales and England's Lost Renaissance.* London: Thames and Hudson, 1986.

Strong, R. C. *The Renaissance Garden in England.* London: Thames and Hudson, 1979.

Swan, C. *Art, Science and Witchcraft in Early Modern Holland: Jacques de Gheyn II (1565–1629).* Cambridge: Cambridge University Press, 2005.

Sweerts, E. *Florilegium tractans de variis floribus, at aliis indicis plantis ad vivum delineatum in duabus partibus.* Frankfurt, 1612–14.

Szafranska, M. "Łąka ze źródłem, czyli o problemach periodyzacji historii ogrodów [The Meadow with a Spring: The Problematic Periodization of Gardens History]." In *Sztuka około 1500,* 343–55. Warsaw: Arx Regia, 1997.

Szafranska, M. "The Philosophy of Nature and the Grotto in the Renaissance Garden." *Journal of Garden History* 9, no. 2 (1989): 76–85.

Tacitus. *The Annals.* Translated by J. Jackson. London: Hackett, 1937.

Taegio, B. *La Villa,* ed. and tr. T. Edward. Philadelphia: University of Pennsylvania Press, 2011.

Tanaglia, M. *De agricultura.* Bologna: Libreria Palmaverde, 1953.

Tapisseries du Roi, où sont représentés les quatre éléments et les quatre saisons. Paris: Imp. Royale, 1670.

Targioni Tozzetti, A. *Cenni storici sulla introduzione di varie piante nell' agricoltura ed orticoltura Toscana.* Florence: Tipografia Galileiana, 1853.

Tasso, T. *Gerusalemme liberata.* Parma, 1581.

Taverner, R. *The garden of wysdom wherin ye maye gather moste pleasaunt flowres, that is to say, proper wytty and quycke sayenges of princes, philosophers, and dyuers other sortes of men. Drawen forth of good authours, as well Grekes as Latyns.* London, 1539.

Taylor, P. *The Oxford Companion to the Garden.* Oxford: Oxford University Press, 2009.

Tchikine, A. "Gardens of Mistaken Identity: The Giardino delle Stalle in Florence and the Giardino dell'Arsenale in Pisa." *Studies in the History of Gardens and Designed Landscapes* 33, no. 1 (2013): 1–13.

Teskey, G., and G. Logan, eds. *Unfolded Tales: Essays on Renaissance Romance.* Ithaca, NY: Cornell University Press, 1989.

Thacker, C. "'Manière de montrer les jardins de Versailles,' by Louis XIV and Others." *Garden History* 1, no. 1 (1972): 49–69.

Tomasi, L. T. "Projects for Botanical and Other Gardens: A 16th Century Manual." *Journal of Garden History* 3 (1983).

Tongiorgi Tomasi, L. "Botanical Gardens of the Sixteenth and Seventeenth Centuries." In *The Architecture of Western Gardens,* ed. M. Mosser and G. Teyssot. Cambridge, MA: MIT Press, 1991.

Tongiorgi Tomasi, L. "'Extra' e 'Intus': progettualità degli orti botanici e collezionismo eclettico tra il XVI e XVII secolo." In *Il giardino come labirinto della storia,* proceedings of an international meeting, ed. Jette Abel, Eliana Mauro, et al., 48–53. Palermo: Publisher, n.d.

Tongiorgi Tomasi, L. "The Flowering of Florence: Botanical Art for the Medic." In *The Flowering of Florence: Botanical Art for the Medici,* exhibition catalogue, ed. L. Tongiorgi Tomasi and G. A. Hirschauer, 15–57. London: Lund Humphries, 2002.

Tongiorgi Tomasi, L. "Francesco Mingucci 'giardiniere' e pittore naturalista: un aspetto della committenza barberiniana nella Roma seicentesca." In *Atti del Convegno celebrativo del IV centenario della nascita di Federico Cesi.* Rome: Publisher, 1986.

Tongiorgi Tomasi, L. "Gardens of Knowledge and the *République des Gens de Sciences.*" In *Baroque Garden Cultures: Emulation, Sublimation, and Subversion,* ed. M. Conan. Washington, D.C.: Dumbarton Oaks Research Library and Collection, 2005.

Tongiorgi Tomasi, L. "Geometric Schemes for Plant Beds and Gardens: A Contribution to the History of the Garden in the Sixteenth and Seventeenth Centuries." In *World Art: Themes of Unity in Diversity,* Acts of the 26th International Congress on the History of Art, ed. I. Lavin. University Park: Penn State University Press, 1989.

Tongiorgi Tomasi, L. *Il Giardino di Flora: natura e simbolo nell'immagine dei fiori,* ed. M. Gallo Cataldi and E. Simonetti. Geneva: Sagep Editrice, 1986.

Tongiorgi Tomasi, L. "L'immagine naturalistica: tecnica e invenzione." In *Natura-Cultura: L'interpretazione del Mondo Fisico nei Testi e nelle Immagini,* Atti del Convegno Internazionale di Studi, ed. G. Olmi, L. Tongiorgi Tomasi, and A. Zanca. Florence: Olschki, 2000.

Tongiorgi Tomasi, L. *An Oak Spring Flora: Flower Illustration from the 15th Century to the Present Time.* Uppervile, VA: Oak Spring Garden Library, 1997.

Tongiorgi Tomasi, L., and A. Tosi, *Flora e Pomona. L'orticoltura nei disegni e nelle incisioni dei secoli XVI-XIX.* Firenze: Leo S. Olschki, 1990.

Trattato di agricoltura di Giovanvettorio Soderini ora per la prima volta pubblicato. Firenze: Stamperia del Giglio, 1811.

Trissino, G. G. *L'Italia liberata dai Goti.* 1547–1548.

Tylicki, J. *Bartłomiej Strobel: Malarz epoki wojny trzydziestoletniej.* Torun: Wydawnictwo Uniwersytetu Mikołaja Kopernika, 2000.

Vallet, P. *Le jardin du roy tres chrestien Henri IV.* Paris, 1608.

Valnay, N. *Connoissance et culture parfaite des tulippes rares, des anemones extraordinaires, des oeillets fins, et des belles oreilles d'ours panachées.* Paris: Laurent d'Houry, 1688.

van Gelder, E. *Tussen hof en keizerskroon: Carolus Clusius en de ontwikkeling van de botanie aan Midden-Europese hoven (1573–1593).* Leiden: Leiden University Press, 2011.

Varoli Piazza, S. "Giardino, Barchetto e Barco della Rocca Ruspoli a Vignanello." In *La dimensione europea dei Farnese [Bulletin de l'Institut Historique Belge de Rome, 63, 1993],* ed. B. De Groof and E. Galdieri, 421–49. Turnhout, Belgium: Brepols, 1994.

Varoli Piazza, S. "Maraviglioso boschetto." In *Bomarzo: il sacro bosco,* ed. S. Frommel, 176–85. Milan: Electa, 2009.

Varoli Piazza, S. "Territorio, ambiente e paesaggio del Parco dei Musei, Valle Giulia e Villa Borghese." In *Villa Borghese. Storia e gestione. Atti del convegno (Roma, 2003),* ed. A. Campitelli, 79–92. Milan: Skira, 2005.

Vasari, G. *The Lives of the Painters, Sculptors and Architects.* Rev. ed. Translated by A. B. Hinds. London: Dent; New York: Dutton, 1963.

Venturi, G. "La selva e il giardino. Tasso e il paesaggio." In *Archivi dello sguardo. Origini e momenti di pittura di paesaggio in Italia. Atti del Convegno. Ferrara, Castello Estense, 22–23 ottobre 2004,* ed. F. Cappelletti, 75–96. Florence: Casa Editrice Le Lettere, 2006.

Venturi, G. "*Picta poësis:* ricerche sulla poesia e il giardino dalle origini al Seicento." In *Storia d'Italia. Annali 5: Il paesaggio,* ed. C. De Seta, 663–749. Turin: Giulio Einaudi editore, 1982.

Venturi, G., and F. Ceccarelli, eds. *Delizie in villa: il giardino rinacimentale e i suoi committenti.* Florence: L. S. Olschki, 2008.

Vérard, A. *Le Jardin de plaisance et fleurs de Rhétorique.* 1501.

Vesme, A., de. *Stefano Della Bella: Catalogue Raisonné,* introduction and additions by P. Dearborn Massar. New York: Collectors Editions, 1971.

Vidler, A. *The Writing of the Walls: Architectural Theory in the Late Enlightenment.* Princeton, NJ: Princeton Architectural Press, 1987.

Vieri, F., de'. *Discorsi delle maravigliose opere di Pratolino,* ed. G. Marescotti. Firenze: Giorgio Marescotti, 1587.

Virgil. *The Georgics.* Translated by L. P. Wilkinson. London: Cambridge University Press, 1969.

Visentini, M. A. "Alle origini dell'architettura del paesaggio: Considerazioni in margine al rapporto tra gli edifici, i giardini e il sito nelle ville laziali del Cinquecento." In *Villa Lante a Bagnaia,* ed. S. Frommel, 190–205. Milan: Electa, 2005.

Visentini, M. A. "The Gardens of Villas in the Veneto from the Fifteenth to the Eighteenth Centuries." In *The Italian Garden: Art, Design and Culture,* ed. J. D. Hunt, 93–126. Cambridge: Cambridge University Press, 2007.

Visentini, M. A. "Il giardino dei semplici di Padova: un prodotto della cultura del Rinascimento." *Comunità* 182 (1980): 259–338.

Visentini, M. A., ed. *L'Arte dei giardini. Scritti teorici e pratici dal XIV al XIX secolo.* Milan: Edizioni Il Polifilo, 1999.

Visentini, M. A. "La chasse dans le duché de Milan a l'époque des Visconti et des Sforza: Les parcs de Pavie et de Milan." In *Chasses princières dans l'Europe de la Renaissance: actes du colloque de Chambord, 1er et 2 octobre 2004,* ed. C. d'Anthenaise et al. Arles, France: Actes Sud, 2007.

Visentini, M. A. *La villa in Italia. Quattrocento e Cinquecento.* Milan: Electa, 1995.

Visentini, M. A. *L'orto botanico di Padova.* Milan: Il Polifilo, 1984.

Visentini, M. A. "A Model Humanist Garden: Villa Brenzone at Punta San Virgilio." In *The History of Garden Design: The Western Tradition from the Renaissance to the Present Day,* ed. M. Mosser and G. Teyssot, 106–8. London: Thames and Hudson, 1991.

Visentini, M. A., ed. *Topiaria. Architetture e sculture vegetali nel giardino occidentale dall'antichità ad oggi.* Treviso: Fondazione Benetton Studi e Ricerche, 2004.

Vredeman de Vries, H. *Hortorum viridariorumque elegantes et multiplices formae, ad architectonicae artis normam.* Antwerp, 1583.

Warnke, M. *Politische Landschaft: zur Kunstgeschichte der Natur.* Munich: C. Hamer, 1992. Translated by D. McLintock, *Political Landscape: The Art History of Nature.* London: Reaktion, 1994.

Waterschoot, W. "Marot or Ronsard? New French Poetics among Dutch Rhetoricians in the Second Half of the 16th Century." In *Rhetoric = Rhetoriqueurs = Rederijkers,* ed. J. Koopmans. Amsterdam: Koninklijke Nederlandse Akademie van Wetenschappen, 1995.

Watson, R. N. *Back to Nature: The Green and the Real in the Late Renaissance.* Philadelphia: University of Pennsylvania Press, 2006.

White, L., Jr. "The Flavor of Early Renaissance Technology." In *Developments in the Early Renaissance,* ed. B. S. Levy, 36–57. Albany: State University of New York Press, 1972.

Whitehouse, H. *Ancient Mosaics and Wallpaintings: Paper Museum of Cassiano dal Pozzo.* Series A: Antiquities and Architecture. London: Harvey Miller, 2001.

Wiley, W. L. *The Gentleman of Renaissance France.* Cambridge, MA: Harvard University Press, 1954.

Wilkinson Zerner, C. "European Convergences: Philip II and the Landscape at Aranjuez." In *Architecture, jardin, paysage: l'environnement du château et de la villa aux XVe et XVIe siècles: actes du colloque tenu à Tours du 1er au 4 juin 1992*, ed. J. Guillaume. Paris: Picard, 1999.

Williams, R. *Keywords: A Vocabulary of Culture and Society*. London: Fontana, 1976.

Williamson, T. *Suffolk's Gardens and Parks: Designed Landscapes from the Tudors to the Victorians*. Cheshire: Windgather Press, 2000.

Williamson, T., and L. Bellamy. *Property and Landscape: A Social History of Land Ownership and the English Countryside*. London: George Philip, 1987.

Wittkower, R. *Architectural Principles in the Age of Humanism*. 2nd ed. London: Tiranti, 1952; 4th ed., London: Academy Editions, 1973.

Woodbridge, K. *Princely Gardens: The Origins and Development of the French Formal Garden*. New York: Rizzoli, 1986.

Wright, D.R.E. "The Medici Villa at Olmo a Castello: Its History and Iconography." PhD diss., Princeton University, 1976.

Wright, D.R.E. "Some Medici Gardens of the Florentine Renaissance: An Essay in Post-Aesthetic Interpretation." In *The Italian Garden: Art, Design, and Culture*, ed. J. D. Hunt, 34–59. Cambridge: Cambridge University Press, 1996.

Yates, F. A. *The Rosicrucian Enlightenment*. London: Routledge, 1972.

Yates, F. A. *The Valois Tapestries*. London: The Warburg Institute, 1959.

Zalum Cardon, M. *Passione e cultura dei fiori tra Firenze e Roma nel XVI e XVII secolo*. Florence: Olschki, 2008.

Zangheri, L. Il disegno del parco venatorio in età barocca." In *Giardini, contesto, paesaggio: sistemi di giardini e architetture vegetali nel paesaggio: metodi di studio, valutazione, tutela*, ed. L. S. Pelissetti et al. Florence: Olschki, 2005.

Zangheri, L. *Pratolino: il giardino delle meraviglie*. Florence: Gonnelli, 1979.

Zangheri, L. *Storia del giardino e del paesaggio: il verde nella cultura occidentale*. Florence: Olschki, 2003.

Zaninelli, S., ed. *Scritti teorici e tecnici di agricoltura*. Milan: Il Polifilo, 1995.

Zimmermann, R. "Iconography in German and Austrian Renaissance Gardens." In *Garden History: Issues, Approaches, Methods*, ed. J. D. Hunt, 97–118. Washington, D.C.: Dumbarton Oaks Research Library and Collection, 1992.

CONTRIBUTORS

Mirka Beneš is a historian of gardens and landscapes and an associate professor of landscape architecture at the University of Texas at Austin. She studied painting and art history at Princeton University and received her PhD in art history from Yale University. She has been a fellow at Dumbarton Oaks and twice a Fellow of the American Academy in Rome. From 1988 to 2005, she taught at Harvard University's Graduate School of Design. Her teaching interests range from Mediterranean antiquity to Islamic gardens to contemporary landscape architecture. Her scholarship focuses on Italian and French Renaissance and Baroque architecture, gardens, and landscape representation in their social-geographical and artistic contexts, with a specialization on Rome, its countryside, suburban development, agrarian history, villas, and parks. Her publications emphasize history of design, methodology, and historiography, and include two co-edited books: with Dianne Harris, *Villas and Gardens in Early Modern Italy and France* (Cambridge University Press, 2001), and with Michael G. Lee, *Clio in the Italian Garden. Twenty-First-Century Studies in Historical Methods and Theoretical Perspectives* (Dumbarton Oaks, 2011). Beneš is currently working on a book on architecture, landscape, and experience in the villa gardens of Baroque Rome and in the landscape paintings of Claude Lorrain.

Raffaella Fabiani Giannetto teaches landscape architectural history and theory at the University of Pennsylvania School of Design. Fabiani Giannetto's research interests focus on the Italian Renaissance garden, its legacy, and its historiography. In addition, she maintains an interest in contemporary landscape architecture, its theory, and its criticism. She is the author of *Paolo Bürgi Landscape Architect, Discovering the (Swiss) Horizon: Mountain, Lake, and Forest* (Princeton Architectural Press, 2009) and *Medici Gardens: From Making to Design* (University of Pennsylvania Press, 2008). *Medici Gardens* was the 2010 recipient of the Elisabeth Blair MacDougall Award. Fabiani Giannetto's current research addresses the reception of the Italian garden tradition in the United States from the colonial period to the early twentieth century. This research is part of her larger book project titled *Foreign Trends on American Soil*.

Elizabeth Hyde is an assistant professor of history at Kean University. She is the author of *Cultivated Power: Flowers, Culture, and Politics in the Reign of Louis XIV* (University of Pennsylvania Press, 2005). The book was the recipient of the 2007 Society of Architectural Historians' Elisabeth Blair MacDougall Award. Elizabeth Hyde is currently researching the cultural and political dimensions of trans-Atlantic botanical exchange of plants, trees, and knowledge in the eighteenth century through the work of French botanist André Michaux and his American counterparts. She is also writing a cultural history of how-to books from the sixteenth through the eighteenth centuries.

Michael Leslie is professor of English at Rhodes College. He chaired the Committee of Senior Fellows in Landscape at Dumbarton Oaks and has published on early modern culture and the intersections among literature, art history, history of science and agriculture, and garden history. Founder of the Hartlib Papers Project and co-editor of *Culture and Cultivation in Early Modern England: Writing and the Land* (Leicester University Press, 1994), his most recent publications are editions of two plays by the largely forgotten seventeenth-century playwright Richard Brome, *The New Academy* and *The Weeding of Covent Garden*.

Luke Morgan is a senior lecturer in the faculty of art, design and architecture at Monash University (Melbourne). His book *Nature as Model: Salomon de Caus and Early Seventeenth-Century Landscape Design* was published in 2007 by the University of Pennsylvania Press, and he is on the editorial board of the journal *Studies in the History of Gardens and Designed Landscapes*. His current research, which is funded by the Australian Research Council and the Graham Foundation, focuses on monsters and monstrosity in early modern landscape design.

Małgorzata Szafrańska is an art historian working at The Royal Castle, Warsaw, specializing in Renaissance Italian garden art, design, and usage, as well as on its effects and reformulations in Poland specifically, but also across Europe. She has written on Renaissance grottoes (*Journal of Garden History* 1989), sixteenth-century plants and gardens (*PACT Journal,* 1995) and "Place, Time and Movement: A New Look at Renaissance Gardens" (*Studies in the History of Gardens and Designed Landscapes,* 2006). As author, translator and editor she compiled the illustrated anthology on Renaissance gardens, *OGROD RENESANSOWY* (Warsaw, 1998), with a range of texts in original languages alongside Polish translations, and an extensive bibliography.

Margherita Zalum Cardon received her PhD from the Università di Pisa, where she studied art history before shifting her focus to garden history. Her current research involves the study of botanical iconography, the history of the garden in the modern age, and baroque architecture. She has been involved in project with Scuola Normale Superiore in Pisa and the Dumbarton Oaks Research Library and Collection. She contributed to the *Theatrum Rosarum* (recipient of the Premio Grinzane Giardini Botanici Hanbury), and to the *Bibliografia del giardino e del paesaggio italiano 1980–2005*, edited by L. Tongiorgi Tomasi and L. Zangheri. In addition, she has curated a volume on the restoration of the hanging garden in Palazzo Agostini in Pisa and has published *Passione e cultura dei fiori tra Firenze e Roma nel XVI e XVII secolo* (2008).

INDEX

Page numbers in bold indicate illustrations.